A History of the English Church

Edited by the late Very Rev. W. R. W. STEPHENS, D.D., F.S.A.,
Dean of Winchester,
and the Rev. WILLIAM HUNT, D.Litt.

VIII

THE ENGLISH CHURCH

IN THE NINETEENTH CENTURY

PART I

MACMILLAN AND CO., Limited
LONDON · BOMBAY · CALCUTTA
MELBOURNE

THE MACMILLAN COMPANY
NEW YORK · BOSTON · CHICAGO
ATLANTA · SAN FRANCISCO

THE MACMILLAN CO. OF CANADA, Ltd.
TORONTO

THE ENGLISH CHURCH

IN THE NINETEENTH CENTURY

PART I

FRANCIS WARRE CORNISH, M.A.

VICE-PROVOST OF ETON COLLEGE
LATE FELLOW OF KING'S COLLEGE, CAMBRIDGE

MACMILLAN AND CO., LIMITED
ST. MARTIN'S STREET, LONDON
1910

INTRODUCTION

INTEREST in the history of the English Church has been steadily increasing of late years, since the great importance of the Church as a factor in the development of the national life and character from the earliest times has come to be more fully and clearly recognised. But side by side with this increase of interest in the history of our Church, the want has been felt of a more complete presentment of it than has hitherto been attempted. Certain portions, indeed, have been written with a fulness and accuracy that leave nothing to be desired ; but many others have been dealt with, if at all, only in manuals and text-books which are generally dull by reason of excessive compression, or in sketches which, however brilliant and suggestive, are not histories. What seemed to be wanted was a continuous and adequate history in volumes of a moderate size and price, based upon a careful study of original authorities and the best ancient and modern writers. On the other hand, the mass of material which research has now placed at the disposal of the scholar seemed to render it improbable that any one would venture to undertake such a history single-handed, or that, if he did, he would live to complete it. The best way, therefore, of meeting the difficulty seemed to be a division of labour amongst several competent scholars, agreed in their general principles, each being responsible for a period to which he has *devoted special attention, and all working in correspondence through the medium of an editor or editors, whose business it should be to guard against errors, contradictions, overlapping, and repetition; but, consistency and continuity being so far secured, each writer should have as free a hand as possible. Such is the plan upon which the present history has been projected. It is proposed to carry it on far enough to include at least the Evangelical Movement in the eighteenth century. The whole work will consist of seven [1] crown octavo books uniform in outward appearance, but necessarily varying somewhat in length and price. Each book can be bought separately, and will have its own index, together with any tables or maps that may be required.*

I am thankful to have secured as my co-editor a scholar who is eminently qualified by the remarkable extent and accuracy of his knowledge to render me assistance, without which, amidst the pressure of many other duties, I could scarcely have ventured upon a work of this magnitude.

W. R. W. STEPHENS.

THE DEANERY, WINCHESTER,
20*th July* 1899.

---

[1] *In a note appended to this Introduction in volume v. and subsequently, it was announced that the series would be extended by adding another volume which would deal with ' The English Church in the Nineteenth Century.' It has been found necessary to devote two volumes to that period (1800-1890): they are written by the same author and are published together as one book.*

W. H.

This *History of the English Church* is completed in the following volumes :—

PREFACE

THE present volume deals with so long a period and so wide a range of subjects, that a writer who undertakes to treat of it lays himself open to the charge of omitting matters of importance or giving undue prominence to what is comparatively unimportant, of bias in politics or religion, and of imperfect acquaintance with what is matter of common knowledge. The standard authorities are few, and most of the facts must be collected from biographies, accounts of transactions in Parliament and Convocation, and the reports and comments of the Press during the greater part of a century. I cannot, therefore, hope to have escaped serious faults of omission and commission.

I have tried to give a truthful picture of the times, and not to write in the spirit of a partisan ; but I am well aware that to exclude every expression of opinion or personal preference is to take away all life from a narrative.

I owe especial obligation to the *Life of Archibald Campbell Tait* by Archbishop Davidson and Canon Benham, and to Canon Perry's *Student's History of the Church of England*, vol. iii., without the help of which books this history could not have been written. Other sources of information are indicated in the lists of Authorities appended to each chapter. It would be too long a task to record the bountiful assistance I have enjoyed, both from the kindness of the Editor, who has spared neither time nor labour, and whose wide knowledge of church

ix

history has always been freely opened to me, and from a large number of friends known or unknown to me personally, who have taken much trouble in giving me the result of their own experience, or pointing out sources of information ; but I desire here to express my gratitude to all who have helped me to carry out, however imperfectly, a lengthy and difficult task.

FRANCIS WARRE CORNISH.

ETON COLLEGE,
December 1909.

N.B.—For all opinions expressed or implied in these volumes the Author alone is responsible.

CONTENTS

CHAPTER I

CHAPTER II

CHAPTER III

CHAPTER IV

CHAPTER V

CHAPTER VI

CHAPTER VII

CHAPTER VIII

CHAPTER IX

CHAPTER X

CHAPTER XI

CHAPTER XII

CHAPTER XIII

CHAPTER XIV

CHAPTER XV

CHAPTER XVI

CHAPTER XVII

APPENDICES

ERRATA

PART I

Page 24, line 27, for " province " read " diocese."

,, 41, line 5 from bottom, for " 1806 " read " 1805."

,, 72, line 11, after " Lloyd," for " 1820 " read " 1829."

,, 302, line 12, for " Thomson " read " Thompson." Delete " (afterwards Archbishop of York)."

,, 307, line 6, for " they " read " some of them."

,, 316, line 12, for " but not " read " as well as."

,, 349, inset, for " Palmer . . . Graham " read " Palmer, Beresford-Hope." Delete " Graham."

,, 355, line 2 from bottom, for " Fanshawe " read " Fanshaw."

CHAPTER I

INTRODUCTION

ALL history is compounded of material and spiritual factors, combined in varying proportions, which depend on a multitude of conditions that cannot be easily summarised or classified. Religious history, so called, is not different from secular history, though looked at from a different point of view. Spiritual and material causes help or hinder each other. We have learnt at length to see the power of political and economical elements in the Crusades, the Reformation, and the Wars of Religion, and the intrusion of ideas such as nationality, liberty, and unity into questions of trade and delimitation. The secular historian is apt to underrate the emotional aspect of his subject; a writer who deals with religious history may easily overlook the external conditions of religious movements, among which may be reckoned the general state of intelligence at the time under consideration, the means of communication and intercourse, the localisation of ideas, as of authority at Rome, equality in France, distribution of responsibility in England; and he must not ignore the workings of self-interest, prejudice, pride, and cowardice in the minds of men whose lives were spent in promoting what they believed to be the cause of religion.

The history of the Church of England is to be viewed in connexion with the general history of England, and of the main currents of thought and action external to the Church.

Religious history a part of general history.

PART I   𝕾   B

It is neither the history of thought nor of piety nor of philanthropy, nor an account of good men and good works, though all these elements are to be found in it; it is also a record of a part of the Constitution, nor to be dissociated from political and social movements.

The beginning of a century is an arbitrary division as applied to history. All such divisions indeed are arbitrary, since at any given date some things which must come under review are ending and others beginning: but, roughly speaking, the centuries have each its own character, and in the history of the Church of England the end of the eighteenth century is a natural period for the opening of a new chapter.

The turn of the century is marked by the growth of a practical and philanthropic spirit. In spite of the dislike which was inspired by the French Revolution, connected in British minds with ideas of anarchy, violence, despotism, and universal war, the bonfire of privileges had not blazed in vain. Some sense of responsibility connected with privilege and position had been awakened; it was more generally felt that the Church owed a duty to the poor; gross inequality of rewards began to be remarked; in short, democratic and humanitarian ideas, which are cognate to those of Christianity, crept into religious life, as doctrines of equality affected politics.

Influence of the French Revolution.

Here, as always, a double influence was felt. All but a few clear-headed men, who were called, and probably were, narrow-minded or fanatical, accepted the practical results of doctrines which they abhorred, much in the same manner as Roman Catholics submit to be taught by the experience of heretics, and Tories adapt themselves to Whig ideas. The strife of principles goes on, but the defenders are pushed farther down the hill. We shall see the dogmatic party taking up new ground, and all parties agreeing in terms of philanthropy, education, and progress on the road towards equality; privilege weakened, dogmatic differences smoothed over, religious interests finding a footing on the secular platform, and secular interference with religion tolerated; all these things may be reckoned among the fruits

Philanthropy and philosophy.

of the French Revolution, and their expression in our country coincides generally with the early years of the nineteenth century.

During the latter part of the eighteenth century questions of personal religion, the relation of the individual soul to God, occupied the minds of Christian professors.   Debates about faith and works, and the refinements of Arminianism and Calvinism, had gone over the Church border into the region of dissent.   The evangelical section of the Church was active and earnest, but not so intent upon preaching the Gospel to the poor as in Wesley's early days.   'Serious' people enjoyed without hypocrisy the world whose pleasures they condemned. Religion invaded society.   Since the reign of James I. or the Commonwealth, religion had not held its head so high nor laid claim to so much attention from the world.   It became almost fashionable to be religious ; and as a natural result, religion was cooled and diffused, and took shape in schemes of philanthropy in which many could be interested.   Religion left the closet and entered the committee room.   It would not be just to call this a mechanical age, an age of 'economists and calculators' ; but it was an age which paid much attention to machinery, and organised many institutions which are still alive and vigorous, and working for good.

If we look at the literature of England during this quarter of a century, we find little directly religious literature, except the works of Hannah More, Wilberforce, and Paley, and in a different region, Coleridge and Wordsworth.   Religious literature.
The literary forces of the age were the poets, not the preachers.   Revivalism gave place to romanticism, high and dry doctrine was breathed upon by Coleridge and melted into new forms.   Men of genius are at all times the lords of the ascendant, and the schools of the poets were leavening the new generation.   The ideas which attracted it were new creeds of universal brotherhood and enfranchisement, dreams of 'pantisocracy,' new births of liberty and equality, not the ancient doctrines of Christianity.   But for the present our business is with the Church and its   The evangelical school.
organisation, especially the evangelical party, the leaders of which stood aghast at Shelley and Byron, and looked with suspicion upon Wordsworth and Coleridge.   The

imagination of the most active among them was limited, their doctrine was strictly orthodox in the narrow way of a moderate Calvinism.   But nothing could be more admirable than the pious energy with which they gave their time and their wealth to raising the level of religion in the mass of the people, and the enthusiasm with which they set themselves to promote the cause of negro emancipation, missionary enterprise, reform of prisons, the spread of pure literature and national education.

If the eighteenth century was the age of philosophical doubt, morality, and personal religion, the nineteenth is the battle-ground of scientific doubt with dogma, and of corporate with individual religion.   In other words, inquiry into theological truth, the relation of the individual soul to God, the search for holiness or virtue for the individual, characterise the earlier period ; in the later, a historical and social view of mankind prevails.   We see the influence of the school of Rousseau.   Man is considered as a member of a civil or religious society.   Associations are formed to promote the general good, both spiritual and secular.   The Evangelicals institute religious societies, the High Churchmen preach Catholicism.   The supreme importance of faith is less dwelt upon, the doctrine of St. James is more in favour than that of St. Paul.   Spiritual energy, which had shown itself in 'enthusiasm,' was now diverted into different channels, and lost some of its early freshness.

At the beginning of the century, Church principles, as they were understood by the earlier and later High Churchmen, were dormant as regards doctrine.   The paramount importance of sacraments, the sanctity of the priesthood, and the validity of Church tradition and authority were neglected if not forgotten.   Dogma was dormant too, for the Evangelical revivalists did not question the doctrine of the Church of England, finding it sufficient for their spiritual needs, and no zeal for dogma had as yet been kindled within the Church itself.   England, cut off from the Continent, was vaguely reckoned among the Protestant nations.   Heresy and schism were words of little account.   Most Churchmen, if asked, would have said that the Church of Rome was heretical, and the

Indifference to dogma.

dissenting congregations schismatical; but such questions belonged to a class of ideas which had no great interest at the moment. The reaction against this state of feeling, when it came, was, like all reactions, a positive movement. A protest against darkness is a cry for light; the strong man armed is driven out, not by his own carelessness, but by a stronger than he. In this conflict of opinion, which was to occupy the greater part of the nineteenth century, the aggres- Churchman- sive force proceeded from a sense of churchmanship, ship and brought into strong relief by the Methodist seces- dissent. sion. The Whig latitudinarianism of the Low Church body had lost vitality. The sleepy orthodoxy of the so-called High Church party, allied with political Toryism and hostile to all religious excitement, had yet retained some of the feeling which had been brought out by the death of Charles I. and the fall of James II., and the light of high Anglican doctrine had never been wholly extinguished. The Wesleyan secession revived it. But the secession also drew attention to the fact that the Church of England, under the conduct of the High Church party, had lost her hold upon the conscience of the poor : whereas at the beginning of the eighteenth century it was reckoned that one man in twenty-five was a Dissenter, the proportion in 1800 was estimated at one in four.

The Church, beyond other established institutions, was looked upon as the great bulwark of stability. Here centred the conservative forces, stimulated by the war The clergy. with France. The clergy were almost unanimous in supporting the war and the Ministry, both from conviction and from fear of change. There was little to distinguish them from the laity. They were not a separate order, but shared the opinions and sentiments of the ruling class. They visited the sick and ministered to the poor ; but many of them did little spiritual work, neglected Church observances, were careless about education, lived throughout the week much as the squires and lesser gentry to whom they preached on Sunday mornings, and administered the Sacrament once or at most three or four times a year. Pluralism, non-residence, and the abuses of translation and patronage were at their height. The official theology of charges and pastoral letters was chiefly directed against Dissenters and Evangelicals.

Controversy took the same line, a line stopping short at the Reformation; the defenders, such as Archdeacon Daubeny, and the opposers, such as Sir Richard Hill, taking their stand upon the Anglican settlement, and reading into its formularies Calvinist or anti-Calvinist doctrines. The attitude of the Church was 'high and dry.' The beneficed clergy upheld the use and wont of the Establishment, the malcontents wished for more vital religion and love of souls; neither party desired much social or political change.

The ecclesiastical abuses which were attacked in 1831 were not confined to one or the other of the two parties in the Church which bore the names of High Church and Low Church. Both alike were opposed to reform, both condemned enthusiasm and methodism. The two parties have greatly changed their character since the evangelical revival of the eighteenth century, when the High Church party did not hold high sacramental doctrine, nor the Low Church strong and clear views of regeneration and conversion. The High Church party was Tory, the Low Church Whig, and respect for the memory of Charles I. on the one hand, and William III. on the other, would be a fair test of distinction. The origin of the term 'evangelical' is obscure; it is not certain whether it was first applied as a nickname or adopted as a watchword. John Wesley's breach with the Church accentuated the difference between those of the revival who seceded and those who remained in communion with the Church of England. The latter assumed or accepted the title 'evangelical'; and after the extinction of the old political latitudinarian Low Church party, or its absorption into Liberalism, the name Low Church was applied, as it still is, to the evangelical portion of the Church of England.

It may seem surprising, when we look back at the distance of a century, that the Churchmen of 1800 did not see the signs of coming change. Even thirty years later the call to 'set her house in order' came upon the Church as a surprise, and the ecclesiastical legislation which followed was carried out in the hurry and confusion of panic. But this blindness was natural enough. The parishioners went to church; tithes and church rates were paid; outward respect was shown to the clergy; their windows were not broken nor their ricks

burnt; they had no reason to feel themselves unpopular.
From the days of Noah to those of the latest revolution it has
been so; the threatened class or institution has never felt the
need of reform till the storm came; disaffection may exist
and increase, and yet find no voice to express itself, till a
common grievance leads to combination, and finds expression
in some emphatic act.   At this time, moreover, the attention of the nation was directed to the war with France, the
condition of Ireland, the volunteer movement, and the widely
spread distress and discontent among the working classes, and
ecclesiastical affairs were in the background.   Pitt's influence
ruled public opinion, and the bulk of the clergy were hearty
supporters of Pitt.

The present writer must ask for some indulgence if he,
goes over ground which has already been traversed, to some
extent, by that volume of this series which treats of the
eighteenth century.   The important figures of the early
nineteenth century cannot be dissociated from the events
of the eighteenth, and a certain amount of repetition is
unavoidable.

The early history of the Church Missionary Society, of the
Bible Society and other religious and philanthropic associations, and of the agitation against the slave trade, High Church
throws a light upon the condition of parties in the   and
Church of England at the beginning of the nineteenth Low Church.
century.   It is sometimes assumed that the evangelical revival
which divided the Church into High and Low had put the
evangelical party in a dominant position.   Nothing can be
farther from the truth.   The preaching of Wesley and
Whitefield produced a deep and wide impression upon the
lower and middle classes, reinforced the 'Three Denominations' of Baptists, Presbyterians, and Independents, by a
large increase of members, and founded a new denomination.
But it hardly touched the clergy, the universities, or the upper
classes.   'Enthusiasm' was a byword among all; the spirit
of the non-jurors was almost dead, though there was still a
remnant who maintained Arminian or high Anglican doctrine;
all but a few held easy Church-and-State opinions, and were
content to leave things as they were, in 'dignified tameness.'
The Low Church or latitudinarian party traced their descent to

the Whigs of the Revolution, and were rather political than religious. The principal cause for distinction disappeared with the Jacobite danger, though before that High Churchmen had become Georgian, and Low Churchmen had become orthodox. Of 'vital religion' there was not much on either side. It must be acknowledged, and Mr. Stock, the historian of the Church Missionary Society, does not scruple to avow it, that the Clapham sect was not dominant in the Church of England. 'It represented a small minority; it was either hated or despised by most Churchmen.' One of the Venn family was excluded, merely on account of his name, from Trinity College, Cambridge; Henry Martyn was kept out of orthodox pulpits; when Hannah More was taken to Clapham in the carriage of Bishop Porteus, with whom she was staying, to call upon John Venn, the coachman was ordered to set her down at the Bull's Head, not at the Rector's door. 'Evangelical' clergy, as they called themselves, few in number but noisy and inconvenient, were looked upon as dangerous innovators and bad subjects. No high promotion for such men was dreamed of, either by themselves or by their supporters. It was with difficulty that they could be provided with humble livings, curacies or preacher-

Unpopularity of 'serious' Churchmen. ships; the universities rejected 'serious' candidates, and bishops scrupled at ordaining them and attacked 'Church-Methodism' in their charges. Even as late as 1810 the lists of subscribers to the Church Missionary Society contain no names of peers or bishops, no support from the cathedrals, nor from the universities, except so far as Simeon's friends may be reckoned. The clergy refused to let its missionaries preach in their churches, the older religious societies frowned upon them, the magistrates were slow to enforce the law in their favour.

But the shouting of preachers, the noise of hymn-singing in the fields, the secession to Methodism of many among the poor and the middle classes, the general shock to established institutions which was sent through the world by the French Revolution, could not but startle the slumbering Church. The instinct of defence was roused; the disturbers of quiet became more unpopular than ever, but more attention was drawn to their doctrines. The

Philanthropic movement.

evangelical school became identified with the philanthropic
movements which mark the latter part of the century, unquestionably the result of Rousseau's influence.

A tradition of holy friendship gives fragrance to the
'Evangelical Succession' of the eighteenth and early nineteenth centuries.   Newton and Cowper, the Wesleys
and Whitefield, the Hills, Venns, Bickersteths, Eminent
Evangelicals.
Thorntons, and Milners, Scott, Cecil, Hannah More,
and in the later generation Wilberforce and the Clapham
circle, Simeon and the Cambridge circle, were friends and
friends' friends, walking in the House of God.   They held
the same doctrines of moderate Calvinism, read the same
books, used the same devotions and religious observances,
maintained and suffered for the same causes, made the same
protest against worldliness both by precept and example;
in all they were supported by the strength of brotherhood.
There was wisdom as well as piety in their course of life, for
consistency always wins respect.   They rescued the old
tradition of Puritan seriousness and strictness of life from the
Pharisaism of respectability into which it had sunk, warmed it
into life by what their opponents called 'enthusiasm,' and
set an example of unobtrusive godliness which, however open
to ridicule and censure, raised the level of family life in
England, and did noble service in the cause of philanthropy.
It was this, more than their influence as religious teachers,
that put easy-going religion to shame.   Judged by their fruits,
they could claim to have revived personal religion in the
nation, and stimulated associated and corporate action.   To
a sensitive judgment they might seem even to incur the
imputation of dependence upon works, so freely cast upon
the Roman Church at the time of the Reformation.   Reliance
upon works was indeed one of the errors against which they
chiefly preached; the doctrine of the hymn 'Rock of Ages'
was their doctrine, and the vanity of secular learning and
charitable works their theme, nor were they ever untrue to
their principles; yet they owed their prominence in the early
years of the century principally to their activity in philanthropic
movements, headed by leaders who showed that strictness in
religion could be combined with efficiency in business.

In doctrine, these 'enthusiasts' were more fervent than

those who called themselves 'orthodox,' the official Protestant
party in possession and secure. Though they were
not 'Catholic-minded,' they gloried in the Prayer
Book, into the origins of which they had no mind
to inquire. Being a compact and militant body, they made
themselves felt within the Church. Influence came to them
by degrees, from the sincerity of their profession and the
honesty of their conduct; they made their way with the
world, and established themselves as a power by unity and
perseverance, not unaided by wealth and respectability, which
took the line of good works; and where simple piety might
have failed, they commanded attention, and took the kingdom
of the world by force. Evangelicalism had no philosophy of
religion but Christ crucified, no Church system
beyond that of the Church of England, with a
general benevolence towards all Protestant sects, no
learning to meet the attacks of deism and liberalism. It
did not hold such doctrines as that of the ultimate salvation
of all mankind, partly because it had never conceived them;
it kept aloof from all rationalising of sacrificial substitution
in the Atonement, or reconciliation of the natural with the
supernatural in daily life. It was uninterested in ecclesiastical history, took no account of the beginnings of historical
criticism, no part in Church organisation.

It may be objected to the evangelical school that its sense
of brotherhood to other Churches was founded on a common
dislike to Rome, a legacy from the Reformation. To base
brotherhood on a position not negative but of agreement was
the ancient Catholic way, which came in again with High
Church teaching, and also re-introduced the ancient Catholic
intolerance. To accept Lutherans and Calvinists as fellow-
workmen in Christ seemed to the Oxford school almost as
profane as it would have been for Athanasius to call Arius
brother. The theology of the Evangelicals was suspected of
unsoundness; they were accused of 'enthusiasm' because
they revered Wesley, Whitefield, and Grimshaw; of revolutionary opinions because they threatened the vested interests of
planters and nabobs in their zeal for abolition of the slave
trade and for Indian Missions; and of Jacobin opinions because
they favoured popular education. These were the objections

Their doctrine. (margin)

Evangelical theology. (margin)

of laymen : the clergy, both dignitaries and rank and file, disliked their toleration of dissent and their willingness to work with nonconformists of the Three Denominations. Bishop Jebb, a moderate and benevolent man, denounced the 'premature and spurious unity of a theologico-political compact' with these as 'an unity of pretence rather than of reality.' The best Dissenters, he thought, like the best Churchmen, were those who kept most strongly to their own doctrines. Thus the same men were accused of fanaticism and indifferentism. They condemned dissent, and held fast to the Church of England, but they admired Rowland Hill and Robert Hall, and looked upon the religious revival of the eighteenth century as the work of God.

Another religious revival was in preparation. Part of its motive power was to be found in the revival of the eighteenth century, which had kindled a flame on High Church altars, and had put lukewarmness and worldliness to shame. Yet those who felt the new warmth did not acknowledge the boon ; and indeed no class of men, lay or clerical, welcomes the sting which disturbs their quiet. The evangelical body disturbed comfortable conventions. It condemned things which those who condoned them were beginning to wish altered ; and when people are contemplating reforms, it is irritating to see them taken up by zealots who do not appreciate the rights of property and convention. There was among the High Church section of the Established Church, besides the High Church clergy. merely conservative and obstructive element, much piety and sincere observance of the old-fashioned order. Many of the opponents of the evangelical doctrines and methods were good Christians nursed on traditional and sacramentarian doctrine, believers in good works after the teaching of St. James, with high views of Church authority, better read in Church history and theology than their opponents, and inclined to despise their unlettered vehemence. The progress in religious activity which marks the nineteenth century would not have taken place without the evangelical revival of the eighteenth century. But having been begun on evangelical lines, it was better continued, at least for a time, by a body of men of a higher intellectual type, who grounded the thought of their school upon philosophy and history, as well as upon religious emotion, and whose action was corporate as well as individual, and speculative as well as practical.

Among the forces which constituted the later evangelical movement one of the most powerful was that notable brotherhood of Christian neighbours which is commonly known as the 'Clapham Sect,' a name given by Sydney Smith and perpetuated by the title of a well-known essay by Sir James Stephen the elder, and of which some account has been given in a former volume of this series.

Clapham sect.

Wilberforce and Stephen in Parliament and society, the Thorntons in the City, Lord Teignmouth and Grant in official life, took away the reproach of obscurity from the party; the friendship of Hannah More and Bishop Porteus adorned it. This knot of friends and philanthropists was bound together by the holy cause of Abolition, and interest in the temporal welfare of the miserable negro race quickened the zeal for its conversion to Christianity. We must admire their independence and courage, their zealous philanthropy, and their sincere and carefully cultivated type of religion; we cannot ignore their shortcomings in theology and Church history, their upholding personal religion to the neglect of united Church action and authority, which subjected them too much to leaders whom they idolised and flattered.

It is an idle question whether the bond which held together this circle of friends was primarily a bond of faith or of works, for the two were inseparable; the faith animated the works, the works were evidence of the faith. They were not men of conspicuous ability, with the exception of Wilberforce, nor scholars, nor even theologians : they were Christian men and women, working out the Christian life according to a common conception, and endeared to each other by common objects, associations, and occupations, and by the tie of friendship and neighbourhood. To Clapham, as to a Protestant Mecca, the evangelical world looked, partly, no doubt, because the Clapham coterie was wealthy and influential, but more because of the beauty of holiness which dwelt there. The Clapham community held aloof from political parties, which nevertheless they could move to their purposes, and from court and society. These saints converted the world to their views, not by poverty, but by the right use of riches. They lived in hand-

some houses, kept horses and carriages, bought and sold,
planted and builded, and thanked God for their good things,
whilst, Zaccheus-like, they gave half their goods to the poor,
and, labouring incessantly, made Mammon serve in their
workshop of philanthropy.

The locality of the new evangel, the 'villa-cinctured
common of Clapham,' the 'holy village,' was fixed by the
fact of its being the residence of Henry Thornton
(1760-1815), banker and Member of Parliament   Henry
for Southwark, 'the living spirit of justice,' the   Thornton.
untitled judge who 'never laid aside the ermine,' a philan-
thropist who gave away much more than the proportion of
Zaccheus, 'a wise, a good, and a happy man.' Thornton
lived in a large and luxurious house, for which his friend
William Pitt planned an oval saloon 'curiously wainscoted
with books.' His next neighbour, and for several years his
housemate, was William Wilberforce, between whose garden
and his own a *pervius usus* was always open. Granville
Sharp (1735-1813) lived close by, and among the neighbours
who shared the same interests were Zachary Macaulay (1768-
1838), the austere and silent father of the greatest talker that
the world has ever known, a man consumed by zeal for the
one absorbing interest of negro emancipation; Lord Teignmouth (1751-1834), the most just and generous but
least inspiring of Governors-General; James Stephen   James
(1759-1832), father, grandfather, and great-grand-   Stephen.
father of distinguished men who inherited his name; to whom
Henry Brougham gave the praise of high oratorical power, of
perfect sincerity, and of 'the strictest integrity and nicest sense
of both honour and justice.' Stephen, as well as his friends,
was an enthusiast for emancipation. 'Of all subjects, that
of the slave trade and slavery most engrossed his mind,' and
his connexion with Wilberforce, whose sister he married, kept
this great subject continually before his eyes.

Another of the friends collected at Clapham was Henry
Venn the younger (1796-1873), whose grandfather, Henry
Venn (1725-1797), the Vicar of Yelling, Hunts, was   The Venns.
one of the saints of the eighteenth century; a man
who preached 'absolute holiness,' and recorded in his diary
the smallest shadow of a sin. So sensitive was his conscience

that he records his conversion from the holiness of obedience
to the holiness of love.   After he had attained this he enjoyed
peace of mind.   Henry Venn the elder, like others of the
Claphamites, was remarkable for the charm of his conversation.
His son John and his grandson Henry were both born at
Clapham, of which parish John was Rector from 1792 to 1813.
Both John Venn and his son Henry were eminent members of
the evangelical party—far removed from Methodism ; Henry
Venn called John Wesley ' that unhappy man '—both were devoted to the suppression of the slave trade and the improvement
of the African race, and consequently to the missionary cause.

Other members of the Clapham society were Charles Grant
(1746-1823), Thomas Babington, and John Bowdler, whom
to name is to praise.   Nor must we omit that other society
at Cambridge, more learned and theological, and also less
wealthy, the spokesman of which was Isaac Milner, and its
spiritual guide Charles Simeon, both of whom were frequent
visitors at Clapham ; nor other visitors, Thomas Gisborne of
Yoxall (1758-1846), the inspired preacher; Josiah Pratt
(1768-1844), who may almost be called the founder of the
Church Missionary Society and the Bible Society ; and
Hannah More (1743-1833), who, though not a
resident at Clapham, was one of the friends always
welcome there.   Hannah More deserves mention
here, not for her position in society and literature, though
that was remarkable enough, but because she exemplifies the
character of the school to which she belonged in the consistent
sincerity of faith and practice, which led her to retire more
and more from the world of religious fashion, in which she
was almost supreme, in order to devote herself more completely to good works.   It may be that she was too conscious
of her own humility, and demanded too much adoration
from the worshippers at her shrine ; but these were blemishes
of taste rather than serious defects.   Her *Sacred Dramas*
and *Cheap Repository Tracts* have had their day, but they
were widely and beneficially read ; her attacks upon the vices
of the rich may not have produced a great effect, but in
making them she risked the imputation of arrogance and
hypocrisy.   Her courage was one of her finest qualities.   She
attacked the fashionable world, she left the fashionable world.

Hannah
More.

She faced clergymen, squires and farmers, and rough miners, from whom for years her life was in danger. An invalid, and subject to severe bodily pain, which seldom left her, she bore all weathers and fatigues. If she was a little affected—very little, considering the adulation she received—she was never censorious.

It would be a mistake to suppose that the evangelical code of manners, severe though it was, was gloomy and sour-visaged. If, as Stephen writes, 'the Clapham festivities were not exhilarating,' where Wilberforce was welcome, gaiety was not excluded. The atmosphere of Clapham was benevolent, not critical; where universal good-will reigned, uncharitable exclusiveness had no place.

The theologians and philanthropists who formed what is called the Evangelical School are now known to the world not by their writings, which are forgotten, but by their lives, which can never be forgotten. Any description of them, therefore, must be chiefly biographical; and the biographies of saints are monotonous, whether the monotony be of a Roman or a Protestant complexion. The saintly halo does not obliterate the human features, but it creates a kind of spiritual family likeness, such as may be observed in the countenances of those who have renounced the world, whether they are monks and nuns, Quakers, Evangelists and Deaconesses, or Salvationists and other visionaries. This expression may be imitated by 'the only power that walks unseen, hypocrisy,' and the character to which it corresponds may also be counterfeited. The lay world dislikes nothing more than official sanctity. Therefore, though no man was less a hypocrite than Charles Simeon or Daniel Wilson of Calcutta, or Edward Bickersteth, we would rather (setting aside men of such eminent saintliness as Legh Richmond and Henry Martyn, and others who lived a heavenly life upon earth) take instances of laymen than clergymen to illustrate the peculiar type of character which was favoured by Evangelicalism.

Pre-eminent among these is William Wilberforce (1759-1833), the saintliness of whose character shed a radiance upon the natural powers and graces which William Wilberforce. made him the most brilliant figure of his time in all kinds of company; the truest and warmest of friends, an orator as persuasive as he was eloquent, a wise and enlightened statesman. Wilberforce may truly be said to have given up to mankind what his friends would have reserved to party. Though he had at his command a great parliamentary position, and could have been the right-hand man, as he was the dearest friend, of William Pitt—and where among the distractions and temptations of public life shall we find a purer name than that of Pitt?—he refused all offers of ambition, being convinced that the service of God, as he understood it, was inconsistent with the service of the State, as that service was understood by those who conducted it. He may have been mistaken, but if so, his mistake was more noble than success would have been. As a party leader he would have had a larger share in the preparation of government measures and passing them through Parliament. But his influence upon Pitt would not have been greater and more wholesome than

it actually was, and he would have lost the benefit,
Wilberforce and Pitt. which was pre-eminently his, of detachment from party ties. He could differ from Pitt, and oppose

him publicly, without impairing the friendship which bound them together as intimately as if they had been brothers ; and he could stand aloof from party without damaging his reputation as a practical statesman, one who abstained, not capriciously, but on conviction, from the exercise of distinguished powers. He felt the strain, both at the outset and at a later period, when he saw himself passed by equals or inferiors, but he never faltered. 'It was his part,' as his son says, 'to give the example of an independent member of Parliament and a man of religion, discharging with activity and fidelity the duties of his trust, and not seeking to render his parliamentary station a ladder by which to rise to a higher eminence.'

The two things which kept up Wilberforce's credit were, first, respect for his honesty, and, secondly, the general belief, brought about by his own course of action, that it would have been impossible for him to give himself both to politics and to the cause of the abolition of slavery. For himself, perhaps the principal reason of his keeping aloof from party—and may we venture to suggest that the religious conscience was here too scrupulous, perhaps unwittingly too self-regarding?—was the feeling expressed in his diary, 'The world is my

snare. I require more solitude than I have had of late.
Early hours night and morning . . . prayer three times a
day at least, and begin with serious reading or contemplation.'
It is impossible to combine the life of a hermit with that of a
member of Parliament; and the sentence which follows shows
that good works, however unregenerate the doctrine, had his
heart. 'Slave trade my main business now.'

The abolition of the slave trade was the subject of
Wilberforce's chief care and thought as long as he lived;
what concerns us here is his inward life, the cultivation of
that temper of mind which he and his co-religionists thought
to be the mind of Christ. He and his friend, Isaac Milner,
while travelling through France, read Doddridge's *Rise and
Progress of Religion*, and in a second journey the New
Testament. In his youth, whilst leading the life of a man of
fashion and going to card-parties, balls, and theatres,
there was in his mind the latent feeling that all this Wilberforce
would have to be given up. In 1786, being then Newton,
twenty-seven years of age, he went to visit John 1786.
Newton at his church in the City, St. Mary Woolnoth. Wilberforce 'got nothing new from him, as how could I, except a
good hint that he "never found it answer to dispute." . . .
When I came away I found my mind in a calm, tranquil state,
more humbled, and looking up more devoutly to God.' A
little later came the conscious sacrifice of which he wrote many
years afterwards : ' By degrees the promises and offers of the
Gospel produced in me something of a settled peace of conscience. I devoted myself for whatever might be the term of
my future life to the service of my God and Saviour, and with
many infirmities and deficiencies, through His help I continue
until this day.'

If there is any difference between this temper of mind and
that of the saints whom the elder Church honours, it is to be
sought in the more introspective attitude of the soul. The
Catholic saint adores and waits for enlightenment, the Protestant
saint seeks and toils for salvation; the blessing of Rachel
rests on one, the blessing of Leah on the other;
it may be said also that the one is tempted to relax Wilberforce's
effort in contemplation, the other to rely on self- active charity.
righteousness. To Wilberforce the sight of human suffering

and sin was an irresistible spur to action. The story is well
known, but will bear repeating, how when he was on a visit
to Hannah More and her sister Martha at Cowslip Green
he was persuaded to go and see the neighbouring cliffs of
Cheddar. 'After breakfast to Cheddar,' he notes in his
diary for August 21, 1789: 'intended to read, dine, etc.,
amongst the rocks, but could not get rid of the people, so
determined to go back again. The rocks very fine. Had
some talk with the people, and gave them something—
grateful beyond measure—wretchedly poor, and deficient in
spiritual help. I hope to amend their state.' Or, as Martha
More describes it: 'When he returned, with the eagerness of
vanity (having recommended the pleasure), I inquired how he
liked the cliffs. He replied they were fine, but the poverty
and distress of the people was dreadful. This was all that
passed. . . . Mr. Wilberforce appeared at supper . . . the
servant at his desire was dismissed, when immediately he
began, "Miss Hannah More, something must be done for
Cheddar."' She goes on to say that from this moment she
and her sister set themselves to consider what could be done,
and with Wilberforce's help the candle was lighted at Cheddar
which threw its beams so far in lighting up the dark places of
the West.

No ties either of politics or friendship could hold Wilberforce against his conscience, as he showed conspicuously in
voting against 'the old firm' on the question of
peace with France in 1792. But neither did he
join the party of Parliamentary Reform. 'You will
soon see that you must join us altogether,' said Fox. Courted
by one party and disowned by the other, he maintained his
lofty and perilous independence.

We need not inquire what would become of party government if there were many Wilberforces. Party government
exists because Wilberforces are few. The moral of his public
life is that sincerity and courage, which are never parted,
always tell in human affairs. If Wilberforce and his friends
had not been Christians, if they had not held a strict form of
Christianity, it is doubtful whether they would have had
courage and force enough to carry their measure. If their
strength had been divided and frittered by separate ambitions,

they would have failed: their strength was in their single-heartedness, and this came from their religion. Not only did they succeed, but they left an example and an encouragement after them for those who will take up philanthropic work in the same spirit. The outward manifestation of this spirit was the courage which took no account of consequences and refused to temporise. Wilberforce in 1792 disdained to withdraw his motion for immediate abolition; and such was his ascendency over Pitt, that Pitt spoke for it 'with more energy and ability than were almost ever exerted in the House of Commons.' This is Wilberforce's own account.

The political courage which he showed on this occasion was sustained by ardent faith and the habit of prayer without ceasing. Private prayer and meditation was the mark of the Evangelical, as recourse to the public offices of the Church was the mark of the High Church school. They rose 'a great while before day' to pray, read, and meditate. 'I was out before six,' says Wilberforce, 'and made the fields my oratory.' Their prayers were deliberate and studied, guided neither by the emotion of the moment nor by the use of manuals. It was the practice of many of them, and Robert Hall recommended it 'on conviction,' to pray aloud. Silent prayer, they thought, became meditation, not petition. It is obvious that the familiarity with God's presence which accompanies continual prayer may easily lead to that kind of spiritual self-satisfaction which is repulsive to the unreligious mind, and which was perfectly understood by Thomas à Kempis. Christians of the traditional schools are restrained by authority, by formularies, and by the confessional, from over-estimating the value of their own convictions and emotions. The besetting sin of the Evangelicals, and Puritans in general, is not spiritual pride, but spiritual vanity. When a man seeks divine guidance on every occasion, and is convinced of his own integrity, it is difficult for him to avoid the belief that he is inspired. Even Wilberforce, 'at all times in good humour and in charity with all men,' is gently reminded by Southey that 'poor creature' is his name for those who have the misfortune to differ from him.

Wilberforce's life was too full of action, of reading, and meditation to afford him much leisure for writing: and his

Practical View, published in 1797, was written in 'occasional
intervals of leisure,' and bears traces of hasty composition, natural in the case of a man who was full of
and familiar with his subject, and eager to speak
his message.   The book is not a treatise on religion, but a
contrast between the religion of the world and 'real
Christianity'; its object is to point out that to those who
accept the Bible as true there is no middle way.   The whole
edifice of evangelical Christianity stands upon the foundation
of the depravity of mankind, the universal sentence of eternal
death imposed by the wrath of God, the consequent need of a
Mediator, the duty and privilege of a full surrender of all to
Christ.   The Christian religion is not a system of morality;
it is an enlistment of the affections and passions in God's
service.   The emotions need practice as much as the bodily
and mental faculties.

The moral, decorous, and charitable world, as it were, pays
a tithe to religion, or makes a composition with God by good
deeds, domestic virtues, and temperate indulgence.   But if
works are enough, why have any dealings at all with faith ?
Christianity is a religion of motives, not of works.   The
ordinary feeling among 'good people' generally is that it is
no great matter; God will not be extreme to mark what is
done amiss; their intention is good, their lives are clean, they
must live in the world, not in a cell.   The world looks upon
the greatest part of human actions as indifferent, and continually encroaches on the religious allotment.   But Christianity lays claim to the whole ground; she does not allow
things to be indifferent, she knows of no 'little sins.'   These
men of sober sensualism, sober avarice, and sober ambition
are outside her pale.   She bids them mortify the flesh; and
they desire a 'soft luxurious course of habitual indulgence.'
They wish for liberty; and her master-principle is to bring
every thought into captivity.   Such a doctrine cannot be com-
promised with.   It is identical with the esoteric teaching of
the Gospel; and if such language is to be interpreted literally,
it condemns the whole course of the world.   So do all other
attempts to reduce human social life to the rule of the
Gospel, from whatever quarter they come.   They are counsels
of perfection, and the holiest men do not carry them out con-

Wilberforce's
Practical
View.

sistently.   But without such ideals there is no salt in the
world ; and such progress in morality as is made comes by
their means ; not by intelligence, nor by force, nor entirely
by the paradox of weakness, but by persuasive power of
goodness.   Wilberforce may not have been a great originator of
ideas, but he gave to what he undertook the stamp of his own
character.   When eloquence, courtesy, and perfect honesty and
courage are combined with perseverance, they are irresistible.

Sir Thomas Fowell Buxton (1786-1845), Wilberforce's
partner and successor in the fight against slavery, and his true
brother in faith, is in some respects perhaps an even
nobler character than Wilberforce.   He had not
Wilberforce's versatility nor his shining gifts, and
therefore not the same temptations.   His massive character
might have been contented with the routine of business and
politics ; touched with the spark of conversion or conviction
he became a hero.   In his case conversion was a certitude
of salvation rather than a sense of sin and pardon.   Like
Wilberforce, he maintained his spiritual life by constant prayer.
His doctrine of prayer was that nothing is trivial—'there are
no little things with Him'—and therefore anything, however
small, may be made a subject of prayer.   Prayer is not
answered as we wish, but it is always answered.   Simeon
held a different language, but not inconsistent with this :
'to construe an inward persuasion of mine into an absolute
promise of God . . . I account it little better than blas-
phemy.'   Buxton, like Wilberforce, based his whole course of
action upon Christianity, like him he turned away from parliamentary honours, like him he disdained the hatred and slander
of his opponents, the supporters of the slave interest ; like
Wilberforce he was inflexible when his mind was made up, and
gained the supreme object of his life by his integrity and
inflexibility.   There is no nobler figure than Buxton in the
noble band of Christians who carried the abolition of the
slave trade, and of slavery itself, against the opposition of all
constituted authorities and vested interests, by the simple
method of unremitting diligence in exposing the wickedness
of the institution, till the nation became ashamed of what it
had supported or condoned.   He carried out in his life his
conviction that what makes the difference between man and

Thomas Fowell Buxton.

man is 'energy, invincible determination'; the direction of
his will, which must in any case have made its way, was due
to his religion, and his religious character was formed by
Christianity of the evangelical type, as he heard it expounded
by Josiah Pratt, the good Secretary of the Church Missionary
Society, whose chapel in Spitalfields he attended as a young man.

Charles Simeon (1759-1836), the friend and contemporary
of Wilberforce, was born in the same year as Pitt, and in-
Charles Simeon. habited Cambridge at the same time with Porson;
and these names illustrate his remoteness from the
world around him. His own world was the other
world; here, he was a stranger and a sojourner, indifferent
to criticism and fearless of opposition and violence. In these
smoother days we do not know such men. Simeon's conversion came from the accident of being summoned by the
Provost of his College to attend Holy Communion. The
youth who could say 'I thought Satan himself was as fit to
attend as I; and that, if I *must* attend, I *must* prepare for
my attendance there,' must have been half converted already,
and his fervours of self-abasement in the retrospect of his
ungodly life are not to be taken too literally. There is
perhaps a little 'dramaturgy' to be suspected in the lurid
descriptions of themselves which converted sinners give, looking back from a state of mind so different that it seems to
the sinner as if he had indeed become another man. It is
difficult to believe in the absolute depravity of Bunyan,
Cromwell, or Cowper. Who can doubt that those who
honoured Simeon had always honoured him, and that those
too near companions who had laughed at and browbeaten
him in the Long Chamber at Eton continued in the little
society of King's to 'buffet and afflict' him to the end?
There was much in Simeon that invited ridicule or dislike:
an affectation, or what seemed like affectation, of manner,
gesture, and speech, as he came 'dancing over the lawn' at
King's; 'the warm and eager manners of a foreigner'; a
face 'grotesque and versatile, and at the same time affecting';
a naturally impatient and restless temper, which now and
then broke out into unsanctified anger; an assumption of
superior knowledge and experience which yet was not inconsistent with real humility; a personal isolation which made

him seem 'not highly sensitive to contemporary currents
of action and thought,' and enabled him to say without
arrogance, 'the servant of God does not live under the
same laws as others'; and a fierce antagonism to worldly
compromises, which made his position as a clergyman in the
town almost unendurable for many years, and was resented so
keenly at home that Fellows of his own college 'would not
walk on the grass plat with him for a quarter of an hour.'
He would seem to have been marked out for an Ishmaelite ;
yet by faith and perseverance he prevailed over every obstacle.
He records that when seeking for guidance by the method
of *sortes sacrae*, he lighted on the verse, 'a man of Cyrene,
Simon by name : him they compelled to bear the cross.'
'Then lay it on me, Lord,' he exclaims ; 'henceforth I
bound persecution as a wreath of glory round my head.'

The facts of Simeon's life are few and simple : he lived
entirely in his rooms at Cambridge, except for the missionary
journeys which occupied some part of every year ; he chose
his manner of life deliberately, for he knew that he was one
born to exercise influence, by personal example, by
private conversation, and by preaching and expound-   His Friday
ing the art of preaching ; and this insistence,   evenings.
in and out of season, as it was the cause of his wide influence,
was also an occasion of offence to those who felt towards
him as the Athenians felt to Socrates. He had, we are
told, the manner of one expected to speak with authority,
an expectation not easily won.   The Friday evening meetings
in his college rooms were constrained and uncomfortable,
and to those who were not in the circle his manner of
conducting them appeared artificial and pretentious, the
consulting room of the ghostly physician turned into an
operating theatre thronged with admiring students ; there
was no ease, no sociable tea-making, no flow of conversation,
nothing of the atmosphere of a *salon* : but those who went
once went again.

It may be questioned whether Simeon completely followed
the doctrine that the servant of God must not strive ; whether
the protest which he made for many years to hold his position as preacher of evangelical religion in Trinity Church,
Cambridge, his presentation to which was notoriously dis-

tasteful to his parishioners, was worth the ill feeling which it cost. There were other pulpits at Cambridge, or if these were closed to him at the beginning, his courage and persistency must at last have gained him a hearing in the town where Isaac Milner reigned, since there he had set up his rest, being rightly convinced that his message was to the young men of the University. It was for their sake that he contended so long at Trinity Church; his design was to build up an evangelical tradition at Cambridge, and to educate clergymen and preachers. To this object he gave up his life and the greater part of his fortune; and *Horae Homi- leticae.* it was for them that he completed his chief literary labour, now dead on the shelf, the *Horae Homi- leticae*, or system of homiletics containing the 'skeletons' of more than two thousand sermons. His aim was to train up with his own hand a body of divines who should leaven the Church. In the same spirit he bequeathed most of his fortune to the institution of a body of trustees, who still make it their business to acquire livings and present evangelical nominees to them.

The young men responded eagerly to his zeal, loved, reverenced, and obeyed him. One after another caught fire at his altar, and went forth, sent by him to preach his doctrine. These were the men from whom he drew his curates, many of whom he afterwards sent out as missionaries; for Simeon made missionary work one of his principal cares, calling India his 'province'; Thomason, Henry Martyn, Daniel Wilson, Buchanan and others were sent by him; and his love for Martyn and Thomason (whose son he adopted) is one of the most beautiful things in his life.

Simeon was too strongly individual in character to be quoted as a type of Evangelicalism. And yet this very individuality bears testimony to the strength of the *Simeon's theology.* evangelical creed and the unity of the brotherhood. There was nothing original in his teaching. His originality was one of character, not of intellect. His doctrine was Bible doctrine of the simplest kind, untheological, narrow, and literal. He never doubted the absolute truth of every word of the Bible in its full, plain, and natural sense; he accepted the whole edifice of doctrine raised upon it by the divines whom his school followed ; acceptance by faith of the propitiatory sacrifice of Christ, and a life with God.   To inquire further was foolish as well as sinful.   The three aims he set before him were 'to humble the sinner, to exalt the Saviour, to promote holiness.'

He held in its completeness the doctrine of eternal re-probation, which, whatever its effects on charity, is a robust doctrine, capable of great effects on the conscience and life. He would speak of the mercy held out to himself, in his 'being out of hell.'   Another favourite tenet was the com-plete depravity of man, and the wrestling of grace and sin in the region of free will and divine foreknowledge.   Such teaching, held sincerely and humbly, could lead to great holiness of life, and Simeon's own life bore witness to it. There are few places which preserve holier memories than Simeon's oratory on the roof above his rooms at King's, where day by day he walked with God, seen by no human eye.   The many hours spent in solitary prayer and meditation prepared him for unwearying labour in saving souls, and en-abled him to overcome the private persecution of his College, the open hostility of the town, the neglect of his superiors, the sneers of the worldly and the learned in the critical society of a university, till in his old age he became an oracle, and his rooms a place of pilgrimage.

Simeon had no exclusive notions in religion.   He could see no important difference between the Churches of England and Scotland, and when he was in Scot-land he preached and received the sacrament in Presbyterian churches.   'Where the King *must* His compre-hensiveness. pray, his subject *may*.'   He put the edification of the congregation before the 'dignity of the pulpit,' and had no scruple, at least as a young man, in preaching in a barn. He was 'no friend to systematisers in theology'; believing that the truth lay between Arminian and Calvinist, that pious men of either persuasion 'approximate very nearly when they are upon their knees before God in prayer,' and that the Gospel which has to be preached to the poor must be plain and simple.   But he disapproved of dissent in all its forms, and was a strong upholder of Episcopalianism, the Church of England, and the Prayer Book.   'I am never nearer to God,' he said, 'than I often am in the reading-desk'; he distrusted extemporaneous prayers as being often barren, an exhibition of 'official fluency' obtained by habit; and 'as for the Liturgy, no commendation can be too great for it. . . . If a whole assembly were addressing God in the spirit of the Liturgy, as well as in the words, there would be nothing to compare with such a spectacle on the face of the earth; it would approximate more to heaven than anything of the kind that was ever yet seen in this world.' Some even went so far as to say that he was 'more of a Churchman than a Gospel man.'

Simeon was the centre and, to some extent, the founder of the evangelical society which made Cambridge a double star with Clapham. Farish (1759-1837), Scholefield (1789-1853), Thomason (1774-1829), Martyn (1781-1812), Kirke White (1785-1806), and Corrie (1777-1837) were his pupils, and some of them his curates. Isaac Milner (1751-1820), the genial President of Queens', was his senior, Farish and John Venn (1759-1813) his contemporaries, the rest were younger; and Simeon's persuading or compelling genius made him by far the most influential member of the group in which Dean Milner was the most commanding personality and the public champion of the Cambridge Evangelicals at the beginning of the nineteenth century. 'The Dean,' Dean Milner. as he was always called, being Dean of Carlisle, as well as President of Queens', held a great position in the University. He has often been compared with Dr. Johnson, whom he resembled in his dictatorship of conversation, his clumsy figure, his emotional and benevolent character, his strong and somewhat eccentric opinions, though the Dean was neither High Churchman nor Jacobite. He was greatly beloved at his two homes, Cambridge, where he ruled half the University, and Carlisle, where he ruled the Chapter and the Bishop. 'He had,' says Sir George Trevelyan, 'boundless good-will for all his fellow-creatures at every period of life, provided that they were not Jacobins or sceptics.' Thomas Macaulay describes his kindness to himself as a boy. In theological opinion he was a moderate Calvinist, counting all 'orthodox' Protestant Dissenters as brethren, and at the same time, like Simeon and most of the Evangelicals of his day, strongly attached to the Church of England, and opposed to all change in her articles, homilies, and liturgy. Milner was not closely associated with the Clapham coterie; the Cambridge group of Evangelicals, though one in spirit with Clapham, had their own field, more directly religious than humanitarian.

In the hagiology of the evangelical section of the Church, the founder of the agitation against the slave trade deserves more than a passing mention. This agitation was originally set on foot by Granville Sharp (1735-1813), 'the first labourer' in the cause in England. His name came prominently forward as early as 1765 in the case of Jonathan Strong, a negro who had been barbarously used by his master, David Lisle; in 1771 in that of another slave, James Somersett, on which occasion Lord Mansfield delivered his famous dictum about the freedom of all slaves on British soil; and later again (1783) in the horrible affair of the *Zong* slave ship, the master of which threw more than a hundred sickly slaves overboard on the plea of danger to the ship; the true reason being that if they died a natural death the loss would fall on the owners, if they were drowned for the sake of the vessel, on the underwriters. 'The law,' said Lord Mansfield, 'though it shocks me very much, is the same as if they had been horses.' The Abolition Society, founded by Sharp, had, as the fundamental article of its creed, the humanity of the black race. Its well-known device was a kneeling negro, with the motto, 'Am I not a man and a brother?' The detestable traffic in slaves was justly described by Henry Thornton as 'war, not trade; a mass of crimes, and not commerce.' Yet it was justified by sensible, humane, and religious men.

What Sharp began, Thomas Clarkson (1760-1846) carried forward. He devoted his whole life and energy to the cause, and lived to see the slave trade abolished in 1807 and the Emancipation Act passed in 1833. His strongest coadjutors were Zachary Macaulay and Wilberforce, who brought into the cause not only his own eloquence and persuasive grace, but the support of Pitt as well as Fox, and the sympathy of all his religious friends. It must not be forgotten that the first suggestion of the idea of abolition came from the Quakers as early as 1727, and that

Slave trade. Granville Sharp.

Thomas Clarkson.

the Committee of Twelve 'for effecting the abolition of the
slave trade' contained nine members of the Society of Friends.
For many years the wicked traffic had been denounced by
moralists and poets, Baxter, Steele, Pope, Cowper, Johnson,
Wesley; but to gather the mass of undefined sentiment to a
head and give to the cause the cohesion and organisation of
a party required a leader.   Clarkson's task was to rouse a
nation against an interest.   With astonishing courage and
persistency, and with a mind bent to this one object, he
made head against the interest, sparing neither his money
nor his health.   On one occasion he boarded no less than a
hundred ships in three weeks' time, to find one witness; he
travelled more than 35,000 miles to collect evidence and get
Progress of signatures to petitions.   The petitions showed the
the emanci- House of Commons its duty, and turned the current
pation move- of opinion; and though the bill for immediate aboli-
ment. tion was thrown out, the language of its supporters,
Pitt, Fox, Burke, and Wilberforce, was triumphant and announced the assurance of victory.   But the interest combined
their forces and fought hard, and victory was delayed.

We notice that the evangelical element on the Committee
for Abolition becomes stronger as the agitation progresses;
Stephen, Teignmouth, Macaulay, Grant, and John Thornton,
all Claphamites, were added to it.   The band of Wilberforce's
fellow workers was led to success through the organisation of
the evangelical party, and especially the laymen of the party.
The clergy of an established Church are likely to be timid in
The clergy supporting large measures of philanthropy or social
and abolition. reform which rouse strong popular feeling or are
opposed by great interests; no agitation was ever
carried on with more bitterness than this; and the clergy
may pardonably have shrunk from putting themselves at
the head of the anti-slavery movement.   This movement had
its first beginnings from the bosom of the evangelical party;
and this was a reason, though an unworthy reason, for the
coldness with which it was met by the bishops and other
dignitaries of the Church.   When the trade in slaves was
abolished, and the abolitionists went on to attack the
institution of slavery itself, the attack was led by laymen;
throughout that magnificent struggle with greed, cruelty, and

stupidity which has raised the names of Wilberforce and Buxton above those of statesmen and generals, there is little mention of the clergy. In the revulsion of public opinion which in both instances, the abolition of the slave trade and the abolition of slavery itself, converted the Government and carried the bills, the clergy followed where they should have led.

The anti-slavery movement became a political question, and it was necessary for its promoters to carry on their campaign in Parliament. Pitt was heartily in its favour, and would have risked more for the cause if he could have been an Evangelical, instead of Pitt and abolition. what Wilberforce called a 'natural' man ; but circumstances retarded his action, in spite of his close friendship with Wilberforce ; the King was against abolition ; so were Dundas and other important members of his Government ; the insurrection of the slaves in St. Domingo in 1791 showed the danger which might follow a grant of liberty to the blacks. Many causes contributed to a reaction of feeling ; fear of Jacobinism made all meddling with established things unpopular, the war with France absorbed public attention, and Parliament was unwilling to irritate the Colonies, especially those which had lately been annexed by war. Pitt, it may be thought, might have passed the measure now or at an earlier date ; but to Pitt, as to other statesmen, politics came before philanthropy, and though powerful, he was not omnipotent. One of his greatest speeches was in favour of abolition ; but he did not make it a cabinet question, nor risk his tenure of office on such an issue. When the success of British arms at sea caused a great development of the slave trade under the British flag, to the extent, it was stated, of doubling the numbers of slaves imported annually in British ships, Pitt took no measures to discourage it. For several years Wilberforce abstained from parliamentary action ; and in 1804, when Pitt succeeded Addington, and the Union with Ireland had increased the abolitionist vote, Pitt did nothing to help him. Fox, who said that abolition was nearest to his heart and peace next, died within sight of victory ; and the Abolition Bill was passed by Grey on February 23, 1807. Similar circumstances attended the second stage of liberation, that of the abolition of slavery itself, a stage implied in the earlier period, but not carried till 1833.

The good things, and with them the scandals, of the religious world, principally belonged to the High Church and Low Church divines whose minds were not set upon reform ; and, as we have already noted, the evangelical party in the Church, though it has had worldly support and been favoured by aristocratic patrons, has never been in favour with the great world. The work done by the Claphamites and their successors in the field of philanthropy was so great

Evangelical party not influential.

that they could not be ignored, but though they were powerful they were not popular. The access of Evangelicals to the high places of the Church was long obstructed. The first conspicuous Low Church bishop was Henry Ryder (1777-1836), a brother of Lord Harrowby, made Bishop of Gloucester in 1815, and translated to Lichfield in 1824; a warm supporter of the Church Missionary Society, and the first bishop who ordained missionaries direct to the country in which they were to work, instead of requiring an apprenticeship in an

Bishop Charles Sumner.

English diocese. Charles R. Sumner (1790-1874), a royal chaplain, but not a courtier only, was made Bishop of Llandaff in 1826, and a year later translated to Winchester, which see he held for forty-two years. His short tenure of Llandaff was a time of great activity, and he changed the whole face of the diocese of Winchester. He set up rural deaneries, required clergy to reside and hold services, insisted on cleanliness in churches and church-yards, and visited all parts of his diocese in person. He deserves to be mentioned with Blomfield of London, Wilber-force, Copleston, and Stanley as one of the 'organisers of the episcopacy.' Sumner, like his brother the Archbishop of Canterbury, gave promotion to evangelical clergymen ; he began the restoration of churches in his diocese, and established a Church Building Society and Diocesan Board of Education, and a special fund for South London, which till a few years ago was part of the overgrown diocese of Winchester.

When the generation of Wilberforce and his friends had passed away, the evangelical party suffered by the absence of a local centre. Clapham had been a centre and a

treasury, and thence had come the impetus which founded
societies.   They had already the Societies which will be the
subject of the next chapter, the Religious Tract Society, the
Church Missionary Society, the Bible Society, the Jews
Society, the Newfoundland Society (1823), the Colonial
Church Society (1838), and the Church Pastoral Aid Society
(1836), which aroused much obloquy by employing lay
evangelists.   There was not much need of new societies;
what was needed was a central organisation and
place of meeting.   Exeter Hall, built in 1831,   Exeter Hall,
had the motto ΦΙΛΑΔΕΛΦΕΙΟΝ engraved over   1831.
the portal; here, in May and June, year by year, Evangelicals from all parts of the world met and arranged their
operations.   Exeter Hall was beloved neither by the world nor
by the Church; but it was the workshop of a practical idea,
and it succeeded.   The Evangelical Societies found a centre
there, and carried on the traditional work of missionary enterprise, besides looking after church organisation and, so far as
possible, supplying churches with an evangelical succession.
The Hall is gone, but the May meetings, which afford an easy
butt for satire, have since that time been a power in the
religious world.   Besides the Church Societies, the National
Society, the Society for the Propagation of the Gospel, the
Church Missionary Society, and the Church Pastoral Aid
Society, many other societies, both denominational and free,
such as the Bible Society, the Religious Tract Society, the
Baptist and other missionary societies, held their yearly
meetings in Exeter Hall, and vast sums of money were collected
there and poured into religious treasuries.

Among the leading men of the early period were Thomas
Dale of St. Bride's, afterwards Dean of Rochester (1797-
1870), Henry Melvill of Camden chapel, 'the Evangelical
Chrysostom' (1798-1871), J. W. Cunningham of Harrow
(1811-1861), Henry Blunt of Chelsea (1794-1843), and Daniel
Wilson of Islington (1772-1858), Bishop of Calcutta in 1832.
It is noted that Wilson introduced at Islington early communions,
saints' day services, and the Litany on Wednesdays and Fridays.

The Evangelicals invaded the great towns and captured
their pulpits.   Hugh M'Neile conquered Liverpool, Hugh
Stowell (1799-1865), Manchester, Francis Close, Cheltenham,

where his power was so great that he was able to stop the town races in spite of all opposition. At Birmingham the patronage of the parish church and three chapelries passed to evangelical trustees. The leading Evangelicals are, to some extent, local names, not men known throughout the country, as were Newman, Pusey, and Manning. M'Neile, Stowell, and Close were men of mark, but M'Neile was the only one who, as an orator, kindled the imagination of the public. Though he was a thorn in the side of the bishops and impatient of clerical control, one of the greatest Churchmen of the last century, if the Church is to be judged by her fruits, was undoubtedly Anthony Ashley, Earl of

Lord Shaftesbury.

Shaftesbury. Apart from the philanthropic work in which his life was spent, the interests of the evangelical party were always a matter of keen interest to Lord Shaftesbury. He was never too busy to take the chair at a meeting ; and no regard for his position as a statesman or the head of a great house prevented him from coming forward whenever he felt that he could be useful ; and therefore he could do what he liked without fear of losing caste. The main facts of Lord Shaftesbury's life, however, belong to a later period, and to social rather than religious history.

It is difficult, when there is so much religious activity abroad in the world, to estimate the comparative progress of a party like the evangelical party, after the original impulse had more or less expended its energies upon negro emancipation and missionary work, and its

Progress of the evangelical party.

first pioneers had died. The principles of the party were the same, but after 1833, the date of the Oxford Movement, the rising tide was with the High Church party, for reasons both secular and spiritual. No one will deny to the Tractarians holiness of life, enthusiastic piety, and zeal for the truth ; they were more learned than the Evangelicals ; they had also on their side the weight which comes naturally to those who have attractive novelties to offer, beauty of services, the revival of religious art, veneration for antiquity, the hope of unity, the enthusiasm of discovery ; whereas the ideal of the Evangelicals was plain-suited, quiet and unadventurous, and their action directed rather to guide and check than to stimulate. ' Catholic ' is a more powerful

word than 'Protestant.'   High Churchmen have borne witness
to the exalted piety of the Evangelicals of half a century
ago, among whom 'everything, down to the minutest details
of action and speech, was considered with reference to
eternity': but their form of piety was growing out of fashion,
and it was not the theology but the good works of Clapham
and Islington that commanded the respect of Englishmen.

The Evangelicals laid great stress on individual religion, as
opposed to corporate religion, and encouraged an undenominational temper.   They cared little for the outward framework
of the Church ; they had little idea of the Church or of the
State as a Divine institution, their business was with personal
salvation ; 'their ethical ideal of the individual Christian was
wanting in wealth and variety' ; they did not, like the ancient
Church, seek to conquer the world in its science and politics
and literature.   They had little zeal or enterprise even in the
search for truth ; they regarded whatever truth was important
as already discovered, and loved truth less for its own sake
than as an engine of salvation.   The love of souls was their
motive, and separation from the world their method ;
for they held the sternest doctrine as to the wicked- *Evangelical
ness of the world and the imminent danger of eternal religion indi-
perdition.   'Save, Lord, by love or fear,' was no vidual, not corporate.
mere form of words with them, but the expression of their
constant thought.   Such severity of teaching and life required
the presence of living teachers and an untiring organisation to
keep it from decline ; and in fact after Simeon's generation it
did decline.   Inelastic and unenlightened, and not curious
of anything which lay to right and left of the strait path of
salvation, Evangelicalism cannot be said to have failed, but it
was little capable of development, and what development it
has attained has come, at any rate in some degree, by reflection from without.

The question which continually recurs is whether the more
enlightened Evangelicals of to-day, within and without the
Church, have the same love for souls which inspired Simeon ;
whether zeal is chilled by the weakening of the motive of fear,
so strong in the early Evangelicals, by whom the mediæval
doctrine of hell was held as strongly as any part of their
creed ; whether the Puritan tradition of belief and manners

has lost its savour by being diluted with laxer views of the importance of a rigid scheme of doctrine, and a sharply-drawn line distinguishing worldly custom and learning from the simplicity of Gospel truth and walking with God. These questions do not affect the descendants of the evangelical school only : they affect all schools of religion, since Christians

Dangers of toleration. first began to question the truth of the proposition that 'the devil would for his purpose rather have a toleration than any other form of falsehood' ; for if Christians may meet non-Christians and Dissenters on neutral platforms, and work with them in a spirit of brotherhood, indifferentism is at the door, and 'zeal and quick-eyed sanctity' are endangered by seeking to 'halve the Gospel of God's grace.' Newman's conflict with Liberalism was conducted in the same spirit as that which made Simeon refuse to vote for his friend's son who was pledged to Catholic Emancipation, the spirit of dogma, which is essentially intolerant. The good-natured relegation of all troublesome personal doubts to the twilight region of 'invincible ignorance' is disturbing even the rigidity of Roman Catholic orthodoxy ; it is thus that the common sense of the world breaks down the strongholds of superstition. Lady Huntingdon would be as impossible in these days as Bishop Bonner ; here and there in a Scotch manse or a Lincolnshire village there may be found a rigid Calvinist uplifted in heart by the doctrine of predestination to eternal death ; but for the rest of the world this doctrine is practically though not theoretically obsolete.

AUTHORITIES : GENERAL.—Overton, *Engl. Church in XIX. Cent.* ; Hore, *The Church in England from Will. III. to Victoria* ; Hunt, *Religious Thought in England in XIX. Cent.* ; Perry, *Student's Engl. Church Hist.*, vol. iii. BIOGRAPHIES : *Wm. Wilberforce*, by S. Wilberforce ; *Charles Simeon*, by Moule, Carey, Brown ; *Hannah More*, by Miss Yonge ; *Annals of a Clerical Family*, by Venn ; *Sir Thos. Foxwell Buxton*, by Buxton ; *Edw. Bickersteth*, by Birks ; *Autobiography*, by Bp. Watson ; *Essays in Eccles. Biography*, by Stephen.

CHAPTER II

IN the formation of religious societies, such as the Bible Society and the Church Missionary Society, the evangelical party took up a new relation to the needs of the time, and a new and permanent position as the promoters of philanthropic and missionary work, and gained in public opinion in consequence. Few religious leaders of the time are worthy to be compared with the friends who promoted the dispersion of the Bible, the growth of Sunday schools, abolition and emancipation, whether Churchmen or Nonconformists, for they now began to work side by side. Two centuries earlier, correctness of dogma was the first requirement of religion ; and the comprehension which distinguishes the Church of England, though designed to include in practice different ways of thinking, in formal terms excludes divergence. The ecclesiastical and philosophical theology of the seventeenth and eighteenth centuries had given place to the emotional theology of the evangelical school. The barriers of religious difference were weakened, and the rising school of politicians were philanthropists as well as Christian believers.

The evangelical philanthropists were not inattentive to the needs of the unenlightened and ignorant at home ; and another Society which owed its existence to them was the Religious Tract Society, founded in 1799. Though the Church of England Society for Promoting Christian Knowledge had been at work for a century, and the undenominational Society for Diffusing Religious

35

Knowledge among the Poor for fifty years, they perceived that the movement for general Christian education needed further development. Wilberforce initiated a Society for the Reformation of Manners in 1787, which distributed tracts. As the number of readers grew larger it was desirable to supply them with pure literature. The example had been set long ago by John Wesley, who gave away 'some thousands' of tracts; Hannah More began the publication of *Village Politics, by Will Chip*, in 1793, and issued from 1795 to 1798 the *Cheap Repository Tracts*, some of which bore titles which are still familiar, such as the *Shepherd of Salisbury Plain, Black Giles the Poacher*, and *Tawny Rachel*; these were sold in immense numbers; Wilberforce's *Practical View* was published in 1797; Magazines were set up, the *Gospel Magazine*, the *Spiritual*, the *Evangelical*; and in 1799, on the occasion of the London Missionary Society's anniversary, a meeting was held to consider the best means of preparing and circulating evangelical tracts. The anniversary sermon was preached by Rowland Hill on May 8, 1799, and after the service he and the Rev. George Burder of Coventry asked a few friends to meet and discuss a plan for the publication of evangelical tracts which had been already prepared by Burder. According to the fashion of those days, it was agreed to meet at St. Paul's coffee-house at breakfast the next morning at seven o'clock. A meeting was held after breakfast, and in two days more the preliminaries were completed, and the Religious Tract Society formed and named.

The Religious Tract Society was established on an unsectarian and evangelical basis. The first Committee, like all subsequent Committees, contained clergymen of the Church of England and other denominations. Joseph Hughes, a Welsh Baptist, minister of a chapel in Battersea, and five years later the founder of the Bible Society, was the first secretary. Among the first helpers were Zachary Macaulay, Edward Bickersteth (1788-1850), Legh Richmond (1772-1827), Dr. Steinkopff, and others whose names are familiar. The Religious Tract Society was only another aspect of their manifold religious and charitable activity. The tracts were to treat of Gospel truth and the salvation of sinners, and exhorta-

Its first promoters.

tion was their main subject; but they were not to be
merely sermons in type. They were to be plain, striking,
entertaining, full of ideas and variety. When the first writers
found that there was a danger of tedium, they published tracts
of a more popular form, after the pattern of Hannah More's
compositions. Such writings as Legh Richmond's *Dairyman's
Daughter* and *Young Cottager* were printed and sold by tens
of thousands. A 'Hawkers' Series' of tracts, both entertaining
and instructive, was begun, and had an immediate success.
In two years' time more than a million had been sold. The
Society's tracts were translated into many foreign languages;
for the missionary zeal of these enthusiasts included foreign
countries. Germany, Sweden, Switzerland, Russia, and even
India and China, were visited by purveyors of tracts.
Auxiliary societies in the United States and Canada and at
home sprang up and increased; the methods of the Religious
Tract Society were the same which had conspicuous success
in the Bible Society, of which this Society was the parent.

A Society had long existed for the supply of Bibles to
the army and navy, and the Society for Promoting Christian
Knowledge also distributed Bibles; but the supply
fell short of the demand, and no enterprising Bible
Societies.
publisher came in to help. As early as 1787 an
unsuccessful attempt was made to get a number of Welsh
Bibles printed for distribution in the Principality. Not only
was the number offered too small, since the Society for
Promoting Christian Knowledge refused to part with more
than 500 copies, but the price, 5s. 6d., was prohibitive.
There was great complaining amongst the poor for want of
Bibles; Welsh Bibles could not be had even for money. The
bishops do not seem to have troubled themselves about
the business. In 1791 the Society for Promoting Christian
Knowledge undertook to publish 10,000 Welsh Bibles on
condition that the price of 4000 copies was guaranteed. So
languid was the bookselling trade, or so faint the interest felt
in the affairs of Wales, that the plan was dropped, the necessary
number of subscribers not being obtained. It was not till
1799, twelve years after the question was first raised, that
the Society for Promoting Christian Knowledge issued
editions of the Bible, New Testament, Prayer Book, and

New Version of the Psalms in Welsh ; and these—for the Society once moved to action was liberal—were to be sold to any inhabitant of Wales at half the prime cost.

No Welsh Bible had been printed for thirty years; and though the whole impression of 10,000 was immediately sold, the number of copies issued was miserably insufficient. The Society for Promoting Christian Knowledge, however, refused to print any more, and the question of providing a larger supply of Bibles was discussed in evangelical circles. Wilberforce and his friend Charles Grant promised their help, and Dr. Steinkopff, pastor of the Lutheran congregation in the Savoy, undertook to make the design known in Germany and Switzerland.　The Rev. Thomas Charles of Bala had come up to a Committee meeting of the Religious Tract Society on December 7, 1802, and had told the story of Welsh Bibles. a little Welsh girl, Mary Jones of Tynoddol, who walked over the mountains every week to read and learn the Sunday's text, since she had no Bible of her own ; and who, when she had saved up pence enough to buy a Bible and had walked thirty miles to get one, found that not a copy was to be had.　The Committee resolved to take steps for stirring up the public mind to the dispersion of Bibles generally ; and it was from this incident that the British and Foreign Bible Society took its beginning.　It was then that Joseph Hughes, the Secretary of the Religious Tract Society, asked the memorable question, ' If Bibles were to be printed for Wales, why not for the British Empire and the world ? ' He also, about this time, printed an Essay on the subject of the more general dispersion of the Holy Scriptures, in which, whilst acknowledging the good work done by the Society for Promoting Christian Knowledge, the Society for the Propagation of the Gospel, and other societies, he proposed that a society should be formed ' for promoting the most extensive circulation of the Holy Scriptures both at British and Foreign Bible Society founded, 1804. home and abroad.'　A meeting was held on March 7, 1804, Granville Sharp being in the chair ; and the first resolution passed was that the designation of the new society should be ' the British and Foreign Bible Society,' and its sole object ' to encourage a wider dispersion of the Holy Scriptures.'　The Bishop of London

(Porteus), 'after a reasonable delay,' gave his approval to the scheme, and recommended Lord Teignmouth as 'an excellent President.' Lord Teignmouth was a fervent Christian and a good man of business. Among the other supporters of the Society were Sharp, Macaulay, Wilberforce, Thornton, Stephen, and Grant. We notice among the first rules of the Society that the English Bibles were to be 'the Authorised Version, without note or comment'; and (a significant fact, when it is remembered that the Society had episcopal sanction from the first) that the Committee, out of thirty-six laymen, included fifteen Nonconformists and six resident foreigners, presumably Lutherans or Calvinists; all ministers of the Gospel, whether Episcopalians or not, had *ex officio* a seat and a vote in the Committee.

The names of the promoters, including as they do those of the prominent members of the Clapham group, as well as the character and description of the Society, announce an evangelical origin. The founders of the Bible Society had no dislike or distrust of Protestant bodies outside the Church of England; there was no 'pious estrangement or consecrated hostility.' But there is no ground for attributing to the Society a dissenting origin or colour. It was in no way sectarian; it claimed to be an association of 'Christians at large'; but it was founded in decided connexion with the Established Church, and to this day the archbishops and bishops are amongst its Vice-Presidents.

Bible Society not sectarian.

We are inclined in these later days to pride ourselves on toleration, and to take credit for meeting religious opponents on social and charitable platforms. But here was a religious question handled on equal terms by Churchmen, English Nonconformists, including Quakers, and members of foreign churches, and hardly a discordant note was heard. It is worth recording that when the President, Lord Teignmouth, proposed that the various nonconformist members of the Committee should add to the list other names from among their own religious connexions, they declined the offer, the Wesleyans saying that they considered themselves represented by the bishops, and other classes of Dissenters declaring themselves contented with the Committee as constituted. This

temper of mind is remarkable, when we remember that twelve
years earlier (1792) Burke had supported Pitt in
opposition to Fox's attempt, favoured by Lord North
himself, to give relief to the Unitarians, and whilst
arguing in favour of religious liberty in general, laid down that
this liberty should be closely defined and limited by law, and
should not extend to a non-Christian association.   Unitarians,
it is true, were in a different category from other Dissenters, and
it may be doubted whether Lord Teignmouth's Committee
would have admitted Unitarians as such, pledged as they were
to political as well as religious unorthodoxy ; but there was no
rule made to exclude them ; and in 1830, when such an
attempt was made, it ended in a schism in the Society and
the secession of a number of members, who formed the
Trinitarian Bible Society.

Religious toleration. (left margin note)

The promoters of the Bible Society were soon attacked
on the score of latitudinarianism, and were ready to defend
themselves.   Steinkopff's labours on the Continent brought
the Society into correspondence with the Reformed Churches
of Germany and Switzerland, Sweden, Denmark, and Norway,
and proposals were made in connexion with the Baptist
Mission at Serampore for translations into the Indian languages,
and also for a Chinese translation.   The Society was rising
in popular esteem : it had episcopal patronage, and
was able to deal with the Cambridge University
press for stereotyped copies of the Scriptures.   It
was now thought well to introduce the newly formed Society to
the notice of the Society for the Promotion of Christian Knowledge and the Dublin Association for Discountenancing Vice.
From the Society for Promoting Christian Knowledge no
answer was received, but the Dublin Society answered with
a friendly welcome.   This action was followed by the despatch
of a letter to the 'parochial clergy, dissenting ministers, and
other respectable persons individually.'   The Society, by the
nature of its constitution, had taken up a pan-Protestant
attitude, and was in danger of attack from that section of
the Church of England which looked upon Lutherans and
Calvinists as schismatic if not heretical bodies.   Accordingly
within a year of the Society's foundation 'a Country Clergyman' published an address to Lord Teignmouth, the President,

Translations of the Bible. (left margin note)

in which he complained of 'associations of discordant principles, combinations of men professedly at variance and in hostility with each other,' as only tending to supply Socinians, Quakers, and Papists with arms against the Church. The bishops investigated facts, and thought the charge unfounded; the pamphlet was withdrawn and the controversy dropped. The circumstance is only mentioned here because the association of 'the Prelate and the Presbyterian, the Lutheran and the Calvinist, the Peer and the Quaker' was not likely to go long unchallenged, still less to put an end to 'the long and disgraceful reign of misunderstanding and hostility among professing Christians.' The whole incident is creditable to the moderation and good feeling of the Society and of the bishops, and throws light upon the moderating influence possessed by cool-headed prelates like Porteus of London and Barrington of Durham.

The Society went rapidly forward. A demand for Bibles having been created, it was difficult to keep pace with it. Within three years correspondence was established with Iceland, Esthonia, Russia, even as far as trans-Caucasia, the East and West Indies, and the Cape, and preparations were made for printing the Bible in the languages spoken in those remote quarters of the world. Meantime at home the Welsh were not forgotten, and many thousands of copies were sent into Wales. 'When the arrival of the cart was announced which carried the first sacred load, the Welsh peasants went out in crowds to meet it, welcomed it as the Israelites did the In Wales. Ark of old, drew it into the town, and eagerly bore off every copy, as rapidly as they could be dispersed. The young people were to be seen consuming the whole night in reading it. Labourers carried it with them to the field.'

The efforts of the Society to send Bibles to India were checked by the jealousy with which the Government of India traditionally regards missionary enterprise. Lord In India. Wellesley, 'the friend of religion and the patron of learning,' left India in 1806, and his successors, Cornwallis and Barlow, were unfavourable. A stockholder of the East India Company, Irving by name, published a pamphlet against propagandism in India. The Society replied that missionary work was not within their province, which was strictly limited

to the printing and dispersing of the Scriptures : and the Court of Proprietors did not think fit to interfere. It is interesting to learn that Warren Hastings, who was not in favour of missionary activity, as tending to disquiet the minds of the natives and make them suspicious of the Government, was a warm supporter of the Bible Society. Irving was answered by Bishop Porteus and Lord Teignmouth, and in anonymous pamphlets, which maintained that the Bible ought to have as fair a chance of being read as the Koran and the Vedas; that a Christian Government, whilst respecting native institutions, ought not to forbid its subjects to become Christians ; and that the excesses which the Hindu religion encouraged and prescribed 'were so horrible that no Christian people can wish for their continuance.'

Controversy about propagandism in India.

The Society was not yet free from trouble ; and it was in truth an aggressive Society, and likely to get into trouble. Its leaders seemed to be upsetting old foundations and building a new church edifice ; they were leagued with un-covenanted Christians of every kind, disturbers of church order and discipline, contemners of bishops. The death of Bishop Porteus in 1809, and the promotion of Dr. Randolph to the See of London in the following year gave an opportunity for a High Church attack, led by Dr. Christopher Wordsworth (1774-1846), Dean of Bocking, and afterwards Master of Trinity College, Cambridge, who published in 1810 a pamphlet expressing objections to the intrusion of an undenominational society on the province of the Society for Promoting Christian Knowledge. He was answered by Lord Teignmouth ; the ground of the controversy was jealousy for the S.P.C.K. ; all seems to have been smoothed over.

Bishop Porteus, d. 1809.

Christopher Wordsworth and Lord Teignmouth, 1810.

A more formidable attack was made in 1811, on the occasion of a meeting held at Cambridge to establish an auxiliary Society there. The authorities of the University saw danger in this, and feared lest, if undergraduates discussed religious questions, it should 'run to politics.' The undergraduates consulted Simeon and Milner, and at their request abstained from

Opposition at Cambridge, 1811.

interference, an incident which shows both the good discipline of 'Simeon's young men,' and his moderation, where it was lawful to be moderate. Dr. Marsh (1757- Dr. Marsh. 1839), Lady Margaret Professor of Divinity, and afterwards Bishop of Peterborough, now joined the fray, a man of considerable learning and a strong partisan. The Society for Promoting Christian Knowledge had been sufficiently vindicated; but Dr. Marsh represented that that Society was alone entitled to the support of Churchmen, as being also a Bible Society, the elder of the two, and patronised by all the bishops, whereas the Bible Society gave no preference to the Church of England. He was answered by Nicholas Vansittart, afterwards Lord Bexley, in the sense that the co-operation of Churchmen and Dissenters in religious matters was desirable, and that such co-operation tended to unite all hearts, if not to reconcile all opinions.

Professor Marsh was not discouraged, and in 1813 renewed his objections to the Society on a new ground ;—the distribution of the Bible alone without the Prayer Book was a danger to the Established Church, as tending to throw discredit upon its Liturgy and encourage dissent, and as showing that the supporters of the Bible Society were no true friends to the Church, and cared little for her formularies. It was difficult for the two parties to understand each other. The Evangelicals accused Marsh of setting up the Prayer Book as a 'corrective' to the Bible. He replied that the Prayer Book and Bible unlearned needed, not a corrective indeed, but a controversy, 1813. guide, and this could be found in the Prayer Book. The 'modern Bible Society' was not a church society ; and Churchmen, who had their own Bible Society, the Society for Promoting Christian Knowledge, ought not to support it. The answer was easy : that the Bible Society was supported by many bishops and a great number of the clergy, and that the demand for Prayer Books had increased fourfold since its institution.

The present generation is not likely to take much interest in so obsolete a controversy. Dean Milner did not love controversy, but he was put forward as a Milner and Marsh. champion of the Bible Society, and in that character had no scruples, and was a hard and somewhat random hitter.

Marsh was a German scholar, who had spent several years at Göttingen, and may be looked upon as a forerunner of modern biblical criticism in his studies of Michaelis and other German writers ; one of Milner's grievances against him is the dangerous character of his speculations on the origin of the Gospels, which appeared to the Dean no less unsound in theology than Marsh's theory of chances was in mathematics ; and truly that controversialist might be thought an easy prey who laid down as axiomatic the proposition that if a particular reading is found in only one of ten MSS. of the New Testament, the chance of its being found in the eleventh is as 1 to 9. Dr. Marsh's object was to strengthen the dogmatic party in the Church and depress the pious but unlearned Evangelicals. The rising credit of the 'orthodox' party was felt in every department ; and here, as in the National Society controversy, which was proceeding at the same time, the forces were drawn out to battle. The scene of war was the same. Isaac Milner wished to work with Dissenters wherever possible. Marsh and his friends said, Draw a line ; give up the Bible Society to the sectaries and apply your own strength to the Society for Promoting Christian Knowledge. Let the denominations carry on their schools and teach such doctrine as they think right; but let us support our mother the Church, and admit no children into the national schools whose parents are not willing to accept the Church's teaching. We can be friends though not partners, and we shall be better friends as well as better Churchmen, or better Dissenters, if we do not pretend a unity which does not exist.

The outcome of the controversy was injurious to both societies, not as regards numbers or subscriptions, but as deepening antagonism between parties ; an antagonism which the reviving fortunes of the High Church party did not fail to embitter.

The history of the origin of the Church Missionary Society, founded in 1799, goes back some little way into the eighteenth century, and here again some repetition is unavoidable, since it is hardly possible to separate events and motives which belonged to a continued course of action.

Church Missionary Society, 1799.

The Roman Church was before the Protestants in the cause of missions. Whatever the reasons may be, the Jesuits preached the Gospel to the heathen before the Protestants thought of doing so. There was some Early missions. evangelising in the early settlement of British America. A Society for the Propagation of the Gospel in New England was established in 1648, and other societies came to fulfilment in the venerable Societies for Promoting Christian Knowledge and for the Propagation of S.P.G. and S.P.C.K. Dr. Bray. the Gospel in Foreign Parts, which look back to Dr. Thomas Bray as their founder. The Society for the Propagation of the Gospel claimed as its mission-field 'the colonies and dependencies of Great Britain,' in which term was included, though not expressed, the conversion of the natives. The S.P.C.K. added mission work to that of home evangelisation, and directed their attention to India in the first place. John Wesley's mission to Georgia John Wesley in Georgia, 1735. in 1735, under the patronage of the Society for the Propagation of the Gospel, is well known. Other missions were sent to Bermuda and Western Africa, but little progress was made in the century which elapsed between the foundation of the S.P.G. in 1701 and the foundation of the C.M.S. in 1799.

The same band of friends, with Henry Thornton at their head, who began and carried through the abolition of the slave trade, saw in the misery of Western Africa Sierra Leone Company, 1791. a hope of redemption. They founded in 1791 a Sierra Leone Company to introduce into that district trade, industry, and Christian knowledge. To set slaves free was useless unless they were given the means of subsistence and taught the rudiments of civilised life, the first essential of which was the knowledge of the Gospel. In the same year the Eclectic Society, an evangelical association founded in 1783, which did much to give the Evangelicals a policy and a voice, discussed the best means of propagating the Gospel in Africa; William Carey William Carey. (1761-1834), the Baptist shoemaker, Sydney Smith's 'consecrated cobbler,' preached in 1793 a sermon which led to the formation of the Baptist Missionary Society; and in 1795 the London Missionary Society was

founded on undenominational lines. The next important
step was taken by Charles Simeon. His interest
in the cause of missions, and especially of his
'diocese,' India, had never slackened, and he
proposed to the Eclectic Society on February 8,
1796, to constitute a Church of England Society
for the conversion of the heathen, and especially for 'Africa
and the East,' since the missionary work of the two elder
Societies was almost entirely confined to the British Planta-
tions in America and the West Indies.

Charles
Simeon
and the
Eclectic
Society,
1796.

'This conversation,' wrote Basil Woodd, 'proved the
foundation of the Church Missionary Society.' Little, however, was done as yet; the majority of those present 'were
afraid of the bishops,' or did not wish to interfere with the
mission work of the two Societies. But the hint given by
Simeon in 1796 was not forgotten. Wilberforce considered
plans with his friends at Clapham. He notes in his Journal
a dinner at Henry Thornton's house on November 9, 1797:
'Simeon, Charles Grant, Venn, there. Something, but not
much, done. Simeon in earnest.' On March 18, 1799,
John Venn brought the question before the Eclectic Society,
and Simeon urged immediate action. It was accordingly
agreed to found a society; and on April 12
a meeting was held at the Castle and Falcon
Inn in Aldersgate Street, John Venn, the Rector
of Clapham, being in the chair. The number
of persons present was twenty-five. It was a business-like
meeting, conducted without much oratory. A Committee and
officers were nominated, and four resolutions were passed;
the most important being one which stated, 'That it is a
duty highly incumbent upon every Christian, to endeavour to
propagate the knowledge of the Gospel among the heathen,'
and another to the effect that though the Society for the
Propagation of the Gospel and the Society for Promoting Christian Knowledge had taken up missionary work,
'there seemed to be still wanting in the Established Church
a society for sending missionaries to the continent of
Africa or the other parts of the heathen world.' Though
the Society was a Church of England Society, one of its
original rules ran thus: 'A friendly intercourse shall be

Foundation
of the
C.M.S
1799.

maintained with other Protestant societies engaged in the same benevolent design of propagating the Gospel of Jesus Christ.'

This new Society was to be connected with the evangelical party in the Church of England. John Venn gave the word for this, 'on the Church principle, not the High Church principle.' The founders of the Society were Churchmen, and entirely in agreement with the decision that it must be founded on 'the Church principle.' They approved episcopacy and liturgical worship, and saw that, though missionaries who differ from each other in doctrine may combine to preach the Gospel to the heathen, a settled church must have a common creed. But they were also guided by the other half of Venn's saying, that the Society must not be based on 'the High Church principle,' an expression which must be understood, not in the light of the later development of High Church doctrine, but as implying that spirituality and evangelical doctrine were essential, but the patronage of bishops was not essential. By 'the High Church principle' was meant the principle of episcopacy and transmitted grace; which carries with it in practice the rule that no mission should be set on foot except under episcopal rule, and that bishops were to be the judges of the fitness of this or that man for the work. In all these beginnings we may see the natural self-assertion and jealousy of interference which belongs to an unpopular party, the highly-wrought religious feeling which leads to exclusiveness and divides by shibboleths, and the unwillingness to be bound by regulations which is characteristic of a young society, ardent in faith, full of enterprise, and not entirely free from spiritual vanity.

Principles of the C.M.S., John Venn.

The tone of thought and expression in all the proceedings is strongly evangelical, and the officers chosen belonged to that section of the Church. It is significant of the low estimation in which the party was then held that of thirteen clerical members of the Committee only four held benefices. The Evangelicals had no access to the Societies under episcopal patronage, the Society for the Propagation of the Gospel and the Society for Promoting Christian Knowledge; they were independent Christians, full of zeal and faith, and wishing to work on their own lines.   They had no thought of compromise, and made no attempt at catching

Evangelicals a popular accent.   The danger was lest the bishops and the old should withhold their sanction from an association Societies. which held out a hand to non-episcopalian bodies, home and foreign, or hamper it by making it auxiliary to the old Societies, or drive it into the ranks of dissent.   The friends of the newly founded society wished it to be a Church society, free from dissenting limitations, and at the same time of evangelical colour.   They succeeded perfectly; and by quiet perseverance the C.M.S. received in due time the patronage of the episcopate, without sacrificing its distinctive character.   It may not be desirable that a church should be divided into parties; but no church has ever existed which was not so divided; and in this case religious zeal, working on two different principles, has had fair play without jealousy or animosity.   The intention of the founders of the Church Missionary Society was to spread the Gospel as they understood it; to take what advantage they could from the ecclesiastical world, but not to bow down to it; in short, to maintain their freedom without outrunning the limits of authority.   They did not set themselves against patronage, but sought the favour of the elder Societies and of the bishops.

A Committee was at once appointed to consider first steps. The original name given to the Society was 'The Society for Missions to Africa and the East.'   The present designation, 'The Church Missionary Society for Africa and

Name of the East,' was not adopted till 1812.   Wilber- the Society. force was elected president, but declined the offer: John Venn was chairman, Henry Thornton treasurer, and Thomas Scott secretary; and John Newton was the preacher chosen for the first anniversary.   The

Committee Committee immediately issued an 'account' of appointed. the Society, and addressed letters to Archbishop Moore, Bishop Porteus, and the Mission Committee of the Society for Promoting Christian Knowledge.   The Society for the Propagation of the Gospel received them without jealousy; the Archbishop gave no answer, but a year later told Wilberforce personally, with some expressions of

sympathy for the work proposed, 'that he would look on
the proceedings with candour, and that it would give him
much pleasure to find them such as he could approve.'
This was taken by the Committee as a favourable Archbishop
Moore.
reply, and they passed a resolution (4 August 1800),
'That in consequence of the answer from the Metropolitan,
the Committee do now proceed in their great design with all
the activity possible.' They did so under much discouragement. The Evangelicals, associated as they were with the
friends of emancipation, were thought to be fanatics West Africa.
and enemies of the rights of property ; the material
difficulties were great ; West Africa, which was chiefly in view,
was not only distant and pestilential, but the voyage there was
exposed to dangers from slavers and French privateers ; and
for some years little progress was made.

Though Africa was the chosen mission-field of the C.M.S.,
the Committee made inquiries in other directions also.
They gave grants of money for procuring translations of the
Scriptures into Arabic and other languages, and the Secretary
wrote letters to his friends asking them to send him young
men who would go out as missionaries or lay catechists, but
without success, though sermons were preached by Scott,
Simeon, Cecil, and others ; till in 1802 Josiah Pratt (1768-
1844) became Secretary. Progress was still slow ; there was a
lack of English volunteers for missions, and the Society did
not refuse the help of fellow-workers from a Lutheran
seminary at Berlin, introduced by Dr. Steinkopff ; Dr. Steinkopff
and the
German
missionaries.
and two Berlin students, Renner and Harting, pre-
sented themselves in 1802 as missionary catechists
for West Africa. They were sent back to Berlin to receive
Lutheran orders, and went out to Africa on January 31, 1804,
to minister to the colony of Sierra Leone, founded thirteen
years before for the reception of emancipated slaves,—the first
missionaries sent out by the young Society. Five missionaries
in all, with their wives, went, and died after reaching the fatal
shore through long delays and perils. The abolition of the
slave trade in 1807 opened a door of hope, but did not, for
a while, remove difficulties.

One of the first rules of the Society was to hold friendly
intercourse with other Protestant missionary associations.

This was in accord with the practice of the older Societies. The Society for Promoting Christian Knowledge also employed Lutheran catechists, both Germans and Danes ; the Lutheran body being at that time regarded, whether from wider charity or less defined theology, as a sister church, with which Anglicans might freely be associated. It is interesting to see how clear a line was then drawn between the Lutherans, whose tenets, being those of a foreign community, did not come into practical conflict with our own, and the Calvinists, whose doctrine, though it more nearly resembled that current among church-people, was connected with ideas of English dissent. The Church Missionary Society has from the first kept up relations with other Societies, such as the London Jews Society, the Bible Society, the Religious Tract Society, the Prayer Book and Homily Society, the London Missionary Society, and the Baptist, Moravian, and Wesleyan missions, as well as those conducted by foreign and American Protestant churches ; for example, the Domestic and Foreign Missionary Society of the American Church, founded about this time.

Intercourse with other missions.

The particularist spirit, if it may be so termed, which has its advantages and disadvantages, is well seen in Josiah Pratt, Vicar of St. Stephen's, Coleman Street, one of the founders of the Society, and for more than twenty-one years its Secretary. Pratt belonged to the straitest sect of Evangelicals, those who resolved that the C.M.S. should be not only exclusively Church of England in spirit, but kept in evangelical hands, and who were more kindly inclined to Lutherans than to High Churchmen. 'The Society,' he writes, 'thankfully acknowledged the zeal and devotedness of a sister church, which put to shame the coldness and backwardness of their own,' and he makes no difficulty about accepting Lutheran ordination, though, as a matter of precaution, Lutheran missionaries were asked not to preach in dissenting chapels while in England, since 'we are surrounded by those who wait for our halting.'

Josiah Pratt, Secretary of the C.M.S., 1802.

Pratt was one of the first to detect the 'deep-laid mischief' of Tractarianism, of which he was a decided and uncompromising opponent. Even in the *Christian Year* he saw formalism and unsound doctrine; in his opinion Newman's Tract No. 90 was 'an act of unprincipled Jesuitism,' and the fourth and fifth centuries, so much praised by the Tracts, 'a seedplot of Popish error.'

But apart from particularism, there were good reasons for adopting an independent line of action. Both the old Societies, which have shown wonderful powers of revival since then, were at the beginning of the nineteenth century at a low point of efficiency, poor in funds and unenterprising in action. The S.P.G. was more concerned with European colonists than with native Christians or heathen; Relations with the older the S.P.C.K. was almost starved out of India for Societies. want of funds; yet the organisation of both was strong enough to have absorbed the new association, if it had not maintained a separate individuality. Moreover, it was likely that any offer of help from an evangelical quarter would have been rejected by the old Societies. Their principles had been fixed for many years, and their methods were such as approved themselves to the bishops, the mass of the clergy, and the respectable laity. The 'serious' clergy and laity had no part in them; and the enthusiasts were too fully assured of the justice and holiness of their cause to sacrifice anything to the hope of patronage.

The four principles laid down by John Venn, the Society's first chairman—(1) 'Follow God's leading,' (2) 'Begin on a small scale,' (3) 'Put money in the second place,' (4) 'Depend upon the Spirit of God'—have worldly John Venn's four wisdom in them; for nothing is more important principles. to a new institution depending on personal effort, not on rule and precedent, than that it should avoid regulations and regulators, take an original and independent line, and be guided by circumstances.

The progress of the Society and the wide scope of its energy may be seen from the reports of these early years, which show it carrying out its activity not only in India, but in New Zealand, West Africa, and in the Mohammedan world. The 'anniversaries' of the Society became more noticed and frequented, as the Bishop Ryder. evangelical school rose in public favour. It is noted in 1814 as an encouraging fact that the anniversary sermon was preached that year by a dignitary of the Church, Henry Ryder (1777-1836), Dean of Wells, who in the following year became Bishop of Gloucester.

The Church Missionary Society has always from necessity been dependent upon gifts; without begging, the great sums of money which were needed for the work could not have been raised. Church Missionary Society associations were quickly formed, and much was hoped for and realised from penny-a-week subscriptions gathered by their members. Among the early associations formed in connexion with the Society may be mentioned that of Norwich, founded by Edward Bickersteth, to which Bishop Bathurst gave his patronage, and that of Cambridge, illustrated by the names of Simeon, Milner, Farish, Scholefield, and Dealtry, besides many younger men whose names are remembered in the annals of the evangelical movement. Another prominent association was that formed in 1813 at Bristol. The city was divided into districts for weekly and monthly collections, and in its first year the Bristol Association collected £2300, a sum equal to the average annual income of the whole Society up to that time. Basil Woodd, in one preaching tour, collected a thousand pounds, and 'returned full of joy and thankfulness.' These were the beginnings of Deputations, which have had good success in providing for the ever-increasing needs of the Society. They were not supported by the authorities of the Church. While the Bible Society had bishops and royal dukes as patrons, the C.M.S. deputations were spoken of by bishops as itinerant preachers who neglected their own parishes.

Methods of the C.M.S.

Deputations.

The subject of India occupied the mind of the Church Missionary Society after the abolition of the slave trade in 1807. The difficulties here were of a different kind from those to be encountered in savage countries, since the ancient civilisation of India rested on a double religious foundation, and to introduce a new religion into the country was thought to be full of danger by those who knew India best.

The C.M.S. and India.

The special difficulties and problems of missionary work among peoples of different races, religions, and states of civilisation do not come within the compass of a work like the present. All that can be done is to summarise very shortly the records and the general results of missionary activity during this period of Church history.

In India, where, if we omit an insignificant number of Buddhists, the vast native population is divided, as regards religion, into Mohammedans and Hindus, and where the simple and unchangeable organisation of the creed of Islam, and the equally unchangeable institution of caste, oppose an impassable barrier, General view of Indian missions. progress has been slow and partial. Conversions from Mohammedanism are rare in every part of the world. The Hindu who changes his creed loses his caste and cannot recover it. The best hope for success is in the conversion of groups of natives, which may grow into a community. In such cases it has been thought that the formation of independent churches not under European control may be the best way to meet the difficulty of maintaining union where no fusion of race is possible.

For more than a century after the earliest settlement the position of the English in India was precarious. We went there not as conquerors or colonists, but as traders dependent on the goodwill of the neighbouring princes. We do not easily realise how little support was given from home to the founders of our The English conquest of India. Indian Empire. At three months' distance from home, on the outermost fringe of an undiscovered continent, of which little was known but that it was thickly populated and ruled by splendid and apparently powerful sovereigns, our Indian factories were too remote to raise much interest or even curiosity. The wealth which Englishmen brought back from India was purchased by exile and estrangement, and few of them returned in sound bodily health. The idea of conquering India was as far removed from English minds as the idea of conquering China is at the present day. Conquest of settled lands is a different thing from occupation of deserts; and never, since the dream of the Hundred Years' War passed away, did the thought of conquest occupy British minds till our rivalry with France created new and imperial ambitions, dimly conceived at first. But though conquest was not the intention of the early visitors to India, to conquest it grew; and one of the many drawbacks to the spread of the Gospel is that Christianity is the religion of the conquerors, and yet uses no force but that of persuasion. The Christian religion conquered the Roman world from below, by persuading its rulers; Islam and the Christian barbarians brought in their religion by the sword; the English missionary in India is disliked as one of the oppressors, and despised because he is not favoured by Government. The natives look for example to their rulers, and the English who rule India show a shining example in justice and integrity rather than in the Christian virtues and graces, though many noble exceptions are found.

Among the difficulties of India, one of the most formidable is the question of caste. It will always be debated between missionaries and civilians, and among missionaries themselves, whether caste and all it involves is to be reckoned with, ignored, or denounced. The Hindus are among the most religious of mankind, and their religion is inextricably bound up with caste. Christianity proclaims universal brotherhood; the principle of caste is the eternal inferiority of one class to another. If the Christian teachers temporise with caste, they give the natives the impression that they are not sincere, since caste cannot be treated as a thing of no importance. If they denounce it, they give up the hope of converting any but those who can afford to live without caste, that is to say, the lowest classes, and a few confessors who are capable of sacrificing all for Christ. The history of the early Church shows that an institution which flies in the face of convention may succeed by the very fact of doing so. The history of the mediæval Church shows the success of an institution which gathered into its net and turned to its own use superstitions and customs as unchristian as caste, and in doing so exorcised the evil spirit in them. A similar difficulty is found in dealing with questions of polygamy among primitive nations, and with questions of colour and race. Some, like Wilson of Calcutta, take an uncompromising line; some, like Colenso of Natal, are disposed to be lenient to customs alien to Christianity, but ingrained in society and carried on without sense of wrong. The missionaries in the South Seas are unable to approve or to abolish the ritual of *tapu*. Both sides can quote Scripture and show historical precedent. Customs connected with religion often survive the religion which created them; and caste, if, as is possible, it prevails against the philosophical and scientific scepticism which, we are told, is undermining Hinduism, may prove a greater obstacle to Christianity than Hinduism itself. But the principle is larger than any instance which may raise the question; and questions of this kind are best decided by public authority, not by the discordance of private judgment.

Sydney Smith's satire, the lukewarmness of the bishops, and the solid opposition of responsible statesmen to missionary endeavour, seemed to unite the Church, the world, and literature in a coalition against the spread of the Gospel. The common indifference to Indian missions was counted by Wilberforce as 'by far the greatest of our national sins.' The question of neutrality, *Indifference and hostility to missions.* which Government officials were inclined to interpret in a sense unfavourable to Christianity, was much discussed. The fear of arousing suspicion and perhaps rebellion among the natives was always *Government neutrality.* present; missionaries were slighted; native Christians were despised as half-converted outcasts, and their low social position, with its accompanying disadvantages, illogically set down as a result of their change of religion. Though the Government officials practised Christianity in private, their public actions ignored it. The disinclination of the Indian Government to favour the attempts made to spread Christianity in India was increased by a mutiny at Vellore in 1806, which was attributed to a supposed suspicion that the English intended to put down the *Vellore mutiny, 1806.* native religion by force. Missionaries were ordered out of the country; others were forbidden to land and sent home. 'One might fire a pistol into a magazine and it might not explode,' said the Governor-General, Lord Hastings, 'but no wise man would hazard the experiment.'

The C.M.S. lost no opportunity of making known the

needs of India. Pamphlets were published and petitions signed to support the agitation for India ; the Society meant to take public opinion by storm, and succeeded, instant in season and out of season, as its opponents complained, who wished for quieter methods. The methods of the Society are such as attract the public eye ; it prefers the housetop to the closet, and is not ashamed to lift up the voice like a trumpet. In 1806 a seminary for missionaries was established at Bledlow, in Buckinghamshire, under the care of Thomas Scott, to which many German students resorted. Among those who were associated with these efforts may be mentioned William Carey, the Baptist missionary, who had already been for some years preaching and translating the Bible in Bengal ; Fountain, another Baptist ; and the 'Five Chaplains' in Bengal, David Brown (1763-1812), Claudius Buchanan (1766-1815), Henry Martyn (1781-1812), Daniel Corrie (1777-1837), and James Thomason (1774-1829), Simeon's foster-child ; and especially among these Martyn and Buchanan. These men were Evangelicals, disciples and friends of Simeon. Claudius Buchanan, a poor Scotch student and itinerant musician, was converted by Simeon, and under his influence was ordained and went out to India as a chaplain in 1796. He was made Vice-Provost of the training college at Fort William, and the greater part of the salary which he received was given to missionary purposes. His idea of forming an ecclesiastical establishment for India was approved by Bishop Porteus and by Lord Wellesley, the Governor-General, but caused great anger and disquiet among the large class of Europeans, who feared nothing so much as unsettling the minds of the natives by proselytising.

Henry Martyn, whose name is famous in missionary history, went out to India in 1805 at the earnest entreaty of Simeon. The most permanent part of Martyn's work is the translations of the Bible begun by him. His fame is due to the nobleness of his character, his lofty spirit of consecration, and his untiring energy, and also to his early death, rather than to the actual results of his missionary labours, which were checked by official and clerical jealousy. 'God measures life by love; and by that measure Henry Martyn's life was a long one indeed.' He was a man of genius as well as a saint, and, as was the case with Wilberforce, his example was commended by an extraordinary personal charm, for those who admired Henry Martyn loved him as much as they admired him.

The evangelisation of India had hitherto been chiefly in the hands of the Baptist Missionary Society. It was the agitation begun by the Clapham friends, and especially by Lord Teignmouth, that opened India to Anglican missionaries; and since that time the episcopalian societies have taken the lead, though nonconformist bodies have not been idle.

Claudius Buchanan's sermons in 1808-1810 on 'The Star in the East,' 'The Light of the World,' and 'Let there be Light,' produced a deep impression. In 1811 a new impetus was given to missionary work by a sermon preached by Melville Hoare, and by the action of Samuel Marsden, the Apostle of New Zealand (1764-1838), and Buchanan; and in 1812, its twelfth anniversary, the Society established its home in Salisbury Square, where its office now is; and at the same time started on a fresh track under the presidency of a soldier, Lord Gambier, and the vice-presidency of Lord Teignmouth, late Governor-General of India; Sir Thomas Baring, Thomas Babington, and Nicholas Vansittart being members of Committee. *Buchanan's sermons, 1808-1810.* *Offices removed to Salisbury Square, 1812.* *Lord Gambier, President of C.M.S.*

The Society saw before it the prospect of evangelising not only India, the Mohammedan lands, West Africa, and the southern hemisphere, but of extending its operations to the churches of Europe and the Levant. Such an ambition might seem chimerical, but was fulfilled in the course of the following century.

The policy of the home and Indian Governments has never been more than neutral, sometimes unfriendly; for among the elements of danger amongst the Indian populations the religious element is one of the most formidable; and the fear of rousing religious panic among the natives of India has made English officials timid. Until 1845 the official deference paid to *Neutrality or hostility of the Government.*

idol-worship in India was felt at home as a continual grievance. The Church, to say the least, has not been favoured. At this day the number of English bishops in India and Ceylon is but eleven, among three hundred millions of souls; less than half the number of Roman Catholic bishops in the same regions.

In 1812 a fresh effort for the evangelisation of India was made, beginning with a meeting held on April 24, at which Wilberforce spoke 'with acceptance,' and *A fresh effort,* the S.P.C.K. followed with a meeting to the *1812.* same end. Another important meeting of the Church Missionary Society was held at the New London Tavern in May 1813, six months after the death of Henry Martyn, at which Wilberforce, Simeon, and Dean *C.M.S.* Ryder spoke, and hopes were expressed that some *meeting,* *May 1813.* recognition of the Christian religion in India might be made by Lord Liverpool's Government, which was then considering its Indian Charter Bill. A number of petitions from all parts of the country were presented to Parliament in favour of the introduction of Christianity into India. A Committee of the House of Commons sat and examined witnesses, among them Warren Hastings and Lord Teignmouth. The fear was expressed that if the Indian Government should show any favour to Christian missions, some compulsion would be put upon the conscience of the natives. In deference to public opinion Lord Castlereagh, on June 22, brought forward among other resolutions one which *Lord* stated 'that it is the duty of this country to promote *Castlereagh's* *Resolutions,* the interest and happiness of the native inhabitants *June 22.* of the British dominions in India, and that such measures ought to be adopted as may tend to the introduction among them of useful knowledge and of religious and moral improvement,' and that facilities to this end should be afforded by law. 'Wilberforce rose at midnight, and spoke for two hours; and at three o'clock in the morning the victory was won. Good men, he heard afterwards, were *East India* praying all night.' The resolution was passed by *Bill, 1813.* 53 votes in a House of 125. After the abolition of the slave trade this was the second great triumph of the evangelical party.

The discussion was repeated in Committee, and it was observed that the opposers of the scheme for christianising India were for the most part men who had resided in the country, and the promoters 'those at home who are distinguished by the name of the evangelical party.' A clause in the bill provided for the appointment of a bishop and three archdeacons. This bill received the Royal Assent on July 21, 1813. 'I am persuaded,' wrote Wilberforce, 'that we have laid the foundation stone of the grandest edifice that ever was raised in Asia.'

Notwithstanding these successes, the Society made way but slowly. The bishops disapproved of the setting up of an evangelical association within the borders of the Church, and showed little favour to the young Opposition to C.M.S. Society, liable as it was to the imputation of Methodism and innovation. The methods of the Society, itinerancy, collections, meetings, special services with singing of hymns, such as 'Jesus shall reign,' 'From all that dwell beneath the skies,' 'All hail the power of Jesus' name,' gave an evangelical character to the Deputations instituted, 1814. movement. The system of deputations, begun by Josiah Pratt in 1814, gave offence. At a meeting held on St. Andrew's Day, 1817, at Bath, a Church C.M.S. meeting at Bath, 1817. Missionary Association was inaugurated with a service at which Bishop Ryder preached the sermon. Notwithstanding this, at a meeting held the next day at the Octagon Chapel, Pratt was interrupted by a formal protest from Archdeacon Thomas against 'factious interference' with the Society for the Propagation of the Gospel. This incident led to a correspondence between Pratt and the Archdeacon, and in the event caused a public discussion and a meeting of the bishops, and roused the dormant energy of the Society for the Propagation of the Gospel into something like rivalry with the younger Society. Pratt revenged himself by bidding the S.P.G. 'most heartily God speed,' and rejoiced when a Royal Letter brought that Society the sum of £45,000. He did more, for he gathered from its reports for a hundred years an account of the good deeds of the elder Society, and published it under the title *Propaganda*. The book had a large sale, and contributed no little to the success of the Royal Letter.

The East India Charter Act (53 George III. c. 155) as passed (21 July 1813), contained provision for the appoint-
E. I. Charter ment of a bishop for the whole of the British
Act passed, territories in the East Indies.   His salary, £5000
1813.   a year, was to be paid by the East India Directors, and his jurisdiction was limited by the letters patent which appointed him.   Three archdeacons, whose salary was to be £2000 a year each, were nominated to Fort William, Fort George, and Bombay.   Letters patent were issued in the course of the year appointing Thomas Fanshaw Middleton (1769-1822) Bishop of Calcutta.   Middleton was educated at Christ's Hospital with Coleridge and Lamb, who describes him as 'a scholar and a gentleman in his teens.'   He went to Pembroke Hall, Cambridge, but did not greatly distinguish himself, being rather a scholar than a mathematician : his work on the *Greek Article*, which appeared in 1808, is a landmark in the history of Greek Testament criticism. Middleton was consecrated at Lambeth on May 8, 1814, and reached Calcutta in November.   In the same year
       four C.M.S. missionaries were sent out to India,
C.M.S.
missionaries two of whom, Greenwood and Norton, were clergy-
sent to India, men of the Church of England ; among the first so
1814.   qualified who were directly appointed to mission work, for hitherto the missionaries sent out by the three Missionary Societies had been in Lutheran orders.   Green-wood had been a Yorkshire blanket manufacturer; Thomas Norton was a shoemaker, and self-taught.

The commencement of the new system was unpromising. The new Bishop went to India against the voice of public opinion, and without the full confidence of the Church.   He was consecrated and sent out almost by stealth, so great was the fear of rousing the fanatical suspicion of the natives.   He obeyed perhaps too faithfully the injunction of Archbishop Manners Sutton, 'No enthusiasm !' for he would have no dealings with the Bible Society, and did not well agree with the Presbyterian ministers whom the Company maintained in their service.   Nor did he actively support missions to the heathen ; his mission was principally to Europeans ; he considered it to be his duty not to make converts, but to organise a church and to establish his own position in it.

Middleton's wish was to train up a native clergy, and with a view to this he founded Bishop's College in 1820. He devoted to the purpose a sum of £5000 presented to him by the Society for the Propagation of the Gospel. The S.P.C.K., the C.M.S., and the Bible Society did the like 'in the same great and common cause,' and these four benefactions made the foundation of Bishop's College possible. The College was built on too large a scale, and was never successful; but money may be well wasted in such experiments.

Foundation of Bishop's College, 1820.

Bishop Middleton died in 1822, at the age of fifty-four. It was something to have established the episcopate with dignity, and to have made a beginning of church organisation in a diocese which comprised the whole of India, and to which, not long after, Ceylon, Mauritius, Australia, and New Zealand were at various times added. Middleton's work has been far outgrown, but his foundation remains, and the Church Societies are still building upon it with unwearied diligence.

AUTHORITIES.—As Chap. I. (p. 34) ; Owen, *The Origin of the Brit. and For. Bible Society* ; Stock, *History of the C.M.S.* ; Allen and M'Clure, *200 Years* (Hist. of S.P.C.K.) ; Pascoe, *200 Years of the S.P.G.* ; Tucker, *Under His Banner*. BIOGRAPHIES : *Daniel Corrie*, by Corrie ; *T. F. Middleton*, by Le Bas ; *Reginald Heber*, by Mrs. Heber ; *Josiah Pratt*, by Pratt ; *Henry Martyn*, by Bell ; *Claudius Buchanan*, by Pearson ; *Wm. Carey*, by Carey.

CHAPTER III

THE OLD HIGH CHURCH PARTY

THE fortunes of the Church of England, closely allied as she is to the State for good or evil, have always been affected by political events. As a national church and bound by somewhat indefinite formulas, she cannot but reflect the opinions of the day ; and it is an imputation often cast upon her that she is, at most, no more than the church of a majority. We have only to pronounce the names of our sovereigns, from Henry VIII. to the present day, to see how the complexion of the Church has varied with the times. The high orthodoxy of Queen Anne's reign, combining with the latitudi-
Religious politics of the eighteenth century. narian tendency of Whig politics, produced a *tertium quid* which faithfully reproduced in the ecclesiastical region the political quietism of Walpole's school. 'No enthusiasm' corresponds to '*quieta non movere.*' The practice of the Georgian clergy was to work with what lay ready to their hand, and distrust all enterprise beyond safe lines ; their theology was not deliberately evolved from study, as that of their predecessors the Caroline divines, nor from emotion and experience working on a biblical ground, as that of the Reformers and the Evangelicals ; but traditional, and rather theoretical than vital. The terms 'High' and 'Low' have changed their meaning from time to time. During
High and Low Church. the eighteenth century 'Low Church' included latitudinarians and Evangelicals, 'High Church' nonjurors and Romanisers, and a large proportion of the 'orthodox' ; which term was applied to Churchmen who accepted the Reformation as a cardinal fact in the history of Christianity, and

condemned the 'errors of Rome' as heartily as Andrewes and Taylor; sacramentalists in theory, but not insisting on high sacramental doctrine, punctilious in keeping to the conventional interpretation of the Prayer Book, but content with the minimum of ritual and observance.

Such were the doctrines and such the practice of those who were called High Church clergy at the beginning of the nineteenth century, and they did not differ very widely from the doctrines and practice of the Low Church clergy. As Alexander Knox said, 'the old High Church race is worn out . . . the majority are men of the world, if not of yesterday.' They belonged to an age when the clergy represented the Church, and the Church the nation, or at least that part of the nation which did not live in towns and was connected with the land. The time was coming when more would be demanded of them in consideration of the worldly advantages which they enjoyed; the duty of greater seriousness was impressed upon them by the evangelical movement, the necessity of action by the liberal movement, which questioned all existing institutions. There were also present higher motives and spiritual forces, which were soon to take form in the stirrings of the Oxford revival. That movement, as its author says, 'was not so much a movement as a spirit afloat.'

In a striking passage in his *Apologia* Newman speaks of the High Church revival as 'a reaction from the dry and superficial character of the religious teaching and the literature of the last generation or century, and as the result of the need which was felt both by the hearts and the intellects of the nation for a deeper philosophy, and as the evidence and as the partial fulfilment of that need, to which even the chief authors of the then generation had borne witness; . . . Walter Scott, who turned men's minds to the direction of the middle ages, . . . Coleridge, who instilled a higher philosophy into inquiring minds than they had hitherto been accustomed to accept. In this way he made trial of his age, and succeeded in interesting its genius in the cause of Catholic truth. Then came Southey, and Wordsworth, . . . one of whom, in the department of fantastic fiction, the other in that

The Romantic School of literature and the High Church revival.

of philosophical meditation, have addressed themselves to the same high principles and feelings, and carried forward their readers in the same direction.' In a word, the Romantic school, with its wistful gaze into past glories and its eager attempt to revive them in art and literature, had its effect on religion also.

Archdeacon Churton's *Life of Joshua Watson*, one of the best Churchmen and best men of his time, throws light upon the principles and methods of the old High Church party, the party in possession, now stirred to activity by the movement of religion and philanthropy, in which all the qualities of the evangelical school were exhibited. The evangelical party, in spite of their loyalty to the Church, were in spirit, though not altogether in theology, the descendants of the ancient Puritans, whose influence upon the nation was to deepen religious feeling, but not to change permanently the foundations on which the Church of England was built. Like the ancient High Churchmen of Elizabeth's time, though differing in many points from them, the 'high and dry' or 'orthodox' party of the latter part of the eighteenth century rested upon dogmatic and historical foundations : they carried on the tradition of a State Church, neither in spiritual nor temporal things inclined to innovation, and thought perhaps too much of the heritage which had descended to them from their forefathers. The progressive High Church party in the nineteenth as in the seventeenth century incurred the reproach of being 'innovators.' The settlement which they disturbed was thoroughly anti-Roman, in doctrine and practice. The doctrine was neither Lutheran nor Calvinist, but nearer that of the more moderate reformers, founded on the Bible, and primitive interpretation of the Bible, so far as it could be ascertained : the practice was the leanest ritual. The theology of High Church divines was anti-latitudinarian as well as anti-Roman ; that of the rank and file, the country parsons who preached Sunday by Sunday, was taken from accredited divines of the Church of England ; all were content with a moderate interpretation of the Bible in the sense of the Prayer Book and Catechism. The doctrine would be thought rather Low Church than High Church in these times ;

marginal note: 'Orthodox' party.

then, certainly, the ritualist teaching and practice of to-day would have seemed to all parties flat Popery. The Protestant Establishment, without the Low Church corollary of Whig opinions, held the field, at any rate since the accession of George III. But Whig politics had leavened public opinion, and in Church as in State there was little approach to Stuartism, and none to Roman doctrine. They had, at any rate on their shelves, the Fathers, the Reformers, the Anglican doctors, and the non-jurors; they did not trouble themselves about the schoolmen or the later Roman divines. The High Church ideal was, in Bishop Copleston's words, 'to preserve the unity of our church, and to make [it] in effect as well as in name a national church'; no doubt by sinking differences within the church, but also by keeping nonconformity at a distance.

A High Church movement was foreseen by an Irish layman, Alexander Knox (1757-1831), a friend and correspondent of John Wesley, who noticed that the 'method' of Methodism was in harmony with the Prayer Book, and as old as St. Gregory, though its theology might be new-fangled; and concluded that what the Church needed was not new doctrine, but assertion and clearer statement of the old, infused with a more vital spirit. Orthodoxy, in short, must become more religious, but in becoming more religious must not become less orthodox, or lose any of the *depositum fidei*. Knox wrote in 1809 of a compensating principle to that of the Protestants' agreement with Scripture, namely, 'the concurrent judgment or tradition of the Church, the *consensus omnium*, the *quod ubique, quod semper, quod ab omnibus*' . . . 'next to sacred Scripture our surest guide.' He held to the Liturgy, 'the pledge of our continuity as a Church,' more than to the Articles, and found in the Liturgy, 'and in that exclusively,' the *decus et tutamen* of the Anglican Church; he preferred the Communion Service in the first Book of Edward VI. to that in the second; yet he was no Ritualist. It is remarkable to compare with these mature opinions those put forward twenty-five years later by the Tractarians, who seemed to be unaware of what they owed to him; not directly, but through the influence of his disciple, Bishop Jebb, a man of learning and eloquence.

The leaders of the High Church movement, when they came to formulate their opinions, pointed to Thomas Sikes of Guilsborough (1767-1834) as their inspirer. Sikes was a Northamptonshire clergyman, a man of retired life but strong personality; one of those men who do not seek for influence, but who are sought because their hold upon principles makes their advice practical; a temper of mind and character which does not necessarily imply wisdom, but which commands confidence. The principle which Sikes put prominently forward was that of the Holy Catholic Church. That Article of the Creed, he said, seemed to him to be suppressed; and to teach the rest of the Creed to the exclusion of that one Article was to 'destroy the analogy or proportion of the faith,' τὴν ἀναλογίαν τῆς πίστεως. 'Our confusion nowadays,' he said, 'is chiefly owing to the want of asserting this one Article of the Creed; and there will be yet more confusion attending its revival, when it is thrust on minds unprepared, and on an uncatechised Church.' There is much meaning in the word *uncatechised*. It looks back to a date when episcopal synods defined the faith, and none were admitted into the Christian fold without instruction as catechumens. The revival of this Article of the Creed 'ought especially of all others to be matter of catechetical teaching and training.' In Sikes's use of the word is implied the whole theory of apostolical succession, of divinely appointed pastors in the Church, of an authoritative guide to interpret Scripture and pronounce upon morals, and of an obedient laity.

Reformed Churches gave this power of interpretation and discipline to the congregation; the Roman Church placed it in the Episcopate, and finally in the Papacy. The Church of England, with its subjection to Royal authority, its theory of fallible churches, and an infallible Bible, as interpreted by antiquity, was in a strait between authority and private judgment, and gave no certain note. The attribution of supreme authority to the first four Councils seemed to make for the right of bishops to define the faith, in a true General Council, that is; for all Protestants professed submission to such a Council, if it could be got together; in a case of necessity the bishops of a single Church might define, but with diminished authority. The right of judgment, which did not ultimately reside in the national episcopate, and could not be conceded to the individual Christian, was practically assumed as prerogative by the Tudor sovereigns, in that tangle of Church and State and arbitrary government in which our institutions are founded. They did not, it is true, set up as divines and define *quod fuit ab initio*; they did not lay down articles or prescribe ceremonies without consent of Convocation or something resembling it; but they settled, as a matter of police, what opinions might be publicly held in the Church which they ruled, and left their subjects free within those limits to adopt the view of primitive authority, or of episcopal authority, or of private judgment, in interpreting the one infallible document.

In speaking then of an 'uncatechised' Church, Sikes appealed to the primitive principle of authority residing in the Church, and to the credentials of the Church, calling upon Churchmen to settle foundations and beware both of State interference and loose doctrine, whether it appeared under the guise of reason, piety, or liberty. This remarkable prophecy was remembered afterwards; and the dictum about the neglected Article of the Creed may have quickened into action a mode of thought unexpressed as yet, but ready for expression. The Oxford movement of 1833 turned principally upon the definition of the Church, its limits and its authority. The answer to that problem was the one object of Newman's search during many years of study and controversy.

What, in short, was the Church? What religious societies were in communion with it? How could a true Church be distinguished from a false one? The ancient distinctions had been blurred or effaced in the English Reformation, our relation to other Churches was arbitrary, and dependent upon fortuitous circumstance; the very Prayer Book and Articles did not proceed from a spontaneous and deliberate act of the clergy in council, but reflected the personality of Tudor sovereigns and the politics of their times. The Catechism and the Articles interpreted the Bible, the Liturgy was a comment upon the Creeds; but who was to interpret the Catechism, the Articles, and the Liturgy?

It was not, however, the question of dogma so much as the question of Catholicity which interested the rising school of High Churchmen. Primitive authority was strong in declaring the necessity of unity, the Reformation was the negation of unity; how could these opposites be reconciled? Episcopacy and the grace of apostolical succession, which to the fathers of the Church of England were matters rather of *bene esse* than *esse*, were now elevated to a prime test of unity. This view was insisted upon by Bishop Van Mildert of Durham (1765-1836), Archdeacon Charles Daubeny (1744-1827) and others; where episcopacy and Catholic doctrine could be traced in an unbroken succession from the Apostles, there was Catholic unity. But since visible unity can only belong to one Church, and since the Church of England never claimed that position, visible unity was disregarded, and Catholicity was looked for in certain points of doctrine and practice, according to the definition of the Confession of Augsburg, adopted in Article XIX.; viz., the pure Word of God preached, and the sacraments duly administered.

Catholicity.

Traditional High Church position.

In these points of discipline and doctrine, episcopacy, pure doctrine, and valid sacraments, the Church of England stood secure, waiting for better times when visible unity should be restored. The difference between the old attitude and the new was this, that the High Churchmen of the sixteenth century to the eighteenth vigorously denounced Roman errors and held out a hand to other reformed congregations; the new High Churchmen of the nineteenth century denied the Catholicity of the continental churches, and began by degrees to look for points of agreement with Rome. Rome had erred, but we too had declined from some points of primitive religion; strict sacramental teaching, prayers for the dead, reverence for the saints, Church authority and discipline. The inquirers turned their veneration from the first reformers to the later fathers of the English Church, who looked to the first four Councils for the interpretation of the Scriptures; Cranmer, Ridley, and Hooper gave place to the Caroline divines and the non-jurors, who showed how this decline from Catholic unity might be made up within the bounds of the English formularies, framed as they were upon the ground of comprehension. To read the formularies in a Catholic sense was no novelty, but it had been the practice of a few, and no one could at that time foresee the tractarian movement and its consequences.

As often happens when a new thought is born, the impulse was given, not by a single leader, a Wiclif or Luther, but from a group of friends. If we find from time to time groups of contemporaries agreeing in opinion, this is not to be set down to accident, nor yet entirely to the 'spirit of the time.' Neighbourhood, family connexion, a common college or university, sets different minds working in the same direction. The spirit of the time is among the conditions ; so is the spirit of youthful opposition to what has become conventional ; so is the voice of personal ascendency ; such men as Bentham, Mill, Newman, Darwin shape the thought of a generation, laying down what seems to it a final form of truth ; a phrase embodying a principle takes possession of many minds at once. *Quod ubique, quod semper* is such a phrase ; *compelle intrare* is another ; and Sikes's ' *neglected Article of the Creed* ' set men thinking, and found answer in a group of friends memorable in the history of the High Church movement, for which they prepared the way, though they did not foresee, and probably would not have approved if they had foreseen, the conclusions arrived at by the younger generation.

A name more venerated than even that of Sikes is William Jones of Nayland (1726-1800), the typical High Churchman of an earlier generation, a clear-sighted and authorita- William tive thinker, as well as a man of holy life and Jones of evangelical poverty, who may be taken as the Nayland. typical High Churchman of his time.

But though it may seem strange that a church movement should owe more to a layman than to the clergy of like mind, if we were to single out one name for special notice in connexion with the High Church revival at this time it is that of Joshua Watson (1771-1855).   He was ten or more years younger than the chief evangelical fathers, Joshua Watson. Simeon, John Venn, Wilberforce, who were now filling the churches and committee rooms.   Half of the religious world was full of their schemes for the benefit of mankind and the spread of the Gospel. The other half wanted a voice, a common cause, and a leader. The time was come for a new brotherhood to arise.

Joshua Watson was sprung from an old stock of Cumberland 'statesmen,' though London-born himself; was a prosperous wine-merchant in London, and, after he had earned enough to be charitable, retired from business at the age of forty-three, and gave himself up to the service of the Church.

John James Watson and Henry Handley Norris. He settled at Clapton, in order to be near his elder brother John James Watson, Rector of Hackney and Archdeacon of St. Alban's, whose brother-in-law, Henry Handley Norris, was also a neighbour, being incumbent of a district formed out of the parish of Hackney. Watson was further connected with the High Church party through his wife, who was the daughter of Thomas Sikes of Guilsborough, and through his uncle, Archdeacon Daubeny. Norris was one of the most vigorous and uncompromising High Churchmen of his time, and was respected, and perhaps disliked, by the Dissenters of East London. He was active in his parish, a constant worker for the Church Societies, a supporter both in money and literary contributions of the *British Critic*, the High Church organ, and a munificent dispenser of a large private fortune. His advice in all Church matters was so much valued by people in authority that he was called by his friends 'the Bishop-maker' and 'the Patriarch.'

Another friend, and of the same way of thinking, was an older man, the biographer and contemporary of William Jones of Nayland, William Stevens (1732-1807), a rich London tradesman, who was active in good works of many kinds, and specially gave his help both in time and money to the old Societies, S.P.C.K. and S.P.G., and to the administration of Queen Anne's Bounty, of which he was treasurer. He was also a man of some learning, and wrote with authority on the Hebrew text of the Old Testament. Stevens was a whimsical character, who delighted in the name of ' Nobody,' published his writings under the title of Οὐδενὸς ἔργα, and founded a bachelors' dining club, which still exists, called 'Nobody's Friends,' and an imaginary association for charitable works, of which he was probably the only member, called the 'Berean Society.'

This company of neighbours and friends supported each other in action, edified each other in principle, gave a large portion of their time and thought to church work, and laid deeper and broader the foundation of a common church feeling, on which the next generation was to build. The Watsons, Norris, and Stevens were nicknamed the 'Hackney phalanx,' or the 'Clapton sect,' in allusion to the 'Clapham sect,' which they resembled in their charitable deeds, though not in their theology. Another member of the same coterie was Archdeacon Daubeny, whose attachment to the Church of England was almost fanatical.

The Hackney phalanx or Clapton sect.

It might be said that the Gospel was preached at Clapham and the Church at Hackney, so large a space in the field was occupied by the Church. From Daubeny's point of view, as set forth in his *Guide to the Church*, a High Churchman means a man devoted to the apostolical government of the Church. Schism is division in the Church, occasioned by a want of obedience to the government established by Christ and His Apostles. The High Churchman does not disclaim private judgment nor admit the infallibility of the Church; he takes his faith neither from Luther, nor Calvin, nor Augustine, but from the Word of God; nevertheless he looks upon dissent as 'separation from the communion of the Christian Church'; and Daubeny did not scruple to call dissenting chapels 'synagogues of the devil.' There was nothing new in the doctrine held at Clapton. What was new was the insistence upon the apostolic succession, and the consequent authority of the priesthood, as an article *stantis aut cadentis ecclesiae*. A tight bond keeps a party together; and the High Church development of the nineteenth century owes much to the knot of friends who, whilst they supported all the practical work of the Church, never relaxed the strictness of their own orthodoxy, or gave way in the smallest degree to any parleying with error.

Archdeacon Daubeny.

These were the friends to whom the terms 'Clapton sect' and 'Hackney phalanx' were in the first instance applied. They gathered round them a group of sympathisers, who added strength to the local society. Among these may be named John Bowles (1725-1810), an early supporter of the National Society; Archdeacon Cambridge (1766-1841); Christopher Wordsworth (1774-1846), the poet's brother, afterwards Master of Trinity College, Cambridge; William Van Mildert, afterwards Bishop of Durham, a scholar and divine of whom Charles Lloyd said that 'he was so great in his knowledge of the exact doctrines of the Church of England that orthodoxy oozed out of his pores, and he would talk it in his dreams'; Bishops Middleton (1769-1822), Broughton (1788-1853), Kaye (1783-1853), Lloyd (1784-1820), and Monk (1784-1856). Among lawyers were Judges Tindal (1777-1840), Richardson (1771-1841), Patteson (1790-1861), and Coleridge (1790-1876). The Hackney brotherhood was a rallying-point for all orthodox Churchmen who wished for clear definition of doctrine and increased activity in church work, combined with the steady political conservatism which brought to their side such men as Gifford and Southey. William Wordsworth too, passing from his ardour of sympathy with the cause of liberty to the side of order, was introduced by his brother into this company of friends, and saw in their teaching a defence which might save the England of his youth from being vulgarised and materialised by liberalism. Though Wordsworth was not a theologian, and though we may be certain that the views developed by the High Church party twenty years later had no acceptance with him, he agreed heartily with the religion as well as the politics of these fathers of the movement.

William Wordsworth.

From whatever source Watson and his friends derived their doctrine, and it is evident that they were no innovators nor preachers of strange doctrine, they were consistent and secure in their belief; which was, as they held, the true primitive creed, supported by the authority of the early Church, purged from mediæval corruption, and not entangled with the unauthorised interpretations of foreign reformers. This belief made them studious, grave, and sober-minded. To the opposite party they seemed lukewarm in faith, because they distrusted personal experience and leant upon antiquity; and believers in works, because they set comparatively little store by preaching, being less eager to save

Their religious views.

souls than the Evangelicals, and opposed both to individualism in religion and to the emotional excesses which attend conversion, and which were conspicuous in the early evangelical revival.

The brotherhood of North - East London may be distinguished, among other characteristics, from the group of earnest Christians on the other side of the Thames by the quiet and sure possession of a complete and settled body of dogma, which taught them to be incurious of novelties. It may almost be said that the Claphamites had one doctrine, the Atonement, preached according to a certain scheme of theology; the Hackney brethren, whilst laying stress on 'the Holy Catholic Church,' did not exalt one article of the Creed above another, but held all bound together by the tenet of Church authority; and this gave them a broader basis for a unity which did not need to be fostered by neighbourhood, or by hearing the same preacher, or using a common language. The High Church school may have had less unction, less glow, less spontaneous warmth of charity; but their piety was of a more solid texture, and had more promise of effective continuance. Its chief fault was the narrowness which is inseparable from a strongly defined dogmatic belief. Joshua Watson did not like the terms 'Established Church,' 'Establishment,' and so on. The worthies who founded the Society for the Promotion of Christian Knowledge, he said, knew of no other church in the country than the Church of England; 'We should like to think that there were no such persons as Dissenters in the world'; and he objected to the custom of the Society for the Promotion of Christian Knowledge of selling books written by Nonconformists, even the *Pilgrim's Progress.* How different from Isaac Milner, who would 'go hand in hand with Dissenters as far as possible,' and the founders of the Bible Society, who admitted them to their Committee on equal terms with Churchmen. We may think this exclusiveness uncharitable, and a narrowing of God's grace; but it makes for unity of doctrine and fellowship within the body, and for those without builds a hedge round the law, keeping indifferentists and sectaries at a distance. This was the attitude of the High Church party, and this attitude they preserved throughout the times of the Oxford movement

and those which followed.   There is strength in definiteness ;
the advance of the High Church party during the nineteenth
century is due not only to the influence of saints and divines,
nor to the reasonableness of their teaching, but also to their
refusal to compromise, and their consistent opposition to
latitudinarianism and dissent.

Of the leaders at the time of which we are speaking
Daubeny is the narrowest, and Watson among the broadest ;
but the difference is one of temperament rather than of
principle.   For all the school there was a high wall built
on the side of dissent and foreign Protestantism, and a less
high wall, though as yet too high to look over, on the side
of Rome.   The denunciations of Rome, which are strong
enough, have an academical sound, as if the writer were
proclaiming his agreement with a received proposition ; the
hostility to dissent and evangelical laxity is more cordial, and
there was reason for this ; the danger from 'poor and loose
theology' was at hand, the danger from Rome was remote.
The challenge of the Roman Catholic divine, John Milner,
in his *End of Religious Controversy*, published in 1824,
drew attention to the weak side of Protestantism, as indicated
by its negative name.   Henry Phillpotts, afterwards Bishop
of Exeter, answered Milner, and another Roman writer,
Charles Butler, who replied to Southey's *Book of the Church*
by the *Book of the Roman Catholic Church*.   Daubeny also
was not unaware of a change in public opinion, and expressed
his anxiety in his archidiaconal charges ; but few, if any,
saw how near at hand the crisis was.   The teaching of
Watson's friends opened a door which could not be shut.
It was handed on by their successors, and it may be safely
said that without the practical foundation laid by them the
Oxford movement would have had a different history.

The Hackney school was active in missionary work.
In 1814 Watson became Treasurer of the Society for
Promoting Christian Knowledge, which was then working
hand in hand with the Lutheran missions in India ; he
and Christopher Wordsworth wrote to the Archbishop ' to
uphold the Protestant missions of India,' and mentioned the
desire of Bishop Middleton to add to the Church of England
six to seven hundred thousands of half-taught Christians.

Under this stimulus the Society for Promoting Christian Knowledge voted £5000 to the Bishop, and the Prince Regent granted a Royal Letter. They were also forward in church building, the movement for which was set on foot by Daubeny; and when, in 1820, Lord Liverpool appointed a Commission to inquire into the subject, Watson and Cambridge were among the Commissioners.

It was by the exertions of these men, and especially Norris, that the *Christian Remembrancer* was founded in 1819. The *British Critic* had its place as a publication which was intended to instruct the country clergy, and which it was hoped would rank with the *Quarterly* and *Edinburgh*, and introduce a more enlightened element into religious literature. It is not easy to estimate an influence of this kind at a time like the present, when newspapers, magazines, and reviews in their manifold variety neutralise each other. The *Edinburgh*, the *Quarterly*, the *Eclectic Review*, the *Christian Remembrancer*, the *British Critic* had their own readers, and did much to direct thought into their several channels, and to instruct in facts as well as to lay down principles. In religious as well as secular politics the importance of the press was daily increasing; the review was taking the place of the sermon. Watson, Van Mildert, and Lloyd wrote in these reviews. Charles Lloyd, afterwards Bishop of Oxford, 'a happy-tempered, wise, and good man'; 'honest Lloyd, bluff and blunt,' a university professor who gave animation and interest to his divinity lectures, well read in the Fathers and in Church history and Roman Catholic literature, an intimate friend of Sir Robert Peel, and a man always mentioned with respect and admiration by Newman, kept Hackney in touch with Oxford, as Christopher Wordsworth with Cambridge. But Watson numbered among his friends and followers men of mark in every line. He appears to have had a sense of proportion, and a statesmanlike instinct of public opinion, which, if he had been a politician, would have been felt in the world. A strong conservative bias is to be noted in all that is recorded of him and his circle. They disliked, by a natural instinct, all innovation, whether in Church or State; the Ecclesiastical

Periodical literature.

Bishop Lloyd.

Commission, the suppression of Irish sees, any concession to Dissenters, whether by admission to the S.P.C.K. or by reform of the Liturgy ; a point interesting with regard both to the past history of the High Church party, and to the great change which took place after 1833.

Note.—For a fuller account of Jones, Stevens, and their friends, see Vol. VII. of this work.

AUTHORITIES.—Canon J. H. Overton's *English Church in the XIXth Century* is the best account of the period from 1800 to 1833. *The Life of Joshua Watson*, by Archdeacon Churton, should be read with this. J. Hunt, *Religious Thought in England in the 19th Century ; Remains of Alexander Knox* ; T. Mozley, *Reminiscences* ; Wm. Stevens, *Life of Wm. Jones of Nayland* ; Sir James Alan Park, *Memoir of Wm. Stevens.*

CHAPTER IV

CHURCH BUILDING AND EDUCATION

THE insufficiency of church accommodation, in proportion to the rapid increase of population in the early part of the nineteenth century, was perceived to be a danger to the Church of England and to religion generally; and among the good works begun and partly accomplished in the early years of the nineteenth century, that of church building is not the least remarkable. It would not be right to impute to any want of self-sacrificing energy the fact that the reproach of want of church room has not even now been done away with. Rather it would be right to praise the liberality which has done and is doing so much. The evil was not created by the indifference of the clergy or laity of the Church. It is true that the gravity of it was not at once perceived; but at no time was it ignored. The growth of population exceeds all that can be done in building churches, especially since Parliamentary grants are no longer made, nor Royal Letters issued.

In 1811 a series of letters on the state of the Church was addressed to the Prime Minister, Spencer Perceval, in which it was stated that in the great London churches, St. Marylebone and St. Pancras, there was not room for one-ninth of the parish population. During the whole reign of George III. hardly a dozen churches were built in London. Perceval himself was active in the cause of church building, so was Lord Liverpool, who succeeded him; but the chief part in initiating the movement for church building

(margin note: Want of church accommodation.)

(margin note: Perceval and Liverpool, 1811.)

77

was taken by the group of friends of whom Joshua Watson
was the principal leader.   Daubeny is credited with
the first inception of the movement; Watson and
Cambridge were also helpers, but John Bowdler
was the prime mover.   Bowdler, with James Alan
Park, afterwards a Justice of the Common Pleas, and two
other friends, and with the warm co-operation of Watson,
Daubeny, and others, wrote a letter to Bishop Howley, lately
appointed to the See of London, dated May 4, 1814, in which
it was stated that in many districts of London and Middlesex,
and also in many great towns in other parts of the kingdom,
not a tenth part of the Church of England population could
be accommodated in churches or chapels.   This want of
opportunity for public worship they believed to be 'one
great cause of the apparent defection from the Church, and
of the increase of Sectarism and Methodism.'   The writers
point to the work done by the National Society, which they
fear will fail of effect if, after the children have been taught
the true religion, they do not find the means of practising
what they have been taught.   They go on to say that a
proposal of this kind would probably be better received if it
were originated by laymen, and they ask the Bishop's sanction
for calling a private meeting 'chiefly of clergy, nobles, and
other excellent laymen,' to draw up a plan which should be
submitted to the Bishop, and by him to the Prince Regent
and his ministers, and the Archbishop of Canterbury.

The meeting does not appear to have been held, but the
subject was not neglected; and in 1815 Bowdler wrote a
letter to Lord Liverpool, signed by about 120
laymen, which stated again the same facts, and
pointing out that 'to cure this dreadful evil, by
providing churches or chapels adequate to the wants
of the inhabitants, is beyond the power of private or parochial
contribution.   Parliament alone can do it.'

Financial reasons prevented Liverpool's Government from
granting this request at the time, but the petitioners and
their friends did not lose heart.   They took steps to form a
church building society, but no hopeful progress was made
till 1817, when a meeting was called and a favourable answer
was received from Liverpool, who himself had a church

*Bowdler,
Daubeny,
and others,
1811.*

*Lord
Liverpool
and church
building,
1815.*

building scheme in prospect, but had been obliged to defer it, owing to the great burden laid on the taxes by the war.

On June 7 another meeting was held, at which it was agreed to form a society for promoting public worship; and a deputation waited on Lord Liverpool, who *Application* gave a friendly answer, and advised that application *made to Lord* should be made to the Archbishop and the Bishop of *Liverpool,* London. The Archbishop and the Bishop having *1817.* given their approval to the scheme, and the Duke of York having consented to be Patron, the Archbishop was nominated President; and the Church Building Society was *Church* formally constituted at a general meeting held at *Building Society* the Freemasons' Tavern on February 6, 1818, at *founded,* which the Archbishop took the chair. The sum *1818.* raised by subscription up to this date was about £50,000; but as the object of the Society was local as well as national, so the money by which church building was carried forward was for the most part subscribed in the places which needed it.

The first lists of contributors show how strong the new Society's patronage was both in Church and State. The King gave in all £1000; archbishops and bishops, deans and chapters nearly £10,000; Oxford £6000, *Large sub-scriptions* Cambridge £3500, the City companies £1500; *to the* several noblemen or rich commoners gave severally *Society.* £1000 or more. The Society was stronger in influence, which is the security of income, than in funded capital; and this was in its favour, since its chosen line of action was to stimulate private liberality, and only give grants in aid, not exceeding one-fourth of the estimated expense. Preference was to be given to those churches in which all or not less than half the sittings were to be free, a matter much insisted upon at this time, when sittings in church were in great measure proprietary, and a clergyman might be robbed of his congregation, as Simeon was at Cambridge, by the locking of pew doors.

On the instance of Archbishop Manners Sutton, mention was made of the deficiency of church accommoda- *Vansittart's* tion in the Prince Regent's Speech from the Throne *proposal,* on January 27, 1818, and on March 16 the Chan- *1818.* cellor of the Exchequer, Nicholas Vansittart, a friend to religion, and President of the Bible Society, proposed that, taking into consideration that part of the speech which referred to the great want of churches in populous places, and in connexion with this the investigations made in various parts of England, exchequer bonds should be issued to the extent of a million sterling, which sum was to be spent in church building by commissioners to be appointed.   He showed that in eighty London parishes the churches would not accommodate one half of the inhabitants, and that in other parts of England things were no better, especially in the dioceses of Chester and York.   Division of parishes into new parishes or districts was another object aimed at by the Government: the clergy of the newly-formed parishes would be partly supported by pew rents, but not to the prejudice of the poor, for whom a large proportion of free sittings was to be provided in the new churches.

The debates upon Vansittart's bill gave evidence both of the paramount importance of the position occupied by the Church of England in the country, and of its inability to meet the claims pressed upon it by the growing population of the towns.   Though the distribution of the Church's revenues was so unequal as to call for some such remedy as was applied in 1834, no one proposed that the necessary money should be paid out of the vast possessions of Durham or Canterbury.   Lord Holland, who spoke for the Dissenters, went no further than to point out the hardship of their having to maintain their own chapels and clergy, as well as paying tithes, and also to contribute towards the erection of churches in which they had no interest whatever; and to recommend the precedent of a former Act of Parliament, passed in 1797, by which two prebends of Lichfield were sequestrated for the purpose of repairing the Cathedral.   The bill went through Parliament with little opposition, and the Church Building Act (58 George III. c. 45) was passed almost on the lines drawn by the Government.   It made a grant of a million, to be spent in building churches and chapels in populous or ill-served places, and provided for division of parishes, and erection of new parishes or parochial districts.   Watson, Cambridge, Christopher Wordsworth, and

Lord Holland's speech.

Church Building Act, 1818.

Richard Mant were named of the Commission for carrying out the purposes of the Act, and their names indicate that the character of the Society was such as Marsh, rather than Stanley, would approve; but its constitution is not open to the charge of narrowness and party spirit.

The impetus given, great progress was made in church building. In 1824 another sum of £500,000 was voted for building churches in England and Scotland. In 1828, the tenth year from its foundation, the Society was incorporated by Act of Parliament (9 George IV. c. 42) and collections made under Royal Letters were ordered to be paid over to it; collections made under brief-letters were by the same Act abolished. Between 1828 and 1851, when Royal Letters were discontinued by Lord Palmerston, the Society received by this means about a quarter of a million more. Bishop Blomfield's work belongs to a somewhat later date; but throughout the second quarter of the century efforts were made to keep pace with the growth of population, with more or less success, but no lack of zeal.

Incorporation of the Church Building Society, 1828.

State aid was largely supplemented by private benevolence; it is calculated that between 1818 and 1833 a sum of at least six millions must have been spent on church building. There were many obstacles; incumbents and parishioners were obstructive, the existing accommodation was not used to the full in consequence of freehold and leasehold rights in pews, and the discomfort of free sittings; the more lively style of the dissenting preachers diverted the congregations from the churches where the clergy, as Sydney Smith said, 'were freezing common sense for large salaries . . . amidst whole acres and furlongs of empty pews.' Bowdler had left it to others to build churches for rich people, and studied economy above everything. Money may be worthily lavished on decoration, after the example of Solomon and the great mediæval builders; but there is room for humble buildings too. Complaints were made that the new churches were extravagantly built, and that such buildings were for the rich, and the poor would be afraid to enter them. Much of the money raised was wasted upon costly and inconvenient build-

Large private contributions.

ings, designed in a pompous classical taste, or a so-called
Gothic style, in which there was nothing Gothic but the
pointed arch. Some of these buildings cost from £15,000
to £28,000, St. Pancras, St. Marylebone, and St. Luke's,
Chelsea, being the most extravagant of all. The poor
were packed into narrow seats at the back of the church,
and few of these provided in proportion to the proprietary
pews. This was the state of things in London
and the great towns, where, nevertheless, great
and beneficial efforts were being made. Church
rates, dissent, and the neglect which fostered dissent,
dried up the sources of liberality and reduced most
of the country churches to a condition which is hardly
credible at the present time, 'scenes of dismal ruin and dank
desolation . . . dirt and damp, crumbling rafters and tottering walls, systematic neglect and wanton mutilation,' says a
writer in the *Christian Remembrancer*, speaking of the state
of the churches in 1841, before the Cambridge Camden
Society, the Oxford Architectural Society, and the writings
of Gresley, Paget, and Pugin had taught a better lesson by
precept, example, and irony.

Bad condition of churches.

An independent witness, Harriet Martineau, writes as
follows some ten years later still : 'The churches were active,
as if trying all this time to heal these social woes.
There was much building of new churches in
London and elsewhere, and while the desperate
poor were emigrating in shoals, . . . exertions
were made by bishops and religious societies to provide for
the endowment of bishoprics in the colonies. Much zeal was
shown by the three great Church Societies for missionary
objects, during the whole of this period, and noble sums of
money were raised. But the misery and crime to be dealt
with were not of a kind to be remedied by a provision for
worship, and it was observable that while the existing churches
bore a very small proportion to the population of their
districts, they yielded more room than was occupied. Churches
come of religion, but religion does not come of churches.'

Harriet Martineau on church building.

These words show a wide difference of sentiment from
the feelings which inspired and directed the church building
movement of which Bishop Blomfield was one of the most

active promoters.   While utilitarian reformers in the middle
of the nineteenth century looked to the advance
of education and to reform in charity, hospitals, Church
building in
the poor law, emigration, and other material agencies, Blomfield's
time.
the clergy, not without reason, looked to church
building as a counterpoise to the spiritual destitution of
which all complained who were interested in the welfare
of the people, whether they were bishops, clergymen, philanthropists, or members of Parliament.   The first thing in the
eyes of the clergy was to bring back the people to the Church
by giving them a place to worship in.   These first church
builders, who to some extent reflected the mechanical spirit of
the time, were succeeded by the Tractarians, to whom the most
sacred ideas were the apostolical succession, the episcopal
system, and the administration of the sacraments; they could
not endure that missionaries should be sent to heathen
countries without a bishop to rule over them, or that there
should be town districts without a consecrated building in
which the weekly or daily sacrifice could be celebrated.   In
the seventeenth and eighteenth centuries the churches all over
England were so full that galleries had to be put up to
contain the congregations.   If churches are half empty now,
the reason may be, not that the world is more irreligious,
but that religion does not come of churches alone.   The
exaltation of services and ceremonies is in its way as
mechanical as the over-confidence in the machinery or
organisation, which is the main mistake of the nineteenth
century.   Both mistakes, however, have borne good fruit in
bringing opportunities to poor people's doors, and both springs
of action are active and beneficent at this day.

Amongst other organisations, the Church Pastoral Aid
Society was founded in 1836 to pay more curates, with the
intention of meeting the difficulty caused by the Church
increase of town populations in England.   This Pastoral Aid
increase of population is one of the capital facts Society, 1836.
of nineteenth-century history, and it is no discredit to the
religious energies of the nation that no efforts to evangelise
have been able to keep pace with it.   Enormous sums of
money have been spent in church building, clergy and missionaries of all denominations have laboured incessantly, and the

problem is nearly what it was in 1818, when the Church Building Act was passed. The Evangelicals claim to have been among the earliest in the field to institute Home Missionary Societies; and in February 1836, Robert Seeley, the publisher, with some friends from the evangelical centre at Islington, formed the Church Pastoral Aid Society, 'for the purpose of benefiting the population of our own country by increasing the numbers of working clergymen in the Church of England, and encouraging the appointment of pious and discreet laymen as helpers to the clergy in duties not ministerial.' The first President of the Church Pastoral Aid Society was Lord Ashley. In its first year the Society made grants for fifty-eight curates and thirteen lay assistants, the greater number of whom were sent to Yorkshire. The founders of the Society applied to Bishop Blomfield to institute a Church Building Society for his own diocese, and offered to raise a large sum of money to be employed in church building, on condition of receiving the patronage of the new churches. The Bishop took an independent course, and drew no strict line about patronage, though both parties tried to win him to their own cause.

Bishop Blomfield issued in 1836 proposals for the creation of a Church Building and Endowment Fund, in which he traced the difficulty to the growth of population, gave instances of parishes with more than 150,000 inhabitants, and church room for 8000. He spoke of church building as a work of prudence not less than of charity, and of the liberality shown in a like cause by Glasgow and Manchester, and asked, not for subscriptions, but for large donations, with the object of 'reclaiming thousands and hundreds of thousands of the poor from practical heathenism and giving increased efficiency and therefore stability to the Church.' At a meeting held at London House in July he urged this appeal upon owners of property in London, City companies, merchants, bankers, and opulent tradesmen. Though corporate liberality disappointed the Bishop's hopes, he was met by the willing labour of local associations, and by the end of the year 1836 the sum promised was more than £100,000.

To those who complained that the new churches were not filled, the Bishop replied that in such districts the work to be done by the Church was of a strictly missionary kind, that the people must be taught the very first rudiments of Christianity, and that schools were needed even before churches. Many churches were built in poor districts, amongst others those of Bethnal Green, Islington, St. Pancras, Paddington, and Westminster. The buildings were neither costly nor beautiful, but they supplied a need. This fund continued to exist till it was superseded by the organisation of the London Diocesan Church Building Society in 1854.

Blomfield and church building.

The Incorporated Church Building Society continues its activity at the head of all the organisations set on foot to improve and multiply the churches in town and country. Branch Societies carry on the work in every diocese, and in the general summary published with the Annual Report it appears that the Society has, since its foundation in 1818, contributed about £10,000 a year in grants. If this does not seem a magnificent sum, it should be remembered that these grants are all grants in aid, and represent many millions given by Churchmen. There is no greater stimulus to individual liberality than the knowledge that there is a Society in reserve which will help its efforts by a proportionate grant. Moreover, the action of the central Society has been multiplied by the work done by diocesan societies in every part of the country, which minister to local needs with the advantage of local knowledge.

Church Building Society, 1818.

Watson and Norris, the founders of the National Society, were wise in their generation, and understood the value of organisation, the management of committees, and the establishment of funds, all the self-sacrificing service of tables by which Christian philanthropy proceeds from sentiment to action. The way had been pointed by the Evangelicals in the Bible Society, the Religious Tract Society, and the Church Missionary Society; and no doubt the zeal which caused the foundation of the National Society, and was beneficent and operative in the other Societies, was quickened by emulation of evangelical philanthropy, and by something like resentment of the encroachments made by unauthorised bodies upon the special preserve of the Church of England, the education of the poor. For,

National education.

as Mrs. Trimmer pointed out, the Act of Uniformity put education into the hands of the clergy, and it was their business, as it had been all along, not that of undenominational instructors, to feed the flock.   The principal educational agency at the beginning of the century was the Society for Promoting Christian Knowledge, which was strictly a Church Society, so strictly that the works of no Nonconformists, not even Bunyan, Doddridge, or Watts, were permitted to be printed at its offices.   It was even a question, incredible as it may seem, whether Dissenters should be allowed to buy its books.   The S.P.C.K. was also a missionary society ; but a wise determination in the year 1825 transferred the management and superintendence of its missions to the S.P.G., which was already the High Church Society, as the C.M.S. represented the Low Church way of thought.

S.P.C.K and S.P.G.

From its institution in 1698 the S.P.C.K. gave attention to education as its primary object, to which the publication of wholesome literature and the evangelisation of the colonies were subsidiary.   This was indeed inseparable from its principles.   Christian knowledge, the antidote to vice and crime, implied readers as well as books, and the home work of the Society had something of a missionary character.   The Society had not only to find funds and supply and organise schools, but also to persuade people that national education was a desirable thing.   The credit is with him who begins ; when this claim was admitted, the work of the Societies was taken up by wealthy men both in the towns and in the country ; but the idea that education is dangerous lingered among the country gentry and the farmer class, and died hard, if it is yet dead.   As early as 1704, within five years of its incorporation, the S.P.C.K. had set up more than fifty schools in London ; in ten years the number had doubled itself ; by the middle of the century the number of S.P.C.K. schools exceeded two thousand.   Other religious bodies were not idle : but the time for their development had not come ; they were not so numerous, wealthy, or powerful as the Church of England, and nonconformist zeal was rather for piety than intellectual progress.

S.P.C.K. and education.

But the zeal of the clergy had cooled, and beyond the

duty of catechising in church, which sat lightly enough upon them, education did not come within what the laity expected of the clergy. Their duties were prescribed by the Prayer Book; and the Prayer Book did not convey the same The clergy. meaning to Parson Trulliber, or even to Parson Adams (who served four churches), as it did to George Herbert. Hannah More was directly opposed by the Somersetshire clergy; at the most some countenance of the village dame was all that was expected of the parson.

Grammar Schools existed, and provided a certain amount of education for farmers, tradespeople, and the poorer gentry; but they were decayed and poor, and their teachers for the most part had neither zeal, learning, Grammar Schools. nor opportunity. These teachers were miserably paid, and such of them as were in orders belonged to that class of the clergy who were glad to get a curacy, and overjoyed if presented to a chaplaincy; for at no time was the distinction more marked between the well-connected or learned clergy, for whom promotion was reserved, and the Poor clergy. humble curates by whom the country churches were served. Thus, then, the chief educational organisation for nearly a hundred years after its foundation was the Society for Promoting Christian Knowledge, a Society which has never become slothful or conventional, though from its constitution it leans to the established order of things, and undertakes no crusades.

A movement in favour of religious teaching was set on foot in 1780 by Robert Raikes (1735-1811), a tradesman of Gloucester, the high-minded founder of Sunday schools, and of much more than Sunday schools, Sunday Schools. Robert Raikes. for the impetus thus given to education spread far. The Sunday School Union, established in 1785, and formed with a mixed committee of Churchmen and Dissenters, taught the children of church people and Nonconformists indifferently. In these schools, the number of which increased rapidly, the hours of teaching were from four to seven a day, besides attendance at church; and general education was included. They were supported by voluntary subscriptions, and chiefly by members of the Church of England. 'The Sunday School,' says Sir James Kay Shuttleworth, 'became the type of the daily school'; *i.e.* the basis of all these schools was religious, and the movement was promoted by the clergy, not the laity. The clergy had it in their own hand to do much or little; and their estimate of the need of education was not much higher than that prevailing among the laity. A Dr. Bray is not born in every generation; and all the zeal in the world would not have warmed parishes which had no resident incumbent, and were served by curates who resembled the Vicar of Wakefield rather in their poverty than their lives.

Education, however, was in the air. *Émile* appeared in 1762, and Rousseau's influence, though not always acknow-

Rousseau's influence.

ledged, inspired such reformers as Thomas Day (1748-1789), Hannah More (1745-1833), Mrs. Barbauld (1743-1825), and Mrs. Trimmer (1741-1810), and following them, Maria Edgeworth (1767-1849). Hannah More was contented with reading, writing, and arithmetic, and a few simple domestic arts. She believed that knowledge has a civilising power, but had no wish to make the savages whose lives she raised from foulness to decency discontented with their social position.

National education was beginning to be reckoned among political needs. In 1802 the elder Sir Robert Peel, a manu-

Sir Robert Peel's Factory Bill, 1802.

facturer on a large scale, carried a Factory Bill, which limited the hours of work for children employed in factories, and required that they should receive instruction in reading, writing, and arithmetic, thus giving the first impetus to the series of laws passed to better the condition of children so employed, from which the name of Ashley derives its greatest lustre.

In 1807 Samuel Whitbread (1758-1815) brought forward a motion in the House of Commons in favour of national

Samuel Whitbread, 1807.

education by the establishment of parochial schools. The plan was to be voluntary; compulsion, he said, would destroy the object of the bill. He was confident that it would soon so work its way that every man in England and Wales, as in Scotland, would feel it a disgrace not to have his children educated. ' In the adoption of a general system of education,' said this enthusiast (and such enthusiasts, however visionary, are more useful to the country than their critics, who see no visions), ' I foresee an enlightened peasantry, frugal, industrious, sober, orderly, and contented because they are acquainted with the true value of frugality, sobriety, industry, and order; crimes diminishing, because the enlightened understanding abhors a crime; the practice of Christianity prevailing, because the mass of our population can read, comprehend, and feel its divine origin, and the beauty of the doctrines which it inculcates: the kingdom safe from the insults of the enemy, because every man knows the worth of that which he is called upon to defend.'

He was heard with little interest; for the country gentlemen of that age, as well as the clergy and the farmers, looked upon national education as a doubtful experiment: Whitbread's and when the bill reached the Lords, it was thrown Bill out on the motion of the Home Secretary, Lord defeated. Hawkesbury, afterwards Earl of Liverpool, on the double ground that the religious clauses of the bill were insufficient, and that the whole scheme was inadequate to so extensive a design.

The 'Bell and Lancaster controversy' presented in a different form the question, which still remains unsettled, in spite of many attempts at settlement, the latest of which are the Education Acts of 1870 and 1902, Bell and and the Education Bills of still more recent years; Lancaster. the question which exists in all countries which have not, like Scotland, a form of religion accepted by the great majority of the nation as the basis of education; the question, that is, whether national education should be religious or secular, and if this is decided in favour of religion, then whether the religious instruction given in schools supported by public funds should be sectarian or unsectarian. The clergy of all denominations will always support sectarian education; the 'clerical' and 'anti-clerical' antithesis can only be got rid of by entirely excluding religion from schools, a remedy which our nation hitherto considers worse than the disease of controversy.

Dr. Andrew Bell (1753-1832), a clergyman of the Church of England and army chaplain at Madras in 1789, volunteered to superintend education at the military orphan asylum there, a beneficent institution insufficiently Andrew Bell. supported by Government; and finding the number of boys growing too great for one teacher to instruct, he hit upon the plan of making use of his pupils themselves as teachers. The discovery, like many other inventions, was brought about by an accident. Dr. Bell saw the children of a native school writing the letters of the alphabet in sand strewed upon the ground. He tried to introduce this plan into his own schools, but finding that his ushers did not carry out his instructions, he set an elder boy to try the experiment of teaching the little ones; which succeeded so perfectly that it was extended to the whole school. This system of 'self-instruction' extended to self-government, and the moral tone of the school was raised. 'As to any purposes of instruction, the master and ushers were now virtually superseded,' their duties were those of general supervision and administration; the school taught itself. 'Every boy is either a master or a scholar, and generally both. He teaches one boy, while another teaches him.' It was found that the attention of the pupils was fixed and occupied, their memory strengthened, and their judgment enlightened, and that keen competition, aided by strict rule and the personal influence of monitors, developed in the pupils habits of industry and order which made it possible for five hundred scholars to be under instruction at once without the smallest breach of discipline. The children, it was claimed, were made religious, thoughtful, obedient, kind, orderly, and diligent. The moral influence of the monitors was most beneficial, and an incidental but important advantage attending the system was that the saving of expense which was effected enabled schools to employ fewer teachers, and to pay them better, than when all the teaching was done by the master and ushers. Thus the number of schools as well as scholars was increased.

Madras pupil-teacher or monitorial system.

This system, known as the Madras system, was introduced successfully into English schools; such as the schools at St. Botolph's, Aldgate, and at Kendal, Dee Bridge, Swanage, and other towns. This was in 1799, by which time the Madras system had been practised for ten years, both in India and at home.

In 1796 Joseph Lancaster or Lankester (1771-1838), a Quaker lad of sixteen, set up a day school in Southwark, which increased so rapidly in numbers that before long there were a thousand children attending it.   As it was impossible for him to teach all himself or provide teachers for them, he cast about for a method, 'stumbled on' a plan similar to that of Dr. Bell, to use his own expression, and found his problem solved.   He was of a sanguine enthusiastic temperament ; he thought he held the key of universal education ; and the rapid growth of his schools encouraged him in thinking so.   Bell's system was pretty well known at this time, and had been described in print ; but there is no reason to suppose that Lancaster borrowed his idea from Bell, though he adopted many ideas from him, and acknowledged obligation. The method was no novelty, but had long been in use at Winchester and Westminster, in Raikes's schools at Gloucester, and probably in other schools ; but Lancaster, like other enthusiasts, was an egotist, and magnified his discovery.   His eagerness to get subscriptions, his Quaker phraseology and his want of deference to superior age seem to have ruffled Bell, a sober and practical Scotchman, who after entertaining him at Swanage for three days found he had had enough of him and his system : and it became clear that difference of principle between the two systems was likely to take a colour from personal rivalry.

Joseph Lancaster.

Bell and Lancaster controversy.

   This system, whether known by the name of Bell or Lancaster, had immense popularity, and was adopted through-out the British Islands.   What has become of it ? the principle was sound, as was proved by its acceptance wherever it was tried.   It has developed or faded into the 'pupil-teacher' system, has become mechanical, and a burden rather than a help to teachers ; but as boys and girls are much what they were a hundred years ago, it would seem that some experiment in the same direction might again be tried, at any rate for elementary teaching.   It is a matter of small interest at the present moment what proportion of credit belongs to Bell and what to Lancaster.   But the 'Bell and Lancaster controversy' came into the theological field, and had important results.   The principal feature, that of pupil-teaching, was accepted on all hands, but a difference of opinion on the question of religious teaching brought in inevitable discord.   Lancaster's principle was that of unde-

The monitorial system.

nominational education ; all distinctive religious formulas were to be excluded from his schools, and the children were taught to regard differences in Christian doctrine as un-

Unsectarian teaching. important. Bell was a Churchman and a clergyman, and held the opinion that unsectarian religious teaching was not worthy to be called religious at all. Lancaster's design was, in his own words, to establish an educational society 'on general Christian principles, and on them only. Mankind are divided into sects, and individually think very differently on religious subjects, from the purest motives. . . . It cannot be reasonably supposed that conscientious men should promote a religious opinion directly contrary to their own ; . . . but the grand basis of Christianity alone is broad enough for the whole bulk of mankind to stand upon, and join hands as children of one family.' A compromise which should secure the teaching of the Scriptures to all children, in the plain sense in which all Christians understood them, and 'make a Bible of a child's memory,' but should exclude the catechisms and confessions which, whilst clearing the grounds of faith, divide Christians, might have satisfied the laity, but was thought dangerous by the clergy.

His principle of education on 'the leading and uncontroverted principles of Christianity' was indefinite. If all controverted questions were ruled out, what was left? the 'broad basis' became a narrow basis. The clergy, however, might have accepted Lancasterian theology, if Lancaster would have admitted the Church Catechism. But the sacramental teaching of the Catechism, though moderate, was unscriptural in the view of the Quaker ; and thus the 'undenominational' teacher defined by excluding definitions.

'Cry out that *the Church is in danger*, and your object is accomplished,' said Sydney Smith ; a cynical but not untrue saying. The note of alarm was sounded by Mrs.

Mrs. Trimmer's Comparative View, 1805. Trimmer, who published in 1805 her *Comparative View*, an attack upon Lancaster's system. The attack was well timed, though the spirit in which it was delivered was neither charitable nor liberal. Mrs. Trimmer countered Lancaster's saying that 'a national vice requires a national remedy' by pointing out that the Church of England had the remedy in its own hands; an unfortunate line of argument, since it suggested the question, 'What is the Church of England doing?' She ignored the existence of dissent, implying that all baptized Christians were bound to the tenets of the Church. She ridiculed some parts of Lancaster's method, and blamed others, as applying to the pupils the stimulus of selfish motives, dread of ridicule, and love of praise, the fear of man not the fear of God. Much of her criticism was true; and there is no doubt that she was sincere in her opposition to Lancaster. The schools prospered; and if both Bell and Lancaster had been free from jealousy and self-conceit the two plans might have coalesced in one, or have gone on side by side, each preserving its own characteristics but working in harmony and mutual respect. As it was, the progress of a movement external to the Church caused church people to make fresh efforts. Lancaster's schools prospered, and the Royal Free Schools in the Borough Road enjoyed the King's patronage and public approval. It appeared as if unsectarian education would carry the day.

Lancaster's schools.

The Royal Lancasterian Society was established (1808) on general Christian principles, and on them only. In Lancaster's view, Dr. Bell's position compelled him 'to push a massive old church and to drag a mighty old steeple after him, a burden beyond his strength.' It turned out that Bell and not Lancaster had the stronger position. Mrs. Trimmer did not stand alone: behind her was the whole force of the Church of England; and within three years (1811) the National Society was founded.

Lancasterian Society, 1808.

We may regret that *odium theologicum* should come into the question. But the Church of England was at that time the national church in a fuller sense than at the present day. Education was supposed by people in general to be the business of the clergy, and even such a reformer as Samuel Whitbread, who introduced Lancaster to the notice of the House of Commons without any mention of Bell, declared for 'parochial schools under the parochial clergy'; and the bill which he brought into Parliament in 1807, but did not succeed in carrying, provided for the establishment of schools the governors of which were

Samuel Whitbread's Education Bill, 1807.

to be the incumbent, the churchwardens, and the overseers of the parish; their action was to be subject to the approval of the vestry and the Justices of the Hundred.

The country was not in earnest about education, though Lancaster's efforts were loudly praised here and there. If anything effective was to be done, the religious parties, church and dissenting, must take up the cause of national education, and the Nonconformists were first in the field. Church people could not but feel that they ought not to allow others to do their work. The Lancasterian School organisation, if it came under the control of the Church, would grow into a system of national education; but it might easily develop into an anti-church association, and headed as it was by a sectarian enthusiast, it must be looked upon with suspicion.

A Charity Sermon preached at St. Paul's by Professor Marsh on June 13, 1811, sounded the keynote which had already been struck by Bell, the word 'National.' The Church of England was the National Church; the Church Education Society should be called the National Society. 'This sermon,' says Canon Overton, 'forms a sort of link between the old ideas of education and the new —for it was preached for the *Charity Schools* (the old system), and just on the eve of the foundation of the *National Schools* (the new); and partly because the title was taken up as the watchword of the new Society.' If the title 'National' seems in these days undescriptive, it is so because of the growth of dissent, the prevalence of the principle of religious equality, and the jealousy with which any appearance of domination is regarded. The Church of England has as good a right to claim the title 'National,' except in point of numbers, as it had then, but public opinion does not, as it did then, allow the claim to be put forward. At this time, however, the Church of England was indisputably the national Church; and though the evangelical party were active, and promised to become influential, a large majority of the clergy belonged to the 'orthodox' or old High Church section, and it was they who rose in arms against the Lancasterian system; for neglect of duty does not carry with it any diminution of claims founded upon the discharge of duty, and the orthodox clergy, no doubt, honestly believed that

Marsh's Charity Sermon, 1811.

unsectarian teaching was dangerous, and the clergy the ordained channel of religious teaching.

Under the reactionary government of Spencer Perceval the Church might feel safe ; the Test Act was still in force, the Church of England was in possession as the national Church, and was not called upon to surrender. Perceval's Government. But the forces which were to upset so many established things in 1832 were gathering, and Liberalism in the form of undenominational education was taking the schools away from the Church. Marsh's attacks upon un- Dr. Marsh. sectarian education, though narrow-minded, were not essentially unfair. If the church monopoly invited aggression, the strength of the Church position made defence both reasonable and easy. Dissenters, he argued, were at liberty to have their own schools, and had no right to demand in the name of common Christianity the weakening of the Church of England by exclusion of its distinctive doctrines from all schools.

The challenge was offered by the Dissenters, and was willingly and successfully taken up. Archbishop Manners Sutton, a sensible and fair-minded man, deserves Archbishop Manners Sutton. thanks from the friends of religious education for having taken positive action in the Bell-Lancaster controversy, instead of repeating the error which the Church made in dealing with the evangelical revival. It is the fate of the predominant body of clergy to undergo capture from external movements. The Reformation, the Puritan movement, the Caroline reaction, the Whig doctrine of the eighteenth century, the Oxford movement, are instances exhibiting strange divergences of belief, but showing that dogma, however high its pretensions, can be modified by public opinion. Education was attracting public notice ; apathy gave place to a reaction against the narrow theology of the Clapham coterie, who had harnessed philanthropy to their chariot, and were threatening church citadels ; and Joshua Watson and his friends, including the sagacious Archbishop, made good use of the advantage of position and the prestige of the Church in founding the National Society, and captured the majority.

Marsh's sermon was meant as a call to arms, and as such it was answered. The Hackney brethren, Norris, Bowles, and

Watson, met at Watson's house and resolved upon the foundation of a society for the promotion of national
education in the principles of the Church of England.   Upon this, meetings were held on October 16
and 21, 1811, under the presidency of the Archbishop himself, and rules were framed.   Watson was appointed treasurer and Norris secretary, and the name chosen
for the Society was that which it still bears, 'the National
Society for the Promotion of the Education of the poor in the
principles of the Established Church.'   The church character
of the Society was impressed upon it from the first, and the
Archbishop's cordial interest in its growth and prosperity
helped this.   The Society was represented at Cambridge
by Professor Marsh, at Oxford by Eveleigh, Provost of
Oriel, and Parsons, Master of Balliol.   Thus founded and
patronised, the Society grew apace ; the clergy welcomed the
new responsibility which increased their activity and enlarged
their wholesome and legitimate influence ; and no imputation
of insincerity or clerical ambition taints their good fame in the
matter of national education.

National Society founded, 1811.

The Lancasterian Society of 1808 was the nucleus of the
British and Foreign School Society of 1814.   Fifteen years
later these schools were in an efficient state, and
the Society is still working vigorously.   To quote
the words of Lancaster's latest biographer :
'Lancaster was the first to show how, with the Bible
as the sole text-book, the schoolmaster could teach the many
great truths on which Christians are agreed.   As Mr. Gladstone
said in 1870, 'the experience of the British and Foreign
School Society, extending over some sixty years, showed that
this offered no practical difficulty.'

British and Foreign School Society, 1814.

The present controversy was whether the denominational
or the undenominational principle should prevail, and whether
the Dissenters should be allowed to dispute the
supremacy of the Church.   The question of the
voluntary system as against the State system in
education was not yet raised, but was coming into
view ; voluntary or compulsory, subscription or rate, sectarian
or unsectarian, religious or secular were terms representing
ideas that would not be kept from disagreeing.   At present

Denomina-tional and undenomina-tional.

the Church of England had undisputed predominance, but the rise and growth of liberal notions was working in every direction against privilege and towards equality and the arbitrament of majorities.

To the National Society and its founders belongs the credit of having formed, as the name of the Society indicates, the first practical conception of a scheme of education to embrace the whole nation ; but, as was inevitable, the scheme proposed by them ignored the existing organisation of the Lancasterian Society, and was in fact erected in antagonism to it. The same antagonism exists to this day, with this important difference, that whereas the Church of England could then claim three-fourths of the population, she now owns barely one-half, including all those who do not profess to belong to any other denomination, and who are therefore reckoned among the adherents to the national Church. In order to the creation of a national system of education it was necessary that the subject should come before Parliament.

Proportion of Church people to Dissenters.

Brougham's application for a Select Committee to inquire into the education of the London poor was granted in 1816 ; a Committee on Endowments followed in 1818, and in June 1820 he brought forward an important Education Bill; the first definite proposal for the education of the people of England and Wales. He spoke in terms of the highest praise of the zeal and alacrity with which the clergy of the Established Church had exerted themselves in collecting information and communicating it to the Committee, and his inference was that the superintendence and execution of the plan which he was about to propose could not be more properly entrusted to any class of men than the clergy, who seemed to be the persons destined by Providence to assist in this great work. Brougham's measure was to apply to England and Wales, and was based on the evidence furnished to the Committee of 1816. He stated that whereas the number of children requiring education was about one-tenth of the population, means of education of any kind were only provided for one-sixteenth or one-seventeenth, and that much of the so-called education was only what was given in dames' schools and other inferior schools. Out of 12,000

Brougham's Education Bill, 1820.

parishes, 3500 had no more means of education than were to be found among the Hottentots. In many districts there were no schools at all, in others none but nonconformist Sunday schools. The county of Middlesex was the worst-educated district in Christendom. His bill required that all teachers should be members of the Church of England, and hold a certificate from the incumbent of the parish ; the parson was to fix the course of teaching; the Bible, and no other religious book, was to be read in all such schools, and no distinctive catechism was to be used. The former provision was likely to alienate Dissenters, the latter Church people ; and the bill, at Lord Castlereagh's request, was not proceeded with after the first reading. But it had done its work in rousing the mind of the nation to this most important subject.

The bill is dropped.

The voluntary system, as locally administered, was in public favour, and Church influence greatly predominated ; but the Dissenters were active in opposition, and saw in any State interference a probable gain to the State Church, whilst the clergy were conscious of an obligation laid upon them, and did not know how to discharge it, owing to the pressure of population.

SUMMARY OF CHURCH BUILDING ACT 1818

AN ACT FOR BUILDING . . . ADDITIONAL CHURCHES IN POPULOUS PARISHES, 58 George III. c. 45 (30 May 1818).

§ 1 Empowers the King to authorise the issue of one million of Exchequer bills to the Commissioners for carrying into execution the purposes of the Act ; §§ 13, 14 to expend money on church building or in aid of church building in places which have a population of not less than 4000 and church accommodation for not more than 2000, or in any place where there are 1000 people resident more than four miles from any church or chapel, regard being had (§ 15) to local circumstances of population, pecuniary ability, etc. Parishes may (§ 16) be divided into new parishes, with due distribution of tithes and other endowments, or into parochial districts to be served by Curates (§ 21), such district parishes being held as Perpetual Curacies (§ 24) and the patronage of them (§ 67) given to the patron of the parish churches. The Crown may grant, or the Commissioners acquire, and parishes are required to furnish, sites for building (§§ 34-55) ; the security for moneys advanced by the Commissioners to be the church rates of the parish, on which security (§§ 58, 59) the churchwardens also may borrow, to build or enlarge churches and chapels (§ 59), but not without the consent of the ratepayers in vestry.   § 62 empowers the Commissioners to build churches and chapels as required and to draw plans for the same, divided into free seats and pews to be let as they think fit, the pew rents (§§ 63, 64) to be assigned as stipends to clergy serving the church.   Arrangements are made (§§ 65, 66) for third services, and for the payment (not less than £80) of curates performing such services.

SUMMARY OF CHURCH BUILDING ACT 1828

AN ACT TO ABOLISH CHURCH BRIEFS, AND TO PROVIDE FOR THE BETTER COLLECTION . . . OF VOLUNTARY CONTRIBUTIONS FOR THE PURPOSES OF ENLARGING AND BUILDING CHURCHES AND CHAPELS.—Statute 9, George IV. c. 42 (15 July 1828).

§ 1 Repeals 4 Anne c. 14.

§ 2 Incorporates the Society for promoting the enlargement and building of churches and chapels.

§ 3. Archbishop of Canterbury to be President, the bishops and twenty-five laymen Vice-Presidents.

§§ 4-9. Constitution of the Society.

§ 10. All sums collected for this purpose under Royal Letters to be paid over to the Society's Treasurer.

§ 11. Accounts to be presented annually to His Majesty.

§§ 12-15. Compensation for Briefs.

AUTHORITIES : GENERAL.—Andrew Bell, *Rise and Progress of Mutual Tuition.*   BIOGRAPHIES : *The New Plan of Education,* by Sarah Trimmer ; *Elements of Tuition,* by Andrew Bell ; *Elementary Education,* by Dean Gregory ; *Bishop Blomfield,* by A. Blomfield ; *Andrew Bell,* by Southey ; *Joseph Lancaster,* by D. Salmon ; *Robert Raikes,* by Alfred Gregory.

CHAPTER V

ABUSES AND REFORMS

IT is difficult in a hurrying age to understand a time when leisure was one of the attributes of high place, and ministers of State and bishops spent their time as they liked. In these days a bishop may be worldly, avaricious, self-seeking, but he cannot well be idle. He must attend a multitude of functions sacred and secular, receive deputations, and answer innumerable letters. At the beginning of the century a Bishop of Winchester could finish his correspondence in the morning and go out to sketch in the park after luncheon. Bishops were not expected even to live in their dioceses, if it was inconvenient to do so. Bishop Porteus (1731-

Bishop Porteus. 1808) held the rich living of Hunton in Kent with the See of Chester, enjoying at Hunton the charms of the country and the company of 'ancient and long-established families' in the neighbourhood, and thus securing for himself what his biographer calls 'a judicious mixture of society and retirement.' 'The smoothest wing,' said Hannah More, 'will be ruffled by the crowd and pressure of the bustling world.' He gave up Hunton when he became Bishop of London, but still was able to spend some months of every year in a cottage in Sundridge in Kent. He had residences also in Cumberland, Lancashire, and Chester. Yet Bishop Porteus was the intimate friend and spiritual adviser of Hannah More, and had a high reputation as an energetic bishop and a conscientious and religious man, and in ecclesiastical politics was in advance of his time. He supported the British and Foreign Bible Society, the Sunday school

40447

movement, the abolition of the slave trade, the cause of missions, the residence of clergy, the better payment of curates ; he wished for some relief both for Roman Catholics and Dissenters, some revision of the Liturgy and the Articles. He came forward at the risk of unpopularity and loss of court favour to protest against the profanation of Good Friday and the fashionable custom of Sunday concerts and assemblies. How are we to judge such a man, or the standards of the society in which he lived ?

Bishop Watson of Llandaff (1737-1816) (of whom a full account has been given by Canon Overton in Volume VII. of this History), an honest man whom his politics and an uncourtly freedom of speech kept from promotion, and if not a pattern Churchman, certainly above the average of the time, would appear, judging by our standards, to have had no sense of obligation. He was made Professor of Chemistry, a subject of which he was completely ignorant, within five years of his B.A. degree, and Regius Professor of Divinity four years later, being as little skilled in theology as he had been in chemistry. *En sacrum codicem* was his answer to inquirers. The Bible is enough. He prided himself on being αὐτοδίδακτος, and cared little for Church authority. His toleration was carried so far as to make him refuse to subscribe to the Society for the Propagation of the Gospel, because he thought its promoters more anxious to convert Dissenters than heathen. He appears to have visited his diocese only once ; he held sixteen livings ; he desired to be remembered as an improver of land and a planter of trees.

Bishop Watson.

The biography of Shute Barrington, Bishop of Durham (1734-1826), is typical as that of a high-born and courtly prelate, who was also a scholar and a Christian. He was the son of the first Lord Barrington, and was born in 1734. He was educated at Eton and Merton College, Oxford. His first promotion was as chaplain-in-ordinary to George II. He was made Canon of Christ Church in 1761, Canon of St. Paul's in 1768, and in 1769 of St. George's, Windsor. The next year, being only thirty-six years old, he became Bishop of Llandaff, and by subsequent translations Bishop of Salisbury and of Durham. Thus his

Bishop Barrington.

whole life was spent in dignified leisure,—for to write 'from two to nine letters daily' would be hardly a holiday occupation for a bishop of this century,—he never stepped down out of the aristocratic class to which he belonged, his courtesy was of the condescending sort; he died, 'full of days, riches, and honour,' and, his biographer adds, 'at the close of a religious and well-spent life,' marked by benevolence, hospitality, and charity, and so full of piety that he gave more than three hours of every day to prayer, meditation, and devotional reading. Such a mode of life may not fit in with a bishop's duty in these days; but the example of a religious life is not wasted. Horsley of St. Asaph (1733-1806) and Pretyman (Tomline) of Lincoln and Winchester (1750-1827) may also be mentioned as bishops who, besides their literary fame, did more in their dioceses than their order and the standard of their time required of them. Horsley, indeed, stood at the head of all the bishops of his generation.

It was no scandal a hundred years ago, though it was beginning to be thought undesirable, for a clergyman to hold three or four livings at once; and it was not considered indispensable that he should supply a curate where he did not reside. A benefice was, in sentiment, as in law, a freehold, and it was no more questionable to hold benefices than to own estates in more places than one. Promotion implied patronage, and it was taken for granted that in dispensing patronage family claims came first. Bishop Sparke of Ely, his son, and son-in-law, are said to have received among them more than £30,000 a year of church money. Archbishop Moore is reputed to have died worth a million; his elder son had £12,000 a year of church preferment, his younger £3000. Archbishop Manners Sutton, 'a mild but rapacious prelate,' presented seven of his relations to sixteen benefices, besides cathedral dignities. Bishop Tomline also did well for his family. Dr. Goodall, Provost of Eton, who died in 1840, was Canon of Windsor and Rector of West Ilsley, a chapter living. And these were virtuous men, of high and well-deserved reputation. It was said that a third part of the clergy were pluralists, and therefore non-residents. We hear of a clergyman with two livings, worth in all £1200 per annum, who got the duty of both done for £84 : and though this may not be literally true, it is probably an exaggeration, not a fiction, for such statements are not made without some foundation in fact.

Elderly men can remember the end of these times, when one part of England was remote from another, when abuses were tolerated because they were not published, and those who profited by them were more envied than blamed ; when duties sat light on incumbents, and clergymen were sportsmen and played cards for money ; when daily services and weekly communions were unknown, and no one thought of 'restoring' the churches ; and they can remember also that with all this neglect of observances there was much quiet attention to simple parochial duty, good preaching and sound learning amongst the clergy. Lathbury of Livermere was the parson of 'an ideal parish,' Sawbridge of Stretton had 244 communicants in his church, out of a population of 610. Had there not been many such clergymen, the Church must have been abolished, not reformed.

Old-fashioned clergy.

Among the noticeable figures of the Reform period is that of Edward Stanley (1779-1849), the father of a more celebrated son, Rector of Alderley in Cheshire from 1805 to 1837, and then for twelve years Bishop of Norwich. In an age of patronage, pluralism, and nepotism he was honourably distinguished by close attention to his duty as a parish priest, and eager zeal for all improvements, both local and public. He aroused, encountered, and outlived the opposition of his parishioners and the neighbouring squires and clergy. His favourite subjects, science and especially natural history, education, and such public questions as Catholic Emancipation and church reform, made him appear a dangerous man to the steady-going clergy and laity, whose own indolence and self-indulgence was rebuked by his strenuous zeal for reform.

Edward Stanley, Bishop of Norwich,

At the present day it would sound strange to give high praise to a country clergyman, still more strange to blame him, for enforcing discipline, by example and command, where it was needed ; for taking constant and lively interest in the parish school, providing it with gymnastic appliances, introducing the study of botany,

as a country clergyman,

geology, and natural history, with examinations and prizes ;
or for regular visiting of the poor, with approval or reproof
according to the condition of their cottages. 'He took so
much trouble in whatever he did,' his parishioners said. He
sold clothing and other necessaries at less than cost price,
lent books, established cottage lectures, waged war against
drunkenness, risked his personal safety to stop prize fights,
and in every way showed himself foremost in civilising and
instructing his flock. The country clergy of a hundred years
ago did not like so wide a divergence from the normal
type; 'though he neither censured in public nor reproved
in private, his conduct testified to a difference of views';
and this is not easily forgiven. It was his public advo-
cacy of church reform in 1831, when he headed a movement among the Cheshire clergy for the abolition of
pluralities, non-residence, and other clerical scandals, that
made him unpopular among his neighbours, and probably
commended him to the notice of the Liberal Prime Minister,
Lord Melbourne, by whom he was appointed Bishop of Norwich in 1837.

As a bishop he did not promise himself peaceful days. A
Liberal bishop was almost a contradiction in terms, though
Whig bishops there had been innumerable. He found his
as a bishop. diocese full of abuses. Non-residence, pluralities,
neglect of services, all the ecclesiastical vices described in the poems of Crabbe were flagrant in the diocese
of Norfolk ; for his predecessor, Bathurst (1744-1837), though
a reformer both in Church and State, and one of the few
bishops who favoured the Reform Bill and Catholic Emancipation, an impartial friend of both Bell and Lancaster, and a
warm supporter of the Bible Society, was of too easy-going
and benevolent a temperament to be a good disciplinarian ;
and the character of the country parson drawn by Crabbe is
taken from the clergy over whom Bathurst presided.
Bishop Bathurst. It should be remembered to his honour that, like
Watson of Llandaff, Bathurst put principle before the
hope of promotion, and that, unlike Watson, he did not complain of the neglect of Ministers. Stanley has been compared
to Sydney Smith, whom he resembled in opinions and in some
points of external circumstances, but not at all in character

or temper.   In their different ways they worked towards the same objects : unity among Christians, effectiveness and purity in the Church of England, emancipation of Nonconformists of every kind, and the general breaking down of barriers and disabilities, ecclesiastical, political, and doctrinal. It is objected to such men that their influence is negative, and that they had nothing positive to teach.   So it is with all reformers :   their business is to say 'thou shalt not,' and to clear the ground on which a new edifice may be built. Their opinions may seem destructive, but their action is not.

Stanley would not endure parishes without a resident incumbent, churches without a regular service, villages without schools, scandalous clergy, pluralities.   He threw new life by his personal presence and interest into ordinations, confirmations, and visitations, ordinances which had little spirit in them under the old system.   In the sermon preached by him at his installation in 1837, at the time of the first flush of the High Church movement, he declared for toleration of dissent, and extension of secular education.   This, and some suspicion of a leaning to unitarian error, caused great dissatisfaction ;   and such expressions were heard as 'the heretical sermon of a Liberal bishop,' 'an enemy of the Church.'   His attitude towards dissent, like that of his son Arthur Penrhyn Stanley, was always friendly, and a charge delivered in 1846, in which he de-

Stanley's toleration of dissent.

nounced the doctrine of apostolical succession, sharpened the anger of the Oxford school, of which he was a determined opponent.   Questions of ritual, such as the use of surplice or gown, he considered merely trivial, but if appealed to, gave his decision in favour of the Rubric.   In 1840 he spoke in the House of Lords in favour of relaxing subscription to the Articles and Liturgy, a measure carried in 1865 without a division.   He made a protest against sacerdotalism by appointing to the Archdeaconry of Norfolk a clergyman who had openly objected to certain parts of the Prayer Book which might bear a sacerdotal interpretation.   In short, the Bishop was so liberal that he was accused of being a partisan of the Oxford school, because he favoured the seemly decoration of churches and the abolition of high pews : like his son he incurred, and probably did not reject, the imputation of latitudinarian opinions.

Samuel Wilberforce has the credit of having led the way in reorganising the episcopal office : but thirty years before him Stanley had been at work on the same method, that of being himself the centre of his diocese at Norwich, and also visiting in person every part of the two counties over which he presided ; so that all institutions, museums, mechanics' institutes, temperance societies, missionary societies, schools and colleges, and not merely those connected with the Church, felt his fatherly hand. 'There were few parishes in which he had not left some monument of his activity and usefulness : very many abuses had been corrected, churches restored, parsonages erected, schools established, the clergy rendered more efficient under his fostering and encouraging influence ; and both clergy and laity throughout the diocese, both rich and poor, felt that they had in him alike a father and a friend.' We must not judge a former age for not producing more men of the stamp of Bishop Stanley ; but if there had been more of them the Church would not have experienced the violent storm which fell upon her towers in 1835.

It does not fall within the scope of this history to treat of the Reform Bill and its causes. But as the Church of England was vitally affected by the causes which produced the Reform Bill, they must be referred to, though briefly. Reform agitation went so far and so deep that the grounds of all privilege and inequality were brought into question ; and attention was called to the anomalies of the ancient church system, some of which dated from the Middle Ages, and had been borne with or imperfectly patched up at the Reformation or the Restoration.

The wave of reform which, in the opinion of many Englishmen, overwhelmed the British Constitution in 1832, threatened to destroy the church Establishment also : for among the institutions, hallowed by time and disfigured by corruption, which the statesmen and popular speakers of the

Reform movement attacked, the Church of England was eminent.

The attitude taken by the bishops and the clergy generally in regard to the Reform Bill caused much discontent; and whilst the question of Reform was still in agitation, this discontent was already growing fast. Pamphlets came out, denouncing the idleness and luxury of the clergy, or drawing comparisons between the wealth of bishops and deans and the poverty of curates. The *Church Reformer's Magazine* appeared in February 1831. Pamphlets were written recommending the separation of Church and State, a notion, it should be remarked, favoured by some earnest Churchmen, such as John Keble, on the ground that the State was no longer Christian.

Question of reform in Church and State.

The school of Bentham, James and John Mill, and the other utilitarians, the scientific secularists who organised the British Association, which held its first meeting at Oxford in 1832—a 'hodge-podge of philosophers,' as Keble called it,—the supporters of undenominational education, the promoters of unsanctified literature, the enemies of religious tests, were all in the same camp. Long pent-up zeal against abuses, violent and undiscriminating, burst forth in all directions and stimulated defence.

Utilitarian school.

The years preceding the Reform Bill are a period unlike any other in the history of England, except those which produced the Reformation and the great Rebellion. Though the measures proposed and carried out were less violent, the contest of opinions was as marked; one party full of zeal against old abuses and fervour for new remedies, the other driven to obstruction by fear of revolution. Since the Church had inherited many inequalities and inconsistencies from ancient times, some of which amounted to injustice, public indignation did not spare it. It was maintained that church property did not belong to the corporations which owned it, but was held on trust for the use of the nation, and might be used for public purposes. The reformers of the day appealed to principle in everything; and the principle of applying particular endowments to general purposes was capable of wide application.

In the year 1831 an anonymous publication, the

Extraordinary Black Book, startled reformers and conservatives

Extra-
ordinary
Black Book,
1831.
alike. It purported to give a truthful account of church revenues and their distribution, and though highly coloured and written in a hostile spirit, it contained much truth, the knowledge of which stimulated the radical propaganda, and served to introduce the ecclesiastical legislation which followed the passing of the Reform Bill. It was an exaggerated expression of a widely-spread feeling. The inequalities and abuses of the Church were notorious ; but the position of the Church was, socially and politically, so strong that it was unassailable, except at a moment when all institutions were being questioned and put on their trial. This attack upon the Church of England begins with the statement, that there was no Church in Europe with more abuses and less real piety than the Church of England. The clergy of the Church of England cost seven times as much as that of France, and yet ministered to no more than eight out of twenty-four millions of English and Irish. The ecclesiastical revenue of the whole of Europe was less than that of England. The revenues of the Church were spent on a few rich men who neglected their duties. The bishops were political nominees, banded against Liberal ideas of every kind : Shipley of St. Asaph, who voted against war with America, and Watson of Llandaff, who voted against war with France, and had advanced views on ecclesiastical revenues, were almost the only exceptions to this. The clergy followed suit. They had no enthusiasm for education ; they would not have encouraged Andrew Bell but from jealousy of dissent ; nor

Alleged
inefficiency
of the clergy.
have helped to found King's College (1828) except as a protest against the London University. They were inefficient as public teachers, had a bad influence in politics, were inert or reactionary in all measures for the good of the people.

The whole of the great ecclesiastical revenue, said this critic, was levied upon the people in the most vexatious way possible, by a burden laid upon the land, of doubtful authority

Incomes of
prelates.
and unequal incidence ; and such even in their own body was the disproportion of merit to reward, that lordly prelates enjoyed incomes of many thousands, while the work of the Church was done by a vast

body of poor labourers.   Church property, he asserts, is public property, it is held on trust for services rendered to the State, and the State has the right to resume into its own hands property which differs from other property, as being held by a service tenure; since the State is the true owner, and private patronage is only exercised under that condition.   Patronage was sold for money as openly as votes at an election.   Gross nepotism prevailed everywhere.   As for pluralism, a third of the whole number of clergy were pluralists, and cases existed where one man held five livings.   The law required all spiritual persons to reside on their livings, but it was notoriously disobeyed; rectors lived where they liked, and handed over their parishes to miserably paid curates.   One incumbent holding two rectories, valued at £900, had no curate at all, and lived two hundred miles away from either benefice.   It was shown by public statistics that the proportion of non-resident to resident clergy was as three to two; even bishops held livings, prebendal stalls, and deaneries, and so little desire of reform was there, that in 1813 a law was passed to indemnify the clergy for breaking the law.   What could be said to justify such episcopal revenues as those of Canterbury (averaging £32,000), Winchester (£50,000), London (£10,000), the deaneries of Westminster, Windsor, and St. Paul's (£12,000 to £7000), or rectories of eight or ten or even of four and five thousand a year?   The most serious part of the indictment was the impunity of offenders; because it showed that those who were responsible for church government did not enforce the law, a sign of a low standard of public duty.   The laws respecting pluralities and non-residence were lax, but the common morality in such things was laxer still.   However extreme the language of the *Extraordinary Black Book* may be, and however exaggerated its statements, the main facts could not be disputed; and when the Ecclesiastical Commission was appointed in 1835 their recommendations followed in great measure the lines here laid down.

The proposals of the writer are simple enough, as irresponsible schemes of reform commonly are. Equalisation of sees and augmentation of poor livings from the suppression of rich benefices; abolition of

Non-residence, pluralism, excessive revenues.

Proposed remedies.

episcopal patronage, pluralities, and sinecures; the tithe to be sold to the landowner or commuted for a land tax;—crude proposals, but not unpractical. The writer did not wish to abolish a State establishment. He would respect vested interests and the rights of patrons, and maintain a beneficed clergy. Ecclesiastical reform, like Parliamentary reform, was to run on constitutional lines. The pamphlet is written in a hostile spirit, and is full of exaggerations and mis-statements. Its historical interest lies in this, that the picture drawn is not that of an ambitious and tyrannical priesthood, but that of a priesthood which has forgotten the sacred character of its office; and that this same clergy was so far from being wholly corrupted that it was willing to accept and apply simple remedies with excellent result. The remedies have worked; and if the clergy of the twentieth century have faults, they are not the same as those of 1831.

A draft scheme was framed by Lord Henley in 1832, which included the appointment of a permanent body of commissioners, in whom all episcopal and chapter property was to be vested, and by them administered, the surplus revenue to be applied to the endowment or augmentation of small or populous benefices. Under this scheme pluralities were to be restrained, residence enforced, translation of bishops forbidden, and new sees erected, the occupants of which would not be lords of Parliament, and would receive a salary of £3000 a year; the revenues of the other prelates were to be fixed from £15,000, the income of Canterbury, to £5000, which was to be the uniform income of all but a few exceptional sees. Some deaneries were to be merged in bishoprics, canons of Cathedrals were forbidden to hold other preferment except a cure in the cathedral city. Lord Henley provided also for the retirement of bishops past work, either by pension or by appointment of coadjutors. The patronage of the Crown was to be vested in a Minister for Ecclesiastical Affairs and ten unpaid commissioners.

To the Tory Peel belongs the credit of the Whiggish measure which produced the Ecclesiastical Commission. He published on December 17, 1834, a straightforward and manly address to his constituents at Tamworth, described by himself as 'that frank exposition of general principles and views which appears to be anxiously expected, and which ought not to be the inclination, and cannot be the interest, of a minister of this country to withhold.' In the 'Tamworth Manifesto,' as it was called, a paper too moderate and honest to please either Tories or Whigs, he declared that he had never been the defender of abuses or the enemy of judicious reforms. He had supported measures for the abolition of church rates, for the marriage of Dissenters in their own places of worship, for diminishing the disqualifications of Dissenters at the universities, for the reform of tithes both in England and in Ireland. As to the great question of church reform, on that head he had no new professions to make. He could not give his consent to the alienating of church property, in any part of the United Kingdom, from strictly ecclesiastical purposes. He would settle the church establishment in Ireland by an improved distribution of revenues and a just commutation of tithes. With respect to alterations in ecclesiastical laws, he would not commit himself further than to say that his Government would give the subject the fullest deliberation, with the sincerest desire to remove abuses, to extend the sphere of the Church's usefulness, and to strengthen its just claims upon the respect and affections of the people.

Sir Robert Peel.

The Tamworth Manifesto, 1834.

Before meeting Parliament in February 1835 Peel's Government appointed a Commission to inquire into the state of the Church in England and Wales, and to suggest a plan of church reform. The Commissioners were the archbishops, three bishops, and four laymen. They were to deal with church territory, revenue, and patronage; to consider the more equal distribution of episcopal duties and revenues, to enforce residence, and diminish pluralities. Peel was never too proud to accept suggestions from others, or to facilitate the carrying out of his own plans by others. In the instructions issued to the Ecclesiastical Commission appointed in 1835, he followed Henley's scheme to a considerable extent.

Ecclesiastical Commission, 1835.

Lord Henley's scheme.

The first report of the Commissioners was presented to the House of Commons on March 19. Their principal recommendations were the erection of two new sees, at Manchester and Ripon, in the province of York, with dioceses

to be taken out of those of Chester and York, and some
other alterations, chiefly designed for consolidation
of dioceses and making them conterminous with
counties. In their scheme the county of Nottingham was transferred from York to Lincoln; the immense See of Lincoln, which extended from the Humber to the Thames, being now confined to the counties of Lincoln and Nottingham; the county of Dorset, in the diocese of Bristol, became part of the See of Salisbury; Huntingdonshire and Bedfordshire went to Ely, Buckinghamshire (from Lincoln) and Berkshire (from Sarum) to Oxford, Leicester (from Lincoln) to Peterborough, Hertfordshire (from London) to Rochester, which was now to consist of the city of Rochester and the counties of Essex and Hertford. The title of Coventry was taken away from the See of Lichfield, with certain districts assigned to Hereford and Worcester, and Bristol became Gloucester and Bristol.

Rearrangement of dioceses.

Under the head of Revenue the whole episcopal and capitular property of the Church, with its enormous disparity, was passed in review. The English custom is to pare and piece out, not to apply a general principle; but in this instance the precedent of the Reform Act was followed, and a consistent scheme evolved, which boldly disregarded local and historical differences, and aimed at equalisation of revenues at the expense of the richer sees. The greatest breach with historical precedent was in the case of the ancient and dignified See of Durham, which was deprived of its secular palatine jurisdiction, and reduced in income to £7000 from an unascertained revenue, estimated at between £17,000 and £20,000. Canterbury was to have £15,000; York and London £10,000 each; Winchester £8000. The maintenance of these large though greatly diminished revenues was justified by the tradition of 'splendour' which attached to the position of a bishop, the ancient and expensive houses which they had to maintain, the cost of dispensing hospitality and charity in a manner suitable to their station, and the necessity of travelling about their dioceses. What was saved by reducing the incomes of the greater sees was to be used in raising the poorer sees to an average of £4000 to £5000 a year. The

Equalisation of revenues.

Commissioners, though thoroughgoing in their proposals, did not wish to lower the traditional status of the bishops : in equalising the emoluments of bishoprics they had in view the abuses fostered by inequality, such as pluralism and frequent translations, with all the jobbery and place-hunting which attended them.

A second report, issued on March 4, 1836, proposed large changes in the capitular bodies. Little regard was paid to the history and local circumstances which had made these what they were, nor was peculiar and individual character considered. Each chapter, with a few exceptions, was henceforward to consist of a dean and four residentiary canons, all other titles, such as Prebendary, Residentiary, etc., being merged in that of Canon ; the lands of the suppressed stalls, sinecure rectories, rich prebends and other benefices were to be vested in the Ecclesiastical Commissioners for general purposes, and applied principally in augmentation of poor livings. It was proposed further that the system of fines on beneficial leases, which was as lucrative to particular beneficiaries as wasteful in respect of good husbandry, should be given up, and a system of short leases substituted for it, money being borrowed upon the capitular lands to tide over the interval. Much of the capitular patronage, that fat pasture ground for clerical families, was handed over to the bishops, whose sense of public duty was likely to be stimulated by a more direct responsibility to public opinion than had been felt by canons residentiary in the comfortable and reciprocal security of their chapters. Yet bishops were not raised above temptation ; and when Bishop Bathurst, on his appointment to the See of Norwich, wished to remit part of a fine of £100,000 in favour of the family in possession, who had held the estate for many years, Dampier of Ely told him that he had no right to give up a penny ; most of his brethren would have said the same, so sacred to the English mind is the duty of property. Sydney Smith, in his *Letter to Archdeacon Singleton*, cried out against the favour thus shown to bishops, who were presumably no less inclined than priests to nepotism, neglect of duty, and greediness.

Peel resigned office on April 3, 1835, and Melbourne's

Commissioners' plan for capitular bodies.

Government took up the question.   The recommendations of
the Commissioners with regard to the limits of
dioceses and episcopal revenues, those referring
to pluralities and non-residence, and to cathedral
chapters and collegiate establishments were embodied in three distinct bills, the first of which, that
dealing with episcopal reforms, was entitled the Established
Church Bill.   While providing for the rearrangement of
dioceses and redistribution of their revenues, it also
incorporated a permanent Board of Commissioners
styled 'the Ecclesiastical Commissioners for England,' who were to administer the law and manage the
property held in virtue of their commission, and from time to
time to lay before the King in Council schemes for carrying
into effect the provisions of the Act, such schemes to become
law when embodied in Orders of Council.

Lord Melbourne's Government. Ecclesiastical legislation, 1835.

Ecclesiastical Commissioners appointed, 1837.

The recommendations of the Commission, coming as they
did with the authority or approval of the two Archbishops, the
Chancellor Lord Lyndhurst, the Bishop of London,
Peel, Goulburn, and the King's Ministers generally,
were accepted in almost all particulars, and under
the titles of the Bishopric of Durham Act and the
Established Church Act became law in 1836.   With regard
to the first, complaints were made that the palatine constitution of the See of Durham was of use to the county,
since the local Court of Chancery was more accessible and
less expensive than the King's Chancery at Westminster,
and it was answered that the court was where the judges
were, and frequently met in London.   It was also said that
it was unjust to alienate so large a sum from the county
of Durham and apply it to general endowments; but this
argument cut at the root of the whole scheme of Church
reform, and could not be entertained.

Bishopric of Durham and Established Church Acts, 1836.

As to the Established Church Bill, it had in its favour not
only the strongest of arguments, a large majority,
but the momentum of 1831, a period when 'youth,
zeal, ideas, and philosophy contributed freely to
legislation';[1] and the measure was so just in itself
that there was no outcry against it on the part of the

Lord John Russell's Established Church Act, 1836.

[1] W. Cory, *A Guide to Modern English History*, Part ii. p. 367.

clergy at the time, nor has there been any desire to repeal it
since.   It may, however, be admitted that the report of the
Commissioners, which was embodied in the bill, would have
been a better report if greater regard had been had to the
particular nature and circumstances of the several corporations
which were modified or destroyed.   For it is truly said that
the Church of England is not a corporation, but an assemblage
of many corporations, distinct in origin and history, and differing according to local circumstances ; and legislation which
tended to make the clergy stipendiaries of the State tended
so far to remove them from the common duties and interests
of laymen, which are closely knit up with local conditions.
The Established Church Bill was introduced (8 July 1836)
by Lord John Russell in a speech which was little more than
a *résumé* of the Commissioners' reports.   Peel spoke in
favour of it.   Fowell Buxton complained that it did not go
far enough ; it left, he said, 3000 livings with an average
stipend of £150 a year, 2000 at £100, 300 at £50.
The revenues of the Archbishop of Canterbury alone
would provide a decent subsistence for 300 poor clergy
who were now starving on two shillings and eightpence
a day.   Charles Buller followed, in the same sense.   There
was little heat in the debate, and the bill was passed
almost unchallenged, its general principle being accepted on
all hands.

One objection may be noticed, viz. to the clause giving the
force of law to Orders in Council.   It was explained that
this provision referred to details only ; but the line between
details and generals is not easily drawn, and such enactments
need careful watching, since an Order in Council is an order
of the Minister of the day.

The recommendations of the Commissioners, contained in
this and subsequent reports, took effect in various salutary Acts
passed in these years ; by the Church Pluralities Act
of 1838 (1 and 2 Vict. c. 106) it was provided that   Church
not more than two preferments should be held to-   Pluralities
                                                      Act,
gether by the same person, nor two, unless within ten   1838.
miles' distance, and with special licence from the Archbishop.
Facilities were given by the same Act for uniting small and
neighbouring parishes, and for dividing, or altering the bounds

of, parishes of inconvenient size or shape; and checks were
put upon the bad custom of non-residence.   Further
regulations were made in the same year (1838) by
the Church Building Act (1 and 2 Vict. c. 106) for
dividing parishes and converting chapels of ease
into parish churches, and *vice versa.*

Church Building Act, 1838.

The Established Church Act, which received the Royal
assent on August 13, 1836 (6 and 7 William IV. c. 77),
had carried into effect the reports of the Ecclesiastical Commissioners, so far as they related to
dioceses and episcopal revenues, and the Act of
1838 had restrained pluralities.   In 1840 Lord Melbourne,
now in his fifth year of office, brought forward a measure
dealing with the capitular bodies on the lines indicated by
the Commissioners, the principle of the proposed legislation
being the application of revenue derived from
diminishing the number as well as the value of
capitular preferments to the needs of poor and
populous districts, especially in the great manufacturing towns.   The failure of the parochial system to meet the
increase of population in such districts was, he said, the cause
of the bill.

Established Church Act, 1836.

Ecclesiastical Duties and Revenues Act, 1840.

After 1836 and 1838 it was not much good to protest;
but some bishops, as was natural, spoke up for their order.
Charles Sumner of Winchester, a moderate man, quoted
Burke on the Long Parliament: ' I see that the confiscations
began with the bishops, deans, and chapters, but I do not
see them end there'; others pleaded the sanctity of their
cathedral oath.   The bill, said Sumner, was supported neither
by the majority of the bishops nor by the universities, nor
by the clergy, and the cathedral bodies had unanimously
petitioned against it.   Archbishop Howley took a more
practical line.   It would be a great calamity, he
said, if the bill which completed the work of the
Commissioners were not passed.   There was much
spiritual destitution; no less than three millions of
souls were entirely without any spiritual care, and against their
claims were set those of four hundred clergymen.   He justified
what some called spoliation by showing that canonries were
not, in fact, commonly given to learned men nor active parish

Archbishop Howley supports the bill.

priests, but to friends and relations of the patrons. He did
not wish to deprive the cathedrals of dignity, nor the dignitaries
of a proper maintenance. The bill cut down the cathedral
establishments to the lowest practical limit, but enough was
left to maintain a dean and four canons, with two minor
canons and assistants. Though opposition might be made by
deans and canons, whose corporate rights, not their personal
interests, were invaded, he did not think the bulk of the
clergy disliked the plan, the principles of which, though it
was not published, were pretty well known. The Church,
if it wished to be supported by the State, must take a share
in its own reform. A hot attack by Bishop Phillpotts of
Exeter called up the Duke of Wellington and Bishop Blomfield in defence, the latter of whom ridiculed the plea of
'learned leisure' in the case of chapter dignitaries who took
upon themselves the duties of parish priests.

How little remained to be said against the bill, now that
the principle of appropriating ecclesiastical revenues had been
accepted in the case of the bishops, may be seen
by the speeches of the Tories in the Commons. *Sir Robert Inglis.*
Sir Robert Inglis, who as Member for the University
of Oxford held a brief against the bill, asked 'why the
number of canonries should be equalised'; 'what virtue was
there in the magic number of four?' Opportunities of learning and general benevolence ought not to be diminished.
If the chapters had so little left to them, they would not be
able to maintain the fabrics of their cathedrals. This was
a good point, and he might have asked that something should
be spared for the endowment of future bishoprics and
chapters. It was, moreover, a bad principle to spread over
the whole country what was the property of one locality.

Peel gave his support to the bill, and said that the
desired reform had been effected by a Commission composed
of friends of the Church; and it was well that the Church
should take reform into its own hand. The bill was passed,
with general acceptance, at the end of the session.

Another reform, much needed, much decried, and at last
thankfully accepted, was the commutation of tithe. There
was, and is still, a persistent prejudice in the minds of many

Englishmen, to the effect that only one-fourth part of the tithe
rightfully belongs to the parson, the other three-fourths
Origin of being respectively due to the bishop, the church fabric,
tithe. and the poor ; and consequently he was grudged the
remainder. The origin of tithe is obscure. The idea of paying
a tenth of produce to God or the Church was inherited from
the Jewish Church ; how and where it became a custom or a
law is matter of debate. In England much tithe had its origin
in voluntary offering, much was attached as an endowment
to churches founded by patrons for the good of their souls.
Such offerings were represented by the clergy as a sacred
obligation. Tithe was paid in kind ; that is, the owner of
the tithe took possession of the tenth part of all that the land
produced during the current year, including live stock and the
produce of labour. The small tithes belonged to the vicar or
incumbent of a parish of which a monastery was the rector ;
the great or rectorial tithes, on corn, hay, and wood, to the
rector if he served the parish, carrying the vicarial tithes with
them in that case ; but often to impropriators, lay or clerical,
principally the owners of secularised church lands, who were
under no legal obligation to the parish except to maintain the
chancels in good repair. In the nineteenth century much
of the tithe belonged, as it still belongs, to corporations
ecclesiastical and civil, and to laymen.

Another reason which made tithe unpopular was that it
was paid to the ministers of religion, and it was felt that they
ought not to be tempted to drive hard bargains
Unpopularity with their flock. It was also uncertain in amount.
of tithe.
If the parson prevailed in the assessment, the
farmer owed him an ill-turn ; if the farmer got the best of
it, he thought the parson a fool. It was looked upon as a
matter of convenience, not of right and wrong. In any case,
the incidence of tithe was precarious, the mode of collection
vexatious, the exceptions and exemptions arbitrary, and
litigation difficult, slow, and costly. The idea that tithe was
an immoral impost was only entertained by Quakers and a
few Dissenters of extreme views, and hardly comes into the
controversy at all. The principle was admitted, and if it had
been disputed, it would have been confiscation to abolish
tithe, so intimately was it mixed up with the tenure of

property : for a large portion of the tithe was owned by inheritors of abbey lands, and never went to the Church at all. The grievance was felt everywhere, and after the Reform Bill was passed many people expected that this grievance, as well as all other grievances, should be redressed at once.

In 1833, Lord Althorp brought forward a measure to settle the payment of tithe on an equitable foot- *Althorp's* ing. The principle of his bill was to give legal *Tithe Bills,* effect to a voluntary agreement between the payer *1833, 1834.* and the receiver of tithe, and, if they did not come to terms, to make an agreement by valuators compulsory. The tithe was to be commuted for a perpetual rent- *Tithe to be* charge, calculated on the price of various descrip- *commuted for* tions of grain by a septennial average. The *perpetual* principle of making the tithe vary with the rent was *rent-charge.* introduced in Althorp's second tithe bill (1834), and also that of redemption at twenty-five years' purchase. These measures were not carried ; and in March 1835 Peel, not *Peel's* unwilling to use the wisdom of his predecessors, *Tithe Bill,* proposed a permanent commission to administer the *1835.* tithe. Tithe was to be commuted for an annual corn-rent, to be estimated from time to time according to a septennial average ; such estimation to be made every seven years by commissioners, who were to act as arbitrators in particular cases. He laid stress on the voluntary principle, as bringing into action motives supplied by local knowledge, common interest, and desire for settlement.

Much tithe (in 2000 parishes it was said) had been voluntarily commuted within some seventy years, *Commutation* such commutation having obtained legal sanction *on septennial* in many instances only by the difficult and expensive *valuation.* process of a private Act of Parliament, which would henceforward be unnecessary. The measure, being permissive, and only professing to give facilities, was objected to on the ground that a corn-rent was not a satisfactory basis, *Change of* and that a voluntary measure was nugatory. The *Government.* real objection to this, as to other parts of Peel's *Melbourne* proposed legislation, was that it was brought in by *Prime* a Government which had not a majority, and the *Minister,* bill was dropped. Peel, as we have seen, remained in office *1835.*

only four months, from December 1834 to April 1835, and was succeeded by Lord Melbourne.

On February 9, 1836, Lord John Russell brought in a Tithes Commutation Bill for England and Wales. He Russell's spoke of tithes as a grievance long ago felt, Tithe Bill, because they operated as a discouragement to 1836. industry, and were looked upon as a mere money payment to the clergy, who must either forego income which honestly belonged to them, or enforce their rights at the expense of their influence upon their parishioners. The method of collecting tithe in kind was condemned alike by payers and receivers of tithe. He referred to Lord Althorp's plan in his first bill (1833) of making a commutation on the principle of a seven years' average of the tithe actually paid in each parish. This had the disadvantage of giving most to those tithe-owners who had been most exacting, and robbing the lenient. Another plan was to strike a seven years' average upon the total amount of tithe paid in seven years, and spread it equally all over the country. This would affect the income of every tithe-owner in the country, and cause great disturbance of all interests.

The objections to Russell's bill were, as Peel said, that it perpetuated inequality, since contiguous parishes might be assessed, one at a minimum, the other at a maximum rate, simply because of two parsons in recent years one had been popular or a good man of business, and the other not; a fair trial of the voluntary principle ought to precede compulsion.

It was also argued by Joseph Hume that the result Joseph of fixing the commutation by the value of corn Hume. would be to rob the landowners, since the value of corn was an artificial value, depending on the corn laws, which were certain one day or other to be repealed; and if it were not to be fixed but fluctuating, then it ought not to be measured by corn, which was selected on account of its stability, for if corn fell in value the clergy would be robbed; a prophecy which has been abundantly fulfilled.

The bill passed both Houses and received the Royal assent on August 13, 1836. By this Act a permanent Board of Tithe Commissioners was appointed; commutation was made compulsory, but might be effected by voluntary arrange-

ment, on an agreement between owners of land and owners
of tithe to the amount of two-thirds in value, which was to be
binding on the minority by the vote of a parochial
meeting of owners of land and tithe ; or finally by the   Provisions
independent assessment of the Commissioners. The   of the
septennial average, to be re-estimated annually, was   Tithe Act,
                                                        1836.
maintained as the basis of valuation. A more far-sighted valuation
would have enlarged the basis ; but at that time a valuation on
the market prices of wheat, barley, and oats was thought to be the
most favourable estimate for the predominant landed interest.
A deduction of 25 to 40 per cent was made in consideration
of the expense of collecting; the profit of this went entirely
into the pocket of the landowner. The principle of the
measure was to interfere as little as possible with natural
economies ; and if it has proved less satisfactory to the clergy
than was expected by all parties, that was the result of causes
not controllable by Parliament in 1836. It is significant of
new relations between the clergy and their flock, and of the
growth of independence generally, that most of the clergy
had already abandoned their right to personal tithe, *i.e.* the
produce of labour, levied on fisheries, mills, wages, etc.

From the date of the passing of this Act, no tithes have
been paid in kind ; tithes, as such, ceased to exist, and were
commuted for a rent-charge made on all land,   Summary of
payable to the tithe-owner, clerical, corporate, or   the Tithe
lay ; that is to say, the universal substitution of a   Commuta-
                                                        tion Act,
money tax for the inconvenient and arbitrary levy of   1836.
a tenth of the produce. Subsequent Acts of Parliament have
modified details ; *e.g.* that of 1891, which made tithe rent-
charge chargeable on the owner, not the occupier personally ;
but the principles of Russell's Act remain unaltered, part of
the series of remedial legislation with which his name is
honourably associated

SUMMARY OF TITHE COMMUTATION ACT
6 and 7 William IV. c. 71 (13 August 1836)

Appoints three perpetual Tithe Commissioners, two to be nominated
by the King and one by the Archbishop of Canterbury, for the purposes
of the Act. Empowers a parochial meeting to be called, at which owners

of two-thirds in value of the land and tithe payable in the parish may agree to assess the annual sum payable in commutation for tithe ; such sum to be thenceforward paid, with consent of the patron and the Commissioners : the owners to appoint valuers ; in case of no such parochial meeting being held, or in case of dispute, the Commissioners to value ; value to be according to the average in the seven years preceding Christmas 1835 of wheat, barley, and oats, and similarly in after years ; orchards, gardens, coppices, etc. being separately assessed. Henceforward all land is discharged of tithe, and subjected to a rent-charge, payable half-yearly.

SUMMARY OF ESTABLISHED CHURCH ACT
6 and 7 William IV. c. 77 (13 August 1836)

Directs the carrying out of the Commissioners' report with regard to the boundaries of old and new episcopal sees ; directs that the members of all cathedral and collegiate chapters in England and Wales be styled deans and canons ; settles the yearly stipends of archbishops and bishops ; gives Durham Castle to the University of Durham ; provides for episcopal residences, nominates and incorporates Ecclesiastical Commissioners ; gives power to the Crown in Council to issue orders for giving effect to schemes drawn up by the Commissioners.

SUMMARY OF PLURALITIES ACT, 1 and 2 Victoria c. 106
(14 August 1838).

§ 2. No two benefices to be held together with cathedral preferment, nor any person to hold preferment in more than one cathedral or collegiate church.

§ 3. No two benefices to be held together unless within ten miles' distance.

§ 28. No spiritual person to farm more than eighty acres without consent of the bishop ; nor (§ 29) to engage in trade.

§§ 38 etc. Conditions and restrictions of non-residence.

§§ 76 etc. Regulations respecting curates, their stipends, etc.

§ 133. Questions to be asked annually by the Bishop of all holders of benefices within his diocese.

SUMMARY OF ECCLESIASTICAL DUTIES AND REVENUES
ACT, 3 and 4 Victoria c. 113 (11 August 1840).

The historical titles of Provost, Warden, Precentor, or Master, belonging to certain ecclesiastical headships, are merged in the title of Dean ; the appointment to deaneries, hitherto elective, is given to the Crown ; canons to be appointed by the bishops, and all prebendaries, canons of the new foundation, and canons residentiary of the old, to be styled indifferently canons (cf. 6 and 7 William IV. c. 77, 1836) ; the number of these, which had varied from twelve to three, now to be uniformly four, except in a few cases. The non-residentiary and sinecure deaneries of Wolverhampton, Middleham, Heytesbury, and Brecon are suppressed; honorary canons, to the number of twenty-four in each cathedral, to have stalls and take rank next after the canons residentiary; the separate patronage of deans and chapters, which by the system of options had become a matter of rotation, is transferred to the bishop of the diocese; benefices in the common patronage of the chapter to be given to canons, archdeacons, or other cathedral clergy. Finally, the Commissioners are empowered to frame schemes which the Crown might ratify by Order in Council, as in the Established Church Act. The sum taken from cathedral establishments and applied to the building of churches and parsonages and the augmentation of small livings was some £300,000 per annum.

AUTHORITIES : GENERAL.—*Histories*, by Sir Spencer Walpole, Herbert Paul, Justin M'Carthy, Harriet Martineau; *The Black Book* (Anon. 1820); *Extraordinary Black Book* (Anon. 1831); *Reports* of Ecclesiastical Commission, 1835-36; Lord Henley, *Plan of Church Reform.* BIOGRAPHIES: *Edw. Stanley*, by A. P. Stanley; *Bishop Watson* (Autobiography); *Bishop Barrington*, by G. Townsend; *Sydney Smith*, by Lady Holland; *Lord Melbourne*, by W. T. McC. Torrens; *Sir Robert Peel*, by Lord Rosebery, C. S. Parker, W. C. Taylor.

CHAPTER VI

ECCLESIASTICAL COURTS

THE question of Ecclesiastical Courts is one of the most complicated problems of Church history. The limits of imperial or royal and ecclesiastical authority have been debated since the time of Constantine, and the debate is still going on.

In England, before the Conquest, civil and ecclesiastical affairs were transacted to a large extent in common. William the Conqueror, with continental ideas of feudalism *Before the Conquest.* and a distinct jurisdiction in matters ecclesiastical *Under William I.* and secular, declared that the ancient English institutions in this matter were both uncanonical and contrary to right government.[1] He divided the ecclesiastical from the secular jurisdiction in matters not strictly spiritual, forbidding bishops and archdeacons to exercise jurisdiction in the courts of the hundred, and bidding them hold their own courts, 'according to the canons and episcopal laws.' He thus substituted the procedure of the Roman civil law, so far as it was followed by the universal ecclesiastical custom of continental Christendom, for the mixed jurisdiction of the English shires and hundreds, and established episcopal jurisdiction over ecclesiastical persons and things. In doing this he did not give up any of the regal authority exercised by his predecessors, but probably meant, like Henry VIII., to reserve his own supreme authority above both clergy and laity. In ecclesiastical legislation also, by the enactment of canons, William

---

[1] *Non bene nec secundum sanctorum canonum praecepta* (Stubbs, *Select Charters*, p. 81).

'did not suffer the primate of his kingdom, the Archbishop of Canterbury, if he had called together under his presidency an assembly of bishops, to enact or prohibit anything but what was agreeable to his will, and had been first ordained by him.' This is not unlike the Tudor supremacy, saving the right of appeal to Rome.

The makers of our Constitution, Henry I., Henry II., and Edward I. and his successors, in strengthening the secular power at the expense of the ecclesiastical, and building up that supremacy which was finally and violently _{In the later Middle Ages.} asserted by Henry VIII., at each step admitted encroachments from the popular will. In spite of the intrusion of canon law and the unsleeping encroachments of the papal curia, the statutes of praemunire and provisors were remembered and put in force when the Bulls *Clericis laicos* and *Unam sanctam* were forgotten, and appeals in certain cases were transferred from the ecclesiastical to the civil courts, in spite of the protest of the clergy. Papal excommunication was not valid, *i.e.* carried no temporal penalties, in England. In short, Henry VIII., by excluding the Pope from jurisdiction in England, extended the limits of the Royal supremacy; he did not invent it. And such is the working of this peculiarly English growth that Henry VIII., in establishing his own autocracy above all orders of subjects, did in the event establish the autocracy of Parliament.

By the English Constitution, ecclesiastical law should be administered by ecclesiastical judges, *i.e.* according to Lord Coke, archbishops, bishops, and their officers who have spiritual jurisdiction, in their provincial and diocesan courts. Convocation also is a spiritual court, and constitutionally has jurisdiction in cases of heresy, and the powers of Convocation are part of the Constitution, whether in abeyance or not. In case of failure of justice an appeal was allowed from the archdeacon's court to the bishop, from the bishop's court to the archbishop, from the archbishop's court to the Pope; the Crown claiming and exercising the right of staying proceedings in ecclesiastical courts by a writ of prohibition when temporal interests were involved, but not in matters of faith, morals, or ritual, which belonged to the spiritualty. Already before the Reformation the abuse of appeals to Rome was intolerable, and Henry VIII. in abating this nuisance, so far deserved well of the nation. The intention of Henry VIII. when he cut himself off from the Roman obedience was to resume to the Crown the jurisdiction usurped, as he held, by the Popes (1) from the Crown, (2) from the Church of England, and also to assert the ancient power and authority of the Crown over the ecclesiastical authority itself, whether Papal or national; in Stubbs's words, 'an undefined power and authority in ecclesiastical matters . . . as fountain of all authority and ordinary of ordinaries.'

Despotism of Tudor Sovereigns.

Henry VIII. did not claim to exercise sacerdotal functions, nor to determine questions of doctrine or ritual. It was left to the body spiritual, when any cause 'of the law divine happened to come in question, or of spiritual learning,' to declare, interpret, and show it. It is further stated in the first Statute of Restraint of Appeals (24 Henry VIII. c. 12) that the spiritualty always has been reputed both for knowledge, integrity, and sufficiency of number 'sufficient and meet of itself . . . to declare and determine all such doubts, and to administer all such offices and duties as to their rooms spiritual doth appertain.' The Royal supremacy, as defined by Acts of Parliament (1534-1537), included the full power to 'visit, repress, redress, reform, correct, restrain, and amend all . . . heresies, abuses, offences, contempts, and enormities . . . which by any manner spiritual authority ought or may lawfully be reformed, redressed, etc.,' and since the ecclesiastical jurisdiction was declared in the same Acts to he held entirely by, from, and under the King, it was difficult for Henry, even if he had been so minded, not to exercise in practice all the powers spiritual, except the administration of sacerdotal offices in church.

Function of the Spiritualty in ecclesiastical causes.

The legislation of Henry VIII. did not repeal the canon law as part of the common law of England. Power was taken to reform the canon law, but the power was never exercised; it remained unreformed as part of the system to be administered by the ecclesiastical tribunals, though no care was taken that canon law jurists should be consulted, or indeed that such lawyers should exist at all.

Canon law.

But a principal novelty created by Henry VIII.'s system was that henceforward no canons could be made by Convocation without the Royal assent, and that canons passed in Convocation had no binding force in law till they had been enacted in Parliament; whilst the Crown was enabled to issue proclamations and injunctions or advertisements having the force of law in ecclesiastical matters.

As a consequence of this legislation two new courts of appeal from the provincial, consistory, archidiaconal, and peculiar courts were erected: (1) the Court of Delegates, created by Statute 25 Henry VIII. *Court of Delegates.* c. 19 (1534), which existed, except during the reign of Mary, till 1832; (2) the Court of High Commission, created by Elizabeth in 1558 (1 Elizabeth c. 1 § 18), and abolished in 1641 by 15 Car. I. c. 11 § 3. By *Court of High Commission.* the Act of 1534 (the Submission of the Clergy and Restraint of Appeals) it was enacted that appeals from the archbishops' courts, which had hitherto been heard at Rome, should thenceforward lie to the King in Chancery, and that upon every such appeal the King should institute a court 'like as in case of appeal from the Admiral's Court,' and that their sentence should be final. The court so constituted came to be called the Court of Delegates; a Commission was appointed for each separate case, usually consisting of three puisne judges and *Composition of the Court of Delegates.* three or four civilians: in special cases lords spiritual or temporal might be added. The Court heard matters of appeal of every sort, and administered cases of ecclesiastical law when such came before it, which was but seldom, by civil law procedure.

The power of the Crown in ecclesiastical matters was extended still further under Edward VI.; after the reign of Mary the strong anti-clerical set of opinion returned, *Edward VI.* coinciding with autocratic doctrines of government and a spirit of subserviency among the clergy, and threw ecclesiastical government into the hands of the Queen. Elizabeth seldom meddled with doctrine, and *Elizabeth.* expressly disclaimed to be a judge of it, though she could interfere in a disciplinary way, as in the instance of the Lambeth Articles in 1595; she left such matters to the

clergy. By the Act of Supremacy (1559, 1 Elizabeth c. 1)
full power of reforming and correcting heresies was annexed
to the Crown, and the Queen was empowered to
appoint Commissioners to exercise this power. This
was the origin of the Court of High Commission,
which, till its dissolution by Charles I., combined judicial
with executive functions.

Act of Supremacy of 1559.

Did the Act of Supremacy, or that of the Submission of the
Clergy, give, to use Mr. Gladstone's phrase, a *directive* or only
a *corrective* power? Did they make the Sovereign
a judge of heresy, or only empower him to correct
and punish heresy? The Act (1 Elizabeth c. 1)
under which ecclesiastical judges, whether commissioners or delegates, were appointed by the Crown, debarred
them from pronouncing any opinion on heresy, except in
accordance with Holy Scripture, the three Creeds, or the
decision of the first four General Councils of the Church, or
of Parliament with assent of Convocation. It follows that
practically laymen might define heresy, since they
had to judge of the agreement or disagreement of
opinions with formularies; and many canonists were
laymen. The High Commission, a legal court though it did
illegal things, and containing both Churchmen and laymen,
took away much ecclesiastical jurisdiction from the ordinary
courts, being, like the Star Chamber, summary in its action
and executive in its functions, and a more convenient instrument for an absolute sovereign than the ordinary process of
the law; but the Court of Delegates continued to exercise its
functions, and it has been noted that out of 1080 appeals in
causes ecclesiastical heard by the Delegates between 1619 and
1639 (for the most part matrimonial and testamentary, and of
small account, since greater matters were heard by the High Commission), the court was in 982 causes composed entirely of laymen. In other causes a mixed commission was appointed;
in none a commission entirely composed of Churchmen.

Limitations to the power of the Delegates.

Action of the High Commission.

In the year 1830 a Royal Commission was issued for the
purpose of inquiring into the practice and jurisdiction of the
Ecclesiastical Courts. The Commission was a strong one,
both officially and personally; among the Commissioners were
the three chiefs of the law, and of the spirituality Archbishop

Howley, and Bishops Blomfield of London, Van Mildert of Durham, and Kaye of Lincoln.   The Commission reported on February 15, 1832, recommending that the Court of Delegates should be abolished, and its jurisdiction in hearing appeals transferred to the Privy Council.

In 1832, accordingly, the Court of Delegates was abolished by Act of Parliament (2 and 3 Will. IV. c. 92), and on the advice of the Ecclesiastical Commissioners of 1831-32, the Privy *Appeals* Council was substituted for it, as being composed *transferred to* of Lords spiritual and temporal, and so seeming, in the *the Privy Council,* Commissioners' words, 'to comprise the materials of *1832.* a most perfect tribunal for deciding appeals from the Ecclesiastical Courts '; and no complaint was raised by bishops or clergy of any intrusion by Parliament on their proper domain. It was also enacted that such judgments should not be subject to a Commission of Review, *i.e.* an appeal from the appeal.

In 1833, by 3 and 4 Will. IV. c. 41, appeals were again transferred from the Privy Council to the Judicial Committee of the Privy Council ; and it has been stated that *Appeals* civil appeals were mainly in view, and that this *transferred to* most important aspect of the case was overlooked *the Judicial Committee of* when the bill was drafted.   Some years later, Lord *the Privy Council,* Brougham gave it as his recollection that the framers *1833.* of the Act had not in their minds the contingency of doctrinal appeals coming before the Committee ; but even if we admit that Lord Brougham's recollection was accurate, the title of the Act of 1832, which is recited in the Act of 1833, is 'an Act for transferring the powers of the High Court of Delegates, both in Ecclesiastical and in Maritime Causes, to his Majesty in Council,' and Henry VIII.'s Statute in Restraint of Appeal is quoted in the preamble ; it was open to any bishop in Parliament or any Churchman out of Parliament to point out the danger of erecting a secular court to decide ecclesiastical causes ; and the Act was framed with the concurrence of the bishops who were members of the Royal Commission by which it was introduced.

No spiritual person is named by the Act in the constitution of the Committee, except so far as leave is given to appoint 'two other persons, being Privy Councillors '; and in the Gorham case (1850) the two Archbishops and the Bishop of London were assessors, not judges.   This is still the final authority.

One addition was made by the Act of 1840 (3 and 4

Concurrence
of secular
and spiritual
judges. Victoria c. 86), which placed upon the Judicial Committee, for appeals from the Archbishop's Court for the correction of clerks, every archbishop or bishop who is a Privy Councillor, and enacted that one archbishop or bishop must be present at the hearing of the appeal.   Bishops, from being assessors, thus became judges, in cases which came under that Statute.   By the Supreme Court of Judicature Act of 1873 power was given to the Queen to transfer all appeals, ecclesiastical as well as civil, to the Supreme Court of Appeal, by Order in Council ; but this never came into effect ; and by the Appellate Jurisdiction Act of 1876 it was provided that no archbishop or bishop should attend the Judicial Committee of the Privy Council, otherwise than as an assessor, and without a vote ; the duties of an assessor being only to advise the Judicial Committee on points on which his opinion is desired.   The combination of lawyers and Churchmen in the Judicial Committee is in agreement with the principle of maintaining the union of the lay and clerical elements in the Church.

It is difficult if not impossible to draw a line between the interpretation of doctrinal statements by lay judges with clerical assessors or colleagues, and the definition of doctrine. If bishops are judges, their decisions may be bad in law ; if the court is entirely secular, its decisions may be unsound in theology.   The conclusion would seem to be that the meaning of words should be determined by secular judges fully instructed by divines, not necessarily bishops, as in cases involving other 'terms of art,' scientific or otherwise.   And to this effect the Royal Commission on Ecclesiastical Discipline (1906) has reported, thus approving the actual state of the law.

The question of ecclesiastical courts, together with other ecclesiastical matters, engaged the attention of Parliament Lord Cotten-
ham's Church
Discipline
Bill,
1838. during the following years, but no legislation took place till 1840.   On July 26, 1838, Lord Chancellor Cottenham, in moving the third reading of the Church Discipline Bill, explained that it was intended to facilitate justice by removing certain cases from the jurisdiction of the diocesan courts to the Court of Arches in London.   On this Bishop Phillpotts of Exeter made one of those emphatic speeches for which he was noted, declaring that such a measure, if it became law, went to deprive the bishops of a power inseparable from their office, and that he would never obey such a law ; he Bishop
Phillpotts. would summon any offending clerk in his diocese before his own court on his oath of canonical obedience ; and if he were contumacious, said the Bishop, ' I shall proceed to that sentence which this bill tells me I am not to pass—I shall proceed to excommunication. . . . You may rob me of my see, you may take from me my robe, but my integrity to heaven I shall maintain inviolate.' Archbishop Howley explained that the bill had been framed with the concurrence of nearly all the bishops, that it was intended to lessen litigation and limit the freedom of appeal, not to take away jurisdiction from the bishops. The bill, however, was withdrawn, and two years passed without legislation. In 1840 the Church Discipline Act was passed (3 and 4 Vict. c. 86), which gave power to the bishop, Church Dis-
cipline Act,
1840. on complaint or *mero motu*, to issue a commission of inquiry in any case of misdemeanour imputed to a clergyman, and to impose penalties by consent. If the party accused did not appear or denied the truth of the articles charged against him, the bishop was to hear the cause with three assessors and give sentence, such sentence to be good in law, or send the case to the Provincial Court of Appeal. Appeal was granted from the bishop to the Provincial Court of Appeal, or direct to the Judicial Committee of the Privy Council, if the case had been heard in the first instance by the Provincial Court. The Archbishop of Canterbury, speaking for the clergy, approved the bill, and so did the Bishop of Exeter, on the ground that it differed in principle from the bill of 1838, in making the bishops the source of jurisdiction. Neither prelate expressed any dislike of the Privy Council as a court of final appeal.

No further legislation on church discipline took place after this till 1874, when the Public Worship Regulation Act (37 and 38 Vict. c. 85) was passed, followed in 1892 by the Clergy Discipline Act (55 and 56 Vict. c. 32), which prescribes the procedure Public Wor-
ship Regula-
tion Act,
1874.
Clergy Dis-
cipline Act,
1892. in all cases of offence by the clergy, except as regards doctrine or ritual.

It is worthy of notice that the validity of the legislation of 1832 and 1833, by which the Court of Delegates was abolished and its jurisdiction transferred, first to the King in Council and then to the Judicial Committee of the Privy Council, depends upon the competence of Parliament to make ecclesiastical enactments without consent of Convocation. Henry VIII.'s Statute of Appeals, quoted above, gives no legislative power to the spiritualty. But Convocation, whether in abeyance or not, has always existed as part of the Constitution, and the question has been raised whether ecclesiastical legislation to which Convocation has contributed nothing is binding on the conscience of Churchmen. In practice, the Church of England since the time of Henry VIII. has been governed by the State. But the Church has always contained a party which has protested against this, and which has gained strength since the High Church revival, and now includes the most numerous and influential part of the clergy; as well as a party which maintains that Parliament has made and may make enactments binding on the clergy, without the concurrence of Convocation, though such concurrence, as all agree, is desirable if it can be had. As Lord Selborne said in Parliament in 1874, there have been fifteen Church Discipline Acts since Henry VIII., on not one of which was Convocation consulted. The function of Convocation is to consider questions of doctrine, worship, and discipline, not to alter the law of the land for the purpose of giving effect to the law of the Church; and Archbishop Tait strongly denied to the clergy in Convocation any right of legislation concurrently with Parliament on matters of legal procedure.

Concurrence of Convocation not considered necessary.

The civil power has encroached upon the domain of the Church. Since the Reformation the jurisdiction in the last resort over all causes ecclesiastical has been acknowledged to reside in the Crown. The Delegates sat under Royal commission, and the Judicial Committee of the Privy Council represents the same authority. 'The three main objections,' says Dr. Littledale, a strong partisan, 'to the so-called Ecclesiastical Courts which have been substituted for the Delegates, apart from the legal objection to their validity as not having been set up by lawful

Question as to the validity of Privy Council judgments.

statutes, are these : (1) that the Crown, in exercising ecclesiastical jurisdiction by and in them, transgresses the constitutional limits of the Royal supremacy,' viz. to act in
spiritual causes through spiritual courts and persons, in
temporal through temporal; '(2) that the Act of Union with
Scotland in 1707 and the Roman Catholic Emancipation Act
of 1829, and later non-Christian legislation' have taken away
the Church of England character of Parliament, so that it can
no longer, as in the time of Henry VIII., claim to represent
the laity of the English Church; (3) 'that there is no provision whatever to secure competent acquaintance with the
subject-matter of ecclesiastical suits on the part of so much as
a single member of the new tribunal,' whereas ecclesiastical
causes brought before a Court of Delegates were argued and
judged by specialists in civil and canon law.

SUMMARY OF 2 AND 3 WILL. IV. c. 92

An Act for transferring the Powers of the High Court of
Delegates, both in Ecclesiastical and Maritime Causes,
to His Majesty in Council (7 August 1832).

Recites Stat. 25 Henry VIII. c. 19, which provides for lack of justice
in the Archbishops' Courts an appeal to the King in Chancery, and enacts
that upon every such appeal the King should direct an appeal to such
persons as he should name, commonly called the High Court of Delegates,
to hear and definitely determine the same, such appeals being removed
from the See of Rome to the King in Chancery; recites also Stat. 8
Eliz. c. 5 (Civil and Marine causes), which Acts are repealed so far as
relates to any power of hearing appeals. Transfers to the King in Council
the powers of the High Court of Delegates. These judgments to be final,
and not subject, as were the judgments of the Court of Delegates, to a
Royal Commission of Review.

SUMMARY OF 3 AND 4 WILL. IV. c. 41

An Act for the Better Administration of Justice in H.M.'s
Privy Council (14 August 1833).

Recites Stat. 2 and 3 Will. IV. c. 92 (1832), which transferred the
appellate jurisdiction of the Court of Delegates in ecclesiastical and
maritime causes to the King in Council, and enacts that such appeals
shall be judged by certain high officials, as the Lord President, the Lord
Chancellor, the Lords Chief Justices, the Judge of the Prerogative Court

of the Archbishop of Canterbury, etc., who shall form a Committee of the Privy Council and be styled the Judicial Committee of the Privy Council, and to whom the King may from time to time add any other two Privy Councillors.

N.B.—There is no mention of ecclesiastical persons except the Judge of the Prerogative Court.

CHURCH DISCIPLINE ACT 1840

An Act for better Enforcing Church Discipline, 3 and 4 Vict. c. 86 (7 August 1840).

§ 3. The Bishop, on complaint or *mero motu*, shall have power to issue Commission of Inquiry of five persons, one being Vicar-General or an Archdeacon or Rural Dean of the Diocese.

§ 5. Commissioners to report on *primâ facie* grounds for action.

§ 6. Bishop may impose penalties by consent.

§ 11. If the party accused does not appear, or does not admit the truth of the Articles, the Bishop shall hear the cause with three assessors, of whom one shall be a lawyer, another the Dean or an Archdeacon or the Chancellor, and after hearing shall pronounce sentence according to the Ecclesiastical Law.

§ 12. Such sentence to be good in law.

§ 13. The Bishop may, if he pleases, on *primâ facie* grounds, but before filing of Articles, send the case by Letters of Request to the Court of Appeal of the Province.

§ 14. In cases where great scandal may otherwise arise, the Bishop may inhibit after fourteen days till sentence is given, and in the meantime provide for the service of the Church, with curate's salary to be assigned, if necessary, out of the proceeds of the living.

§ 15. Party aggrieved by sentence of (1) Bishop or (2) Provincial Court of Appeal, may appeal (1) to Provincial Court of Appeal, (2) to Judicial Committee of Privy Council when the case has been heard in the first instance by Judge of Provincial Court of Appeal [*i.e.* there is no second appeal when the case has been heard (1) by the Bishop, (2) on appeal from the Bishop by the Provincial Court of Appeal].

§ 16. No appeal to be heard by the Judicial Committee, unless one Archbishop or Bishop (being a Privy Councillor) be present at the hearing.

§ 20. No suit to be instituted unless within two years from the commission of the alleged offence.

Authorities.—Bishop Stubbs, *Constitutional History*, and *Select Charters*; *Appendices to Report of Royal Commission on Ecclesiastical Courts*; Hansard's *Debates*; *Annual Register*, etc.

CHAPTER VII

ATTACKS ON ASCENDENCY

THE ethics of religious toleration, as they are discussed in a different sense by every generation in every country, are subject to much vicissitude, and strongholds of liberty may become castles of robbers. The history of religion in England is a record of the English rebellion against Popery, the persecution of Papists, the oppression of Dissenters, the turning of the tables upon the Established Church. The history of religion in Scotland resembles that of England, but drawn in stronger colours, till the victory of Presbyterianism and the union of the crowns brought about mutual toleration among the contending sects. The history of religion in Ireland is a history of turbulence and spoliation. The wars and rebellions of the Tudors and Stuarts, the 'curse of Cromwell,' the Protestant settlement under William III., all the massacres and burnings which under the name of religion devastated Ireland for three centuries, left deep-seated in the minds of Irishmen the conviction that the English people were enemies to their religion as well as their liberty. Till near the end of the eighteenth century it was assumed by Protestants both in England and in Ireland that Papists had no rights; but the disaffection of Ireland forced the religious difficulty into prominence, and the emancipation of the Roman Catholics in both countries became towards the end of the Whig policy century part of the accepted policy of the Whig in Irish party, which, ever since the Revolution and till within affairs. a recent period, had been opposed to all concession. Sir George Savile carried a Relief Bill for English Catholics in 1778, and another was passed in 1791, with the approval of

Pitt and the full consent of the bishops, which took away many of the existing disqualifications ; but these were toleration acts, not acts of emancipation, and did not satisfy Fox, who declared that only the actions of men, not their opinions, ought to determine their position in the State.   The half-insane opposition of George III. deferred for many years the hope of the admission of Roman Catholics to Parliament, and Pitt failed to overcome the King's fixed idea that to consent to Catholic Emancipation would be to break

Pitt defers to George III.

his coronation oath.   Pitt, unable to redeem his pledges, left office ; but on Addington's resignation in May 1804 he became Prime Minister again, with the understanding that the question was not to be raised again during the King's life.   Statesmen for the most part take secular views of religious questions ; and Pitt may be forgiven if, in the existing condition of home and foreign politics, he thought it his duty to take up the burden of office in 1804 at almost any sacrifice.   In 1805 he opposed firmly, though unwillingly, Fox's motion to take into consideration the Irish petitions which were presented to both Houses, a like motion having been made by Lord Grenville, and the motion was lost by 336 against 124.   The question was treated by both sides as affecting party politics rather than national welfare ; 'a switch for Mr. Pitt' rather than the assertion of a high principle.   It may be doubted whether the stubborn mind of George III. would have resisted to the end if his Minister had stood firm ; possibly if he had been pressed his reason would have given way ; but to have passed Catholic Emancipation a quarter of a century earlier would have made the history of Ireland a different story, and given an additional lustre to the name of Pitt.

After Pitt's death in 1806, the hopes of the Catholics were revived by Grenville's Whig administration.   But Fox would

Grenville's administration, 1807.

make no promises, and advised delay, and his 'neutrality' was severely commented upon.   In 1807, after Fox's death, Lord Grenville proposed to bring in a bill to admit Roman Catholics to military rank in the army.   The King consented to this step, provided it were the last.   Some difficulty of interpretation arose, or something

more than the King meant was urged upon him, in consequence of which the King's friends, headed by Lord Sid-
mouth, intrigued for the fall of the Ministry; the King
retracted his supposed consent, and the Ministry withdrew
their bill. This, however, did not save them, for the King
required them to make an unconstitutional promise never to
offer him advice on the subject of Catholic concession. On
their refusal he dismissed the Ministry (18 March
1807); the Duke of Portland became Prime
Minister, with Eldon and other Tories in his
Cabinet, as well as Canning. A dissolution followed, and
the King's policy was confirmed by the elections.

*Portland's ad-
ministration,
1807.*

Not long after this Sydney Smith wrote the *Letters on
the Catholics from Peter Plymley*, the argument of which is an
appeal in the first place to justice, in the second
to common sense, and in the third to fear. Justice,
he said, demanded that a small minority should not
be able to give the law to the majority; common
sense declared the absurdity of imposing an oath in order to
exclude Roman Catholics on the ground that they were not
to be trusted on their oath; fear of invasion from Ireland, or
of insurrection in Ireland if England were invaded from the
Continent, counselled conciliation; for with a hostile population
in Ireland, a large part of the English force must be stationed
there. Finally, he appealed to good feeling, and a sense of
common national interest, which mutual acts of good-will
would quickly develop, and which centuries of oppression
had not entirely destroyed. The *Letters* were published in
1807-1808, when the power of Napoleon was at its height,
and the danger of England most imminent; the effect
which they produced was neutralised for the present by the
return of the Tories to power, and their continuance in
power till 1827; for though Castlereagh and Canning favoured
the cause, it was not as yet one on which to break up a
party. Unsuccessful attempts to remove Roman
Catholic disabilities were made from time to
time, as by Grattan, since the time when he first sat in
the Union Parliament, and notably in 1819; but the
cause of emancipation gained ground; and when in 1826
Sydney Smith published his *Letters to the Electors on the*

*Sydney
Smith's
Peter Plymley
Letters,
1807-1808.*

Grattan.

Catholic Claims, he found that what he had written nearly twenty years before was not wasted, though the words might be forgotten.

The agitation for Catholic Emancipation did not directly affect the condition of the English Church in England; for the number of Roman Catholics there was inconsiderable, and their political power counted for nothing; but it was of vital interest to the Established Church in Ireland, the position of which was so mercilessly exposed by Sydney Smith; and what was of vital interest to the Irish Church could not be indifferent to the English Church. Catholic Emancipation was, in the minds of some Churchmen, a capital danger to the Protestant religion, and concerned all Englishmen as a matter of national politics; but it comes into English Church history only as a subject of second-rate importance, one which divided Churchmen into camps and deepened lines of disagreement, but led to no immediate ecclesiastical disturbance.

The term 'Catholic Emancipation' meant many different things, but one above all, and comprehending all, the admission of Roman Catholics to Parliament. As happens when an agitation is carried on for a long time with an increasing prospect of success, the approaches to the last stand of the defenders were given up one by one. The penal laws, as Canning said, had been growing for two centuries, and had been in their decline for half a century. The laws were abolished by degrees, the disabilities one by one removed. Catholic Emancipation came to the front as a practical problem early in the reign of George IV. On February 28, 1825, Sir Francis Burdett moved that the House of Commons should resolve itself into committee 'to consider the state of the laws affecting the King's Roman Catholic subjects,' and six resolutions were agreed to, affirming that certain Roman Catholic disabilities should be repealed, saving the Protestant succession and the Established Churches of England and Ireland and of Scotland; and a Roman Catholic Relief Bill was brought in by the same member on March 23, 1825, to give effect to the resolutions. This bill proposed the repeal of disabilities and

Meaning of the term Catholic Emancipation.

Sir Francis Burdett's motion, 1825.

a State endowment for the Roman Catholic clergy. One of its
most important provisions was that the new form of oath
proposed contained no disclaimer of spiritual, but only of
temporal authority, exercised by the Pope in the United
Kingdom. The bill was supported by Canning and opposed by
Peel, and passed the second reading in the Commons (on April
21, 1825) by 268 to 241. The Reform Bill was beginning to
cast a shadow. It was on this occasion that the
Duke of York, in presenting a petition to the Lords   The Duke
(25 April 1825), made a violent and indecorous   of York.
speech, in which he declared, 'so help him God,' that he
would maintain and act up to the principles of his illustrious
and beloved 'father to the latest moment of his existence,
whatever might be his situation of life.' These brave words,
addressed by the heir presumptive to the throne to an
assembly which remembered how successful the opposition
of George III. had been, encouraged the Lords, not unwilling,
to resist ; and the second reading of the bill was negatived
on the 18th of May by a majority of forty-eight in a House
of 308. In this division three archbishops and eighteen
bishops voted against the bill : only two, Stanley
of Norwich and King of Rochester, supported it.   Bishops'
The Duke of York gave a dinner to celebrate his   votes.
victory—he was not used to victories—at which the toast
was 'the 48, the year 1688, and the glorious and immortal
memory of William III.': and 'the glorious 48'   'The 48.'
and 'the ladies who locked up their husbands'
(whilst the voting was going on) became Protestant toasts in
consequence. The Dissenters were unfavourable to the
Roman Catholic claims, both on the broad principle of
Protestantism, and because Canning did not include them
in his zeal for emancipation. His inconsistency was less than
it seemed, for the Catholic grievance was more serious and
real than the nonconformist grievance.

No progress was made in 1826. The Government had
enough to do at home to meet the distress of the poor,
especially in the manufacturing districts ; the mutual suspicion of Roman Catholics and Dissenters was increased
by Canning's unequal treatment ; it was not likely that the
Lords would be soon converted, and it was believed that

time was on the side of emancipation, and that, if time were given, the rest of the Cabinet would come round to Canning's views.

On March 5, 1827, Sir Francis Burdett, in presenting a Catholic petition, moved a resolution that the affairs of Ireland required immediate attention. Canning supported the resolution: but the recent elections had altered the composition of the House, and the motion was lost by four votes (7 May 1827). Canning, who became Prime Minister on April 10, 1827, was unable during his short tenure of power to further the cause which he had so much at heart. He died on August 8, 1827, before anything more was done for the Catholics, and Lord Goderich, his ineffective successor, gave place to the Duke of Wellington in January 1828. In May 1828 Lord John Russell proposed the repeal of Test and Corporation Acts for the relief of nonconformists. This was carried in the Commons by a majority of forty-four; Wellington thought it better to give way, and the bill passed both Houses. Whatever the Ministry might wish, the King's opinion about emancipation tied their hands and made it difficult for them to explain their position. George IV., as the Duke of Wellington said, could not hear the Catholic question mentioned 'without his mind being disturbed'; and no more was done till O'Connell's election for Clare in June 1828 convinced Wellington that emancipation must be granted, to prevent worse consequences. Peel went with him, and resigned his seat for the University of Oxford, to which Sir Robert Inglis was elected. By March 1829, principally in consequence of Peel's determination to stand by Wellington, and to support and even conduct through the Commons a measure which he had hitherto consistently opposed, the King's objections were overcome, and a speech from the throne was prepared, in which George IV. recommended to the Parliament that they should 'review the laws which impose civil disabilities on His Majesty's Roman Catholic subjects.' The Emancipation Bill was brought in by Peel on March 5, 1829.

Marginal notes:

Canning's administration. His death, 1827.

Wellington's administration, 1828.

Repeal of Test and Corporation Acts.

Clare election.

Oxford University election.

The arguments for and against the bill were the same as from the beginning. The Duke of Wellington said plainly that he would not run the risk of civil war. Some of the speakers supported the bill on the ground of justice, some on that of necessity. The chief arguments were drawn from the inequality of the present system in a country in which five-sevenths of the population were Roman Catholics, and the difficulty, if not the impossibility, of maintaining coercion without a state of siege. It was time to try the experiment of generosity. Peel, in concluding his speech, declared his belief that the course which he proposed would give better and stronger securities to the Protestant interest than any other course which could be taken, and avert evils and dangers impending and immediate. Speakers on the other side appealed to the Protestant Constitution of England, rescued at a great price from the Roman Church, a church the principles of which are unchangeable, and which would make all concessions a ground for further aggression; the preservation of the Protestant monarchy; the danger to the Protestant establishment both in England and in Ireland; the evil of yielding to fear what was not demanded by justice; the certainty that Irish disaffection would not be extinguished by concession; these were the arguments brought against the bill.

The Emancipation Bill passed the Commons on May 30, 1829, by 320 votes to 142; and the Lords on April 5, by 217 to 112. Thirteen bishops voted with the minority, one with the majority. The exception was a remarkable one, Charles Lloyd, Bishop of Oxford, once the tutor and still the intimate friend of Peel: *Emancipation Bill passed, 1829.* 'Of all my friends in the University of Oxford,' Peel writes, 'the one with whom I had maintained the most unreserved intercourse after quitting the University.'

It is impossible to deny that the ascendency of the Church of England suffered a severe blow by the passing of Catholic Emancipation, both in England and still more so in Ireland. In Ireland the victory of the national cause led to further demands; in England the Dissenters were encouraged to ask for more and more, never satisfied while falling short of complete equality. But whether or not equality is justice, the inconveniences of ascendency outweigh its advantages, and the change was inevitable. The Irish Church was established on a principle of intolerance; its founders believed that it was a sin to suffer the existence of popery. By degrees the numerical principle prevailed over the religious argument; the Emancipation Act foreshadowed disestablishment, but the forty years which came between 1829 and 1869 were years of advance and improvement, and it was freely acknowledged, when the time for disestablishment came, that the only grave fault to be charged against the Irish Church was that while receiving the endowment of a national church it ministered to a tenth part of the nation.

The long course of agitation which brought about the Reform Act of 1832 did not cease with the passing of that measure, and the removal of abuses in England drew fresh attention to abuses in Ireland. The Protestant episcopal clergy of Ireland were supported by glebe, tithe, church-cess or rate, and first-fruits or annates, collected, chiefly in minute sums, from the poor, nine-tenths of whom were Roman Catholics. When the clergy and the people are of the same religion, a system of small payments in kind, though vexatious, is tolerable; but the Irish system drew attention at every moment to the anomalous position of the State Church, and added a third bitterness to the grievances of race and land. The clergy collected their shillings, pence, and farthings themselves, or employed collectors; the collectors were murdered, the police called in to protect them were fired upon; the people, in short, would not pay the church dues, and the clergy were impoverished and even in danger of starvation. In 1832 a Parliamentary Committee reported in favour of the entire extinction of tithe by a commutation charge upon the land; and Lord Grey's Government, on the motion of the Irish Secretary, Stanley, afterwards Lord Derby, advanced £60,000 to the poor clergy on the security of arrears of tithe due. The arrears could not be collected. Out of £104,000 due, Government, with the assistance of cavalry, infantry, and artillery, gathered in only

Irish Church reform.

Revenue of the Protestant Church in Ireland.

Stanley Irish Secretary, 1832.

£12,000.   Mr. E. J. Littleton, who became Irish Secretary
in 1833, had to deal with arrears of nearly a million ;
a million was granted (5 August) as a loan to the   Littleton
Irish landowners on the security of these arrears,   Irish
which the Irish Government was empowered to col-   Secretary,
lect.   The State thus became 'tithe-proctor for the whole of
Ireland' ; but without much prospect of recovering.   'The
pretended loan,' it was said, 'would be converted into a gift,
and England, besides paying its own tithes, would likewise be
paying those of Ireland.'   The grant, however, passed both
Houses, and the subject was dropped for a time, to be taken
up soon afterwards as part of a larger measure ; a measure, it
may be remarked, brought in not only on the ground of
general justice and expediency, but because the Irish Church
grievance was a chief cause of outrages which made Coercion
Acts inevitable.

Lord Althorp, Chancellor of the Exchequer in Lord Grey's
Government, brought in an Irish Church Bill in
February 1833, which it was hoped would at least   Althorp's
diminish the evils connected with 'the great griev-   Irish Church
ance of Ireland.'   Althorp's bill did not deal with   1833.
glebe lands or tithes.   It abolished first-fruits and church
cess, and imposed instead of them a graduated tax upon all
ecclesiastical incomes above £200 a year.   The annual sum
to be raised thus was to be appropriated to the augmentation
of poor benefices, and the building and repairing of
churches and parsonages.   The bill also diminished   Suppression
the number of archbishops and bishops from   of Irish sees.
twenty-two to twelve, thus saving £60,000 more, which Lord
Althorp wished to appropriate to general expenditure.   Strictly
speaking, no bishopric was suppressed, but dioceses were
united, some of which had already been held together for
long periods ; Irish sees were originally donative, and some
of them had been joined or held together *in commendam* both
before the Reformation by papal authority, and since the
Reformation by the sole authority of the Crown.   There were
Tudor and Stuart precedents for the amalgamation of dioceses ;
and, but for an article in the Act of Union regulating the
number of Irish bishops to sit in the House of Lords, the
matter might have been settled by Royal prerogative.   Owing

to Parliamentary delays, the result of hurry on the part of Ministers, the bill had to be put back till resolutions could be carried. The debate brought out serious differences of opinion ; the cries of the Church in danger, Property, Sacrilege, the Coronation oath, were heard ; the Government, on Stanley's motion, withdrew the appropriation clause, which transferred to Parliament the disposal of the revenues of the bishoprics which were to be suppressed ; and with the appropriation clause went, as Sheil said, 'the life, heart and soul, all that gave the measure its vitality and spirit.' The bill passed on July 30, and the bishoprics were suppressed, causing an outcry at Oxford, the echoes of which are sounding still ; but the grievance was not removed.

Irish Church Bill passed, 1833.

In 1834 the Irish Secretary, Littleton, proposed to commute the tithe, reduced by one-fifth, into a land tax payable to the State : in other words, the ecclesiastical persons and lay impropriators having a right to tithe were to receive it from the State, not from the landlords, who were henceforward to pay their tithe, now commuted into a land tax, to the State, for distribution among incumbents and other tithe-owners. O'Connell agreed to the principle of the measure ; but Lord John Russell 'upset the coach' by again raising the question of appropriation ; that is, application of church revenues to secular purposes. 'If,' he said, 'the State should find that the revenue of the Church was not appropriated justly to the purposes of religious instruction . . . it would then be the duty of Parliament to consider of a different appropriation.' This was taken up by Ward, a private member, who moved a resolution on May 27 to the effect that the Church of Ireland ought to be deprived of part of its temporalities. The tithe system, he said, was the source of all the troubles of Ireland. The truce bought by the grant of a million in 1833 would expire in November 1834. The cost of the Irish Church Establishment was a million every year for the benefit of 600,000 persons, and this million was divided in a scandalously uneven manner among the clergy ; the number of non-residents was more than half that of the residents. Parliament, he declared, had a right to apply an ecclesiastical surplus to

Proposal to substitute a land tax for tithe, 1834.

secular purposes. The important question of appropriation was thus raised; and the debate came to a sudden end, for a ministerial crisis was proceeding, owing to Stanley's resignation, which was followed by that of Richmond, Graham, and Ripon, and by the ministerial changes which became necessary in consequence. Ward's motion was rejected. The King appointed a Commission of Inquiry into church property and church affairs generally in Ireland. In consequence of intrigues and misunderstandings, not connected with the Irish Church, Grey resigned office, and Lord Melbourne became Prime Minister on July 16. The Ministry and the Commons accepted O'Connell's proposal to remit arrears and convert tithes into a rent-charge; but the Lords threw out the bill, and with it the hope of a permanent settlement (11 August). The result of unsuccessful attempts to legislate was to discredit the Ministry, to diminish the dignity of the Irish Church, and to sink the clergy 'into a deeper slough of popular hatred.'

Question of appropriation.

Grey resigns. Melbourne Prime Minister, July 1834.

Melbourne's Ministry was dismissed by William IV. in November 1834, and Peel became Prime Minister in December. In his 'Tamworth Manifesto,' issued on December 17, Peel, as we have seen, declared his intention of maintaining the Irish Establishment, and his fixed objection to the alienation of Church property from 'strictly ecclesiastical purposes.' The Government could not command a majority, and was beaten on a resolution of Lord John Russell on March 30, 1835, to consider the temporalities of the Church of Ireland, with the intention of applying surplus 'locally to the general education of all classes of Christians.' As the Government did not resign, Russell, on April 3, 1835, proposed and carried another motion asserting the principle of appropriation, and so condemning the Tithe Bill which Sir H. Hardinge, the Secretary for Ireland, had in hand; Peel resigned office on April 8, and Melbourne came in again, with Russell as leader of the House of Commons. On June 26, 1835, the Secretary for Ireland, Lord Morpeth, afterwards Earl of Carlisle, brought in his Tithe Bill, by which the tithe was converted into a rent-charge upon land, on a scale

Melbourne's Ministry dismissed. Peel Prime Minister, Dec. 1834.

Morpeth's Tithe Bill, 1835.

which gave the tithe-owner something less than 75 per cent of his legal due. The effect of this change was that the land-owners were to pay the tithe, instead of the tenants, and recover it in the form of rent. The bill was thrown out by the Lords, as infringing the principle of applying surplus to other than church purposes. Again, on April 25, 1836, Morpeth brought in a bill; the appropriation clause was carried with difficulty (4 July); the Lords repeated their action of the previous year; the Commons did not accept their amendment, and no legislation took place.

Morpeth's second Bill, 1836.

In 1837 (1 May) Morpeth brought forward what he said was the fifth measure in three years dealing with Irish tithe. He proposed that 70 per cent on the composition already agreed to should be levied as a rent-charge on land, and that this should be collected from the landowner by the clergy, not by the Government officials. Ten per cent of all ecclesiastical revenue in Ireland was to be applied to purposes of general education, in view of a law of Henry VIII., by which every beneficed clergyman was bound to 'teach, or cause to be taught, an English school.' Such education was, according to Morpeth's bill, to embrace all sects and denominations. William IV.'s death (20 June 1837) put an end to the bill, before the discussion of it had gone further, and nothing effectual was done in the matter of Irish tithes till 1838; but during all these years the country, under the wise control of Thomas Drummond, the under-secretary, learnt that good administration is possible even under bad laws.

Morpeth's third Bill, 1837.

In the next session (1838) Lord John Russell, the leader of the House of Commons, introduced a plan which resembled former plans in proposing to convert the existing tithe composition into a rent-charge of 70 per cent of the nominal value, to be secured to the existing incumbent; to purchase this rent-charge, and to remit the loan of a million, which had been made to the clergy in lieu of tithe arrears in 1833. The appropriation clause, under which surplus was to go to secular purposes, could not be insisted upon by a Government which had but a small majority; and thus the Minister who had turned Peel out

Russell's Tithe Act, 1838.

upon the appropriation clause passed a bill through both
Houses which was nearly identical with Peel's bill of 1835,
thrown out by his own Government.   According to Russell's
plan the existing tithe composition (*i.e.* the payment of a sum
of money agreed upon instead of a payment in kind) would be
converted into a tithe rent-charge at the rate of 70 per cent
on the compositions then existing (the figure was altered to
75 per cent in the passage of the bill through Parliament),
and the rent-charge, saving existing interests, would be purchased by the State at the rate of sixteen years' purchase
(£1600) on each full sum of £100 due as tithe composition.

The money received in redemption of rent-charge was to
be invested in land, or otherwise, as the Irish Ecclesiastical
Commissioners should determine ; and the rent-charges
themselves, when purchased, would go towards a fund out
of which certain sums would be payable for purely Irish
purposes of police and education, and the surplus, if any, to
charitable purposes.

The result then was that the tithes, diminished by 25
per cent, were changed into a rent-charge ; *i.e.* the payment
of tithes was transferred from the tenants to the landlords,
who recouped themselves by raising their rents *pro tanto*.
The Act (1 and 2 Victoria c. 109) received the Royal
assent on August 15, 1838.

Some years later a somewhat similar dispute arose in the
case of the Canadian Clergy Reserves, lands which had been
reserved in 1791 for the benefit of 'a Protestant
clergy,' with the object of attracting Protestant   History of
                                                      Canadian
settlers to the country.   Circumstances had greatly   Clergy
                                                      Reserves.
changed since then.   Disputes arose between the
various denominations, which rose to such a height as to
become a contributory cause of Papineau's rebellion in 1837.
In the Union Act carried by Lord John Russell in 1840, it
was provided that no further reservations should be made ;
and by another Act of the same date the Colonial Government
was empowered to sell or grant clergy reserves under certain

conditions. In 1853 the Under-Secretary for the Colonies,

Frederick
Peel's Clergy
Reserves
Bill,
1853. Frederick Peel, brought in a bill to subject all the clergy reserves to the control of the Canadian Legislature, so as to enable the colonial Government to deal freely with the whole amount, the matter being not of imperial but of colonial concern.

There was little doubt that the ultimate result of that course of action would be the secularisation of the reserves ; there was also little doubt that to reject the bill would be to risk the loss of Canada ; for since Lord Durham's Report and the Act of Union all had been changed, the Dominion had become a nation, and to treat it as a mere dependency was impossible. The question was not a simple one. Settlements which purport to be final are affected by changes of external circumstances and changes of opinion. In this case the population of the Canadas had multiplied itself many times in half a century, and conditions were altered. The corporate vested rights of the clergy could not but suffer. The clergy of the English Church favoured neither concurrent endowment of religion nor endowment of education at their expense ; and they were upheld by the aristocratic and official party. But they were overruled in the end ;

Sir John
Macdonald's
Act,
1854. and after much difficulty and discussion, which produced more ill-will than in proportion to the cause, Sir John Macdonald finally (1854) carried a measure by which the Reserves were handed over to the municipalities for secular purposes, with compensation for personal vested interests.

The chief interest of these events lies in the fact that though principles remain the same, political changes alter their application. Sacrilege is a crime ; but appropriation of church property, as of lay property, may be just and necessary in certain circumstances, and it is rash to determine by *a priori* arguments whether, *e.g.* Henry V. was justified in laying his hand on the possessions of the French alien priories, and Henry VIII., and not only Henry VIII. but almost every European Government, in confiscating monastic property. The English Parliament, when they made submission to the Pope in the reign of Mary, did not restore to the Church the abbey lands impropriated or granted by

Henry VIII.   It may be similarly held that it is sacrilege to apply endowments made before the Reformation to Protestant uses, or to the 'endowment of error,' or to charitable and humanitarian purposes, or to education.   In the debate on the Irish Church Bill in 1869, Bishop Thirlwall laid down the contrary principle in an impressive manner.   He denied that the property of the Irish Church was in any special sense the property of God.   Those grants, whether of a church or of a market, were, he held, most peculiarly gifts to God, which were most beneficial to man.   This was the test, and not the sanctity of the particular destination.   We can get no nearer to a definition than this; for the very term 'beneficial to man' eludes definition.

The interests of the Protestant Church in Ireland were thus settled for the time.   But part of the Irish religious grievance lay in the condition of the Roman Catholic clergy, whose flocks had to support them besides contributing towards the maintenance of the Protestant clergy.

The mediæval Church in Ireland, as in other countries, was supported by tithe, glebe, and private bounty.   It had fallen into decay before the Reformation.   The monasteries suppressed by Henry VIII. held much land, and half of the tithes over the whole kingdom ; so far, that is, as tithe was paid at all.   During the Reformation and afterwards, large quantities of church land were granted to lay impropriators.   The impoverished Church was re-endowed by the Stuarts both before and after the Restoration, with tithe forfeited to or vested in the Crown, and with glebe land in every parish, out of land which had been taken into the King's hand during the troubles of more than half a century. *Mediæval Church in Ireland.*

As to numbers, the Protestants in Ireland were at this time about one-fifth of the population of Ireland, the members of the Established Church were little more than one-tenth.   The opposition between Popery and Protestantism coloured the whole history of the country, and 'obscured, in sentiment and in practice, the sense of a common Christianity.' *Disproportion of population.*

The existence of an established Protestant church in Ireland was a confessed anomaly.   It was created at a time when toleration was unknown, and was intended to be the church of an anglicised and protestantised nation. The nation had become neither English nor Protestant; the agitation for emancipation raised the hopes and expectations of the Irish Roman Catholics, and pointed the way to religious equality; Protestant ascendency could not be maintained for ever; the practical question was how to reconcile the just claims, founded in practice or in sentiment, of Protestants and Catholics alike.   From the Reformation onwards a large proportion of the native Irish clergy, being unable to find facilities for clerical education in their own country, had frequented foreign seminaries, and especially those of France and Belgium, and the Irish college at Salamanca.   Though Roman Catholics were not excluded from Trinity College, Dublin, they did not come there in large numbers; and few of those who did were clerical students, since the education of the Roman clergy is not easily combined with the ordinary course of university life and study.   One result of this was that many of the Roman Catholic clergy, though chiefly derived from the class of peasants, were men of considerable culture, not bigoted in religion, and disposed to live harmoniously with their Protestant neighbours.   They had seen a larger and a more civilised world than the bulk of the Protestant clergy; they were less prejudiced and better educated; and their high morality, combined with intellectual superiority, gave them unbounded influence over their flocks.   But side by side with these was a class of clergy of a very different kind, poor curates and mendicant monks, who used all the influence they possessed to inflame national hatred.

The continental war closed foreign seminaries to the Irish students, and it became necessary to provide for the education of the priesthood in Ireland.   The Catholic bishops petitioned Lord Westmorland in 1794 for the endowment of a seminary in Ireland.   It is to the credit of Lord Fitzwilliam that he should have proposed the expenditure of public money for the education of Roman Catholic priests.   The Act by which Maynooth College was constituted was passed in 1795 by both Houses of the Irish Parliament without a dissentient voice; a grant of £32,000

Marginal notes:
Claims of religious equality.

Irish priesthood.

Maynooth College, 1795.

was made for the building; and for nearly fifty years a sum of about £8000 was annually paid for its maintenance by a vote of the British House of Commons. The principle of 'concurrent endowment' was implied in the *Regium Donum*, or Government payment to the Presbyterian clergy, which was augmented in 1792, and about the time of the Union negotiations were begun which resulted in a further considerable increase in 1803. Religious inequality could only be redressed by disendowment of the Established Church or endowment of other religious bodies, whether the cost of the process was borne by the State, or the voluntary principle was adopted.

The Roman Catholic clergy, however, though educated were not provided for. The British Government was not unwilling to purchase the goodwill of the priests, in view of the Union, and negotiations with the leading clergy were set on foot with that object. Immediately after the passing of the Act of Union in 1800 Pitt applied his mind to this problem. He attempted in vain to persuade the King that the native clergy, in the event of emancipation being granted, could be attached to the Government _{Pitt and George III., 1800.} by making them 'dependent for a part of their provision, under proper regulations, on the State.' The resistance of George III. postponed Catholic emancipation, and with it all schemes for endowment, for many years.

In 1825, when emancipation was the question of the day, a resolution in favour of State endowment of the Roman Catholic Church in Ireland was moved in the House of Commons on April 29 by Lord Francis _{Proposed State endowment, 1825.} Leveson Gower. He proposed to pay an annual stipend of £1500 to each of the four Archbishops, of £1000 to each of the twenty-two Bishops; and to the clergy stipends ranging from £300 to £60 per annum. He estimated the whole annual expense at about a quarter of a million. O'Connell, as well as the heads of the Roman Church, whilst disclaiming any desire to enrich their own body by despoiling the Established Church, spoke in favour of a State endowment which, said O'Connell, would preserve the fidelity and attachment of the Catholic clergy by 'what I call the golden link, a pecuniary provision. . . . The consequence would be that the Catholic clergy would become in the nature of officers belonging to the Crown.' This resolution was carried by 205 to 162, but no further action was taken. On June 14 in the same year Joseph Hume, supported by Brougham and Burdett, moved for a select committee to consider the present state of the Irish Church, and in doing so stated the principle that property held by the Church was public property, and applicable to public purposes. The motion was negatived without a division. The question of religious equality might, it would seem, have been settled at that time on the principle of concurrent endowment, leaving the Established Church untouched. The agitation of the following years took the line of affirming a principle of equality, not of redressing a practical grievance ; and when emancipation was passed, the sense of wrong survived the remedy. To Irish Roman Catholics it appeared that the boon was granted from motives of fear rather than of goodwill : it was another instance of the selfishness and conceit of wisdom which vitiated all English attempts to deal with Irish grievance.

Hume, Brougham, and Burdett.

The proposal to endow the Roman Catholic clergy was heard of again from time to time. Nassau Senior, in 1843, gave it as his opinion that 'the first effectual step towards the recovery of Ireland is to relieve the Catholic population from the irritating and mis-directing influence to which both the laity and the clergy are subjected by the loss of the original endowment of their Church.' The Roman Catholic Church in Ireland was not endowed ; and the apostolic poverty of the Irish clergy endeared them to their flock, who were for the most part sprung from the same class as themselves. The endowed Church did not grow in popularity as it declined in power. It was ripe for reform, if not for removal.

Nassau Senior on endowment.

Meantime the maintenance and improvement of the Roman Catholic seminary at Maynooth was not forgotten. Strong Protestants both in Ireland and in England spoke of it as endowment of idolatry. Statesmen thought it a convenient sop to the Roman Catholic interest ; and it had the sanction of three Acts of Parliament, two before the Union and one in 1807, which with the approval of Spencer Perceval raised the annual grant from £8000 to £9250.

Increase of grant to Maynooth.

Throughout the emancipation period attempts were made to improve the condition of Maynooth, as for instance in 1824; but the first serious action was that taken in 1845 by Peel, then Prime Minister.

The Maynooth Bill was the most prominent parliamentary measure of the session of 1845. Public meetings were held in all parts of the country and innumerable petitions presented for and against the bill. The whole question of Protestant *v.* Catholic was hotly discussed, and the most sacred principles invoked on both sides. *Peel's Maynooth Bill, 1845.* Irish disaffection, as at other times, was the stimulus to English goodwill or policy. Peel introduced the bill himself, and without going deeply into questions of principles, stated that the present vote of £9000 a year was just enough to discourage and paralyse voluntary contributions. He described a condition of squalid and involved inefficiency. The present course was only justifiable on the ground that a flagitious contract had been entered into, which could not be broken, but under which no further obligations ought to be incurred. The only reasonable course was to improve the education of the Roman Catholic clergy in Ireland; and to do this he proposed to incorporate Maynooth and enable the Corporation to acquire and hold land, and asked for a permanent endowment of £26,000 per annum, and an immediate grant of £30,000 for building and repairs.

Sir Robert Inglis and other Conservative members waved 'the flag of Protestantism,' but the bill was supported by some Conservatives, and, of course, by Irish members. Lord John Russell referred to Leveson Gower's proposal in 1825 for the endowment of the Roman Catholic clergy in Ireland, and said that if that had been accepted, 'the House would no more be talking now about agitation in Ireland than about agitation in Yorkshire or Middlesex.' Gladstone, who had left Peel's Government on this *Gladstone.* question, on the ground set forth in his book *The State in its Relations with the Church*, that the State ought not to endow error, allowed the present grant, as under a previous contract; but, as Peel showed, there was no difference of principle between £9000 and £26,000; if the one was wrong, so was the other; £9000 was miserably inadequate, £26,000 was a tolerable provision ; and whether rightly or wrongly, the country was committed to the maintenance of Roman Catholic services and the teaching of Roman Catholic doctrines.   Macaulay dealt with the whole question in a masterly speech, which left no room for any answer except that of necessity, a plea which will excuse anything.   It was obviously the interest of both countries, he said, that the clergy who ministered to nine-tenths of the Irish people should be educated.   The Irish people were not likely to be converted to Protestantism ; the best way to civilise them was to civilise their priesthood.

The illogical but salutary position taken up by those who favoured Catholic emancipation has ruled the relations of England and Ireland in religious matters ever since.   Liberal doctrines bid us give power to a party which will exercise power in discouraging Liberal doctrines.   We press forward, in order to strengthen the champions of retrogression.   That is the situation ; and no Liberal Government can escape from the dilemma.

While the bill was in Committee, H. G. Ward, Member for Sheffield, endeavoured to make a diversion by proposing that the pecuniary provision for Maynooth College should be taken from the funds of the Irish Established Church.   The inequalities and anomalies of the Irish ecclesiastical settlement were exposed by Lord John Russell and other members, but the Prime Minister would not allow so far-reaching a design to come in by a side-issue, and Ward's amendment was negatived.   The debate in the Lords was specially remarkable for the speeches of the Archbishop of Dublin (Whately) and the Bishops of St. David's (Thirlwall) and Norwich (Stanley).   The Duke of Cambridge and the Duke of Wellington spoke in favour of the bill, the Bishop of London (Blomfield) against it.   But it would be tedious to recapitulate speeches in which no new arguments could be brought forward.

The principal provisions of the Act (8 and 9 Vict. c. 25, 30 June 1845) by which Maynooth College was incorporated and endowed were as follows : The Trustees of Maynooth College were incorporated and declared capable of holding property and lands not exceeding £3000 annual value. The college was furnished with officers and professors, and five hundred free studentships; and a building grant of £30,000 was made.

In the same session another bill dealing with university education in Ireland was introduced by Sir James Graham. The object of the bill, he said, was to frame a *Sir James Graham's bill for Queen's Colleges, 1845.* system for education in Ireland, without making any attempt to influence or disturb the religious tenets of any sect or description of Christians. The present system of national education was denominational with a conscience clause, children of all religions being educated together. This national system applied to primary schools had been successful in Ireland; the system of separate education had failed. He would extend this to the children of the middle and higher classes, and therefore proposed the establishment of three colleges in Ireland—at Cork, Galway or Limerick, and Derry or Belfast. As in the metropolitan colleges of London and Edinburgh, no religious tests were to be applied. There would be no theological faculty, and therefore no professorships of divinity in these colleges, but facilities would be given for the voluntary endowment of theological professorships. He did not intend to interfere in any way with Trinity College, Dublin. That institution was founded by Queen Elizabeth for Protestant purposes, and for the education of the clergy of the Church of England, and it would be unjust and impolitic to meddle with it. Roman Catholic and nonconformist students would be able, as now, to take degrees at Trinity College, Dublin, but not to hold fellowships.

Exception was taken on both sides of the House to the non-religious character of the proposal. Sir Robert Inglis, especially, described it, in words which have been remembered, as a 'gigantic scheme of godless *Sir Robert Inglis.* education.' The usual arguments were heard. The 'religious difficulty,' of which so much was soon to be heard in England, was insoluble in Ireland, and Lord John Russell advised, with much show of good sense, that the system in the new colleges should be entirely secular, except that in the halls for resident students, which it was intended to establish, there should be no religious restrictions, so that they might privately assume a sectarian character without compromising the unsectarian principle of the public institution. He recommended that counsel should be taken with the Roman Catholic hierarchy of Ireland, and much weight given to their opinion. Mr. Gladstone supported the bill, which included facilities for religious education, though it enforced none, on the model of University College, London. Such a plan he thought better suited to Ireland, where religious discipline was strict, than to England, where religious discipline was lax. The Roman Catholic members, with O'Connell at their head, protested against the scheme. The clergy could not approve it, even if their advice had been asked. They considered the bill to be a 'penal and revolting measure,' it omitted religion altogether, and only permitted it to be taught.

Gladstone.

In the Lords, Lord Brougham denied that the bill excluded religion because it provided only secular instruction. Could not religion be taught to the youths by their parents, or the pastors of their own profession? A 'godless' system meant no more than a 'priestless' system. In saying this, Lord Brougham forgot that a priestless system must be abhorrent to a Roman Catholic nation. But, said Lord Brougham, he did not like the plan of the Government the less because it might tend to the endowment of the Roman Catholic clergy. As to the assertion that they would reject an endowment, '*credat Judæus.*'

Lord Brougham.

The Act (8 and 9 Vict. c. 66, 31 July 1845) gave the Queen power to found one or more new colleges, and to charge the Consolidated Fund for that purpose with a sum not exceeding £100,000. Lecture-rooms might be provided in the colleges for the use of such religious teachers as should be recognised by their several governing bodies; but no student was to be compelled to attend such lectures, or be subject to any religious test; persons *in statu pupillari*, who must dwell under proper disciplinary conditions in buildings licensed by the college, might be required to attend such public worship as their parents should approve. Three colleges were accordingly established in the same year at Cork, Belfast, and Galway, which are known as the Queen's Colleges.

Queen's Colleges Act.

SUMMARY OF ACT TO ABOLISH COMPOSITION FOR TITHES IN IRELAND, AND TO SUBSTITUTE RENT-CHARGES IN LIEU THEREOF, 1 and 2 Vict. c. 109 (15 August 1838)

§ 1. All tithes or compositions for tithes shall wholly cease and determine.

§ 7. All lands subject to the payment of tithe compositions are charged with an annual sum by way of rent-charge equal to three-fourths of the compositions, computed on the gross amount.

§ 27. Rent-charges to have priority over all other charges on the lands chargeable.

SUMMARY OF ACT FOR THE BETTER GOVERNMENT OF THE COLLEGE ESTABLISHED AT MAYNOOTH, ETC., 8 and 9 Vict. c. 25 (30 June 1845)

§ 1. Trustees of Maynooth College appointed.

§ 4. Provision made for payment of salaries to officers of the college, and increasing the number of the professors.

§ 6. Provision for endowment of senior and junior studentships.

§ 10. Grant of £30,000 for building.

§ 14. Appointment of visitors.

§§ 17, 18. Visitorial power in matters of religion to be exercised exclusively by Roman Catholic visitors.

SUMMARY OF ACT FOR FOUNDING NEW COLLEGES IN IRELAND, 8 and 9 Vict. c. 66 (31 July 1845)

§§ 1-9. Grant of £100,000 for building new colleges in Ireland, and applied by the Commissioners for Public Works in Ireland.

§ 12. Grant of £21,000 annually for endowment of the new colleges.

§§ 14-20. Provisions for founding and maintenance of lecture-rooms, boarding-houses, and halls for students.

AUTHORITIES : GENERAL. — Walpole, Martineau, M'Carthy, etc., as above. Sydney Smith, *Peter Plymley's Letters* and *Letters to the Electors.* BIOGRAPHIES : *Canning*, by A. G. Stapleton ; *Peel*, by Lord Rosebery, Sir L. Peel, and J. M'Carthy ; *Althorp* (3rd Earl Spencer), by Sir Denis Le Marchant ; *Russell*, by Sir Spencer Walpole ; *Sir James Graham*, by C. S. Parker.

CHAPTER VIII

CHURCH RATES AND UNIVERSITY TESTS

By the common law of England every parish was bound to maintain the fabric of the parish church, with the exception of the chancel, the repairs of which fell on the rector; and this was fair to all, so long as all the King's subjects were members of the Church of England. But it was one of the earliest complaints of Dissenters that they were called upon to contribute for the maintenance of a church which had cast them out; and the grievance grew with the growth of dissent. That the grievance, though real, was not intolerable, may be judged by the fact that in 1811 the 'Protestant Society for the Protection of Religious Liberty' expressly ruled church rates out of the scope of their activity, for the reason that they were not considered an injustice to Dissenters. But the proportion of Dissenters to church people increased, as the large towns increased; and in a like proportion grew the strength of nonconformist hostility. The Dissenters saw no reason why they should pay voluntary contributions for the support of their own chapels, and at the same time be taxed for the repairs of buildings which they never entered, buildings, too, which they looked upon as the outward symbol of ascendency and oppression. The rate was in many cases refused by individuals, who suffered in consequence distraint of goods or imprisonment. It was therefore not merely a sentimental grievance. The objection was twofold; on the score of conscience, that they should be compelled to contribute for the maintenance of what they believed to be a superstitious

Universal incidence of church rates.

Growth of the dislike to church rates.

158

form of religion, and of justice, that they should be compelled
to pay for that which was of no use to them.   The obligation
was unjust, and should be removed by statute.   The best
argument on the other side was that the Church kept open
doors and repelled none ; that the clergy were willing to
minister to all who came to them ; that the churches, being
the property of all, and used by all for baptisms, marriages,
and burials, the maintenance of them might be fairly charged
upon all.

As a matter of law, the obligation was admitted, but
authorities were not agreed as to how it should be enforced.
The Court of King's Bench had on one occasion   Church
refused to grant a *mandamus* for compelling a   rates
parish to make a rate for the repair of the parish   refused.
church, on the ground that action belonged to the ecclesiastical
courts.   In point of fact, no *mandamus* would ever be issued
for such a purpose.   The only remedy provided was an
interdict ; a remedy which, even if it could be conceived
possible, would punish the Churchman by shutting up his
church, but not touch the Dissenter.   When it was once perceived that the legal obligation could not or would not be
enforced, it became clear that the voluntary principle would
ultimately be applied to church rates.   Quakers might suffer
in silence, but the Nonconformists as a body were increasing
in number and influence, and were in no peaceful temper.
Religious questions are always used in English politics as a
stalking-horse for party ; and once brought into a ministerial
programme, it was not likely that the church rate question
would be lost sight of.

The equalitarian doctrines of 1832 affected ecclesiastical
as well as civil politics during that period of disappointment
and disillusion in which it became matter of experience that
new laws do not abolish ancient grievances.   Reformers who
wished to reform everything at once were disappointed at
being checked by the inertia of Parliament when   Divett's
such motions were brought forward as Mr. Divett's   proposal,
(18 March 1834) to abolish compulsory church   1834.
rates in England and Wales.   To prove a grievance to
the satisfaction of Parliament is a slow process, and it is a
slower process still to devise a remedy which Parliament will

accept. Mr. Divett, in moving his resolution, spoke of church rates as a tax of ' infamous character,' which produced more than half a million out of nine and a half millions, the amount of general local taxation. He desired the abolition of this tax principally on account of the hostile feeling of the Dissenters, which he believed would be greatly diminished if his measure were passed ; there was ' no subject which created more heart-burnings than the compulsory assessment of church rates.' The difficult questions connected with the existence of an established church were not disentangled in the course of the debate, but it was represented that the tax was unjust and inexpedient, both in the interest of Dissenters and Roman

Althorp's resolution, 1834.

Catholics, and on general grounds of religious equality ; and also because the working of the law was unsatisfactory to the Church itself. Lord Althorp had already given notice of a motion on the subject, and on April 21 moved a resolution to terminate church rates altogether after a fixed time, and in their stead to charge a quarter of a million annually upon the land tax, to be expended on the repair of the fabrics. The sum raised by rate was nearly double this, but it was got with great and increasing difficulty ; moreover, the money would be administered by the Ecclesiastical Commission, who were to be made a permanent body ; and the Commissioners would be likely to make repairs more economically than the local authorities, who were charged with extravagance. It was, however, not self-evident that the Commissioners would administer the fund better than the local authorities, who at least knew what they wanted. Parish churches belong to the parishes, not the State. The weak point in Lord Althorp's argument was that if the principle of paying for the maintenance of churches out of public money were upheld, the Dissenters' grievance, so far as it was one of principle, would not be removed by halving the sum to be paid.

Althorp's moderate proposal, though the resolution was carried in Parliament, pleased neither party. The time for moderate proposals had not come ; both parties were putting their armour on, and were in no temper to accept compromises ; the Dissenters hoped to abolish church rates altogether ; the Churchmen thought the grant too small, and the

security insufficient, and disliked parliamentary interference
with ancient church property.   Church rate, they said, was
as clearly defined an incident of property as poor rate, or any
other established impost, paid indifferently by Churchmen and
Dissenters.   One man's conscience should not be allowed to
interfere with another man's right.   The whole amount of
the rate did not amount to more than threepence in the
pound on the landed rental of the country ; and of this threepence the Dissenters did not pay one-quarter of a farthing.
But Dissenters did not complain, said Joseph Hume, of having
to pay much or having to pay directly ; they complained of
having to pay at all.   It was a question of conscience, not
of money.   If the bill passed, the Dissenters would not be
relieved ; they would only have to pay the tax-gatherer instead
of the churchwarden.

The Government carried the first reading by 256 to 140,
but went no further with the measure.

On March 3, 1837, Spring Rice, the Chancellor of the
Exchequer, moved the consideration of the question of church
rates.   It appeared, he said, that the opposition   Spring Rice's
to the rate was increasing, and was so bitter that   bill,
in some places, Manchester and Sheffield, for in-   1837.
stance, it was impossible to levy it.   In 1833 at Manchester
there was a majority of one on a poll of 7000; in 1834
11,000 out of 15,000 voted against the rate, and none
was levied.   A tax on the members of the Establishment
was impossible, a tax on ecclesiastical benefices was unfair
and unjust.   Lord Althorp's proposal to impose an annual
tax of a quarter of a million would also fall unequally.   Spring
Rice's own plan was to take the whole property of the bishops,
deans, and chapters out of the hands of those dignitaries,
and to vest it in the hands of eleven Commissioners, ecclesiastical and lay, partly persons of high official rank, partly
nominees of the Crown and the Archbishop of Canterbury.
It was thought that an improved method of management, by
granting leases for terms instead of for lives, with fines on
renewal, would save at least £250,000 per annum, the
same sum as that which Althorp had proposed to raise by
taxation, and that the present holders of church dignities
would not suffer.

When the House went into Committee on March 13, Sir Robert Peel made an attack upon the bill. He said that

Peel's speech.

he disbelieved in the financial soundness of the plan, as well as its justice. He also contended that to remove the impost from those who never complained of it would gratify only a small number of Dissenters; that the proposal affected the independence and dignity of the bishops and the stability of the Church, and that if a surplus should be realised out of the property of the dignitaries of the Church, it ought to go to the augmentation of poor livings and the building of new churches, not to the relief of large landed proprietors, the chief payers of church rates, for this was the real principle of the measure. But why should church people be relieved of a burden which, for the most part, they were willing and proud to bear? Admit this precedent, and church rates would be followed by tithes, tithes by the Establishment altogether. This measure dissolved in principle the connexion between Church and State.

The arguments used on the side of the Radicals and Dissenters were, briefly, equality and conscience. The practical grievance was small, but only those who felt it could estimate the sentimental grievance. All wish to disestablish the Church was disclaimed : but in the case of a privileged body like the Church of England each outwork of prescription broken down weakens the position.

Some of the bishops had already met at Lambeth on March 9, and by a unanimous vote disapproved of the proposed

Archbishop Howley.

measure, and Archbishop Howley spoke strongly against it in the House of Lords. He represented that if it were necessary for church property to be touched at all, the sum diverted from the cathedral establishments ought to be applied to church extension. There were in England, he said, two millions of souls entirely destitute of spiritual instruction. The plan proposed would reduce church dignitaries to the position of mere annuitants, dependents on a board of Commissioners appointed by Government. Lord Melbourne, who though a theologian did not understand ecclesiastical objections to secular policy, was indignant, rated the Archbishop for 'undue haste and precipitation,' and assured him that his opposition would not alter the action of the Government, which he considered as just in itself, advantageous to the Church, and beneficial to the community at large. The Bishop Bishop
Blomfield. of London replied in the same strain as Archbishop Howley, but more strongly. He said that the Dissenters looked upon the abolition of church rates as a step to the abolition of tithes. The Dissenters were a small minority ; they had inherited property, well knowing all its liabilities. It was neither just nor politic to relieve from the rate a body of men who scarcely felt the burden, and at the same time to neglect the spiritual wants of two millions of Churchmen.

The question of the sacrosanctity of ecclesiastical property had already been decided by the appointment of the Ecclesiastical Commission in 1835. So too had the principle of relieving the gentry at the cost of the Church, by the Irish legislation of 1833. The debatable points at this crisis were, whether the bishops and cathedral clergy were unfit to be entrusted with the management of their property ; whether, if it were taken out of their hands, they would lose dignity and influence ; whether the church rate was unjust as well as inconvenient ; and even if it were so, whether a small measure of justice to Dissenters did not involve a great injustice to the Church in transferring church property to the relief of members of the Church of England, who now paid church rate in respect of landed estates. The motion to consider the question was passed by a small majority. It was a question not to be settled till many years had passed, and then on the voluntary principle.

The second reading of Spring Rice's bill was moved on May 22, 1837, when it became clear that the Spring Rice's
bill
dropped. measure would not go forward in the face of the opposition certain to be encountered in the Lords. It passed the second reading by a majority of only five, and was then dropped.

To the year 1837 belongs the notorious 'Braintree case,' which vexed the law courts till its final decision Braintree
case,
1837-1853. in 1853. The parish of Braintree, in Essex, contained large numbers of Nonconformists, who for some years in succession refused to make a rate for the repair of the parish church. In 1836 the majority in vestry post-poned the rate for a year. On June 2, 1837, the Vicar and churchwardens proposed a rate, the church being now almost ruinous, but were met by an amendment which was carried by 207 against 70, to the effect that church rates were an unjust imposition. The meeting was then broken up, but a week later the churchwardens, by their own authority, made a rate of three shillings in the pound in order to raise the sum of £488 : 10 : 4, the amount of the estimate for repairs. A parishioner named Burder was sued for his quota of the rate in the Con-sistorial Court of the diocese of London, and the judge (Lushington) declared the rate to be good. Thence the case (Burder v. Veley) was carried to the Court of Queen's Bench, where Lord Chief Justice Denman (1 May 1840) declared the rate so levied to be 'altogether invalid, and a church rate in nothing but name.' He held that if the parish, being summoned, would not act, the churchwardens might act. In that case the churchwardens are the vestry. Here the case was different ; the meeting was called and the parishioners attended it. If they did not do their duty—a duty which no one denied—there ought to be power to coerce them, or there would be a wrong without a remedy, an anomaly abhorrent to the law of England. The lawful remedy, the offence being against ecclesiastical law, was excommunication of particular persons or interdict in general. These censures and the penalties incurred under them were obsolete ; it did not follow, there-fore, that the common law could interfere, or that the churchwardens could act in default of the proper authorities.

Burder v. Veley, 1840.

Denman's judgment, 1840.

The case was then taken to the Exchequer Chamber, and judgment was finally given on February 8, 1841, by Lord Chief Justice Tindal, who held that the church-wardens could not make a rate, by their sole authority, and without holding a vestry meeting. The courts of common law could not interfere, as the matter was for the spiritual court, and involved spiritual censures. He therefore confirmed Denman's judgment, and held that the rate was not good, as not having been made by a competent authority.

Tindal's judgment, 1841.

A few weeks later (13 May) the churchwardens of Braintree held a vestry meeting in due form in order to make a rate, and the second Braintree case began to run its course. A rate of two shillings in the pound having been proposed and seconded, a silk and crape manufacturer named Courtauld moved and carried an amendment against the general principle of church rates by a majority of nearly five to one.

Second Braintree case, 1841.

Lord Chief Justice Tindal, in his judgment on the first case, had thrown out a suggestion that possibly, though the churchwardens could not levy a rate by their own authority and without a vestry meeting, they might do so with the concurrence of the minority and at the same vestry meeting. Acting on this hint, the churchwardens and the minority, after asking whether any other rate was proposed, made a rate of two shillings, against which the majority entered a protest at the same time. When the churchwardens proceeded to collect the rate, a farmer named Gosling refused payment, and was proceeded against in the Consistorial Court of the diocese of London (Veley *v.* Gosling). The judge (Lushington) gave it in Gosling's favour, and the churchwardens appealed to the Court of Arches. The Dean of Arches, Sir H. Jenner Fust, decided that the rate was good.

Veley v. Gosling, 1841.

The case then went to the Queen's Bench, where Lord Denman gave judgment in favour of the churchwardens, and confirmed the judgment of the Court of Arches; his argument being the same as that of the Court of Arches, that the majority who made an irrelevant amendment threw away their votes, and that therefore the minority had a right to act for them. The next appeal was in Error to the Exchequer Chamber; and there too the same judgment was given, on the ground that the persons who voted for the amendment, since the amendment had no reference to the object of the meeting, must be considered as having left the question in the hands of the remainder; the rate, therefore, was legally made, though not put formally to the vote. The judges were divided in opinion, Maule, Cresswell, Alderson, and Platt declaring for the rate; Wilde, Parke, and Rolfe (weightier names than the others) against it. Wilde gave it as his opinion that 'it does

Judgments of Lushington, Jenner Fust, and Denman.

Exchequer Chamber decision.

not do to torture the law to find a remedy for the consequence
of certain misconduct where no such remedy exists.   Here no
such remedy does exist.'

The case was taken to the Lords on appeal for final decision ;
the judges attended on June 25, 1852, and gave their opinion
Lords' at length, after which, but not for more than a year
judgment, later, Lord Truro (Wilde) gave final judgment (12
1853. August 1853) that the rate was invalid.   A valid rate
can only be made by an actual or constructive majority of
the parishioners present in vestry.   'The resolution refusing
a rate, though denominated an amendment, was in effect
a direct negative of the original proposition, preceded by
irrelevant reasoning.'   You cannot presume absence and non-
interference when the dissentients were present throughout
the proceedings, and protested at the close of the meeting.
The power of imposing a rate when the majority has (unlaw-
fully) refused to make a rate does not devolve upon the
minority.

The Braintree cases had now proceeded through eight
courts of law, had been pronounced upon in elaborate
judgments by seven judges, and in lengthy opinions by
fourteen more, and had lasted from 1837 to 1853 ; and after
all justice was not done, and the law of church rate was
not made clear.   Two modes of imposing a rate were declared
invalid ; it was laid down that all parishes were bound to
repair the parish church, but that there were no means of
compelling any parish to do so, nor of enforcing the payment
of a rate on any parishioner.   The law of England abhors
a wrong without a remedy, but in this case the ecclesiastical
remedy had been lost at the Reformation, and the secular
courts could do nothing to provide one.   The only points
satisfactorily established appeared to be that the churchwardens
are not a vestry, that a minority is not a majority, and that
persons present at a meeting cannot be assumed to be
absent.

But real issues sometimes turn on such points as these.
The result of the Braintree cases was to show that no power
was given by the law of England to compel the payment of
church rates ; it was clear that Parliament would not supply
this power ; consequently the only way out of the dilemma,

the only way of preventing the churches from falling into ruin, was some arrangement of a voluntary kind.

Another church rate dispute, 'Thorogood's case,' is an instance, not of the 'hard cases' which 'make bad law,' but of those which show the badness of the existing law. In 1839 John Thorogood, a shoemaker living at Chelmsford, a Nonconformist and in politics a Liberal, refused payment of five shillings and sixpence, at which sum he was Thorogood's assessed for church rate, and was committed to case, prison for contempt of court.   He was a trouble- 1839. some man, and Chelmsford was 'a great conservative citadel'; and public opinion seldom favours martyrs.   He was not treated with exceptional severity; but the fact that a man should be punished for a conscientious scruple, not by distraint of goods, but by bodily imprisonment, showed an unsound state of law.   Moreover, there was no power that could release him, short of the passing of a special Act of Parliament, or the exercise of the dispensing power which was tolerated in Charles II., when he let 460 Quakers out of prison, but which was put an end to by the Revolution. Sir Robert Inglis visited Thorogood in prison and thought him fairly well treated; Lord John Russell lamented that the Queen had no power to release him; Sir Robert Peel said that there would be no laws if there were no penalties.   As for trying the issue at law, the Consistorial Court could not be set in motion for five shillings and sixpence without the payment of court fees to the amount of six pounds. The ecclesiastical courts had survived the Reformation; Archdeacon's Court, Consistorial Court, Court of Arches, of Peculiars, of Prerogative, of Delegates, Commission of Review, here were seven traps to catch a misdemeanant, and in all, fees and costs made justice slow, uncertain, and expensive.

In reading the enormous verbiage of judges in the tedious progress of the Braintree cases through every zigzag of the law courts, one is tempted sometimes to wish for the swift and final decision of a judge in the gate, a cadi, or a Court of High Commission; for the ecclesiastical courts have outlived the reasons of their existence, and call even now for a radical reform.   In the case of Thorogood all that a well-disposed House of Commons could do was to pass, by 42 to

Resolution
of the
House of
Commons,
1839.
22, a resolution (30 July 1839) condemning his 'cruel and unjust' imprisonment, and calling upon the Legislature, 'at the earliest possible period of the next Session of Parliament,' to make alterations in the existing laws for levying church rates. But resolutions of Parliament do not always lead to action, and Thorogood remained in prison. His was not the only hard case; and the importance of cases like his lies in their effect upon public opinion. When Peel, Russell, and Sugden could only defend the existing state of things by explaining that the law was so, it was clear that the law would have to be altered, and its opponents were greatly strengthened. Thorogood's case showed the impotence of ecclesiastical law to deal with the conditions of modern life, and the need of secular legislation to amend it; the Braintree case pointed to complete enfranchisement as the only means of escape from mediæval trammels. But the remedy was not applied till 1868, nearly thirty years later, when it was acknowledged that the law of England contradicted common sense and had become ridiculous in practice.

The church rate question was not brought prominently forward for some years. The Liberal vote for abolition could be counted on, and between 1855 and 1858 several abolition bills passed the Commons. At the beginning of the session of 1858 Sir John Trelawny, Member for Tavistock,

Trelawny's
bill,
1858.
brought in a bill for the total abolition of church rates. He represented the measure as one brought forward in the interests of peace; for since the beginning of the Braintree case parishes were liable at any moment to be involved in strife and litigation, whilst the church fabric fell into disrepair. The grievance from being a Dissenters' grievance had become a Churchmen's grievance. The deadlock was confessed on all sides; but no remedy for the evil could be found except in abolition, and Conservatives were unwilling to commit themselves to the voluntary system, which seemed likely to extend the prevalence of pew rents and other questionable sources of income, and pointed to ultimate separation of Church and State. The Home Secretary, Sir George Grey, preferred to retain church rates where they could be levied, but to exempt

conscientious Dissenters from payment; in other respects
he proposed to leave the law as it was, but to empower
churchwardens to levy pew rents, and landholders to charge
their estates with a rate for the maintenance of churches.
Another proposal was that already brought forward in 1834
by Lord Grey, to substitute a rent-charge for
a rate, church rate being, in fact, a charge upon   *Proposed
property. This was objected to by Sir George   amendments
                                                          of church
Cornewall Lewis, as a general, new, and compulsory   rate law.*
charge upon the real property of the country for the benefit
of the Church.   The alternative was not between the old rate
and a new plan of levying a rate, but between abolition and
some working compromise to save what was left of the rate.
Why, said some, disturb the existing situation, which was tolerable though unsatisfactory?   Why make a present of £300,000
a year to the landlords, who did not ask for it?   Gladstone spoke optimistically of the position of the Church in
country districts; the rate, he said, was regarded there as a
fixed charge upon property, and caused little discontent.   He
was not prepared on speculative grounds to make a wholesale
importation of the voluntary principle to displace an old
principle that worked well.   If church rates were abolished,
tithes would follow; but there need be no practical difficulty
in framing a scheme which would both preserve the rights of
the Church and not force consciences.

Sir John Trelawny's bill, though not a Government measure,
was passed by a majority of sixty-three, and sent up to the
Lords, where (2 July) the second reading was
moved by the Duke of Somerset.   He reviewed   *Trelawny's
                                                bill passed by
the history of the movement since 1834; Grey's the Commons,
proposal in that year to abolish the rate for   1858.*
maintenance of the church service, but to preserve the rate
for the repair of the building by laying the charge upon
the land tax, *i.e.* the Consolidated Fund; Melbourne's proposal in 1837 to make the revenues of the Church bear
the burden by a different distribution; and another scheme
under which Dissenters were to declare themselves, and so
be exempted.   But Dissenters were in no hurry to declare
themselves.   They did not like to give up the rights of
vestrymen, nor even in some cases the exclusive property in

a pew which the owner did not occupy but let at a rent, whilst at the same time he voted against a church rate. This
Duke of
Somerset's
speech. scheme also had fallen through. The Archbishop of Canterbury, said the Duke of Somerset, had brought forward in 1855 a bill to abolish church rates in any parish where they had been twice refused ; but, as another speaker said, this would be 'a premium on agitation.' His conclusion was in favour of the voluntary system, which had built some 20,000 dissenting chapels, in comparison with 14,000 churches, though the Dissenters were taxed for the support of the churches of the Establishment.

The chief arguments on the other side were that if the rate could be properly assessed and recoverable through the civil courts, it would generally be paid ; for a thing once settled is accepted, but subject to the chance of a vote, is a cause of perpetual dispute ; that the obligation to repair parish churches was one of the primæval institutions of the country, as old as the Heptarchy ; that the voluntary principle cut at the root of the national character claimed by the Church, and by making the clergy the servants of their flocks tended to diminish their independence. Under this system, it was said, the churches would fall into ruin, and the clergy come into contempt.

The House of Lords did not think the time opportune for settling the question, and the bill was dropped. But such debates are not wasted in the end ; they guide public opinion, if they do not make it ; and subsequent history shows that
Result of
the dispute. thenceforward the introduction of the voluntary system was only a question of time. The Braintree case had not in vain shown the weakness of a position which relied only on the sanction of ecclesiastical law. Since that contest began, church rates had been refused in more than 1500 parishes, where they would never be levied again. The decision of a vestry could abolish the payment in any parish. Before it was gone it would be well to accept a compromise, if that could be called a compromise where the party in possession was called upon for an absolute surrender.

The subsequent parliamentary history of church rates gives evidence of much fluctuation of opinion. The abolition of compulsory church rate, carried by Trelawny in the House of Commons in 1858, was lost in 1859; in 1860 it was carried by nine votes, in 1861 defeated by the Speaker's casting vote, lost again in 1862 and 1863. No less than four bills for abolition or compromise of church rate were introduced into the House of Commons in the year 1868, though a Conservative Government was in power: one by Hardcastle (Bury St. Edmunds), for complete and unconditional abolition; one by Hubbard (Bucks), allowing Dissenters to declare themselves and claim exemption; one by Newdegate (N. Warwickshire), to charge the rate upon property instead of persons; and one by Gladstone, who had changed the view which he had held in 1866.

In Parlia ment, 1858-1868.

Gladstone's Compulsory Church Rate Abolition Bill, founded upon a suggestion of John Bright, took away the power of legally enforcing any claim for the recovery of church rate, but permitted assessments to be made by agreement, such agreement being legally enforceable upon the contracting parties in respect of money paid or obligation incurred on the faith of it, in the same manner as contracts to subscribe to a charity, a religious society, or a dissenting place of worship. Thus the grievance of the Dissenters was removed by the bill, while the existing machinery of the vestry was left, on a voluntary basis. The bill was not opposed by the Government, and was accepted by all parties as a working measure. It was passed by the Commons on May 24, 1868, by 131 to 28, and was referred by the Lords to a select committee. An interesting debate took place on a motion made by the Bishop of Oxford (Wilberforce), that none but those who paid the rate should be permitted to vote upon the expenditure of any money for church purposes; this was opposed by Archbishop Thomson of York, as tending to alienate from the Church Dissenters who were not hostile and might return to the Church. Protests were made from both sides of the House against a bill which redressed an unreal grievance at the expense of justice, pointed to disestablishment, and after all would not conciliate Dissenters. But the principle of the bill having been accepted, Conservatives and Liberals were agreed to make the

Gladstone's Church Rate Bill, 1868.

details effective, and it was passed by both Houses with the Lords' amendments, and became law.

Among the disqualifications most keenly resented alike by Roman Catholics and Protestant Dissenters were those imposed by the Test and Corporation Acts; a monument of ancient dangers in Church and State, capable of affecting timid minds, even when no longer real; and a badge of privilege and inequality, as much disliked by Nonconformists as prized by uncompromising Churchmen. Under the Corporation Act, passed by the royalist Parliament at the Restoration, all office-bearers in corporations were required to swear adherence to the doctrine of passive obedience, to renounce the Covenant, and to receive the Sacrament in the English form; and by the Test Act, passed in 1673, all persons holding any temporal office whatever were required to take the Sacrament according to the rites of the Church of England, and to subscribe a declaration against transubstantiation.

Corporation Act, 1661.

Test Act, 1673.

The first of these laws was directed against the Presbyterians; the second, passed in a moment of alarm and distrust caused by Charles II.'s Declaration of Indulgence and his intrigues with Lewis XIV., was directed against the Roman Catholics; both were two-edged measures, designed and maintained for the defence of the Established Church by the isolation of Popish Recusants and Protestant Dissenters. Since the accession of the House of Hanover the Roman Catholics had become harmless or loyal, and the Dissenters friendly; the latter were admitted freely to places of trust and honour: but the laws remained on the statute book, though an annual Act of Indemnity was passed to render them ineffective; and the sense of injustice and the hope of remedy lived on from generation to generation, as an abiding heritage of nonconformist families.

Among the grievances put forward by Dissenters in the eighteenth century was their exclusion from the universities, and consequently, to some extent, from the liberal professions. In 1771 a society called the Feathers' Tavern Association was formed by Archdeacon Francis Blackburne,[1] for the pur-

[1] See vol. vii. p. 209.

pose of obtaining relief for Dissenters by the abolition of clerical subscription, and a petition was also pre- sented (1772) to the House of Commons by Sir W. Meredith, signed by 250 persons, of whom 200 were clergymen, and the rest lawyers and doctors, praying

Feathers' Tavern Association, 1771.

that students in the universities might not be compelled, as a condition of matriculation, to sign the Thirty-nine Articles. The signatories were for the most part Cambridge men, among them Dr. Watson, Professor of Divinity at Cambridge, and afterwards Bishop of Llandaff. The petition was also approved by Paley, who some years later dealt with the ques- tion in his *Moral Philosophy* as a problem in casuistry.

It is interesting to note that in the debates which ensued, the same arguments were used which have been used, with hardly any additions, on every occasion till the final abolition of university tests, exactly a century later, in 1871; the triviality of the Dissenters'

Arguments for and against.

grievance, the rights of the Church, and the danger to religion; and on the other side, the inefficiency of the Articles as a system of theology, the absurdity of requiring subscription from boys of fifteen or sixteen, the right and duty of private judgment, the dangers involved in the principle of priestly authority, the temptation to dishonesty offered by attaching emoluments to the profession of opinions, the duty of enlarging the borders of the Church. There was nothing left for a later generation to add, except the slowly growing and only partially accepted theory that the universities belong to the nation, not to the Church of England. This petition, and a motion to the same effect two years later, were rejected by large majorities, and the question slept for many years.

Meanwhile at Cambridge in 1772 a declaration of *bona fide* churchmanship was substituted by a Grace of the Senate for the more rigid subscription; and this regulation continued in force till recent years. But indeed, if the tests had been removed, the religious disabilities would not have been removed. No undergradute could reside in either university without being a member of a college, and the government of all colleges was in the hands of clerical heads and fellows, who enforced attendance at chapel services, and even reception of the Holy Communion, as a part of college discipline.

The rivalry between Church and dissent, the immovability of the University, and the growth of secularism produced public action in 1825, when, in consequence of a letter written by Thomas Campbell, the poet, and Henry Brougham, a meeting was held in London, Brougham being in the chair.

Proposal of a non-sectarian college, 1825-1826.

Campbell was present, as well as Lord John Russell, Joseph Hume, Sir Isaac Goldsmid, and other public men. It was resolved to invite subscriptions for the foundation of a non-sectarian college in London, at which university studies might be pursued at a moderate expense. The capital required for the plan, which was estimated at £200,000, was to be raised by the issue of £100 shares. In December a Council was elected, including, besides the persons mentioned above, Zachary Macaulay, George Grote, James Mill, and other prominent Liberals. A deed of settlement was drawn the next year, and by 1827 the land near Gower Street, on which University College stands, was bought, and the foundation-stone of the new building was laid on April 30 by the Duke of Sussex.

Foundation of University College, London, 1827.

In 1828 the college was opened as the University of London, and received students in the course of the same year, the first lecture being delivered by Charles Bell. The name of 'University' was prematurely given, since the new institution had no power to confer degrees; and the grant of this power was delayed for some time, owing to religious difficulties and the opposition of other chartered corporations.

University of London, 1828.

Not long after these events, some of those who had supported the movement, fearing the effects of its unsectarian character, raised funds for the institution of a Church of England College. King's College, the college thus founded, received in August 1829 a charter incorporating it as a college in which instruction should be given in the doctrines of the Church of England; and when the charter of University College was granted in 1836, King's College, with several other institutions, was named as one whose students were entitled to present

King's College founded and incorporated, 1829.

themselves for degrees to be granted by the new University of
London.

The Reform Bill and the change of political equilibrium
which accompanied it increased the importance of the
Dissenters. Though numerically much inferior to
those who called themselves Churchmen, many of
them were wealthy, intelligent, and active, and they
belonged for the most part to the newly enfranchised
middle class. The history of nonconformity since
the Revolution is a history of successful struggles against
disabilities. The repeal of the Test and Corporation Acts
in 1828 abolished religious subjection; possession of power
led the Nonconformists to work for legislation which should
abolish religious inequality. National education, tithe, church
rate, the establishment of the Church with the precedence
and property belonging to it came under review, and weak
points were chosen for attack. The hostility of the
dissenting churches was implacable; but it must
not be forgotten that the Toleration Act of William
III. perpetuated the disabilities of Nonconformists which the
Comprehension Bill would have removed, and made it a
point of honour and a family tradition to work for the removal
of all inequality between the Established Church and other
religious communities. The Church of England was twice
helped—in 1660 and in 1667—by the Nonconformists, men
for whom Churchmen, as Neal in his *History of the Puritans*
says, 'would not move a pin nor abate a ceremony'; the
legislation of the Tories in 1662 and the Whigs in 1689
perpetuated inequality, the removal of which might almost
have put an end to nonconformity itself.

The precedent set by the repeal of the Test and Corporation
Acts and the removal of Roman Catholic disabilities led the
friends of religious equality to hope for further legislation;
and the same causes which produced the movement for church
reform naturally brought into notice the Nonconformists'
objection to ecclesiastical monopolies. Though private
teachers, being Nonconformists, were no longer subject to
penalties, all access to schools and universities was closed,
except so far that the University of Cambridge allowed
Dissenters to be students in its colleges, while refusing to

Reform Bill. Increased political importance of Nonconformists.

Traditional nonconformity.

admit them to degrees, scholarships, or fellowships.   At Oxford the exclusion was complete : no one could matriculate without

University grievances of Non-conformists. signing the Thirty-nine Articles, and similar tests, even more stringent, were imposed as the condition of a degree in Arts.   The London University was waiting for its charter ; in the meantime Nonconformists who wished to practise as lawyers or medical men had to get a degree from Germany, Holland, France, or Scotland, or lose much time for want of one.   Many petitions were presented to Parliament, in which the university grievance appeared in company with other nonconformist disabilities, incidents of 'toleration,' which pointed the difference between that and religious equality.

At Cambridge the question of university tests was argued in 1834 by Connop Thirlwall of Trinity, afterwards Bishop of St. David's, in a letter addressed to Dr. Turton, then Dean of Peterborough and later Bishop of Ely, chiefly on the practical, if ironical, argument that very little religion was taught at Cambridge, and that what divinity lectures were given had 'so little of a controversial or polemical character that a Dissenter might attend them without fearing any shock to his religious sentiments,' whilst the theological examinations had 'in fact scarcely more to do

Thirlwall and Whewell, 1834. with theology than any part of profane literature. The more [the Dissenters] know of us, the more they will be convinced of the perfect harmlessness of our . . . divinity lectures.'   Nor did Whewell, Thirlwall's brother-fellow and tutor, in answering him, deny the almost total absence of religious teaching ; he hoped for improvement ; but he could not take up the strong line of a dogmatic believer maintaining the defences of apostolic doctrine and order, as the Oxford apologists did.

The movement for university relief came from Cambridge, where a small body of residents, 'sincere Churchmen,' as they

Cambridge petition, 1834. declared themselves to be, petitioned Parliament on March 21, 1834, for the abolition of 'every religious test exacted from members of the University before they proceed to degrees.'   Among these were some of the most honoured names in the University, both old and young,—Airy the astronomer, Sedgwick the geologist, Musgrave, afterwards Archbishop of York, Thirlwall, Peacock, afterwards Dean of Ely, and Farish, Jacksonian Professor of Mathematics, and one of the leading Evangelicals.   Attempts had been made to bring the subject under the notice of the Caput, a permanent committee, resembling the Hebdomadal Board at Oxford, and like that able and willing to block the way whenever the Church seemed to be in danger.   The petitioners said that the restrictions then maintained were imposed by Royal mandate in the reign of James I., and re-imposed at the Restoration, that their legality was doubtful, and that non-graduates laboured under disabilities if they wished to practise as medical men or solicitors.   The petition bore a small number of signatures, and the great majority of the Senate was opposed to it, as was shown within a month by a counter-petition presented by a much larger and more influential body of subscribers.

The Cambridge petition against tests was presented by Earl Grey, and supported by Lord Chancellor Brougham, who argued that equality was sure to come, and might as well be granted now as later; a convenient argument for reformers, but one which did not carry much weight with Conservatives.   There was no petition from Oxford.

At Oxford the atmosphere was more electrical than at Cambridge.   The challenge was given from the Liberal camp by Dr. Hampden of Oriel, who towards the end of the year 1834 printed some *Observations on Religious Dissent*, which gave an opportunity to the High Church party to make objections, as no doubt he expected them to do.   Hampden's *Bampton Lectures* of 1832 were passed by 'not only unanswered but with high applause,' as Whately said, and might have been forgotten; Hampden was now White's lecturer in Moral Philosophy, and a person of authority in the University, and was at the same time a conspicuous member of the latitudinarian party.   All this had attracted no adverse comment; he may have been thought unorthodox, but he was left unmolested till the publication of the *Observations*, which could not be ignored by the High Churchmen.   The progress of the Hampden controversy and its sequel will be narrated in its place in connexion with the progress of the Oxford movement.

The question of nonconformist grievances was brought under the notice of Parliament by Dr. Stephen Lushington on March 11, 1834. Such were the want of general registration, difficulties connected with marriage and burial, exclusion from the universities, and liability to rates and other compulsory levies for the maintenance of the Established Church. Lord John Russell introduced, but did not carry through, a bill for permitting Dissenters to be married in their own licensed places of worship, instead of going to church as heretofore.

Dr. Lushington on Dissenters' grievances, 1834.

The measure which especially roused the anger of Churchmen and Conservatives at Oxford and Cambridge was the University Tests Bill, brought in by George Matthew Wood, Member for South Lancashire, 'to grant to Her Majesty's subjects generally the right of admission to the English universities, and to equal eligibility to degrees therein, notwithstanding their diversities of religious opinion, degrees in Divinity alone excepted.'

Wood's University Tests Bill, 1834.

The debates were conducted on the ordinary lines of such discussions. The supporters of the motion said that no harm had been done by the admission of nonconformist students at Cambridge, which dated from 1772, and that it was unjust to refuse them degrees ; there was no danger of their demanding votes, fellowships, and headships, which rightly belonged to the Church of England. They dwelt on the hypocrisy of religious subscription, and argued that the admission of Dissenters to the universities would help to heal divisions and be beneficial both to those who gave and those who received instruction.

Debates in Parliament

The opponents of the motion held a much easier brief. They said that the Dissenters would not rest till they had gained admission to all the prizes of the universities ; there was no finality in such legislation, and every concession would be used as a lever to effect the prime object of the Nonconformists, the destruction of the Establishment. Religious education would become a mockery ; it would be based upon a meaningless or dishonest compromise. The Duke of Wellington—whose arguments for leaving things alone were always effective, since they were always sensible, dealt with things as they were, and raised no difficulties which did not exist in fact—remarked that the University of Oxford was a corporation with power to act for itself, and the sixty-three petitioners were a dissatisfied minority, though consisting of most respectable individuals. Why should the legislature, on such showing as this, override the wishes of the corporation? Lord Durham, in reply, used an argument which the Duke would appreciate: Did the Duke of Wellington ask whether his officers were members of the Church of England before sending them into action, and was there any good reason why a doctor or a lawyer should be orthodox? Bishop Blomfield doubted whether the proposed change was really desired by the Dissenters. In his view religious education, which all parties desired, could not be and ought not to be colourless. Bishop Phillpotts bluntly said that to remove disabilities was to persecute the Church of England.

In the Commons, where the debate was interrupted by scenes of the greatest disorder, the argument most keenly urged and combated was from the national character of the universities. They were founded for the good of the nation, and attached to the Church at a time when the Church included the whole nation, whether before or since the Reformation. Now that the Church of England, though still the Church of a majority, was no longer, except by law, the national Church, it could not fairly lay claim to a monopoly in a national institution. This argument, as was seen when disabilities were removed many years later, applied equally to the M.A. university franchise, to scholarships, fellowships, tutorships, and headships in the colleges, and to professorships and other places of emolument and dignity in the University. But for the present no one proposed to touch the colleges, nor to admit Dissenters to more than public examinations and titular degrees. Other speakers complained of the disadvantage to the sons of business men at Liverpool or Manchester, many of whom were Unitarians, who could not give their sons the educational and social advantages of University life.

The argument from Founders' intentions was difficult to meet; for, as James II. said, the heads and fellows of colleges were bound by their unrepealed statutes to say mass every day for the souls of their benefactors. Daniel O'Connell, who took part in the debate, accepted the Protestant character of the University as an established fact, but contended that a Protestant Church had no exclusive right to pre-Reformation endowments.   Other speakers said that the universities were places of religious education, and seminaries for the clergy ; *Dominus illuminatio mea* is the motto of Oxford.   The newly-founded Liberal University of London had admitted no religious teaching within its walls, and the measure proposed pointed the same way, and would go far to unchristianise the universities and with them the country.

The House of Commons passed the bill by 164 to 75 (28 July) : the Lords rejected it four days later by a majority of 102.   This defeat seemed final.   The first impulse had spent itself, and reaction had begun.   Oxford and Cambridge, it seemed, were to be as heretofore the property of the well-to-do classes, and in particular the nursery for the Anglican ministry. In holding this position, the Conservatives did not think they were doing any injustice to the Nonconformists.   Their view, which had much to commend it, was that the reformed Church of England had a full right to the property and the position of the mediæval Church of England, a right which was a sacred trust, to be administered in the interest of true religion.   Toleration of dissent was not an act of justice, but a concession of charity or policy.   The admission of Dissenters to university lectures and examinations, already conceded, gave them no claim to a share in college or university endowments and duties.   This was the doctrine which prevailed at both universities, and any changes in the present system of government must be carried from outside or not at all.

University Tests Bill thrown out by the Lords, 1834.

For some years no further step was taken : but university reform was not forgotten when a more favourable time came.

The rejection of Lushington's bill gave the Liberals an argument, which was pressed home upon Peel's Government by Wm. Tooke, Member for Truro, Lord John Russell, and others, namely, that it was reasonable to give Dissenters the opportunity of obtaining degrees in arts and medicine, even if of less dignity than those conferred by the ancient universities, and that this was more urgent under the present Government than when Lord Melbourne's Ministry were willing to remove obstacles at Oxford and Cambridge. It was also suggested that King's College, as well as University College, should be incorporated in one general London University, which should confer degrees by its own examinations, independently of the professors of the two colleges.

Lord Melbourne came into office in April of the same year, and the charter asked for by the Duke of Somerset, Chairman of the Council of University College, was granted on August 19, 1835. The object of the Government in conceding it was announced in an official document to be 'to provide a mode for granting academical degrees in London to persons of all religious persuasions without distinction, and without the imposition of any test or disqualification whatever.' It was stated that students of other bodies similarly incorporated would apply to University College for degrees in arts, law, and medicine, through the medium of a Board of Examiners, who were to receive a charter of incorporation under the title of the University of London. The arrangement thus initiated was accepted, and the principle established that the University should be an examining body and confer degrees on qualified students, and that the duty of teaching should be left to the colleges. The charter was accordingly granted on November 28, 1836. The Earl of Burlington, afterwards Duke of Devonshire, a distinguished scholar and man of science, and afterwards Chancellor of the University of Cambridge, was nominated by the Crown as Chancellor; and Lord Brougham, Bishops Maltby, Stanley, Thirlwall, and Otter, Hallam, Macaulay, Cornewall Lewis, Arnold, and Grote were elected among the members of the Senate. King's College thus became incorporate with the University, retaining its own staff of professors, and preserving intact its connexion with the Church. Henceforward religious differences had no place in the history of university education in London.

London University charter granted, 1836.

AUTHORITIES: GENERAL.—As in Chapters V. and VII. For the Braintree case, Walpole and Paul, *Histories*. R. D. Hampden, *Observations on Religious Dissent*; Lewis Campbell, *The Nationalisation of the Universities*.

CHAPTER IX

THE LIBERAL MOVEMENT

THE various interests of the new century may be judged by a glance at the literature of the time. Cobbett and Bentham, Ricardo, Malthus, the Mills, Erasmus Darwin and the geologists stand queerly by the side of Words-worth and Coleridge; we have also the literary critics, as Hazlitt and Lamb; the company of poets, at the head of whom stand Byron, Scott, Keats, and Shelley; and the writers of fiction and romance, lurid and fantastic, or domestic and realistic. In all directions the ancient bands of sentiment and tradition were being weakened; in religion, literature, and politics the ideas which attracted the age were new creeds of universal brotherhood and enfranchisement, dreams of 'pantisocracy,' new births of liberty and equality; the name of liberty was in all mouths. The world cannot go on without dogma, it must have a belief to live by; and those who cried loudest for liberty were the apostles of a new dogma, as intolerant as any which preceded it, the dogma of science. Whether the field of their efforts was theological, historical, political, or literary, they were at work in pulling down old faiths and clearing the ground for a new faith, or rather a new set of principles for faith to deal with, one of the first being the ancient Greek saying, μέμνασ' ἀπιστεῖν, 'be not too ready to believe.' The sentiment of the time showed itself in emotional religion, whilst the dogmatic temper asserted itself by exalting ancient authority, or sought to settle historical principles, and so to lay the foundation for a new deduc-tive philosophy. This involved much pulling down as well

Various currents in literature.

as building up, and to the orthodox it appeared that the
Liberals, as they called themselves, were merely destructive.
The struggle over the history of Biblical and Orthodox
Christian origins came at a later point; the and Liberal
Liberals of the early part of the century were more criticism.
occupied in the practical work of philanthropy and the
destruction of privilege than in discussing theological problems.
Of liberal theology little appears in the first part of the century.
The religious world was busy with the abolition of slavery,
missions, education, the poor law, church building, the condition of the poor, the removal of religious disabilities, the
condition of Ireland, and all the social and economic questions
which came to a head in the Reform period. The clergy,
almost exclusively educated at Oxford and Cambridge, were
deeply imbued with university prejudices, as were also the
educated gentry, who formed a large proportion of the House
of Commons. It was a time of learning new facts and the
application of them, rather than of speculation. Since the
French Revolution the world seemed to have been born again
before men's eyes. The French Revolution, so much of it,
that is, as the English nation could assimilate, had come across
the Channel, and though English people do not love theory,
they could not help applying to their own circumstances some
of the theories which came in from abroad.

The High Church school and the reformers came to a
contest first upon education, then upon parliamentary reform,
in which the clergy were with few exceptions opposed
to change, then upon the admission of Noncon- Education
formists to the universities. In the discussions and reform.
concerning national education, abolition of tests, removal
of ecclesiastical privileges, such as tithes and church rates,
redistribution or alienation of church property, the clergy
were of necessity on the defensive side, and could not
easily disentangle lost or bad causes from good, nor see
where the old leaders might suffice or where the Church
might justly call for new. To stand stiff or to yield frankly
requires courage at a crisis; and it would be unfair to charge
the bishops with cowardice because they did not desert
the interests of their own order, when attacked by
antagonists who did not always distinguish between just and

unjust possession, and who were sometimes animated as much by dislike of privilege as by love of equity. Religious inequality was undermined before political equality was gained, principally because the privileged classes cared less for the rights of the Church than for their own; but the successful assaults made upon the outworks of the Church in the years preceding the Reform Bill showed plainly enough what might be expected when the main attack should be delivered on the centre of the position. The Church felt itself threatened by the same spirit which threatened the State, the spirit of Liberalism, with all its attractive catchwords, equality, purity, simplicity, removal of abuses, and so forth; the spirit which denied constituted authority and made light of respect due to God or Caesar. When statesmen threatened the Church and appealed to the vulgar 'Protestantism' of the mob; when the 'Society for Promoting the Diffusion of Useful Knowledge' was disseminating such unreligious literature as the *Penny Magazine*, the *Penny Cyclopædia*, the *Library of Entertaining Knowledge*, and the like; when the London University was being founded on undenominational principles; when the Birmingham Union men were talking of sending an army of 200,000 men to London, and the Duke of Wellington could order the Scots Greys to rough-sharpen their swords, but could not be sure that they would use them if ordered to do so; when to most wealthy men reform meant revolution, while reform was as irresistible as the Atlantic, to which Sydney Smith compared it in a famous speech at Taunton; it was natural that Churchmen should look about them and prepare for war.

Liberalism.

The statesmen and theorists of the Reform movement of 1830 directed their attack against privilege and property. Privilege and property are only the material strongholds of authority, the external vested interests of the system in possession. The liberalism which Newman spent his life in combating made war upon the internal and spiritual privilege of established ideas, and assumed the right of interrogating all that claimed authority by prescription. As is always the case, the forces of conservatism were drawn out in more compact order than those of liberalism. This may be

expressed by the formula that truth is discovered by independent experiment, or by the formula that truth is one,
and error manifold.   In the years which immediately preceded and followed the Reform Bill, the reformers were in
touch with each other politically ; in theology and historical
criticism they took their several lines, but, even so, their
ventures were all within orthodox limits.   The earlier Liberals,
such as Bishops Bathurst and Watson, did not lean to
heterodoxy.   Marsh, a champion of High Church orthodoxy,
was one of the first to introduce German Biblical criticism into
England, and his translation of Michaelis's *Introduction* (1802)
opened the door more widely than perhaps he intended.
Hartwell Horne's *Introduction to the Critical Study of Holy
Scripture*, published in 1818, was also an enlightened work.
The attention of English scholars once directed towards
Germany, the influence of German thought was increased,
though most English divines did not read German books till
they were translated.   Pusey's *Inquiry into German Rationalism*,
published in 1828, and his studies in Schleiermacher worked
in the same direction, though not with his will.   But the
citadels of orthodoxy were as yet unassailed.   The Oxford of
1820 resembled, so far as the times suffered it, the Oxford of
Johnson and Gibbon.   The University was entirely governed
by clergymen.   Every head of a college, every professor and other
office-bearer in the University was a clergyman, every fellow of a
college was bound to take orders within a prescribed time or to
resign.   The resident members of the University were sufficiently numerous to form a body of public opinion, and though
all were not learned, there was enough learning at Oxford to
make this public opinion respectable.   The current mode of
thinking was entirely old-fashioned, orthodox in religion and
Tory in politics.   Oriel and Balliol were to some extent a focus
of liberalism ; elsewhere the new gospel had no access.   Yet
young men came up year by year to Oxford full of the
ideas which cost Shelley his place there.   In course of time
Arnold's pupils leavened Oxford, but it took many years to
break down the Tory fences in politics, and more to give
admittance to the idea that the theology as well as the politics
of the ruling classes was vulnerable.

The attack upon privilege was led by enthusiasts and

economists who sympathised with the sufferings of the voiceless poor. Hunger made the poor discontented, not theories of equality. They struck at what was nearest, the machines which took the bread out of their mouths. Without leaders they might have suffered in silence; that power and wealth should belong to the owners of land was to them a law of nature. But theories once set afoot grow quickly, and long before 1830 it was becoming clear that the reign of ancient toryism was approaching its close. When the parliamentary monopoly was destroyed, the ecclesiastical monopoly followed; the claim of the Church to a monopoly of ideas came next to be attacked, and of this monopoly the universities were the headquarters. But as the universities were also workshops of thinking, the attack upon antiquated modes of thought came from within the walls as well as from without.

The 'Broad Church' school of thinkers—since no better term exists to include men differing greatly among themselves—may be divided both intellectually and chronolog- Broad ically into two sections, the philosophical and the Church critical or historical. The first may be said to begin theology. with Coleridge and end with Maurice, from whom Westcott descends; the second derived their impulse from the sceptical inquiries of German theologians into the history of religion, and produced in England the literature of which Arnold was one of the harbingers, though he did not extend his inquiries into forbidden regions, and Milman, whose bold inductions roused the antipathy and disgust of Newman and the Tractarians. Henry Hart Milman (1791-1868), Fellow of Brasenose, appointed Dean of St. Paul's in 1849, became conspicuous by his *History of the Jews*, published in 1830. His comparison of Abraham to an oriental Emir or Sheikh opened a vista in Biblical study, not to be closed again. He said himself that the book had been written 'fifty years too soon.' He wrote 'rather as an historian than as a religious instructor'; he was the intellectual father of Stanley and the liberal school of religious historians. The influence of the *History of the Jews*, and, to a less extent, the *History of Christianity* (1840), on the thought of the time cannot easily be exaggerated.   The admission of historical perspective into the field of sacred history had far-reaching and unexpected consequences.   Theologians and philosophers may confute each other without interesting many readers outside their own circle : progress in the history of religion and in the knowledge of the Bible is made not by theologians but by historians. The advance, whether in truth or error, which has been made in the last century, is due to the historical and comparative method of discovering facts in textual, Biblical, and historical science.   This movement necessarily came in with the study of physical nature and the development of the comparative method.   Broad Churchmen or Latitudinarians are those who in every age accept scientific conclusions and endeavour to adapt traditional beliefs to them.   Coleridge and Maurice believed themselves to be orthodox and conservative ; Milman and Mark Pattison knew that limits could not be set to inquiry, and believed that their duty was to look forward, not back.   Such thinkers approach problems of faith from different points of view and in a different spirit ; but their paths converge, and the upholder of Biblical or ecclesiastical authority instinctively knows them for his enemies.

What is called a Movement is commonly the gathering up of ideas floating in many minds by some powerful interpreter, who gives them expression, whether or not he possesses the intellectual and moral qualities which make a party leader. Side by side with the ideas which led to the Reform Bill were other ideas which may be called reactionary or reconstructive. Both these tendencies were working at Oxford in the years preceding the Reform Bill, and their time bore fruit of two kinds, the tractarian movement and *Liberal tendencies at Oxford.* the liberal movement, of which two movements Newman and Arnold are the prominent figures.

Cambridge was less prominent than Oxford, less alert and active.   But at Cambridge as well as at Oxford at this time there was much intellectual activity, especially in Trinity, of which college Thirlwall was one of the tutors, Thompson, afterwards Master, another, and Julius Hare and Adam Sedgwick, the famous geologist, fellows.   Sterling, Maurice, Archbishop Trench, *Cambridge reformers ; Thirlwall, Thompson, etc. at college.*

Tennyson, John Kemble, Charles Buller, Monckton Milnes, and their associates, that company of brilliant young men who called themselves or were called the 'Apostles,' held the Liberal faith and illustrated it by their genius. The air was full of promise. There seemed no end to the prospect open to religious and political freedom. Thirlwall's translation of Schleiermacher's *Treatise on St. Luke* (1825), the *Guesses at Truth* of the brothers Julius and Augustus Hare (1827), the translation of Niebuhr's *History of Rome* by Thirlwall and Julius Hare (1828), took effect in shaping the thought of the younger generation and giving inquiry an entrance into subjects which had been closed by the spirit of authority, religious or political; and Tennyson's early poems bear witness to the same spirit of liberty, or revolt, which was abroad.

For some years Oriel, which, under Provost Eveleigh, was the first of the colleges to throw open its fellowships to competition and to favour the institution of university class-lists, was the home of a succession of able men who differed from each other in many respects, but agreed in one, the claim to dispute freely and express their opinion boldly on all subjects of controversy. These men were commonly

The Oriel Noetics.

known as the Oriel 'Noetics,' *i.e.* 'Intellectuals,' a title the origin of which is obscure, but which was probably given by detractors, annoyed by a supposed assumption of superiority which they may have felt but would not acknowledge to be well founded. Oriel, says Newman, 'from the days of Dr. Copleston to Dr. Hampden, had had a name far and wide for liberality of thought'; it was looked upon as 'the school of speculative philosophy in England.' Among

Oriel men, Provosts Copleston and Hawkins.

the older generation of Oriel men may be mentioned the 'august and commanding' presence of Provost Copleston (1776-1849), and his successor Hawkins (1789-1882), who saw the Romeward tendency of the 'Apostolicals,' who dismissed the three tutors of the college, Newman, Froude, and Robert Wilberforce, and always spoke of Tractarianism as 'that unhappy movement.' His

Whately.

despotic rule did not check the growth of High Church opinions, but altered the character of Oriel. Archbishop Whately (1787-1863), who was a fellow of Oriel in

1811, a great name in his time, and one of the hard-headed and negative-minded men whose influence in a time of change is more conservative than their opinions, was, as he claimed to be, a former of men's minds. He was too independent and original to be a party man or work in harness, but so far as he may be classified he is to be reckoned among the Liberals, as was decidedly his friend and pupil Samuel Hinds (1793-1872), afterwards Bishop of Norwich. John Davison (1777-1834), also a Fellow and Tutor of Oriel, and one of the creators of that brilliant society, was not suspected of heterodoxy, but suggested heterodox conclusions in his *Discourses on Prophecy*, the first English work which approached the Hebrew prophetical books from the side of historical and linguistic criticism, and showed the way to others who went further than he did himself. Thomas Arnold (1795-1842), whom, if he had lived, intellect, honesty, and force of character pointed out as the leader of the reformers, not only at the University but in the Church generally, left Oriel early, and for some years his voice was not heard at Oxford. His office was pastoral and prophetical, not controversial, though he did not shrink from controversy. In his *Principles of Church Reform* (1833) a pamphlet which was read with interest, but greatly disliked by the orthodox, he put forward a plea for religious union on the ground that the divisions of Christians do not go so deep as is generally supposed, and he proposed to 'christianise the nation' by comprehending all sects in one national Church, with the exception of the Roman Catholics and Quakers, whom the epithet 'national' would exclude, and the Unitarians, whom he would not describe as Christians, since they could not join in addressing Christ in the language of prayer and praise. Under this scheme all ministers of the Church were to receive episcopal ordination, and all services were to be held in the parish churches, whilst less formal worship than the Liturgy was to be admitted at certain hours and days. This would have made the Church national; but High and Low Churchmen questioned whether it would have been a Church at all, and whether such a scheme would have satisfied any one; at any rate, of all forms of liberalism the High Church and the Evangelicals alike thought religious liberalism the most dangerous. Truth, said Arnold, should be the object of all parties, not victory. In place of inventing formulas to serve as a test of latent error, the object in framing articles, creeds, and prayers for public use should be to provoke the least possible disagreement. It was said wittily of Arnold that he 'woke up every morning with the conviction that everything was an open question'; that is, that the tendency of his mind was to question all authority, to accept probability as his guide, and not to fear conclusions. He was less clearsighted than his pupil Stanley, but of a more commanding character.

Arnold's idea of the Church as coextensive with the nation met with little more acceptance from Liberals than from Tractarians; his detestation of the doctrine of apostolical succession, which he termed 'a profane heraldic theory,' 'a bugbear,' 'an idol,' brought him nearer to the Evangelicals, but his views of inspiration were opposed to theirs. His influence upon liberal thought was felt more through the men whom he trained at Rugby than through his own writings; he died early, before his prejudices had been modified by experience of life. Had he lived longer he would have attained in the world the stature which his pupil and biographer Arthur Stanley truly discerned in him at Rugby. His High Church contemporaries lamented his want of fixed principle; Newman asked, 'but is Arnold a Christian?' They could not conceive of religion separated from dogma, nor appreciate Arnold's zeal for the removal of barriers to religious or political, intellectual or spiritual liberty. Arnold's pupils, Stanley, Clough, Lake of Durham, Thomas Hughes, his own son Matthew, belong to a later period, but he was their true spiritual father: and though he was not a great original thinker, he had the Socratic power of stimulating the thoughts of others.

To the Noetics belonged also Renn Dickson Hampden (1792-1868), a much misunderstood man, of whom more will be said later; he was made a controversialist by circumstance, not by choice, and sustained more obloquy than he deserved.

Hampden.

Another Oriel man who may be counted among the

Noetics is Baden Powell (1796-1860), a man of wide scientific
and literary learning and beneficent sympathies, one of
those of whom it is written, as his friend W. Tuckwell
says, *sciunt ut operentur*. His Essays on Rational Religion
and kindred subjects disturbed orthodox minds, and
that on Scripture Miracles in *Essays and Reviews* Baden Powell.
was violently attacked. Powell deserved a hearing,
because he belonged to the class, never a numerous class, of
religiously minded men who have enough scientific knowledge
to form an opinion about the limitations of authority and
evidence ; a subject full of *odium theologicum*, since the temper
of authority is always the same, however its postulates may
change.

The influence of Cambridge, with the notable exceptions
of the Christian Advocate, Hugh James Rose (1795-1838),
and Professor W. H. Mill, was chiefly evangelical
or liberal. Julius Charles Hare (1795 - 1855) Julius Charles Hare.
cannot be reckoned as belonging to any acknow-
ledged school of theologians. His place is with the theological philosophers, Maurice, Erskine of Linlathen, and
Frederick Robertson, both in date and in meaning between
Coleridge and the critical school ; a Broad Churchman, but
a defender of the written Word. He held that earlier
systems, Roman and Protestant alike, had been faulty so
far as they were mechanical, in reverencing the framework
of religion as if it were religion itself. The voice of God,
heard in the Church, heard in the Bible, is also heard in
external nature and in the human conscience. This is
agreed by all : but the Roman Catholics deify the Church,
the Protestant reformers the Bible, natural theologians the
phenomena and sequence of nature, sentimental Christians
and mystics of all colours their own experiences and emotions.
As the theology of the Reformation was a reaction against
that of the Middle Ages, setting up Biblical authority against
Church authority, and, incidentally, private interpretation
against traditional interpretation, so the decorous sacramentalism of the old High Church school from Hammond
onwards was a reaction against the fanaticism of the
English Puritans and Scottish Whigs. The test proposed was
one of sacraments and ordinances as opposed to inward

illumination. 'Of all of them it may be said that they appear to concentrate and condense the operations of the Spirit into a single magical movement, an electric transmuting flash, and continually disregard the perpetual abiding influences and operations.' This formalism was at its height in the Georgian period, when evidences seemed almost more important than the truths to which they bore witness, and when the effort to repress Wesleyanism and dissent left little room for more positive religious activity. The Evangelicals who followed were also in their way literalists, as were the Tractarians who protested against them.

Coleridge, to whom the succeeding generation looked as to a prophet, held that the framework of the Temple was sound, but that the presence of God would only be found in the Temple if the spirit of man inhabited it also. Reason, the divinely enlightened spirit of man, not 'understanding,' which is a lower function of the soul, tests truth by its rationality, that is, its correspondence with rational, moral, and spiritual ideas implanted by God in the human conscience. The Scriptures and creeds, and the framework of the Christian Church, bear this test. It is not necessary to look for verbal inspiration in the Bible, or infallible truth in the Church. 'In the early church the words of a dead Apostle were not more inspired than the words of a living Bishop.' This doctrine, that God's Spirit lives in the Church and in the conscience of man, though no new thing, became in Coleridge's hand a message of freedom. For if the truth of revelation is not to be laid down by the living Church, but tested by the written Word, and that again by external evidences, the centre of gravity is shifted from authority to assent; and if ordinances are channels with which God may dispense, the human conscience may question them.

Coleridge.

Thomas Erskine of Linlathen (1788-1870) was not a disciple of Coleridge, but trod a parallel path. He believed Christianity because of its human interest and response, not as a religion imposed by authority. Religion, he held, must be self-evidencing. He is called by Principal Tulloch an apostle of Christian consciousness, opposed alike to formal orthodoxy and formal rationalism

Thos. Erskine of Linlathen.

—the latter 'a bastard form of reason,' which had cut the heart out of all religion and reduced it to a *caput mortuum*. His religion was practical holiness, not theology. He was not a professed scholar or theologian; but his personality gave him influence and authority.

Hare stood between the 'Bibliolaters' and the 'Ecclesiolaters,' opposed to both as making religion mechanical. It is the old antagonism of the letter and the spirit, which shows itself in infinite variety. He too, as well as Maurice, would not bind the Spirit to a book, a church, or an ordinance. 'In Christ Jesus neither episcopacy availeth anything, nor non-episcopacy, but a new creature.' His limitations may be seen in his attacks upon Newman. It is easy to show that Newman was inconsistent—his own Retractations fill many pages; that he was a master of deductive logic; that he argued from assumptions as if they were proved facts; that he used invective, sarcasm, and equivocal terms in the place of sound reasoning; but Hare was not able to take in the vast idea of Catholicism, or see that the Roman system must be attacked, not by opposing to it the variety and dissension of Protestant systems, but by meeting its extreme assumptions with the negative of antecedent improbability.

Hare and Maurice.

Opinions are spread and schools of thought formed as much by the personal intercourse of friends as from books. Frederick Denison Maurice (1805-1872), set on his way by Hare, was himself a stronger and more subtle spirit; he went beyond his teacher, and by the magnetism of his character coloured the thought of all with whom he came in contact. He carried on and added to the thought of Coleridge and Erskine. With Coleridge he upholds the Church, though in no sectarian spirit; with the Evangelicals he finds in the Bible an answer to human needs, but he does not, as they did, deify the letter. His *Theological Essays*, addressed to the Unitarian community, in which he had himself been brought up, raised many questions by asserting ancient doctrines in such a manner that to readers who did not look far below the surface he seemed to contradict them. Because he set forth the character of God in Scripture as love, he seemed

Frederick Denison Maurice.

to deny the wrath of God against sin. Sin, according to the orthodox, is an act of the will; Maurice represented it as a condition of humanity, and found in man not only a natural depravity but a natural righteousness, owing to the indwelling of the Son of God. According to Maurice, the Atonement is not the acceptance by the offended Creator of a vicarious victim, the innocent for the guilty, but the fulfilment of the law of righteousness by the perfect obedience of the Son, whose will is one with the Father's, and who shares the sufferings of those whose Head he is. Baptism is the declaration of sonship, not the introduction of a new relation between Creator and creature. Eternal death is not punishment continued through unending time, but the essential alienation of man from God by unrepented sin. The word 'eternal' has nothing to do with time, but belongs to another order of ideas. Revelation is not the laying down of a law by an exterior authority, but the unveiling of the nature of God to the soul of man, in aid of the intuitive knowledge of God which exists, or may exist, in the soul. Thus Maurice restated ancient formulas in a new sense, and claimed, like Hampden, to be orthodox.

The difficulty or obscurity of Maurice's language exposed him to misrepresentation, which his elucidations did not always clear up. Bishop Wilberforce, who took an active part in his defence in 1853, put before him in writing his own interpretation of Maurice's doctrine, viz. that to speak of torments through never-ending extensions of time is to transfer to the eternal world the conditions of this world, since eternity is not time prolonged, but rather time abolished, and thus to misrepresent the character of God, and open a way to the introduction of unwarranted palliations for sin; that the happiness of the creature consists in his will being brought into harmony with the will of God; that free will wrongly used leads to misery in body and soul here, and that our state here is the seminal principle of what it is to be in the world to come; that hardened separation from God with its consequent torments is the 'death eternal' spoken of in the Scriptures, concerning which we must not dogmatise as if it were subject to earthly conditions, nor therefore on the one hand forget to contemplate God's exceeding love, nor on the other hand to conclude that after a certain period God's vengeance would be satisfied and further suffering remitted. Maurice accepted these definitions as 'a full and most satisfactory exposition' of his meaning.

There was no confusion in Maurice's mind. But when he dealt with 'plain men,' and seemed to be following the same object with them, it often appeared that he was on a different quest, finding their formulas at variance with one or another of the principles which were sacred to him. He was misunderstood in his hostility to utilitarianism, which substitutes success or happiness for the sense of right and wrong as declared by conscience; in his dislike of all parties, sects, and systems, which divide under pretext of uniting; in the strong distinctions which he drew between such terms as religion and theology, system and method, system and science, Protestantism and Anglicanism, catholicity and catholicism, regeneration and change of nature, historical religion and Church history, ecclesiastical system and Christian Church, critical faculty and criticising spirit, terms which to careless hearers seemed not opposite but identical; in his maintenance of paradoxes such as these, that subscription is no bondage, but a defence of liberty; that Broad Church is Narrow Church; that submission of the reason is good for the reason's sake; that the spirit of liberty is incompatible with the lust for independence; that episcopacy is essentially necessary to the idea of a church, and yet that the Scots were right in resisting it; that the difficulty of believing arises from the necessity of believing; that he himself was to be a man of war against all parties, in order that he might be a peacemaker between all men. This temper of mind isolated him, though he was severally claimed by the Evangelicals, the Tractarians, and the Latitudinarians as their own, till he showed that he would subscribe to none of their formulas; it would have isolated him more, had it not been for his sincerity and ardency, and the need of all who came into contact with him to drink from his perpetual well-spring of fresh thought and sympathy.

Maurice's writings and personal intercourse were felt in a wide circle of friends and disciples, among whom Frederick Robertson, Kingsley, Hort, and Westcott were conspicuous. His influence has not changed the spirit of religion, but has contributed to modify the form of theology. Much thought has travelled over the bridge which he helped to build between old beliefs and new. What he wrote on Baptism, Vicarious Suffering, and the Last Judgment, by its action upon the thought of his time, did something to bring about the profound difference which exists between the current belief on these topics now and that which prevailed in the middle of the nineteenth century.

It would be idle to inquire how much these men of the later generation owed to Carlyle. Though he constructed little, his early writings may be reckoned among the greatest forces of liberation working in those years. Whilst the schools of the economists were laboriously demolishing, brick by brick, the homes of prejudice and superstition, Carlyle's battering-ram made such a noisy assault upon them that all were bound to listen. His discordant summons was not merely a menace; it conveyed a promise also, the condition of which was honesty of thought. The prophet was true to his message. His stimulating influence pervaded all the thought of the time, rousing bitter opposition and fervent discipleship, bidding all men 'nor sit, nor stand, but go.'

AUTHORITIES: GENERAL.—As before. *Works* of Julius Charles Hare, Thos. Erskine of Linlathen; F. D. Maurice, *Theological Essays*. BIOGRAPHIES: Bishops Marsh, Watson, Bathurst, Stanley; *Pusey*, by Liddon; *S. T. Coleridge*, by Traill; *F. D. Maurice*, by Maurice; *Thos. Arnold*, by Stanley.

CHAPTER X

NATIONAL EDUCATION, 1833–1843

AFTER Brougham's Bill in 1820,[1] no further progress in national education was made for more than ten years. The abolition of slavery, the repeal of the Test and Corporation Acts, Catholic Emancipation, and Parliamentary Reform occupied the mind of the nation. It was not till 1833 that Roebuck, seconded by George Grote, asked the House of Commons to pledge itself for the next session to a scheme of national education. As this move was likely to embarrass the Government, the Chancellor of the Exchequer, Lord Althorp, himself proposed that a grant of £20,000 for national education should be made, the sum to be divided between the National Society and the British and Foreign School Society. This was the first public money voted for the purpose of education; 'a small fraction of the revenue of one day,' said Carlyle. No sum was to be contributed from the grant, unless an equal amount were raised by voluntary contributions. The principle of religious equality was stated by one party, and controverted by the other; the old rivalry of the Societies broke out: but it was said then, as it might be said at this day, that 'there is not practically that exclusiveness among the Church Societies nor that indifference to religion among those who exclude dogmatic instruction, which their mutual accusations would lead bystanders to suppose.' It should be remembered that this was the era of the 'Useful Knowledge' movement, set on foot by Brougham

Parliamentary vote for education, 1833.

---

[1] See p. 97.

in 1825, and that the cause of progress was at that time reinforced by secularism, an alliance greatly dreaded by Churchmen and conservative politicians. The common ground of agreement is disregarded by combatants; and in this instance it might be said that both parties desired religious education, but neither party desired religious liberty, which is one of the conditions of religious education.

On May 21, 1835, Lord Brougham reviewed the progress of national education since 1818, when the appointment of an Education Committee of the House of Commons had caused much dismay, and he himself had been accused in connexion with that appointment of 'sowing the seeds of revolution and aiming at a dictatorship.' In the meantime, he said, the number of children under education had more than doubled in the voluntary schools, whilst in the endowed schools, notwithstanding the stimulus given by the Bell and Lancaster systems, the number had diminished. He would therefore support the voluntary system. 'Let the tax-gatherer, or the county assessor, or the parish collector but once go his rounds for a school-rate, and I will answer for it that voluntary assistance will soon vanish away.' He compared the number of children at school, not much more than one-twelfth, with the right proportion, about one-ninth. He spoke of the need of beginning education early; of 'the irrepressible curiosity of infancy . . . a perpetual course of induction; a series of experiments, which begin when the child wakes in the morning, and only ends when he falls asleep.' He enlarged on the miserable quality of the education commonly given; an ill-delivered and inefficient course of reading, writing, and arithmetic, nothing more, was the staple of most schools, and that in face of the wonderful results achieved by Lancaster's Borough Road school; and in conclusion he moved a set of Resolutions, deploring the deficiency of elementary schools and the poor quality of the education given in them, and urging the need of infant schools, training schools or seminaries to train teachers, and stating the necessity for parliamentary aid in support of voluntary effort; and he asked for a Commission. The Prime Minister, Lord Melbourne, cordially agreed, and Bishop Monk of Gloucester gave his blessing to

[marginal notes:]
Brougham's speech, 1835.

Brougham's education Resolutions.

the scheme, provided all that was done were connected with the Church of England. Again, in December 1837, Brougham brought in an Education Bill on the voluntary principle, stimulated by the incentive of grants in aid from the Treasury, to be distributed by a Board of Commissioners. Unsectarian religious teaching was to be given ; and any parish might form a school committee and levy rates for school purposes. This bill was dropped for want of time, and, in 1838, a similar proposal made by Mr. Wise, chairman of the Central Society for Education, also fell through.

The next landmark in the history of national education is the creation of the Education Committee of the Privy Council. The policy of Melbourne's Government was summed *Education* up by Lord John Russell, Home Secretary, in a *Committee* letter written early in 1839, as 'a temperate atten- *of Privy* tion to the fair claims of the Established Church *1839.* and the religious freedom sanctioned by the law'; and on February 12, he announced the intention of the Govern- ment to establish, by Order in Council, a special *Lord John* Committee of the Privy Council, with a staff of officials, *Russell's* who would form a permanent Board of Education, *plan.* responsible to Government and Parliament. The arguments by which he supported the creation of an organised State system of national education in place of the inadequate and irregular action of voluntary boards of management, are now familiar, and need not be recapitulated. But it is interest- ing to note that so thorough a reformer as Russell could neither hint at a policy of uniform education under State con- trol, nor dissociate the teaching of the people from the para- mount claims of the Church of England. He assumed that the distinction of Church schools and British schools was unalterable. The ideas which at that time held the field were the voluntary principle, and the division of all schools between the two societies ; no statesmen then looked forward to the substitution of State schools for voluntary, to religious instruc- tion in which all sects should meet on a ground of common Christianity, to division of religious instruction by denomina- tions, or separation of secular from religious teaching ; or if any did, they were theorists, not practical statesmen.

Yet at this very time a movement was proceeding for

solving the problem, by setting religious teaching apart from
Education, secular, and leaving the various churches to settle
religious their differences apart from the State, a movement
and secular,
denomina- actively promoted by an association called the
tional and
undenomina- Central Society of Education, and approved not only
tional. by Mill and Spencer, but by more moderate reformers also. Moreover, it was not likely that the strong
organisation which had created the British and Foreign School
system, a system pledged to the principle of combined as
opposed to sectarian education, would accept such a solution
as that supplied by Russell's plan. In the latest attempts
at educational reform in England the danger has appeared
to be lest the undenominational principle should destroy
the Church schools. Then, the chances were the other
way; the likelihood was that the Church's organisation,
backed by the Church's wealth, would be too strong for
the nonconformist churches to resist, when education should
come to take its place among the political and parliamentary issues of the time. The Church, though she had
not fully discharged her duties, was too firmly in position
to be set aside; and the feeling of Churchmen generally agreed with the words of Bishop Blomfield, written
Strength in 1838, that no system of compulsory national
of Church education would be tolerable 'which should not be
feeling. in conformity with the principles of the Church of
England, and worked by its instrumentality.' Peel, always
in favour of moderate and constitutional reform, expressed
the sense of the majority when he disclaimed anything which
would violate perfect liberty in education, but at the same
time asserted the right of Churchmen to insist upon Church
teaching in their schools. The quarrel was inevitable. Either
party can appeal to principle with sincerity; neither can
escape the prejudices engendered by a long history of social,
political, and religious inferiority on the one hand, and on the
other the habit of oppression or at least detraction. Nor was
it unnatural that the nonconformist bodies, connecting their
troubles with the existence of a Church establishment, should
make all their action in politics and education subordinate to
the main object of pulling down the fabric of establishment.

The grant of £20,000 made in 1833 was increased to

£30,000, and an Order in Council, bearing date April 10, 1839, appointed a special Committee of the Privy Council to administer it.   This was the origin of the Board of Education, which has now become a Department of Government.   A staff of officials was appointed, at the head of which was placed the able and energetic Dr. Kay, and by the perseverance of many years in the face of difficulties, a system of national education grew up, directed by an able succession of administrators, who worked under instructions from the Department, and without interference from Parliament.

Education grant of £30,000 and appointment of Committee of Privy Council on Education, 1839.

The establishment of the Committee of Council on Education was a long step in the direction of national recognition. In consequence of this, education has to some extent been removed from the strife of parties, and the Board of Education, as it is now commonly termed, has been able to extend its executive operations so as to take the place of the Legislature in the gradual development of a national system of education, for the most part in a secular direction.   The progress of secularism in the nation and the freedom of action assumed by the Board have worked together in the direction of dissociating education from the Church of England.   Education is only incidentally and secondarily a part of church history : but it will be well to set down in order a few of the chief steps in the development of national education in this relation.

New organisation of the Board of Education.

The Committee lost no time in putting out regulations, among which were the following : that the Committee should administer parliamentary grants in concert with the National Society and the British and Foreign School Society ; and that other schools not connected with those Societies should also be entitled to receive Government aid.   It was laid down that the right of inspection should in all cases be retained by the Committee, 'in order to secure conformity of the regulations and discipline established in the several schools with such improvements as may be from time to time suggested by the Committee.'

Regulations of Education Committee, 1839.

The policy of encouraging voluntary aid was so far successful, that the amount contributed from local sources for school purposes between 1839 and 1844 was £230,000, which was met by grants of public money amounting to £170,000. Contributions were made in various ways : by voluntary rates, by gifts from landlords, and by parents' school fees, but most of all by the clergy, who showed much liberality and devotion in the cause of education.

With a view to providing a training for teachers in its schools, the National Society in 1838 opened a Model School at Westminster on church principles, and entered into correspondence with the Committee of Council on Education, hoping to get a building grant. As the Committee insisted in coupling this with the condition of Government inspection, this design was not carried out; but in the following year (1839) it was decided that a training college for young persons of fifteen years of age and upwards should be instituted for the training of teachers in parochial and national schools, by giving them a sound general education, and bringing them up as attached and intelligent members of the Church. Accordingly, St. Mark's College, Chelsea, was built, and received students in 1841. A similar college for girls, Whitelands, was also founded. The first Principal of St. Mark's was Derwent Coleridge, son of the poet, a scholar of distinction, and a man of genial and enterprising character, who by his personal qualities drew much attention to the training of teachers, and inspired enthusiasm for the work. The spirit which animated the founders of St. Mark's College has been compared in this respect to the ardour and hope with which a similar work was begun at Oxford when Keble College was founded in 1868. The College was started at a happy moment in the history of the Church of England, before the secession to Rome had begun, and when the High Church clergy and laity were full of hope and aspiration for the future of the Church, and large designs were entertained for the extension of the Episcopate and for the evangelisation of the heathen. The College was founded on a High Church model : the 'keystone of the arch' was the College Chapel and its daily services ; 'the labours of the house, the field, and the garden were intended to elevate, not to depress ; the studies of the schoolroom not to exalt, but to humble.'

In 1840 Dr. Kay and some friends founded an un-

Church training colleges ; St. Mark's, Chelsea, 1841.

denominational Normal School at Battersea for training teachers to instruct pauper children.   He and his associates, getting no support from Government, spent their own money upon the scheme, and arrangements were made for the reception of fifty apprentice students.   The course of study was both literary and practical, and included instruction in gardening and household work.   The scheme could not be worked economically; in 1842 the Committee of Council voted £1000 towards liquidating the debt incurred on this school; and in 1844 the Battersea College was handed over to the National Society.   Colleges connected with the Church of England were created at Salisbury and Chester, and in other dioceses; in all, thirteen for male students, seventeen for female.   The students were *Education in the training colleges.* chiefly schoolmasters, clerks, shopkeepers and assistants, artizans, and even labourers, the sons of small tradesmen, servants, and superior mechanics.   The low level of their education at entrance is particularly remarked upon, and everything was done in Dr. Kay's school at Battersea and in other colleges to stimulate intelligence as well as to impart knowledge.   There was to be no attempt to foster ambition by educating the future teachers 'above their station': as Derwent Coleridge, the Principal of St. Mark's, said, 'the object was to produce schoolmasters for the poor, the endeavour must be, on the one hand, to raise the students morally and intellectually to a certain standard, while, on the other hand, we train them in lowly service'; and with this view domestic labour, both indoors and in farm and garden work, formed part of the course.   The female students came from the same classes: teachers, shop-girls, milliners, and domestic servants.   Where the level of education was low, the standard of results could not be high; the teachers themselves were imperfectly trained, methods were defective, and the salaries offered for elementary school teaching were so small as not to attract the best students.

A Normal School or National Training College for teachers was to be founded, on an undenominational footing, 'in which candidates for the office of teacher in schools for the poorer classes might acquire the *Normal training college.* knowledge necessary to the exercise of their future profession, and might be practised in the most approved methods of religious and moral training and instruction.' Within this normal or training school there was to be a model school for children between the ages of three and fourteen. The religious instruction was to be on the 'combined' system; that is, the same general religious instruction was to be given to all, but special religious teaching was to be given by teachers of the several denominations. The clergy claimed the right of training and licensing teachers under the Canons of 1604, and did not approve of the equality thus granted to Nonconformists. Churchmen and Dissenters alike raised so violent an opposition to the undenominational character of the proposed college, which seemed to imply pure indifferentism, that the Government abandoned the experiment of a training college for teachers on definite and systematic lines. One reason for this abandonment was a vote of the National Society passed at a large meeting, held under the presidency of Archbishop Howley: 'that it is an object of the highest national importance to provide that instruction in the truths and precepts of Christianity should form an essential part of every system of education intended for the people at large, and that such instruction should be under the superintendence of the clergy, and in conformity with the doctrines of the Church in this realm, as the recognised teacher of religion.' Another reason was an address to the Queen carried by the Archbishop of Canterbury in the House of Lords by a majority of nearly two to one, deprecating the handing over to any public authority without consent of Parliament so important a matter as the arrangements made for the religious instruction of children, and praying that no general plan of national education should be established without giving the House of Lords, as one branch of the Legislature, an opportunity of fully considering the measure.

Meeting of the National Society.

The policy of the Committee of Council was to aim at religious equality, but to work through the various religious communities and organisations. They were introducing into the politics of education a new principle, that of national responsibility for national education; and they must take political and religious conditions as they found them existing.

A policy of neutrality, such as was now adopted, was a novelty. It was not entirely the fault of the Committee, if in consequence of the trend of politics neutrality turned to the advantage of the Nonconformists. *Religious neutrality.*

A minute of Council, dated June 3, 1839, divided the funds diverted from the Normal School between the National Society and the British and Foreign School Society, and established the principle of inspection; a principle which may diminish voluntary zeal in subjecting it to State regulation, but which is a necessary condition of efficiency. The general instructions to inspectors given in 1839-1840 were to the effect that they were to pay special attention to the religious teaching, but abstain from interfering with the religious instruction, discipline, or management of the school, their duty being to collect facts and information, and to report to the Committee of Council on Education. *School inspectors appointed, 1839.*

In August 1840 further instructions, sometimes known as the 'Concordat with the Church,' were given by the Department to the inspectors in Church of England schools. It was agreed that no inspector should be appointed without the consent of the Archbishop, the British and Foreign School Society exercising a similar right with regard to their own inspectors. The inspectors were to inquire in Church Schools whether the children were properly instructed in the doctrines and principles of the Church of England, whether they attended church regularly, and had proper accommodation there, whether the teaching of Bible and Catechism was satisfactory, whether they were taught private prayers for use at home, whether attention was given to senior as well as junior pupils. Reports were to be sent by the Board to the Archbishop. Thus, in the Church of England schools, nothing was done to withdraw the religious teaching of the children from the control of the clergy; whilst, as regards other schools, care was taken not to give any colour to a charge of favouring one sect above another. *Church Concordat, 1840.*

In March 1841 William Ewart, Member for Dumfries, moved for an address to the Crown to appoint a Minister of Education, such minister to be a member of the House of Commons. He desired more and better *Ewart's proposals, 1841.*

schools, schoolmasters, and methods, and especially demanded
normal schools for the education of teachers. The whole
population, he said, required a provision for their instruction,
a great proportion of them, in the rural districts, being in a
state of 'benighted and besotted ignorance.' He would have
a yearly exposition of the state and progress of education, like
the budget of finance. A wise and moderate speech; but
far in advance of public opinion, which at that time was hardly
beginning to allow a national responsibility for the national
evil of ignorance, as in our times it hesitates to allow a
national responsibility for the national evil of intemperance.
It was necessary at that time for Peel to defend himself
against the charge of irreligion on the ground that he had
advised the formation of Mechanics' Institutes and the spread
of useful knowledge, and so encouraged 'that utilitarian spirit
which trusted rather to scientific instruction than to religious
training for the improvement and elevation of the working
classes.'

The question of national education was again brought
forward in 1843 by Lord Ashley, afterwards Earl of Shaftesbury,
who was then commencing the career of philan-
thropy which gives him a foremost place among the
statesmen of the nineteenth century. He moved
in the House of Commons, on February 28, a
resolution to address the Queen with the prayer that she
would 'take into her instant and serious consideration the best
means of diffusing the benefits and blessings of a moral and
religious education among the working classes of her people.'
A sound moral and religious education, he said, would help
to direct the growing spirit of democracy. His plan for the
education of factory children included religious teaching by
ministers of the Anglican, Roman Catholic, and Protestant
nonconformist communions. He estimated the number of
boys and girls of the age for education at something under
two millions, more than half of whom were without any daily
instruction. He gave an appalling account of depravity and
brutish ignorance among young people in great towns. In
spite of all that had been done by the National Society and
the dissenting bodies, there still remained 'a terrible wilder-
ness of spiritual destitution.' After speaking of neglect and

bad example on the part of the rich, he exclaimed passionately:
'Only let us now declare that we will enter on a better course,
that we will seek their temporal through their eternal interests,
and half our work will be accomplished.   There are many
hearts to be influenced, many minds to be instructed, many
souls to be saved.   *O patria ! O divum domus !*—if we engage
in such a task, the blessing of God will rest on our labours,
and the oldest among us perhaps may live to rejoice for himself
and his children at the opening dawn of the immortal because
the moral glory of the British Empire.'

The address was agreed to, and was graciously answered
by the Queen on March 8, 1843.   Sir James Graham on the
same day introduced his Factory Bill, and opposition
to the education clauses contained in it immediately   Sir James
began, on the ground that in the manufacturing   Factory Bill,
districts, where Dissenters and Roman Catholics   1843.
were numerous, they would be excluded from most of the
benefits of the new law, since the clergyman was to be the
chief trustee, the masters were to be appointed and the
inspectors approved by the bishop, and the choice of books,
the conduct of inspection, and the teaching of the Bible would
all be worked to favour the Church.

The Dissenters throughout the country raised an alarm of
Church domination, held meetings in the principal towns,
drew up petitions against the bill as founded on principles of
injustice, and as interfering with the rights of conscience,
because the proposed schools were to be under the superintendence of the Church of England.   The Roman Catholics
also objected to the bill.   Graham pointed out that the safeguards provided were so carefully and fully drawn that no
religious grievance remained, except, of course, if that was a
grievance, the existence of an established Church : the very
fact that it was established presumed a preference, and the
demand for equality was unreasonable.   But though he could
not entirely give way here, he had afforded under the bill
every facility and security to Nonconformists.   *Beati pacifici* ;
it is their portion to be attacked by both sides.   Sir Robert
Inglis, Member for the University of Oxford, declared that
the bill did not tend to place the Church in so prominent
a position as from its character it deserved ; nonconformist

members claimed for the Dissenters not only protection from oppression, but equality; Roebuck objected to any attempt on the part of the State to inculcate peculiar religious opinions; both parties, he said, were to blame, the Churchmen were greedy of power, the Dissenters refused to co-operate; the Legislature ought to stand aloof from the question altogether, and let the minister of religion in. Only Sheil, the Irish patriot, speaking in the interest of the Roman Catholic schools, to which the use of the Douay version of the Bible seemed likely to be denied, in favour of the Authorised Version used by Protestants, rebuked the timidity of objectors :—

'Why,' he said, 'are you for ever crying out, in reference to popery, that your Church is in danger, and giving way to the most fantastic fears? . . . Your Church is incorporated with the State, supported by the interests of the higher orders and by the faith of the humbler classes. It lifts its mitred head amidst courts and parliaments; it possesses vast revenues . . . it has retained all the pomp, pride, and glorious circumstance of the establishment of which it is a perpetuation—archbishops, bishops, deans, cathedrals, golden stalls. It is distinguished by a prelacy eminent for learning, and a clergy distinguished for every activity, and an organised spirit of confederacy. Such is your establishment. . . . This ague of apprehension for your Church is idle, and would be ridiculous but for the fatal results it produces, and the constant injustice it works. I have heard much, in the course of this discussion, of the dogmas of theology. I do not profess to be conversant with them; but I sometimes read my Bible . . . and it strikes me, if there be a passage in which the character of our Saviour is described in a peculiarly amiable light, it is that in which He is represented as desiring His disciples not to forbid little children to come to Him; and I cannot help thinking that if among that little group on whose heads He was invoked to lay His hands, there had been the child of a Sadducee or a Samaritan, the God of mercy and love would not have put the little schismatic aside. Do not imitate the example of those by whom the children were rebuked. Suffer them to approach Him; let them have access to the sources of pure morality, and of that truth which is common to all

Sheil's speech on education, 1843.

Christians. . . . Act on the precept contained in the divine injunction : Suffer the little children to come to Me and forbid them not : for of such is the kingdom of Heaven.'

About the same time Charles Greville, whose view of public affairs is always valuable, from his position outside party and his complete acquaintance with all the actors in politics, as well as from his own shrewd- ness, moderation, and good sense, wrote in his journal, under date November 29, 1843 : '[The Govern- ment] will not burn their fingers with any more bills, but are going to extend the present system and dispense more money. . . . The fact is, [the Dissenters] are not to be conciliated. Their success in defeating the Government measure last session has increased their notions of their own consequence, and nothing will satisfy them now but being put on a level with the Church. I have for some time past expected that the Government would be driven to cast themselves entirely on the Church, and it would be no bad thing for them if they were. . . . They would then at least act on an intelligible principle, and would have the support of the most powerful and influential interest there is.'

Charles Greville's opinion.

We may call to mind here some remarks of Cobden, made ten years later, which are as true now as in 1853 or in 1841. As to the religious 'bogey,' he said, he did not believe that there could be got together one hundred decent and respectable men in any part of the country, to discuss the subject of education, into whose heads it would ever enter to do anything inimical to the cause of religion. He held that 'the religious question' was a mighty bugbear, a bubble which would burst the moment they touched it with their fingers. He had been told by the Secretary of the British and Foreign Schools Society that though he had heard a great deal of talk about the religious difficulty, he had never met with it in practice.

Cobden on the religious difficulty, 1853.

Harriet Martineau also, who cannot be suspected of partiality to the Church of England, wrote as follows : ' In order to judge of the Government scheme and the opposition to it, it must be remembered with what difficulty any beginning whatever had been made ; how jealous was the Church of any admission of

Harriet Martineau.

Dissenters to the public funds for educational purposes, and how unacceptable to the Dissenters was the idea of compulsory education at all. . . . It ought to be acknowledged on every hand that here was a call for magnanimity all round. It was an occasion for the Church to acknowledge her neglect, and hasten to repair it. It was an occasion for the Dissenters to be modest about their much greater exertions for the education of their own members in the large towns, in consideration of the vast deal which it was not in their power to do. . . . The Church was more equal to the occasion than the Dissenters. The Church yielded more than she had ever offered before to the conscience of Dissenters ; and when the Dissenters threw out the educational part of the Government scheme, the Church set vigorously to work to raise funds by voluntary subscriptions, for the extension and improvement of the national Church schools. The opposition of the Dissenters prevailed. The opportunity was lost of taking the Church in a genial and liberal mood, and of providing for the children of various sects being reared as brethren, while instructed each in the doctrine of his own communion. All that was possible was done for the perpetuating of sectarian rancour, and for hounding on ignorance and bigotry to new assaults on the innocence and peace of society.'

Already in 1843, Joseph Hume had proposed the establishment of schools to be supported by public funds, in which secular and moral training should be given, but the religious instruction should be provided apart from the school. He proposed this not from any wish to discourage religious education, but because all attempts to combine secular and religious education had failed. This bill was lost ; the idea of secular education being then even more distasteful to English people at large than it is now. The opposition to the scheme of education contained in the Factory Bill, chiefly on the ground that it gave too much favour to the Church, was so strong that the Government found themselves obliged to withdraw the education clauses (15 June 1843); the rest of the bill soon followed, and when Sir James Graham reintroduced his bill in the following year, the education clauses were omitted.

Joseph Hume's proposal of secular schools, 1843.

Graham withdraws the education clauses, 1843.

The Dissenters gained courage from their victory; the Congregational Union resolved to accept no State aid, and the nonconformist associations set themselves to collect voluntary offerings, in doing which they had great *Voluntary efforts.* success. At the same time Church people began to form a special fund for the purpose of extending and improving church education, and even raised a large sum of money, which was employed by the National Society in providing more schools as well as better methods of teaching, and especially in increasing the number of training colleges. The Education Department gave in return large building and maintenance grants. The voluntary principle was working well, and was still in accordance with the public opinion of the time, which disapproved of compulsion. But much time was lost, and many thousands of children went without education for want of compulsion; and it was soon remarked that it is easier to raise a large sum of money by a special appeal for donations than to meet a growing demand by regular subscriptions.

The simplest, most logical, and in some respects most effective plan of national education is that which prevails in America and in some of our colonies, where the State provides secular education for all, and leaves religious *The secular method.* instruction to be furnished by the various sects for those pupils whose parents desire it. By this means religious friction is removed, and children of all creeds can be educated together without difficulty. But logical considerations are not everything; and those who uphold religious teaching for all do so on the ground that a Christian State ought to provide Christian education, that a religiously minded teacher will create an atmosphere of reverence in the school, and that if religious friction is absent, so is religious warmth. In England sixty years ago, the secularist plan was impracticable, and the choice lay between the 'combined' or undenominational method, based upon the precepts of a common Christianity, and denominational teaching, with the safeguard of a conscience clause, to be imposed upon all schools aided by the State. Denominational teaching was what the Anglican clergy claimed as their right; and if they could have met the pecuniary need by voluntary subscriptions, they might have made their claim good. The policy of the

Education Department was to maintain the voluntary principle, whilst bringing the schools by degrees into closer and more systematic relations with the central authority, by regulation of grants for building and apparatus, institution of training schools, extension of the system of inspection, and adaptation of means to ends in meeting the ever-growing problems presented by the increase of population in the towns. The general relation of the State to the schools and their managers, with respect to financial matters and the religious question, remained for the present unchanged.

AUTHORITIES. —Gregory, *Elementary Education* ; Kay Shuttleworth, *Four Periods of Public Education* ; Craik, *The State in Relation to Education* ; *History of the National Society* (published by Nat. Soc.).

CHAPTER XI

THE OXFORD MOVEMENT

THE English nation had in the last quarter of the eighteenth century received such impression as it could take of the destructive and constructive philosophism which preceded the French Revolution, and of the equalitarian doctrines of 1789. The nation, as a rule, rejected all serious negation of Christian doctrine, though a latitudinarian and sceptical tendency underlay the mode of thinking which prevailed in educated society, which was to have its development later under the wing, not of philosophy but of science, in Agnosticism without the religious pale, within it, in liberal or Broad Church theology. A natural reaction against this sympathy with a philosophy which had been seen to culminate in the orgies of the Goddess of Reason tightened the bands of religious dogma and a regulated morality; and hatred of the French Revolution, and its principles and their results in action, made serious people combine to resist the attacks of infidelity and immorality. Religion was defended not so much now, as fifty years earlier, on the evidential side, but as a safeguard of morality and social order; and the religious world became at once more fervent and less argumentative.

It is impossible to tell anew in fitting terms a story which has been told by Newman and Church, and with which the world still rings. The motive power in the Oxford Movement of 1833 was the feeling expressed by the principal actor in the following sentence, a feeling which makes all intelligible, and without which all that was done must seem extravagant or puerile: 'I have

Last quarter of the eighteenth century.

The Oxford Movement of 1833.

ever kept before me,' writes Newman in the *Apologia*, 'that there was something greater than the Established Church, and that was the Church Catholic and Apostolic, set up from the beginning, of which she was but the local presence and organ.' The earlier school of High Church reformers, Watson, Knox, Sikes, and others mentioned above, were pioneers of a larger movement than they could foresee.

The need of action to men who thought like this was, it seemed to themselves, forced upon them from without. They were not innovators ; *stare super antiquas vias* was their ideal : but a new force had arisen in the world, the spirit of Liberalism ; new it appeared to be, but new it was not, for it was only another name for the old spirit of rebellion, against which the Church had always testified. The Oxford Movement had its roots in the past, in the *depositum fidei* preserved by the High Church school ; but, like all political and religious movements, it owed its form and colour to contemporary events. Pre-eminent among these was the growth of Liberalism, aggressive and combative, demanding of each settled institution to show its right to exist.

'I thought,' says Newman, 'that it was both incumbent on us, and profitable to us, to meet that onset of Liberal principles, of which we were all in immediate anticipation, whether in the Church or in the University.'

The conjunction of Keble, Hurrell Froude, and Newman produced the Oxford Movement of 1833. Other men, Hugh James Rose, William Palmer of Worcester College, Arthur Perceval, and many others counted for something : but without these three it would not have been, or would have been wholly different.

Keble, Froude, and Newman.

A course of public action such as that which has received the name of the Oxford Movement owes so much to its leaders that it seems necessary to introduce here some notice of the individuals whose teaching or personal character gave impulse or direction to the course of events. Among the first of these, according to Newman the 'true and primary author of it,' was John Keble (1792-1866), the son of a Gloucestershire rector, sprung from a family in which traditional High Church principles animated a very sincere and somewhat Puritan form of religion, and himself a man

John Keble.

of strong and impressive character. John Keble went up to Corpus Christi College, Oxford, with no training but that of his father, who himself had been scholar and fellow of the same college, and gained a scholarship there at the age of fourteen in December 1806. Before he was twenty he had obtained a double First Class, and was made Fellow of Oriel, his friend Richard Whately being elected at the same time. Even at that early age great deference was paid to Keble in the Common Room; a deference which he retained throughout his life, based less upon the brilliancy of his intellectual power, though that would have accounted for it, than the purity and saintliness of his nature. We are reminded of Milton at the same age, called 'the Lady' of his college, and of Father Paul Sarpi, called 'la Sposa,' in whose presence no unfitting word was ever spoken.

There was also in John Keble, as in the Puritan poet and the Venetian friar, a sternness of fibre. He calls for 'due severity in our religion'; 'without a severe religion,' he says, 'I fear our Church will practically fail.' His intimate friend, Sir John Taylor Coleridge, tells us that the intensity of his spirit and the authority of his character made it difficult to argue with him; a tendency to think that he was probably right was strengthened by the conviction that he was most completely in earnest, whatever his playful manner might seem to say. His shrinking modesty could on occasion give way to fiery zeal, and his gentle and playful courtesy to words of grave rebuke spoken in public or in private. Of the sterner side of his mind a few instances may be given. He called the Divorce Bill of 1856-57 'a Bill for legalising adultery.' He had no tolerance for Bishop Colenso, or the writers of *Essays and Reviews*. He took part in all the action of his friends in their attacks upon Hampden in 1836 and 1848. He held the strongest possible view of eternal punishment, asking, 'Where is then the stay of contrite hearts?' whose hope departs with the sinner's fear, and he printed a *Litany of Our Lord's Warnings*, which startled many who did not push things to conclusions. Keble never shrank from conclusions; it was characteristic of the tractarian school and of himself personally. Things which might seem trifles to others were 'stuff of the conscience' to him. Absolute sincerity was the foundation of his character, a quality which implies courage no less than clearness of vision. No one who knew Keble could doubt that if a question presented itself to him he would take pains to understand it and to state it clearly—his Aristotelian training had taught him this,—that he would judge it by the light of principle and religion, hold his opinion strongly and act upon it fearlessly. The only apparent exception to absolute truthfulness, and that this was only apparent his own letters testify, is his consistent belittling of himself, which sometimes in a person of such high gifts, so highly appreciated, borders on Socratic εἰρωνεία.

It has been said that to the Oxford Movement Newman gave genius, Pusey learning, and Keble character. The whole spirit of *The Christian Year*, Keble's appearance from time to time at a crisis, coming out from the retirement of his parsonage, the tone of authority which breathes through his letters of counsel as well as in the sermons which he preached before the world, show him to have been a man whose advice was widely sought, and who deemed it his duty never to avoid responsibility, but who knew also how not to be too busy. It is characteristic of these two aspects of his mind that he would not read Newman's *Essay on the Development of Christian Doctrine*, written immediately before the author's secession to Rome, till questions were asked him, which made him feel it to be his duty to study what he would rather have left alone. His natural impulse was neither to controversy nor speculation. He says himself that the influence of his father and his brother Thomas had saved him from eclecticism. He moved in a narrow path, securely ; holding fast to the apostolical tradition according to the ancient Anglican acceptation of it, and to the belief that the Church of England, though fallen on evil days, had God's blessing, and that the saints of that communion had died or were living in God's favour. It was the knowledge of Keble's stability in one set of opinions, which is also evidence of want of elasticity of mind and narrowness of view, that made so many turn to him as an oracle.

Keble's brilliant career at Oxford and his action in the tractarian movement might have been forgotten, but for the wide authority and reverence which came to him through

The Christian Year, and the confidence, which his steadfast
character inspired, that he would remain true to the
Church of England, whatever others might do. He was
deeply pained by the secession of his friends to Rome, and
above all of Newman, whose loss he never recovered ; and
although he would look wistfully in the direction of Rome and
unity, there is nothing to show that he had at any time of his
life the smallest temptation to leave the Church of England.
He thought that political events might necessitate a secession
like that of the Nonjurors, for whose doctrine and practice
he had a strong affinity ; but his mind had been formed by
the study of the Fathers, Hooker, and the other English
divines, and he wanted no more. Modern extensions of
dogma, such as the Vatican definitions, merely repelled him,
and Newman's Essay on Development, though the method of
argument was one with which he could sympathise, left him
unmoved. There were principles in his mind which were
unshakable, and he never looked beyond them.

Richard Hurrell Froude (1803-1836) was, by the account
of all who knew him, one of the most beloved and loving of
men. His friend Frederick Oakeley describes 'a
form of singular elegance ; a countenance of peculiar
and the highest kind of beauty . . . manners the
most refined and engaging.' He was master of the hearts
of his friends ; and though he could not compare in loftiness
of intellect and authority with Newman, nor with Keble in
steadiness of character, nor in learning and industry with
Pusey, his audacity and combativeness, his uncompromising
love of what he held to be truth, his brilliancy of reasoning
power—for he was a mathematician and scientific inquirer
as well as a logician—his poetic insight and wide reach
of imagination marked him as a man of unusual gifts.
Froude was less moved than Newman, much less than Keble,
by personal and historical associations : he was more hard-
headed, but also more impulsive, assertive, and paradoxical.
The men exercised a various influence upon each other. As
Froude himself said, 'Keble is my fire, but I may be his
poker.' 'His influence over Keble's fearless intelligence,'
says his biographer, Miss Guiney, 'felt from the first, was
ultimately very great.' The same writer compares Froude and

[margin note:] Richard Hurrell Froude.

Newman to the bow and the arrow, an inseparable relation
defying analysis.   Froude was 'not a leader, but born to prompt
leaders.'   Whilst Keble worshipped in the sanctuary of the past,
and Newman carefully and with tears gathered up the elements
of his belief, and steadfastly refused to look forward or to
take any step without sure footing, Froude, irresponsible,
fearless, careless of respectabilities and conventions, will have
no half-truths or half-measures, exposes fallacies, breaks idols,
tears open shutters, 'sends up rockets'; he does not disguise
his antipathies and sympathies; he hates the 'wretched
Tridentines' no less than the Reformers; his destructive
criticism moves Newman from conservative ways of thought,
his growing reverence for Rome also moves him, but at first
only to be more fierce against Rome.   'He taught me,' says
Newman in the *Apologia*, 'to look with admiration towards
the Church of Rome, and in the same degree to dislike the
Reformation.   He fixed deep in me the idea of devotion to
the Blessed Virgin, and he led me gradually to believe in the
Real Presence.'   Froude accepted the notions of a hierarchical system, sacerdotal power, the authority of tradition,
the excellence of virginity, the principle of penance and
mortification, the reality of 'miraculous interference as occur-
ring in the early and middle ages.'   In general 'he was powerfully drawn to the mediæval church, but not to the primitive,'
and thus helped to bridge over the gap caused by Newman's
anti-Roman writings.

If we ask what was Froude's share in the movement, the
answer is in the effect of his personality upon Keble and
Newman, and especially Newman.   Froude stirred Keble to
action, but Keble's action was on his own lines.   He showed
Newman the tendency of his own thought, gave him fresh
principles and fresh points of view, to which he returned
after his study of the Fathers; the very difference of their
studies brought these two nearer to each other; Froude's fire
brought out the latent heat in Newman.   What Froude in his
life had been to a few he became to many more in his
Remains; the attraction and repulsion stronger, the influence
more permanent.   The extreme High Churchmen of the
present day, though they may not acknowledge it, are followers
of Froude rather than of Newman or Pusey.

Unfortunately for Froude's reputation, Keble and Newman, the editors of his *Remains*, allowed themselves and were allowed by his family to reveal to the world his most secret perplexities and self-distrusts, and petty details Froude's *Remains.* of mortifications self-inflicted to satisfy an oversensitive conscience.   Of certain passages caught up and covered with not unnatural ridicule, it has been remarked that no one who remembers the keen humour of Keble and Newman can easily imagine how these passages survived the proof-reading.   The public can understand Froude's heart-searchings as little as Keble's self-distrust ; they think the one unmanly, the other affected.   In the same way Froude's fierceness of attack, his denunciations of those who differed from him, have led so acute a critic as Dr. Abbott to speak of him as one 'without love of man as a fellow man,' 'a champion of holiness, though essentially, if charity be essential, not a Christian' ; though he allows that Froude's harsh words were interpreted, to those who knew him well, by his bright and graceful personality.   Extravagant opinions intemperately and violently expressed may defeat their own object ; but when they are put forth by a man of great personal power their extravagance is forgotten, and they attract that class of mind which is inclined to think that truth lies in one or the other extreme, not in any *via media.*   It is not sufficiently appreciated how the magic of personality can harmonise contraries, how tenderness and fierceness, sweetness and severity, humble self-depreciation and strong invective, morbid asceticism and free enjoyment of life can lodge together.   Froude's personality contained all the contradictions which made his *Remains* a puzzle to those who did not know him.

Of John Henry Newman (1801-1890) so much more must be said in the course of this history that it would be waste of labour to attempt to portray him once for all. This much may be set down here ; that his intellectual and moral superiority to most of his fellows drew attention to all that he said and wrote ; his silence and his speech, his plain words and dark sayings, his irony and sarcasm, his pride and his humility, his fierceness and his gentleness, his friendships and his antipathies, his isolation in the midst of devoted friends, his power to attract and to repel, made him always and to all an enigma of the greatest interest. His bringing up was evangelical, and his first and most lasting religious impressions came from that quarter. The spirituality which was natural to him received its first impulse from an evangelical source ; hence he derived assurance of personal salvation, the fear of sin, and the sense of the seriousness of religion. He had no fellow-travellers in his thought ; *tecum habita* might be said to have been his motto. He was always in the presence of the Unseen ; and there came to him what the Greeks called 'voices,' hints and omens to which he listened and gave to them a divine and moral meaning, though they affected him primarily through the intellect. No article in his creed was held more firmly than the belief in divine guidance ; and this worked with his naturally imperious character to make him take an individual course and not lean upon human advice, though he was susceptible to the influence of human character. Logical subtlety and acuteness of mind, clear sightedness, fearlessness, and self-control made him a leader, though he never wished to have followers.

The leaders of the new movement were not merely political partisans or polemical theologians. They may have brought forward an obsolete theology and gone against the traditions of English history. Much that they wrote may now seem antiquated, narrow, superstitious, even childish : but their deep seriousness and the holiness and severity of their spiritual life were to be seen in daily intercourse as well as in the sermons which they preached and the writings which they put forth. No one could be in company with Keble and not feel the power of saintliness ; no one could hear Newman read the Lessons and preach in St. Mary's, and not be aware of a rare genius and a unique and intensely religious personality ; the excitable intellect of Froude was infused with the fire of religious conviction.

The character of all these men, in their various ways and according to their different temperaments, was one of the deepest and severest piety. Newman's self-repression, Keble's self-distrust, Froude's asceticism, Pusey's consistency rested upon a full and clear acceptance of revealed religion, the need

Common characteristics of the leaders.

of rigid self-discipline, fear of God in His judgment, complete submission to His will and obedience to His command. They had no love for the idea of freedom ; to obey was to them the highest happiness, and their tenderness of conscience was exercised by every means which could be suggested by love and fear. Their actions seemed arrogant, but only to those who did not know the depths of self-abasement, which they revealed to none. 'To these men,' says Dean Church, 'religion really meant the most awful and most seriously personal thing on earth'; and those who would understand the character of the Oxford Movement must read its history with this background. The 'serious governance of life' was among the most vital of their aims ; self-discipline, as the means to self-control ; the doctrine of humble obedience added to the emotion of the Evangelicals.

Dislike of their doctrines ought not to have blinded their liberal, latitudinarian, or evangelical opponents to the spiritual virtue which went out of them, and in time altered the face of the Church. If not their earnestness alone, for that is common in fanatics, yet the nobility and elevation of their characters, the high standard of their intelligence and education should have preserved them from misconception. But disputants in general misconceive or ignore the sincerity of their opponents : Arnold put himself out of court, when in his invectives against the 'Oxford Malignants' he made use of such expressions as 'moral wickedness,' 'the mingled fraud and baseness and cruelty of fanatical persecution,' 'a conscience so blinded by wilful neglect of the highest truth or so corrupted by the habitual indulgence of evil passions that it rather aggravates than excuses the guilt of those whom it misleads,' and so on.

Harshly judged by opponents.

The tractarian leaders—and we may add to the names mentioned above those of Hugh James Rose of Cambridge, Isaac Williams, William Palmer of Worcester College, Charles Marriott, Arthur Perceval, Robert and Henry Wilberforce, Thomas and James Mozley, and many more—were as much in earnest as the Evangelicals of a former generation, though their doctrine was of a different order, setting a higher value on worship than edification, on sacraments than preaching, on tradition than exegesis. All felt in

Other tractarian leaders.

their measure the same conviction which was felt so powerfully and expressed so eloquently by Newman, that they 'had a work to do.' They believed that God was employing them for His ends, and this was the foundation of their security and boldness; but at the same time they were not careless about the means; they employed the arts of rhetoric and the methods of party; and Newman in particular, as his correspondence shows, possessed and used the power of making other men work his way without compromising his own freedom. 'Newman's way,' says Isaac Williams, 'was to do things quickly and successfully.' Quick and successful action is for the most part single action; and to act alone requires confidence not only in one's powers but in one's convictions. This confidence was the outcome of a sincerity of conviction which brushed aside the scruples of weaker men, and sometimes alarmed even Keble. It is not given to every one to say 'if God be with us who can be against us?' Newman could say it, and carry into the service of God his natural advantages of boldness, ascendency, command, pride, sarcasm, irony, reserve, caution, and 'economy'; an unusual combination of party leader, enthusiast, poet, and saint.

It is usually said—Newman in his *Apologia* said it first—that Keble's sermon on 'National Apostasy,' preached at Oxford on July 14, 1833, was the starting-point of the Oxford Movement. As a matter of fact this was the match set to the pile: but as the growing volume of Liberal action in Church affairs seemed to culminate in the Irish Bishoprics Act of 1833, so the sermon of 1833 grew out of a settled feeling of sorrow and resentment, of which the first popular expression was *The Christian Year*; now comparatively little read, once almost as well known to church people as the Prayer Book itself. *The Christian Year*, published in 1827, *fons et origo*, as Newman called it, far more than the sermon of 1833, marked Keble out as the mouthpiece of that deeply-felt disapproval of the modern theories of religion and politics which are summed up in the word Liberalism. To Keble, as to Newman, liberalism was the latest device of the Devil, and one of the worst. *The Christian Year* was a protest against liberalism. It was not a polemical work. In its sincere serenity it

The Christian Year.

assumed the truth of the teaching which liberalism attacked, without adopting an attitude of defence. It claimed to teach *quod fuit ab initio*, not to trumpet a new creed or a new view; and by its great and immediate popularity and wide circulation it created its own atmosphere, and prepared churchmen to defend the doctrines which it set forth in a peculiarly attractive and endearing manner, by connecting them with the parochial and domestic religion of English church people. It was accepted as a guide by those of the High Church party who had watched events; it prepared those who were not entirely settled in opinion for resistance, and gave them what they had never had before, an *enchiridion* or weapon of war to be used against liberalism. The quiet church people of England had loved the Prayer Book, but had never understood that it meant any more than it said, or set forth a consistent scheme of religion. Henceforward they learnt that there

Its special value to church people.

was a unity in the Prayer Book, 'a sober standard of piety in matters of practical religion,' specially suited to the times, —'times of much leisure and unbounded curiosity'; they learnt the lesson of 'quietness and confidence'; they learnt that the old High Church tradition had more consistency than they had supposed, that it represented a theory of religion which only needed interpretation to become again a guide of life. In this gentle, mystical, rather obscure poetry there was a practical meaning, not only because of the sincerity of the writer, but because it pointed to a rule of life which could be followed. The book arose out of no settled intention; it did not 'furnish a complete series of compositions,' but it was written from the fulness of the heart; and the heart of English church people responded to it. The key-note of 'quietness and confidence' is struck in the Morning Hymn, which many simple Christians know by heart; lessons of seriousness, watchfulness, reverence, and purity are in every page. It is no easy religion that is here preached, as some may have judged from their knowledge of the tranquil and monotonous life led by Keble for so many years in his quiet Hampshire parsonage at Hursley; the spirit of *The Christian Year* is stern and uncompromising towards sin and error, deeply afflicted by the sorrows of the Church, as much impressed by fear as love. The poet's own natural gaiety of heart brightens all he writes; but no prophet of Israel was more profoundly conscious of the dark side of the picture, the fall of man and the need of penitence, discipline, and holy fear.

The Christian Year is a work of unequal merit, but never contemptible; it sometimes rises to a poetical height not unworthy of the saintly aspiration which breathes in every page. It is not easy for the present age to understand how it came about that a man like Keble, so fastidious and retiring as he was, and so inflexible in his religious and moral judgments of causes, actions, and persons, should have attained at once a popularity so great that he himself was pained and troubled by it; the more, because there was nothing common or *bourgeois* in his poetry. A writer of no great elevation of character may capture the popular ear by expressing something a little above or beyond that which the popular mind is thinking. Keble did more than this. He turned the minds of ordinary church people in the direction of his own thought, and showed them that there was the answer to their questions. *The Christian Year* is not sentimental, but it has its sentimental side; and probably it was the tone of quiet and serene sentiment that chiefly endeared it to the peaceful homes in which it was accepted as next in authority and spiritual power to the Prayer Book.

There is in *The Christian Year* no hint of ritual, no hankering after Roman doctrine, no exaggeration of sacramentalism. The response which it called out was evidence of a healthy condition in the Church, though not of great activity. Church people were taught the meaning of that neglected article of the Creed, 'the holy Catholic Church,' and the value of the Prayer Book; which, interpreted in the light of Church authority, apostolical succession, and the sacramental system, was brought into contrast with the views of both Evangelicals and Liberals. *The Christian Year* did more than any other book to create and spread abroad the tone of thought and religious feeling which the *Tracts for the Times* and Newman's Sermons put in more directly theological form. Keble was contented with the Prayer Book and the Church of England, and had no wish

Its place as poetry.

Its effect.

to search into its origins, or to revive mediæval usages which the Reformers (whom, however, he did not love) had abolished. It was enough for him that he could find all essential catholic truth in the Prayer Book, without inquiring how it came there. His temper of mind was conservative ; Newman and, still more, Froude were iconoclasts.

Another work, the influence of which tended in the same direction, and which was read by the same public, was *Lyra Apostolica*, published by Newman in November 1836. The poems now collected under this title had appeared from time to time in the *British Magazine*, and were already well known to all High Church-men. The collection contains some of Newman's most finished work : he speaks of having ' re-written some parts an incredible number of times.' Out of one hundred and seventy-nine poems, more than a hundred are Newman's (δ) ; of Keble's (γ) there are less than half that number ; about twenty-five are by other writers, Bowden (α), Froude (β), Robert Wilberforce (ε), and Isaac Williams (ξ). The note of severity which characterises the whole work, and is indeed the leading note sounded by the early ' Apostolicals,' is expressed by the well-known poem ' Liberalism ' (No. CIX.), to which Jehu and the golden calves in Bethel and Dan supply the heading.

Lyra Apostolica.

> Ye cannot halve the gospel of God's grace ;
>   Men of presumptuous heart ! I know you well.
>   Ye are of those who plan that we should dwell,
> Each in his tranquil home and holy place :
> Seeing the Word refines all natures rude,
> And tames the stirrings of the multitude.
>
> And ye have caught some echoes of its lore,
>   As heralded amid the joyous choirs ;
>   Ye heard it speak of peace, chastised desires,
> Good-will and mercy,—and ye heard no more ;
> But, as for zeal and quick-eyed sanctity,
> And the dread depths of grace, ye pass them by.
>
> And so ye halve the Truth ; for ye in heart,
>   At best, are doubters whether it be true,
>   The theme discarding, as unmeet for you,
> Statesmen or sages. O new-ventured art
> Of the ancient Foe !—but what if it extends
> O'er our own camp, and rules amid our friends ?

Political events showing the increased strength of Liberalism forced the Oxford brotherhood into publication. The evangelical party had been principally associated with philanthropic work of every kind, the High Churchmen had followed their lead, but timidly and suspiciously ; so far as the Evangelicals were political, they voted with the Whigs ; but both parties were united in opposition to Catholic emancipation. The latitudinarian and liberal clergy, among

The Liberal clergy.

whom Whately of Dublin, Arnold of Rugby, and Stanley of Norwich were eminent, were few in number, though powerful intellectually and in popular support. High Church and Low Church united their forces at Oxford in 1829 to resist Catholic emancipation. Peel, when the Duke of Wellington's Government adopted Catholic emancipation as part of their policy, resolved to relinquish the representation of the University of Oxford; and on February 4,

The Oxford Election, Sir Robert Inglis returned, 1829.

1829, he wrote to the Vice-Chancellor to announce this resolution. His supporters at Oxford, however, thought it right for the honour of the University to put him in nomination, and accordingly an election took place, resulting in the return of Sir Robert Inglis by a majority of 146 (20 February). 'Two-bottle orthodox men,' hot Evangelicals, and ascetic students of the Fathers found themselves unequally yoked on the same committees, pledged to turn out Peel from the representation of Oxford, though they might not all agree on the question of Catholic emancipation. The strength of the 'Apostolicals' lay not so much in their combination to resist the advance of liberalism as in their positive teaching. But a common dislike brings men together for a moment, and is a useful engine in party politics. In the politics of the moment was found the motive power, the call to unity, the division into two camps, the challenge to pronounce for one side or the other. The Oxford election stamped the 'apostolical' party as opponents of liberalism, it separated friends, and created new combinations. The question at issue, whatever the personal and party details might be, was understood by the High Churchmen of the new school to be one of principle, churchmanship against political dictation ; it was to prove 'the independence of the Church and of Oxford'; that is, the determination of the Church and of Oxford to take their own line, undisturbed by thoughts of political expediency. Catholic emancipation was but one step in the advance of liberalism from which the Oxford malcontents formally dissociated themselves, by refusing to re-elect Peel as member for the University. The Duke of Wellington resigned in 1830, and Lord Grey's Ministry brought in and carried the Reform Bill of 1832.

Henry Phillpotts, Bishop of Exeter, was the champion of the clergy in this quarrel, and his courageous if intemperate language was approved outside the walls of the House of Lords. Measures of reform are always a com- Bishop Phillpotts. promise ; the revolutionary party in England were displeased by the opposition of the Lords, and showed their displeasure by violence and outrage. Peace-loving English-men were reminded by these events that the first step towards Jacobinism in France had been taken within constitutional forms ; the overthrow of the old regime in France by the Revolution of July 1830, and the fury of the mob at Bristol, Nottingham, and other towns in 1831 taught the same lesson. These excesses were an irregular expression of the people's feeling, and could not be ignored : but they cast discredit on the doctrines of Bentham and Mill, which brought all authority into question and seemed to make doubt the principal intellectual virtue. Newman, writing of this time in his *Apologia*, says : 'I had fierce thoughts against the Liberals. It was the success of the Liberal cause which fretted me inwardly.'

One symptom of the Liberal success was the Irish Church Bill of 1833, by which church property was dealt with as if it belonged to the State, and the number of Irish Irish Church Bill, 1833. sees was reduced by amalgamation from eighteen to eight.[1] The High Church party saw in this legislation an Erastian attempt to claim for the State the right, not merely to dispose of temporalities, but to dictate to the Church in spiritual matters. They did not admit that the Crown granted jurisdiction, and denied the power of Par-liament to interfere with the election and consecration of bishops, though as a matter of history it was known that

[1] See p. 143.

Irish bishoprics were donatives of the Crown; and all the more because, since the Emancipation and Reform Acts, Parliament could no longer be considered to represent the Church. Such high ground as this was not taken in Parliament even by bishops or university members; but it was taken by the Oxford party, not solely on the ground that the Government proposed to apply church property to secular purposes, a proposal struck out of the bill in the course of debate, but that it was not competent to Parliament to legislate on ecclesiastical subjects, even in the interest of the Church, without the consent of the Church: and if Convocation was hardly mentioned in this connexion, it was only because Convocation was regarded by all parties as obsolete, even for the purpose of an argument from archæology.

AUTHORITIES. — Newman, *Apologia pro vita sua*; *Letters*, edited by Mozley; Church, *The Oxford Movement*; Coleridge, *Church and State*; Gladstone, *The Church . . . in its Relations with the State*; Palmer, *Narrative of Events*, etc. BIOGRAPHIES: *Isaac Williams* (Autobiography); *R. H. Froude*, by Guiney; *Memoirs of J. H. Rose* (from *British Magazine*); *Pusey*, by Liddon; *Newman*, by Hutton; *Keble*, by Coleridge and by Lock. Keble, Sermon on *National Apostasy*.

CHAPTER XII

'TRACTS FOR THE TIMES'

ON July 14, 1833, John Keble preached his celebrated Assize Sermon on 'National Apostasy' in view of impending danger; and in the preface to the sermon, published at the same time, he writes, 'Since the following pages were prepared for the press, the calamity, in anticipation of which they were written, has actually *Keble's Assize Sermon, 1833.* overtaken this portion of the Church of God. The Legislature of England and Ireland (*the members of which are not even bound to profess belief in the Atonement*) this body has virtually usurped the commission of those whom our Saviour entrusted with *at least one voice* in making ecclesiastical laws, as matters wholly or partly spiritual.' Henceforward the apostolical Church established in this kingdom was in the eye of the State no more than 'one sect among many.' He spoke of the growing indifference to other men's opinions; 'the supposed decay of what they call an exclusive system'; neglect of voluntary oaths; disrespect to the successors of the Apostles. The natural tendency of the course of action now begun by the State with infringement of apostolical rights, would end, he prophesied, in persecution of the true Church under colour of toleration, State security, and sympathy with popular feeling. That Parliament should act in this way is considered by the preacher as a 'direct disavowal of the sovereignty of God,' and its acceptance by the country as an act of National Apostasy; and the question is raised, 'How are good Churchmen to regard the position of, consequently their connexion with, a Church whose Government

is now avowedly Erastian?' The answer is, by 'earnest inter-
cession with God, grave, respectful, affectionate remonstrance
with the misguided man himself.'

'National Apostasy' may seem a hard name for the
acquiescence of the nation in a parliamentary measure which

'National
Apostasy.'
applied to ecclesiastical purposes revenue hitherto
appropriated to the families of prelates. But no
consideration of expediency and no historical
precedent had force with Keble and those who thought with
him. They held the Church to be a divine institution, the
government of which, though it might be associated with
the State, belonged to the clergy, of divine right and by
apostolical succession, and was independent of the State;
association with the State might be matter of convenience and
expediency, but could not touch the question of authority.
Arbitrary action in the past could not create a precedent, and
the spiritual authority usurped and exercised by the Papacy
must revert to the clergy, not to the Crown; the root of
the evil was in the Act of Catholic emancipation, which
strengthened Romanism at the expense of the Church of
England, and in the Reform Act, which gave legislative
power to a class containing a large proportion of Dissenters.
Mischief was done, and more would be done, for the bad
principle was still at work. Friends of the Church must
bestir themselves to resist it. The clergy and laity must be
instructed in right doctrine, and a check put upon anti-church
legislation.

In December 1832 Newman left England in company with
Froude, whose health was already broken, and with him spent
some months in the south of Europe. They were at Rome
together, and Newman, like Luther, was repelled by what he
saw there. Newman visited Sicily alone, and fell dangerously
ill of a fever, in the fits of which he continually repeated, 'I
shall not die, I have a work to do.' He returned from his
Italian journey on July 9, 1833, a few days before Keble's

Newman's
return to
Oxford.
sermon was preached, and saw that the hour was
come. He was 'a man who would set well at the
mark'; a leader, not a follower, nor to any great
extent a co-operator. He came back to England filled
with a new vigour of body and mind, and with an exaltation

of spirit which belongs to a man who is conscious of a mission—

Hope elevated, and joy
Brightened his crest.

He says in the *Apologia* : 'My health and strength came back to me with such a rebound, that some friends at Oxford, on seeing me, did not well know that it was I, and hesitated before they spoke to me.   And I had the consciousness that I was employed in that work which I had been dreaming about, and which I felt to be so momentous and inspiring.   I had a supreme confidence in our cause.'   He felt himself possessed by a prophetical fire ; he was the chosen leader to deliver the Church of England from Reformation bondage, the zealous and passionate Froude was his Joshua ; the aims of ordinary men, their compromises and half-measures, their formulas and articles of association seemed to him petty and insufficient, though at the same time he was willing to use the carnal weapons of controversy and combination.   Newman was never more himself than at this moment ; ardent, subtle, vigilant, dangerous ; always keeping his own hand and foot clear of entanglement ; though willing to adopt and use the ideas of others, he would not be bound by rules of associations or the vote of a majority ; he was willing to work with others on conditions of freedom, in sympathy but not under control.

On his arrival in England he found a league already forming, not by his means, but in God's providence for him ; the wood was laid in order, waiting for the fire.   Such thoughts as these must have been in his mind, allying themselves with his strong personal dominancy, an element in his character akin to pride, but controlled by the humility which all through his life he imposed upon himself, and which fitted into his frame of action by leading him to look upon himself as an instrument in the hand of God.   Keble, says Church, 'had given the inspiration, Froude had given the impulse, then Newman took up the work, and the impulse thenceforward and the direction were his.'

Keble's Assize Sermon kindled the flame.   Froude and William Palmer of Worcester, who were in Oxford at the time, and constantly meeting in the Common Room at Oriel, came to the conclusion that it was necessary 'to unite and associate . . . in defence of the Church, of her violated liberties and neglected principles.' Froude applied for advice and approval to Keble, and Palmer consulted Hugh James Rose, Rector of Hadleigh in Suffolk, then Christian Advocate at Cambridge, a powerful preacher and a man of weight and dignity, and of strong and noble personal character. It was arranged, on invitation from him, that Keble, Newman, Arthur Perceval of All Souls, and Palmer should go to Hadleigh as the guests of the Rector, and hold a conference. The conference was held, but neither Keble nor Newman attended it. 'It afterwards appeared,' says Palmer, 'that Newman and Keble had no confidence in meetings or committees'; Keble, with all his boldness, was never rash, and would do nothing without episcopal sanction; and Newman's habit was to act for himself. Froude, Perceval, and Palmer spent some days at Hadleigh at the end of July, and agreed that combined action was desirable, as well as the circulation of publications on ecclesiastical subjects. They did not, however, formulate any specific plan of action, or come to a clear understanding among themselves. 'The Hadleighans could not agree,' wrote Keble in August; and Newman,—'I fear they did not get on very well at Hadleigh'; but the meeting was not unfruitful.

The meeting at Hadleigh, 1833.

Rose's connexion with the first stage of the movement ends here. He went down to Durham to take up his professorship there, and his failing health and consequent exile from England prevented him from taking an active part in what its enemies called a conspiracy against the Protestant religion, and its promoters a combination in defence of the Church; though indeed the friends among themselves familiarly used the word 'conspiracy.' Rose died in January 1839.

Death of Hugh James Rose, 1839.

The following extract from one of Newman's letters shows his relation to the movement at this stage of progress, and may therefore find place here. He writes to Keble on August 5, 1833: 'Do you not think we should act in concert, as nearly in the way of a Society as possible? *i.e.* to take measures for the circulation of tracts, pamphlets, etc., and to write systematically to stir up our friends.'

Palmer and Froude on their return to Oxford, and after much discussion with Newman and Keble, decided on the terms of an Association of 'Friends of the Church,' (1) 'to maintain pure and inviolate the doctrines, the services, and the discipline of the Church; that is, to withstand all change which involves the Association of 'Friends of the Church,' 1833. denial and suppression of doctrine, or innovation upon the apostolical prerogatives, order, and commission of bishops, priests, and deacons.' (2) 'To afford Churchmen an opportunity of exchanging their sentiments, and co-operating together on a large scale.'

A few days later, August 14, Froude wrote to Perceval, 'Since I have been back to Oxford, Keble has been here, and he [Palmer] and Newman have come to an agreement that the points which ought to be put forward by us are the following:—

'The doctrine of apostolical succession as a rule of practice; *i.e.* (1) that the participation of the Body and Blood of Christ is essential to the maintenance of Christian life and hope in each individual; (2) that it is conveyed to individual Christians *only* by Doctrine of apostolical succession. the hands of the successors of the Apostles and their delegates; (3) that the successors of the Apostles are those who are descended in a direct line from them by the imposition of hands; and that the delegates of these are the respective presbyters whom each has commissioned.'

This doctrine occupies so important a place in the tractarian armoury that it is desirable to examine it rather closely. It was put forward by the Oriel friends as their chief weapon. Their intention was to exalt the Church, to lay stress on the superiority of corporate to individual religion. To disparage private judgment and to refer all doctrine to authority was the best way, as it was the truest way, to repel the attacks of latitudinarian and infidel opinion, whether delivered by open enemies, as the followers of James Mill and Bentham, or by foes within the camp like Hampden, Arnold, and perhaps Whately.

The doctrine of apostolical succession, then, as taught by the Oxford school, is this: that when Christ established the Church He committed its government to the Apostles, giving them power to ordain others. The Apostles ordained the seven deacons, and consecrated St. James Bishop of Jerusalem. Paul and Barnabas, Timothy and Titus were bishops, and had authority to ordain priests and deacons. This order, founded by Christ Himself, and continued by the Apostles under His direction, has existed from the beginning, and only those who are duly appointed under it have power and authority to consecrate and administer the Sacraments, through which the whole life of the Church is communicated.

The opposite contention is clear enough. No one would deduce from the Bible alone the doctrine of an exclusive episcopal succession. Granted that our Lord's commission to the Apostles included the perpetual ministry, and that this was conferred only by imposition of hands, there is nothing in the Bible which limits the rights and duties of particular churches to an episcopal succession. There must be an inward call and an outward commission from the rulers or elders of the church or congregation; but it cannot be certainly proved from Scripture that these elders were a separate class, a clergy as opposed to the laity; nor that there was an essential difference between elders and overseers, as between priests and bishops; nor that there was any universal and indispensable manner of appointment. The rejoinder is by an appeal to tradition. If Scripture is infallible, the canon of Scripture was settled by tradition, and its infallibility depends upon the infallibility of the authority which created the tradition in virtue of which it is received; the only escape from this argument is by supposing the Apostles and Evangelists alone to be inspired; and this is an assumption not upheld by the history of the Church. All parties agree in giving value to tradition; but Rome finds in Church tradition an infallible guide, Protestantism a guide to interpretation both of doctrine and history, but not an infallible guide. The argument for church authority, as against biblical authority or latitudinarianism, was clearly and forcibly drawn out by Newman in Tract 85 ('Five Lectures'), one of the most powerful and closely written of the series. The writer's conclusion is that there is no escape from the intellectual difficulties of the Bible but in acceptance of the church system. The burden

of proof lies on the objectors.   Thus the doctrine of tradition
was closely interwoven with that of apostolical succession,
and Keble's sermon on Primitive Tradition, preached on
September 27, 1836, may come under review here, as containing the mature tenets of the High Church party formulated
after some years of hot controversy.

In this sermon Keble expresses the view that the
παρακαταθήκη (1 Tim. vi. 20), a word which is translated by
the Vulgate *depositum*, and by the English translators
'that which is committed to thee,' was a body of
doctrine, not a pastoral charge.   So the Thes-
salonians are charged to keep traditions (παραδόσεις)
at a time when in all probability no part of the New Testament
was written down.   So also the Fathers 'refer to the tradition
of the Church as to something independent of the written
word, and sufficient at that time to refute heresy, even alone.'
Church tradition is parallel to Scripture, not derived from it ;
sin against tradition is the same kind of sin as sin against the
New Testament.   God's unwritten word, if it can be by any
means authenticated, 'must necessarily demand the same
reverence from us ; and for exactly the same reason : *because
it is His word.*'   The true conception of Church tradition
will discourage 'every intrusion of speculative doctrine' and
novelty in religion, all attempt to treat theology like any
human science, and look for development and advance in
it.   He finds fault with 'the growing Nominalism of our
days'; a blow aimed at Hampden, who had praised the
mediæval Nominalists, nominalism being to Keble a synonym
for liberalism.

Keble's
sermon on
Primitive
Tradition,
1836.

Once admit the authority of tradition to a place side by
side with that of Scripture, and apostolical succession is made
so probable that it may easily be accepted, first as a fact,
and then as a doctrine.   The latter tenet was a useful engine
against Latitudinarians and Dissenters ; the doctrine of tradition, which lay behind it, was a more dangerous weapon to
handle, and it broke in Newman's hand.   The doctrines of
apostolical succession and concurrent tradition necessarily drew
the Church of England nearer to Rome, and further from
Geneva and Germany.   Outside the churches which have their
succession direct from the Apostles, though grace may be given,

it is not by covenant, and those Christians who have not the suc-

Anglicans and Protestants.

cession are outside the Church. The high Anglican thus looks upon the Protestant Dissenter in the same way as he himself is regarded by the Romanist, so far as Orders are concerned. It is one thing to enact, whether for the sake of validity of ordination or for decency, discipline, and avoidance of dispute (*legitime, recte, ordine,* as Jewell says), that the Anglican Ordinal shall be required in all cases which come under the Act of Uniformity of 1662 ; it is another to deny the validity of all other Orders, and break the common bond of Protestantism and the historical unity of the revolt from Rome. The latter, however, was what the Tractarians deliberately intended : Froude's letters are full of it ; Newman's journey in the South made him see Catholicism in a new light ; Pusey came back from Germany with gloomy views of the state of Christianity in Evangelical and Lutheran lands ; Keble formulated the statement that sacramental grace in the Eucharist is conveyed to the individual Christian only by the hands of the successors of the Apostles and their delegates. The whole tendency of the party was to dissociate the Church from sympathy with the early Reformers and their traditions, and repudiate the idea of a common Protestant cause, such as was acknowledged by Charles I. and Laud, who died with the word 'Protestant' on their lips.

The next step was to circulate an address, for presentation from the clergy to the Archbishop of Canterbury, expressing

Address to the Archbishop of Canterbury, 1834.

in general terms the assurance of their 'devoted adherence to the apostolical doctrine and polity' of the Church of England, and their confidence in the episcopate in any action which might be required to revive discipline, to strengthen the connexion between clergy and laity, and to promote the purity, the efficiency, and the unity of the Church. This address, drawn up by Palmer, was presented to the Archbishop in February 1834, with the signatures of 7000 clergymen. It was characterised by a supporter of the movement as 'the greatest victory that has been achieved since the battle of Waterloo.' The address was followed up by a declaration of the laity expressing attachment to the Church and uncompromising support of the policy of Church Defence ; no pains were spared to circulate

the declaration in every part of the country ; and it was
signed by 230,000 heads of families.

William Palmer, the author of the *Narrative of Events
connected with the Publication of Tracts for the Times*, published in 1843, tells us that this action caused
some misapprehension and jealousy, partly on the
ground of the actors' youth ; and it may be noted
that of the five men who took up so weighty a responsibility,
the eldest, John Keble, was not more than forty-one.   For
such actions young men are required : but it is unusual to
find youth engaged on the side of orthodoxy and conservatism, and opposing the general trend of contemporary
thought.   With all their learning and piety, Froude, Keble,
and Pusey could not have carried the world with them.   Only
the genius of Newman could make retrograde notions seem
beautiful, even at the moment of emancipation and reform,
and thirty years later give fresh force and vitality through
the *Apologia* to a system of theology which he himself had
discarded.

Palmer's Narrative, 1843.

Of the two methods of action put forward by the band of
Oxford friends, who in time came to be known by the name
of 'Tractarians,' and who among themselves used
that of 'Apostolicals,' the first was to form an Association of Friends of the Church, and the second
to issue individual Tracts without more than a general agreement and responsibility.   Newman preferred the latter method,
and took pains to keep the Tracts separate from the Association.   He had no faith in action by a vote of a majority,
and he had confidence in himself.   The Association came to
little.   The Tracts came to much.   He writes from Oxford,
on August 31, 1833 : 'We have set up societies over the
kingdom in defence of the Church. . . . We do not like our
names known.   You may say as much as you will to any
one about the fact of the societies and their object.   They
are already started (in germ) in Oxfordshire, Devonshire,
Gloucestershire, Berks, Suffolk, and Kent ; the object being
"to make the clergy alive to their situation, to enforce the
apostolical succession, and to defend the Liturgy."   We
mean to publish and circulate tracts.   I have started with
four. . . . I am pleased to find we are called enthusiasts—

Tracts for the Times, 1833.

pleased, for when did a cause which could be so designated fail of success?'

The *Tracts for the Times*, the first of which was published in September 1833, were Newman's work. Though they were anonymous, and at the same time issued each by its author, without any joint responsibility, it was no secret that Newman was their prime mover and also the chief contributor. His was the design and his the execution: his temper of mind was the inspiring genius, zeal against modern thought and the danger to religion which came with it. The form in which this danger appeared was the secularisation of the Church and the alteration of the Prayer Book in a latitudinarian sense, by authority of Parliament. The doctrines chiefly insisted upon in the Tracts were those of apostolical succession and sacramental grace, in opposition to the evangelical theories of conversion by means of prayer and preaching. The first Tract, 'respectfully addressed to the

Newman's Tract 1, 'to the Clergy.'

Clergy,' strikes this note at once: cold, austere, and unrhetorical in form, it calls upon the clergy for seriousness and unworldliness, and a just view of their commission. Not without irony, when we consider the episcopate of that day, and the condition of the clergy in general, the anonymous but not unknown author calls upon the priesthood to be shield-bearer to the bishops, and to stand by them even if it came to the spoiling of the bishops' goods, and their martyrdom; not to rest upon 'that secular respectability, or cultivation, or polish, or learning, or rank, which gave them a hearing with the many'; to put away the notion 'that present palpable usefulness, produceable results, acceptableness to their flocks,' are a test of their divine commission. The Tract is intolerant, exclusive, uncompromising; as designedly provocative as Keble's sermon; and pointing, though by a different road, to the same result, the exaltation of the kingdom of God through the spiritualising of the Church.

A modern reader finds this Tract cold and unimpressive, and wonders why it was found to be so effective. Tracts and articles were fewer seventy-five years ago than now, and much was read then which would now be thought unreadable: but the first Tract must always have been repellent to many who read it. It attracted attention by its matter, not its

(margin note: Doctrines)

manner, though when it is read carefully we see that not a
word is wasted nor a point missed. The matter was a deliberate assault upon all that was conventional in the Church,
an appeal to ages of superstition, asceticism, and intolerance,
in full agreement with its author's conviction, a conviction
expressed in similar words by Keble also, 'that it would be
a gain to this country, were it vastly more superstitious, more
bigoted, more gloomy, more fierce in its religion, than at
present it shows itself to be.'

The sermon from which these words are taken is entitled
'The Religion of the Day,' and words could not have
been better chosen to express the principle put Keble's
sermon, 'The
forward by the writers of the Tracts, which was to Religion of
the Day.'
set up against the religion of the day the religion
of other days as they conceived it. The religion of the day
had forgotten ancient doctrine, they brought a reminder of
Christian antiquity; the religion of the day had lost faith
in the apostolical succession, they exalted the apostolical
succession to a high place in doctrine; the religion of the day
ignored the Fathers and the Councils, and cared nothing for
tradition, they put the authority of tradition, interpreted by
the Fathers, the prophets of the new dispensation, side by
side with that of Scripture; the religion of the day, as
represented by the Church of England, had submitted to the
yoke of the State, they upheld the Church as a divine
institution independent of the State; the religion of the day
held no clear course between Rome and the Protestantism
of the reformed Church, they drew a strong line between
episcopal and non-episcopal communities; the religion of the
day looked back no further than to the Elizabethan settlement, they appealed to Pentecost and the first Pontificate and
primitive Councils; the religion of the day was content with
compromises, and considered what was practical, they abhorred
compromise and preached first principles. The times, for
which they wrote, were against them; but they represented
union against division, clearness against confusion, conviction
against doubt; and they succeeded. Other writers, Keble
and his brother Thomas, Pusey, Isaac Williams, Froude, and
Bowden, contributed to the Tracts, but the voice of all was
Newman's voice.

There was also present another, and, according to Church, Shairp, and James Mozley, a more powerful influence, certainly a more intimate and inspiring influence, that of the sermons which Newman preached at four o'clock on Sunday afternoons at the University Church of St. Mary the Virgin, of which he was Vicar. 'The world knows them,' writes Dean Church, 'has heard a great deal about them, has passed its various judgments on them. But it hardly realises that without those sermons the movement might never have gone on, certainly would never have been what it was. Even people who heard them continually, and felt them to be different from any other sermons, hardly estimated their real power, or knew at the time the influence which the sermons were having upon them. . . . They made men think of the things which the preacher spoke of, and not of the sermons or the preacher.' Those who heard the sermons speak of the quiet remote manner, the absence of action, or even modulation of a voice which had great range and sweetness, the intense earnestness which communicated something of itself to all who heard him. There are no sermons like them, even to read; but what must they have been to hear, when every word was like a deed, charged with the intellectual power and personal character of the speaker. 'While men were reading and talking about the Tracts,' writes Dean Church, 'they were hearing the sermons; and in the sermons they heard the living meaning, and reason, and bearing of the Tracts, their ethical affinities, their moral standard. The sermons created a moral atmosphere, in which men judged the questions in debate.' The *Parochial and Plain Sermons* are still read. *Cor ad cor loquitur* was Newman's heraldic motto; and no religious writer has known the human heart more intimately, or judged it with more experience and charity.

Newman followed up the argument of Tract No. 1 by applying it to practical politics in Tract No. 2, 'The Catholic Church.' Is the State the Church? has the State a right to create a clergy, send forth missionaries, arrange dioceses? The Article of 'the Holy Catholic Church' was in the Creed from the beginning. It cannot be only an assertion that there is a number of sincere Christians scattered through the world; for why should such a truism 'be placed as an article of faith, after the belief in the Holy Ghost? Doubtless the only true and satisfactory meaning is that which our divines have ever taken, that there is on earth an existing society, apostolic as founded by the Apostles, catholic because it spreads its branches in every place; *i.e.* the Church Visible, with its bishops, priests, and deacons'; to belong to which is the only way to eternal life. 'It is,' says the writer of the Tract, 'the unanimous opinion of our divines, that, as the Sacraments, so communion with the Church is "generally necessary to salvation" in the case of those who can obtain it.' Thus the result of the dogma of apostolical succession is to invalidate the power of the State in matters of religion, and to deny to all Christian bodies not episcopally governed communion with the Church of Christ. Tract No. 2 was a defiance to the civil power and to the evangelical and latitudinarian sections of the Church. So it was meant, and so it was understood.

'The early tracts,' says Church, 'were intended to startle the world, and they succeeded in doing so.' He remarks that such productions were unusual as coming from 'distinguished University scholars, picked men of a picked college; and from men, too, who as a school were the representatives of soberness and self-control in religious feeling and language.' They were an appeal to Anglicanism against liberalism. There were hopeful and ambitious theological Liberals, who recognised in that appeal to Anglicanism the most effective counterstroke to their own theology and policy; Arnold, for instance, wrote to Pusey, 'I fear you are lending your co-operation to a party second to none in the tendency of their principles to overthrow the truth of the Gospel. . . . I stand amazed at some apparent efforts in this Protestant Church to set up the idol of tradition.'

Tract No. 3, also by Newman, is directed against all attempts to get the Liturgy altered; on the ground that few would be pleased and many pained, that alterations would open the door to criticism and scepticism, *Tract No. 3, on alterations* would extend from non-essentials to essentials, and *in the* this to please objectors who disliked the doctrine *Liturgy.* rather than the form of the Liturgy. 'In a day like this,' he goes on, 'there are but two sides, zeal and persecution, the Church and the world; and those who attempt to occupy the ground between them at best will lose their labour, but probably will be drawn back to the latter.   Be practical, I respectfully urge you.'   In these words is the expression of their writer's character.   He would have no compromise, no lukewarm followers.   He did not seek for leadership, but he accepted it joyfully, with all its dangers and responsibilities, including, as he was soon to feel, the charge of inconsistency and apostasy.

Newman did 9.

Of the twenty Tracts published in 1834, nine were written by Newman.   All were anonymous, but their authorship was not kept secret; and Newman's handiwork, though he had not as yet attained the fulness of that style which puts him among the masters of English, must have been evident to intelligent readers.   The Tracts aimed at plainness of style, and were addressed, some *ad populum*, some *ad clerum*, but not to the specially learned.   They drew attention to the duty of fasting, to the importance of primitive doctrine and early church history, but above all to the dignity of the sacred office of bishops and priests, and to their apostolical commission.

The trumpet had been blown with no uncertain note.   In his anonymous preface to the series of Tracts, Newman admonished his brethren in the sacred ministry that the times were very evil, and that it was time to unlearn 'that idle habit which has grown upon us, of owning the state of things to be bad, yet doing nothing to remedy it.'   The attack which followed was rapid, open, and unreserved.   The doctrines of the apostolical succession, of baptism, of the eucharist were set forth in unhesitating terms.   Dissent, interpretation of Scripture, fasting, prayers for the dead, the controversy with Rome, rationalism in religion, daily prayers in church, were successively treated; in all, the teaching of the primitive Church and of the Anglican Fathers was appealed to, and large extracts from authorities were compiled.   Eighteenth-century doctrine and practice were exploded, and the nineteenth century was bidden go back to learn of the Caroline divines and the Fathers from whom they had learnt.

[margin note: Newman's preface to the Tracts, 1833.]

The end of the year 1833 was marked by the accession to the tractarian company of Pusey, one of the most learned of Oxford theologians, a man of wealth and good family, honoured by all for his good life and liberality. Pusey, though he said 'I will not be one of you,' printed his initials at the foot of the Tract on Fasting (No. 18), which he contributed to the series on St. Thomas's Day, December 21, 1833. The Tract was published in January 1834, with his initials. 'He at once,' says Newman, 'gave to us a position and a name. Dr. Pusey was a Professor and Canon of Christ Church, he had a vast influence in consequence of his deep religious seriousness, the munificence of his charities, his professorship, his family connexions, and his easy relations with university authorities. . . . In 1829 Mr. Froude, or Mr. R. Wilberforce, or Mr. Newman were but individuals ; . . . but Dr. Pusey was, to use the common expression, a host in himself, he was able to give a name, a form, and a personality to what was without him a sort of mob. . . . He was a man of large designs ; he had a hopeful, sanguine mind ; he had no fear of others ; he was haunted by no intellectual perplexities. . . . If confidence in his position is (as it is) a first essential in the leader of a party, Dr. Pusey had it.'

Dr. Pusey's adhesion to the tractarian movement.

Such language from Newman, applied to a person only a year older than himself, and his inferior in almost all respects except learning and university position, may seem overstrained, almost ironical. But Newman was no flatterer ; his common name for Pusey was ὁ μέγας. He may, from modesty, self-imposed humility, or chivalrous conviction, have overstated it : the world's imagination settles upon the shining figures like himself, and rightly, for they can inspire as well as guide ; but Pusey's adhesion unquestionably gave stability and coherence to the party, which, like all newly-formed parties, was in danger from partial views and hot-headed projects. Pusey's gravity and the ascetic piety of himself and his household impressed all who knew him, even Newman. 'Pusey's presence,' says Isaac Williams, 'always checked Newman's lighter and unrestrained mood.' He could be relied upon to give the movement the weight of his learning and character ;

Pusey and Newman.

he did not willingly enter into controversy, though he sometimes provoked it; he had none of the nimbleness or the
'fierceness' of Newman, but the confidence which he inspired
helped to defend the Tractarians against the imputation of
Romanising. Pusey and Keble never wavered, but maintained
to the end the *via media* doctrine with which the movement
began. As far as this point, at any rate, the anti-Roman
note is clearly sounded by Newman too. The following
expressions, taken from No. 20, would have satisfied Simeon
himself. After speaking of 'the papistical corruptions of the
Gospel,' he continues, 'Truly, when one surveys the grandeur
of their system, a sigh arises in the thoughtful mind, to think
that we should be separate from them; *cum talis sis, utinam
noster esses*! But, alas, AN UNION IS IMPOSSIBLE. Their communion is infected with heterodoxy; we are bound to flee it,
as a pestilence. They have established a lie in the place of
God's truth; and, by their claim of immutability in doctrine,
cannot undo the sin they have committed. They cannot
repent. Popery must be destroyed; it cannot be reformed.'

The use of the term 'Puseyite,' which may seem almost a
misnomer, since the Oxford Movement owed its inception not
to Pusey but to Keble and Newman, may be accounted for
by two considerations: first, the fact that Pusey's official
position at Oxford, the acknowledged centre of the movement, as well as his personal character, directed attention
to him; and secondly, after some years had passed,
the gradual retirement of Newman from Oriel. He left
his college rooms in 1842 and migrated with a few disciples, Bowles, Stanton, Dalgairns, and St. John, to some
cottages which he had fitted up at Littlemore near Iffley as a
religious retreat, a μονή, as he called it; thus, as it were,
abdicating the leadership of the party. Pusey was at as little
pains to take the lead as Keble himself, whom he resembled
in the definiteness of his opinions, and the courage with
which he expressed them, as well as in humility and self-
distrust. Nor indeed was he well fitted to take the lead.
He was a student, not a man of business; he was not
always in the front of progress; he had not much practical
foresight, so as to judge of the tendency of events, as
appeared in the events connected with St. Saviour's, Leeds,

the Jerusalem bishopric, and the publication of Tract 90, matters which will be treated in later chapters; or of the mutual action of doctrine and practice, as in the case of ritual observance; and his want of discretion on some occasions in connexion with conventual institutions brought him into undeserved discredit.   He would take a first view and act upon it, and cause embarrassment to his friends when he saw reason to change his mind.   In some cases, where Pusey was found fault with by both parties, he was really consistent, and displayed both firmness and generosity.   He was not a man of extraordinary wisdom, nor of extraordinary power of mind; but he had great tenacity of purpose, a most tender conscience, and a single-hearted piety in which there was no guile.   He could be impulsive and rash, when it was a question of action, but he could also be determined, when it was a question of belief.   He was always ready to be appealed to on questions of history and doctrine, he accepted the responsibility which attends learning, and gave his opinion maturely and decisively.   When he saw he saw clearly, and no considerations of diplomacy or self-interest prevailed to warp his honesty and fearlessness.   He held back at the very beginning, and let others show the way.   Other men originated ideas and methods of action, but brought them to Pusey for ratification.   He accepted what he did not invent, and he was a firm supporter of what he had once accepted.   His 'immovably conservative theology,' whilst going great lengths towards Rome, was inflexibly limited; and the certainty of this made him trusted, as the influence of his holy life made him venerated.   When the time of separation came, no one that knew Pusey thought he would follow Newman and Manning to Rome; as long as he and Keble held together, and they were never parted, the road to Rome was barred.   The weak side of his character leant to superstition and an exaggerated asceticism, in which, however, there was no censoriousness nor gloom.   His home was cheerful, and he was beloved by children.

The Tracts changed their character when Pusey joined the party.   The earlier numbers had been intended to rouse, alarm, and irritate; they were short stirring appeals, addressed to Churchmen generally.   They now aimed more definitely at instruction, especially the instruction of the clergy, and became long and learned treatises. It was never the intention of the tractarian leaders to make things easy and smooth over differences. Froude, always in extremes, wanted to make 'a blow-up': his object was 'to dictate to the clergy of this country,' to attract attention and provoke opposition.

The first volume of Tracts, forty-seven in number, was published in November 1834, 'with the object of contributing something towards the practical revival of doctrines, which, although held by the great divines of our Church, at present have become obsolete with the majority of her members, and are withdrawn from public view even by the more learned and orthodox few who still adhere to them.'

Five more volumes followed, the second in November 1835, containing Nos. 48 to 70. In the preface to the third volume, issued in 1836, the editors say that the first Tracts 'were written with the hope of rousing members of our Church to comprehend her alarming position . . . they were written, as a man might give notice of a fire or inundation, to startle all who heard him . . . to infuse seriousness into the indifferent. . . . Now, however, discussion became more seasonable than the simple statements of doctrine with which the series began; and their character accordingly changed.' The editors therefore added to the Tracts treatises by Anglo-Catholic divines, and 'Records of the Church, consisting of patristic works, such as Cyprian *On the Unity of the Church*, and Vincent of Lerins *On the Tests of Heresy*. They also inserted a *Catena Patrum*, select passages from the Fathers and from Anglican divines explaining or elucidating points of doctrine; forms of prayer, such as those in the Breviary, and the private devotions of Bishop Andrewes, translated by Newman; and treatises on formal theology.

For the clergy rather than the laity were intended such Tracts as that of Pusey on 'Baptismal Regeneration' (1835), of Isaac Williams on 'Reserve in communicating Religious Knowledge' (1838), and of Keble on the 'Mysticism of the Fathers' (1838). To the same period belong also Newman's *Prophetical*

Office (1837) and *Lectures on Justification* (1838). Froude's *Remains* appeared in February 1838; Pusey's Letter to the Bishop of Oxford a year later. These publications instructed the clergy, but alarmed them too. A sense of insecurity was in the air, especially as to the attitude of the writers towards Rome. Accusations of disingenuousness began to be made. Williams's Tract was, in Church's words, 'like the explosion of a mine.' 'The word "Reserve" was enough. It meant . . . that the real spirit of the party was disclosed; its love of secret and crooked methods, its indifference to knowledge, its disingenuous professions . . . its *disciplina arcani*, its conspiracies, its Jesuitical spirit.' Though these accusations were unjust, there was some colour for them. Newman's denunciations of Rome did not conceal the fact that the tractarian party contained 'a Romanising section,' and that Newman was beginning to lend an ear to what might be said in favour of Rome; though at the same time he was 'saying hard things against Rome,' even collecting such sayings, as he tells us in the *Apologia*, and publishing them with the advertisements of the Tracts.

The Tractarians had two strong points in their favour. They had men of the first rank as spokesmen, Newman, Pusey, and Keble, and they knew their own mind; whereas, of their chief opponents, Hampden was clumsy, Arnold was thought to lack stability of conviction, Thirlwall had no love of controversy, Whately had other interests; all were living away from Oxford, the focus of heat and the chosen battle-ground of opinion; and it would have been difficult to find a formula to include all their views in one. They were good for attack, not for defence; for pulling down, not for building up; it was an unexpected turn of events which put the defenders of antiquity in the position of innovators, and left the defence of established conventions in the hands of Liberal politicians credited with latitudinarian opinions. The Tractarians shared the interest of the world with the Utilitarians and the Romantics. The Tracts, the *Westminster Review*, and 'Useful Knowledge' publications, and the Romantic literature represented three different tendencies of thought and sentiment, all interesting to young men, all dissociated from one another, all destined to unforeseen development. The very extravagance of the opinions put forward in the Tracts made them popular. Here, at all events, was clear statement and hot religious zeal.

From the centre at Oxford the cry went out into the whole country. 'It is hardly too much to say that wherever men spoke seriously of the grounds and prospects of religion, in Oxford or in vacation reading parties, in their walks and social meetings, in their studies or in common room, the "tractarian" doctrines, whether assented to or laughed at, deplored or fiercely denounced, were sure to come to the front. All subjects in discussion seemed to lead up to them.' When Dean Church says this, he is speaking as one who was an undergraduate at the time, and his evidence is of the highest interest; but what he says of Oxford was true in its degree of London also, and not of London only, but of country places far remote from Oxford, untouched by Hampden controversies and appointments to bishoprics and professorial chairs. This response to views which seemed extravagant and chimerical as well as dangerous was indeed, in Newman's words, 'the result of causes far deeper than political or other visible agencies, the spiritual awaking of spiritual wants.' Throughout the country *The Christian Year*, the *Plain Sermons* set in circulation by Isaac Williams, Newman's sermons and lectures, the *Library of the Fathers*, Froude's *Remains*, and the Tracts themselves were doing their work among the clergy, and a new generation of laymen was rising, among whom Gladstone, James Hope and Beresford Hope were eminent. The clergy learnt from the 'apostolical' teaching a new conception of their office and position. They began to adopt a new style of dress and speech, and entered less freely into mixed society. The humdrum age of weekly services and occasional communions was passing away; daily services and weekly celebrations became common; the Cross was no longer looked upon as a popish symbol. Antiquarianism now joined hands with theology; William Gresley of Lichfield, and his neighbour Francis Paget, Rector of Elford, and other writers, and from another point of view Pugin, the Oxford Architectural Society, and the Cambridge Camden Society drew attention to the neglected state of cathedrals and parish churches, and attempts at 'restoration'

[margin note: Spread of the movement.]

Architectural effect

began to be made.   The 'Gothic Revival' began, with all that
was implied in it.

Political events came quickly on in these years ; it was the
time of public attacks upon tithes and church rates ; the Irish
appropriation clauses were brought into Parliament, the Ecclesiastical Commission was appointed, the Quakers' Affirmation Act
passed.   In 1836 occurred the appointment of Dr. Hampden
as Regius Professor of Divinity, the permanent establishment
of the Ecclesiastical Commission, the Dissenters' Marriage Act,
the incorporation of the University of London, the union
of the dioceses of Gloucester and Bristol.   The forces of
liberalism were actively at work ; it was not without significance
that the publication of *Lyra Apostolica* bears the same date.

Besides the Tracts, many other publications were put forth
to support the new doctrines, in accordance with Newman's
original plan of making them known as widely as   Other
possible.   His own works on the *Prophetical Office*   tractarian
of the Church, on the *Arians* and on *Justification*   publications.
came out in 1837 and 1838 ; his share in the Tracts has
already been mentioned, he wrote much in periodicals also,
and his sermons were the most interesting event of every week
at Oxford.   From the first there were two tendencies among
the Oxford friends, one of which may be called Roman, the
other, Anglo-Catholic ; the former was as yet undeveloped ; the
latter has been termed by Isaac Williams, who saw the danger
of division and of too brilliant a leader, 'the Bisley-Fairford
School' ; that is, the school of the Kebles, the school of quiet
duty, severity, and consistency, of the old church habits of
mind which aimed at no effects and expected small results.
The series of *Plain Sermons by Contributors to the Tracts for
the Times* was begun by Williams in January 1839, with the
intention of quieting excitement, and guiding those who did
not know which way to look.   The first volume of the *Library
of the Fathers* was published in 1838, and fifty volumes came
out in succeeding years.   The object of this publication was
to bring the mind of the clergy back to the teaching of the
primitive church 'before the division between East and West.'
Charles Marriott was the working editor, and gave much time
to the labour, esteemed cheaply by himself and not sufficiently valued by his friends ; and he and Pusey, with whom

Keble and Newman were associated, set their friends to work to produce translations from the Greek and Latin Fathers, more exact than elegant, for grace of style was not much regarded, and the work was pushed on rapidly. The *Library of Anglo-Catholic Theology*, another of the tractarian publications, appeared about this time, and helped to form a body of intelligent opinion outside the University. The volumes contained the works of most of the notable English divines of the sixteenth and seventeenth centuries ; the publication of such series was in accordance with the fashion of the time, which put out ' Libraries ' of Entertaining Knowledge, and the like, as cheap literature came to be demanded by the public. The *British Critic* was the chief organ of the school, to which in 1844 the *Christian Remembrancer* succeeded. There was no fear that the Anglo-Catholic candle should be put under a bushel, whether or not Keble desired so much publicity.

In harmony with these more serious works may be noted the appearance in these years and later, of publications bearing no controversial or directly theological character, which were intended to extend the spirit of Anglo-Catholicism as set forth in *The Christian Year*, and did not aspire to the ideal of the more ascetic, polemical, theological, or poetical works of Newman and the other contributors to the Tracts, the *Lyra Apostolica*, and the *Library of the Fathers*. The echoes of these more learned works reached the unlearned ; country congregations were startled by being referred to the works of St. Cyprian, St. Basil, and other saints whose names they hardly knew. Church fashions also began to change under a like impulse ; daily prayers, Saints' day services, and early communions were introduced, as, for instance, the daily prayers at St. Giles's, Oxford, which Newman used to attend, and at some London churches ; but for the most part the long-established Sunday usage held its ground.

A movement, however, was proceeding which was to disturb uniformity, and it was helped by the spontaneous rise of a popular literature, the culminating point of which was reached by Miss Yonge's famous novel *The Heir of Redclyffe*, published in 1853. Among these books may be mentioned the publications of Parker, Mozley, and Masters, domestic stories, church

histories and legends of saints, sacred allegories, collections of
religious poetry, such as *Church Poetry*, *Days and*
Seasons, Keble's *Lyra Innocentium*, Isaac Williams's
Cathedral and *Baptistery*, and Church magazines,
Burns' *Magazine for the Young*, the *Monthly*
Packet, and other serials ; publications which, if
they did not reach or aim at the highest literary pitch, were
widely read, and disposed the minds of young people to take
the direction to which the more serious works of the tractarian
leaders pointed.   Among the books of this sort most widely
known at the time were Miss Sewell's *Laneton Parsonage*
and *Amy Herbert*, Mrs. Mozley's *The Lost Brooch*, William
Gresley's *The Siege of Lichfield*, H. C. Adams's *The Shadow*
of the Cross, Samuel Wilberforce's *Agathos*, Edward Monro's
The Dark Mountains, and other allegories, John Mason
Neale's *Christian Heroism*, and many other stories, Paget's
St. Antholin's, or Old Churches and New ; but the chief part
in this domestic propaganda is to be assigned to
Charlotte Mary Yonge, whose quiet influence was
felt in every one of the homes described from a
different point of view by Trollope, in his novels ; homes where
the lesser virtues flourished, where kindly, wholesome, un-
eventful lives were spent, to which this literature brought a
new emotion and a fresh impulse to duty.   When the scientific
period began, about the middle of the century, the paths
divided, and the younger generation forgot Miss Yonge and
read George Eliot.

Sunday stories and religious poetry, magazines, etc.

Charlotte Yonge.

AUTHORITIES.—As Chapter XI.   Keble, Sermons on *Primitive Tradi-*
tions and *The Religion of To-day* ; *Tracts for the Times* ; *Plain Sermons* ;
Library of the Fathers ; *Library of Anglo-Catholic Theology.*

CHAPTER XIII

OPPOSITION TO THE MOVEMENT

THE Hampden Controversy is a landmark in the history of the Oxford Movement, not so much on account of its intrinsic importance as because it gave the zest of an Oxford quarrel to a dispute which affected the Church generally, and because it bound the tractarian party together by a new tie.

In the year 1832 Renn Dickson Hampden, appointed Bampton Lecturer for that year, chose for his subject 'the Scholastic Philosophy,' and included in the scope of his lectures the origin of dogma. Starting from the position of the infallible authority of Scripture, he found himself in the old difficulty of finding an authoritative interpreter. *Hic liber est in quo quaerit sua dogmata quisque*; all heretics and schismatics appeal to the Bible; who is to judge? The primitive Church, and that Church which claims to be infallible, answer that the Church has authority. The Church, in this aspect, may be defined as the congregation of the faithful, or the clergy, or the episcopate in a General Council, or the Pope speaking *ex cathedra*. Protestant churches were content to affirm the supreme authority of Scripture. In doing so, they declared the fallibility of Church authority, and logically made every man his own interpreter. The Church of England appealed to antiquity, but did not define antiquity, unless the reference to the first four General Councils made in the Act of Supremacy (1 Eliz. c. 1) may be taken as such a definition. Article XX., 'of the Authority of the Church,' is disciplinary, and subordinates all traditions and ceremonies to the authority

Hampden's Bampton Lectures, 1832.

of the Bible.   Article XIX., if it pronounces at all on Church authority, gives that authority to the congregation, not to the clergy alone, and says that churches are fallible both as regards ceremonies and doctrine.   The same is ruled of General Councils by Article XXI., and the reason is given, that 'they be an assembly of men, whereof all be not governed with the Spirit and Word of God.'

Thus, according to the rule of doctrine to which clergymen of the Church of England are bound by subscription, there is no infallible authority but that of Holy Scripture ; and interpretations of Scripture made by fallible men have an inferior authority to the word of Scripture itself.

Dr. Hampden argued that the Church from age to age spoke in the terms of contemporaneous philosophy ; that therefore what was true to one age was not true to another, if expressed in the same terms ; and that in fact the Church of Rome had adopted the methods *Dr. Hampden's view of authority.* and in some cases the conclusions of the rationalists whom she denounced, as Peter Lombard, Albertus Magnus, and Thomas Aquinas himself.   Hampden, in this line of argument, was taking a line resembling that of Döllinger, namely that Church authority is not consistent, and therefore cannot be infallible. In Protestantism is involved the negation of an infallible church, and Protestant churches do not claim to be infallible, though they may claim obedience to their dogmas and proscribe heresy even under pain of death.   The dogmatic principle was too firmly established in Christendom to allow Protestants to see how untenable in argument their position was.

The Bible, said Hampden, reveals facts, not doctrines. Doctrines are built upon revealed facts by uninspired men. They are therefore subject to revision, since the form they take is imposed upon them by the necessity of combating, in the theological language of the time, erroneous doctrine expressed in the same language.   As thinkers can only express their thought in a language intelligible to themselves, theological language is necessarily coloured by philosophical language ; and as new systems of philosophy arose, so did new definitions of dogma.   The Manichæan and Gnostic systems, the various schools of Alexandrian philosophy, all the heresies which arose and were combated, have left their mark upon theology. According to the Roman view, this was ordained as the providential order by which a harmonious scheme of doctrine was unfolded. Scholasticism pressed Aristotle into the service of the Church, and quoted him as a Father of the Church, and almost an inspired prophet. In a legal age everything takes a forensic form ; logic, as formerly rhetoric, invaded theology. The false conception of natural philosophy as deductive science corrupted mental and moral philosophy, and the Schoolmen were chiefly employed in constructing syllogisms which referred facts to principles, according to Aristotelian methods.

Hampden's object in his diffuse and cumbrous work appears to be to show that church authority is a collection of the opinions of fallible men putting forward different views and using different methods at different times ; not a consistent school of doctrine preserved from error by divine providence. The conclusion to be drawn from the work was that church authority was a consensus of private judgment, to be respected, but not to be looked upon as a co-ordinate authority with Scripture ; that it was subject to change, and therefore not to be regarded as final. It may be remarked in passing that Hampden was believed by some who professed to know to have been indebted for some of his learning to Blanco White, formerly a Roman priest in Spain, a man of scholastic study and brilliant but unstable intellect, who left Oriel and Oxford about this time, and whose lapse into heresy and unbelief was already suspected.

These remarks will serve to introduce Dr. Hampden, whose notoriety as a controversialist is out of proportion to his importance as a thinker or a leader. We pass on to the year 1834, when, it will be remembered, the proposal to admit Dissenters to the universities by abolishing subscription to the Articles became the battle-ground of the opposing parties, when Hampden came forward as the Dissenters' apologist, and when the bill for relief, as was stated above, was thrown out by the House of Lords, and both parties were considering from opposite points of view the probable results of concession and the practical steps to be taken. The assertion of a principle

Proposal to admit Dissenters to University, 1834.

carries results with it; the results cannot be foreseen, and the concession of the principle does not take away the power of guiding, delaying, or averting them. Some results which were anticipated came about in course of time, such as the granting of degrees and fellowships to men who made no religious profession; but prophecies of destruction were not fulfilled, and after seventy years the universities are not unchristianised, the college chapels are still frequented, the Vice-Chancellor still goes to Sermon accompanied by the Doctors and Heads of Houses in their scarlet, and Oxford is still the nurse of thought, which, though it is less dogmatic than of old, has not ceased to be religious.

Hampden's pamphlet, *Observations on Religious Dissent*, came out in 1834, more than a year after his Bamptons, and came with more authority than those. The doctrine was the same: the unimportance of dogma as com- *Hampden's Observations, 1834.* pared with religion, the admixture of scholasticism in the formularies of our Church, the advantage of toleration as compared with exclusion, the difference between religion and theology, one being a bond of union, the other a cause of discord. 'In religion, properly so called, few Christians, if any, really differ,' he says; and he does not deny the name of Christians to Unitarians.

The tractarian leaders were not inclined to lose so good a quarrel as that which was offered to them by the proposal to abolish religious tests; and they took this opportunity to retrieve an omission made two years before, when Hampden's Bampton Lectures were allowed to pass unassailed. It was not without some reason that Newman, writing to Hampden himself about this pamphlet, spoke of it as 'the first step . . . taken towards interrupting that peace and mutual good understanding which has prevailed so long in this place.' Yet he might have remembered that he himself with his friends was occupied with 'defences' and 'tactics' to meet the impending onset of Liberal principles, and that since the passing of the Reform Act and the publication of Hampden's Bampton Lectures in 1832, Keble's Assize Sermon had been preached, the meeting at Hadleigh Rectory had been held, the addresses to the Archbishops presented, the *Tracts for the Times* begun. It matters little in warfare who is responsible for the actual *casus belli*, when each side is waiting for its opportunity.   The High Church party at Oxford and throughout the country was organised and strengthened, they were aware of their power, and were preparing for war and ready for defence or attack.

Shortly before the publication of the *Observations* Hampden had been made Doctor in Divinity, and appointed White's Lecturer in Moral Philosophy by the Vice-Chancellor, the Proctors, and three Heads of Houses, Dean Gaisford, Routh President of Magdalen, and Wynter of St. John's, as *religionis sinceritate commendatus* ; a sufficient testimonial to orthodoxy, it might seem.   But his University Lectures, delivered in 1835, were soon objected to.   Rose wrote to Newman in January 1836 : ' *Quousque tandem ?* how long are such books as Hampden's to come forward from Professors and Heads of Houses ?   How long are they to come forth unreproved ?   Hampden's lectures are such an aggravation of the offence of his former book, are in themselves so mischievous and so anti-Christian, that it does seem to me something very like a calamity that they should be allowed to pass with no rebuke more weighty than an anonymous review.   For several years the same injurious policy has been pursued—the policy of silence—of trusting that the books would not be much read, and that the poison would not work.'   This letter, sent by Pusey to Newman, woke in him the fighting spirit.   ' In such a state of things,' he writes (the English Church bound together by the imposition of Articles and the inducement of State protection, not by ἦθος and a common faith, the authorities of Oxford ignorant or incurious of theology), ' surely it is better for *us* to have the opportunity of speaking our mind. . . . Is not ours a state of hope ?   Have we not started the game ?   Is it not better to fight in light than in darkness ? . . . It is as if Providence were clearing the μεταίχμιον, and forcing men to choose their side.'

Hampden's Moral Philosophy Lectures, 1835.

His proposal to relax terms of subscription defeated at Oxford, 1835. Hampden, impenitent, and now by force of circumstances a leader, supported in 1835 the substitution of a declaration of general agreement for subscription to the Thirty-nine Articles, which had the approval of Whately and Arnold, but was thrown out in Convocation on May 20 by 459 votes to 57.

Such proceedings attract the attention of Ministers, and in 1836 Hampden was appointed by Lord Melbourne as Regius Professor of Divinity. His appointment was well understood to have a political meaning, and also to be a counterstroke to the Romanising movement going on at the University.

Hampden appointed Regius Professor of Divinity, 1836.

Melbourne did not fix upon Hampden without considera-tion. His first list of names for the Divinity Professor-ship, drawn up by Archbishop Howley, included Newman, Keble, and Pusey, not Hampden. Whately, to whom the list was sent, had already been consulted, and had recommended Samuel Hinds (afterwards Bishop of Norwich) and Hampden. Melbourne doubted between Hampden and Arnold; when he had decided upon Hampden, his choice was confirmed by Bishop Copleston, late Provost of Oriel. Melbourne was himself something of a theologian, of the latitudinarian way of thinking, and took interest in ecclesiastical politics. Learned clergymen were scarce, and learning was chiefly to be found among the High Church clergy. But it was not to be expected that Melbourne would appoint any one but a Liberal, still less that he would go out of his way to appoint a Tractarian. The choice was limited ; and a Prime Minister is likely to think more of rewarding a political follower than of propitiating university clamour, which, like other clamour, usually subsides when an unpopular appoint-ment is justified by its results ; especially as university opinion is not always in agreement with public opinion, the statesman's guide. But further inquiry would have shown Melbourne that the dislike of Hampden was not confined to the High Church party, and that the interest in religious questions raised by the new teachers had infected the rising generation of university men, and was spreading in every direction, especially in London, and likely to increase. If he wanted a champion of Liberal ideas, Arnold, a man of greater capacity and stronger character, would have been a better man to appoint than Hampden. Melbourne had a high opinion of Arnold, but thought him indiscreet, and believed that his promotion would be used as 'a handle against his Government.'

The political character of the appointment was emphasised

by Melbourne's refusal to accept his nominee's honourable offer to resign the professorial chair when he found how great a stir the appointment made, 'so instantaneous, so strong, and so unusual.' He had considered Hampden 'the safest choice,' when the question of his promotion came forward in October 1835; a strange opinion from a man so well informed about ecclesiastical matters as Melbourne; and the opposition which his appointment aroused did not alter his opinion. The outcry at Oxford had affected the timid mind of William IV., and a letter from him made Melbourne speak out, as indeed was his way. He reminded the King that to withdraw a recommendation touched the honour and character of the Minister who had made it, was a slur upon Hampden, infringed upon the right of private judgment and free inquiry, and tended to diminish the royal prerogative. 'Is his faith to be denied upon such grounds as these—"an impression upon the minds of many"? . . . There are innumerable impressions upon the minds of many, but who ever considered such impressions as any proof against the person whom they affected?' The Minister does not disdain the *argumentum ad hominem*; but he writes with conviction, and was not likely to change his mind.

[margin: Melbourne and William IV.]

Since Melbourne would not give way, Hampden's opponents were driven to take other steps. A meeting was held hastily, and, as enemies said, secretly, in the Common Room of Corpus on February 10, 1836, a committee appointed, consisting of Newman, Pusey, Palmer, and three others, with an Evangelical, Vaughan Thomas, as chairman; and a petition to the King not to confirm the appointment was drawn up and sent to Archbishop Howley. Newman sat up all night writing a pamphlet, *Elucidations of Dr. Hampden's Theological Statements*, which was published on the 13th. War was formally declared. The *Elucidations*, an examination of all Hampden's questionable writings, but especially the Bamptons, was a masterpiece of pamphleteering, ingenious in detecting heresy, close in argument, merciless in logic. A loose or confused arguer was Newman's favourite quarry; and the vigour of his attack was not modified by the fact that his opponent knew more about scholasticism and metaphysics than he did himself,

[margin: Newman's Elucidations, 1836.]

[handwritten margin: Newman's attack on Hampton's writings.]

nor by any considerations beyond the strict rules of the game. Polemical writing, if it does not always serve the interests of truth, brings men of a party together, and the labour spent upon the *Elucidations* was not wasted.

Pusey followed on March 12 with a learned and elaborate examination of Hampden's religious errors, and several attempts were made to set the university authorities in motion against him. The 'new political union,' as Arnold called it, petitioned the Heads of Houses to propose in Convocation an address to the Bishops, and a censure of the errors advanced in Hampden's works. The correct method of procedure, after the petition to the Crown had failed, was to select passages from Hampden's published writings, and bring them under the notice of the Bishop; or to promote the office of the Vice-Chancellor, with the assistance of six doctors of divinity, after the manner of an impeachment before the constitutional judges. Hampden's opponents preferred a method which may be described as an Act of Attainder, a procedure only justifiable, if justifiable at all, when the judges are corrupt or incapable; a course which condemned the culprit without giving him an opportunity of defence. 'A *vote*,' said Arnold in his *Edinburgh* Article of April 1836, 'they knew, might give them what they could never dare to hope from a *verdict*.'

After much hesitation the Heads of Houses framed a Statute to inhibit Dr. Hampden as Divinity Professor from exercising the vote in the selection of university preachers which belonged to him in that capacity, for the expressed reason that the University 'did not feel confidence in him in theological matters.' The proposed statute condemned the person, not the doctrine. The petitioners were dissatisfied, but accepted the action of the Heads as being in their opinion neither unjust nor unprecedented. The statute was brought forward on March 22, 1836, although the Proctors announced their intention of vetoing proceedings. Hampden's opponents were active in summoning their supporters, and the country clergy, 'in black gaiters,' appeared on the spot, ready to vote, and sure of an overwhelming majority. But the Proctors, Bayley of Pembroke and Reynolds of Jesus, uttered the solemn

A petition presented. Statute brought forward in Convocation, 1836.

formula, *Nobis Procuratoribus non placet*, and so stopped the vote on the statute. The Proctors went out of office; and two months later (5 May) the statute was passed by four to one in a full house, though it was probably illegal, certainly irregular, most certainly the cause of much bitterness and hostility. It is probable that Hampden would have been forgotten if he had been left alone: but the University wanted an opportunity of protesting against liberalism, and they made Hampden a martyr, and afterwards a bishop.

Hampden was himself orthodox; but when his name came into controversy on the subject of university tests, his lectures were examined and found to be inconsistent with the principles of orthodoxy, and to involve a denial of the authority of tradition. Controversy clears issues; and in the Introduction to the Bampton Lectures, published in 1837, and in the *Lecture on Tradition*, two years later, published in answer to the objections taken to the Bampton Lectures, Hampden stated his position more definitely. He asserted that his inquiry into the mode of statement in which Christian doctrine is presented left the matter of Christian doctrine untouched. The criterion of doctrine is Holy Scripture alone—'a supposed divine tradition of doctrines and interpretations and rites' he did not consider probable; but he was 'most ready to concede very great importance to tradition . . . as an authentic collection of doctrines, interpretations, and rites existing in the Christian Church by the side of the Bible. But then,' he adds, 'I attribute no *divine* authority to it in itself. It is divine only as it is shone upon by Scripture, a guide, not an oracle.' The sufficiency of Scripture authority was 'a fundamental principle of the Reformation itself.'

Hampden's Professorial Lectures, 1839.

In the *Observations on Religious Dissent*, Hampden, taking the question from a different point of view, had laid it down as his opinion that articles of religious communion, as they assume an immovable character, are 'fatally adverse to all theological improvement'; and that the real causes of separation among Christians are to be found in 'the confusion of theological conclusions and opinions with religion.' In short, he believed that religion had suffered by the accretion of doctrines based upon church authority; that the sufficiency of the Bible alone was a fundamental principle of the Reformation, and that Christians might differ in doctrine and yet be one in religion. Such opinions were abhorrent to the Tractarians, who had no great respect for the early Reformers, and whose sheet-anchor was the authority of church tradition ; and Hampden made no secret of his hostility to the tractarian movement, though he was surprised and hurt when attacked, and took much trouble to show that his own doctrine was harmless. His opponents objected that he explained at great length, but retracted none of his errors ; his explanations explained nothing, because he did not make his own criterion of doctrine intelligible. He had accepted the doctrine of the Creeds and Articles on authority, and they approved themselves to his reason on reflection ; but he did not make it clear whether he believed on authority or by reason.

One sentence of Hampden's would have furnished his opponents with a sufficient weapon. 'This opinion of the dependence of moral theory on religious truth is in fact a remnant of the philosophy of the Middle Ages.' This is to deny the dependence of morals on faith ; a position arguable, but not reconcilable with church teaching, Catholic or Protestant. It is pure rationalism. Hampden had also the serious disadvantage of being unreadable. In every point he was a contrast to Newman. He was laborious, conscientious, and anxious ; Newman was combative, alert, unsparing ; his correspondence at this time reveals in every line the keen party man. Liberalism was what he most hated, and Hampden represented one aspect of liberalism, as Arnold represented another, and the Government, with their ideas of rewarding political services, a third.

Two attempts to rescind the vote failed. The University had censured the lecturer, and the lecturer's appeal to the Archbishop of Canterbury received a cool reply. Archbishop Howley was a temperate man, much respected for Howley and piety. He put his refusal of support on the ground Hampden. that, being discredited by the University, Hampden was not 'a safe guide' in theology. The tone of the Archbishop's letter is that which is easily provoked by a person who has the misfortune of being always misunderstood, a circumstance

irritating to people in authority.   Hampden could not understand being misinterpreted ; and throughout his life he seems
to have been wanting in that kind of intellectual sympathy
which enables a man to conceive that difference from himself
in opinion need not mean moral obliquity.

It should be noticed that the vote was not a party vote on
religious lines, Evangelicals as well as High Churchmen having
concurred in it ; the issue was political as well as religious,
and was so understood by all the actors.   'The condemnation
of Dr. Hampden,' says Palmer, 'was not carried by the tractarian writers ; it was carried by the *independent* body of the
University.'   Dean Church is right in fact when he says that
'it was assumed in those days to be the most natural and
obvious thing in the world to condemn unsound doctrine
and to exclude unsound teachers. . . . The reproach of
persecution must be shared by all parties.'   It is one of the
recurring incidents of theological controversy.   In proportion
to the belief in the importance of correct belief must be the
desire to silence the professor of 'unsound' doctrine, from the
days of Elijah to our own ; and it is one of the disadvantages
of what Father Paul used to call 'doxolatry,' that it tends not
only to produce bitterness and uncharity in controversy, but
to bring about coercive action, such as the 'persecution' of
Dr. Hampden.   The action of persecutors is justifiable on the
ground that dogma is infinitely important : the indignation
of Liberals against persecutors rests upon the belief that dogma
is not infinitely important.

'The *privilegium*,' says Church, 'passed against Dr.
Hampden was an act of persecution, though a mild one
Ethics of
persecution. compared with what afterwards fell on his opponents
with his full sanction.   Persecution is the natural
impulse, in those who think a certain thing right
and important or worth guarding, to disable those who,
thinking it wrong, are trying to discredit and upset it, and
to substitute something different.   It implies a state of war.'
The question could not be put more fairly.   But war cannot
be carried on without bloodshed, and the tractarian party
meant war ; and Hampden was a fair object of attack.   It
is told of him that he came into the Oriel Common Room one
day holding in his hand the first Tract, and saying, 'These

gentlemen, without even knowing it, have crossed the Rubicon'; nor did he ever dissemble his dislike of the movement, or fail to point out its Romeward tendency.

It is not desirable that innovation, religious or political, should be made too easy. The existing frame of things has at least possession in its favour, and it is right that innovators should feel responsibility for their actions; a responsibility which is best brought home to them by experience or fear of consequences, which it is the business of an Opposition to enforce. Both Hampden and the Tractarians appeared in the light of innovators, and were proceeded against, unwisely perhaps and irregularly, but not unfairly, by those who disliked innovation—the majority in every society, whose guiding star is common sense, without whose opposition the victories of genius could not be won.

The stormy year 1838 was signalised by a plan, set on foot by opponents of tractarianism, to bring the Oxford Protestants into line by agitating for the erection of a memorial to the 'Oxford Martyrs,' Ridley, Latimer, and Cranmer. It was known that this was intended as a counterblast to Hurrell Froude's *Martyrs' Memorial at Oxford, 1838.* *Remains*, which had just come out, and as a flag of division. It might have been supposed that all sections of English Churchmen were at one in wishing to honour the memory of the brave men who for the Protestant cause, in Mary Tudor's reign, perished by fire in front of Balliol College. But the word 'Protestant' was hateful to the Tractarians; Ridley, Latimer, and Cranmer, though two of them were among the compilers of the Prayer Book, which was almost an idol of the High Church brotherhood, had held unsound opinions on controverted questions, akin to those preached at Geneva and Zurich; they were hearty enemies of Rome, and the Tractarians wished to regard Rome as an erring sister. The idea of erecting a memorial or in some way commemorating their death at Oxford had too Protestant a colour, and was closely connected with the Oxford controversies of the day.

Newman, Pusey, and others were invited to subscribe: Pusey was at first inclined to give his name to the project, but Newman and Keble and their friends kept aloof and held him back, though the bishops *en masse* subscribed to the memorial. It was represented that the project was intended to divide; Golightly (1807-1885) of Oriel found in it an opportunity for prosecuting his anti-tractarian crusade; a meeting was held at his house, and the Tractarians were put on their guard. In Dean Church's words, coloured perhaps by youthful recollections, 'they were either to commit themselves to the Reformation as understood by the promoters of the memorial, or they were to be marked as showing their disloyalty to it.' . . . Pusey thought that a church might be built and a memorial tablet erected recording thankfulness for religious freedom and the English Bible. If it were decided to put up a cross he would accept that gladly, provided it was made clear that no direct homage were paid to the so-called martyrs; *non martyribus, sed Deo martyrum.* But on the whole he decided to stand aside, lest he should seem to set the Reformers against the Fathers. Keble said, 'Anything which separates the present Church from the Reformers I should hail as a great good.' Newman took the same line. It would have been more magnanimous, though it might have been bad party tactics, to accept the proposal on its own merits and not as a challenge, as it may be presumed the bishops did: but such was not the spirit which prevailed at Oxford in 1838, and the Martyrs' Memorial, which a few years before would have united all parties, stands as a symbol of disunion.

The Tractarians do not support the proposal.

Other omens were not wanting to show that the way of the Tractarians was not the way of the church authorities. In June 1841 the Chevalier Bunsen, a friend of Dr. Arnold and an enthusiast for universal peace and goodwill, inclined, as enthusiasts are, to ignore difficulties and prejudices, was sent by the new King of Prussia, Frederick William IV., to arrange with the English Government for a joint Anglo-Prussian protectorate of those Christians in the Holy Land and adjoining regions who were not included in the Capitulations under which the Latin, Greek, and Armenian communities were protected. It might seem possible that the Anglican and Lutheran Evangelical Churches should be joined under one ecclesiastical head, and form a branch of episcopal

Bunsen's plan for a Protestant Bishopric of Jerusalem, 1841.

Protestantism; for it was believed that a movement was proceeding for uniting the Calvinists and Lutherans in Prussia under the rule of bishops. This was no doubt the idea of the Prussian King and his envoy, and more or less that of the court of Great Britain, under the influence of Bunsen and Prince Albert. It was also thought desirable to establish for Syrian Christians some influence which would diminish the authority of Russia, both because the Syrian Christians did not like Russian protection, and probably for ulterior political reasons.

The King of Prussia, who was more of a religious sentimentalist than a statesman, instructed Bunsen to inquire whether the Church of England would accord to the evangelical National Church of Prussia 'a sisterly position' in the Holy Land. Evangelical Christendom could do nothing in the East, unless as one united body; and to further the plan the King was willing to allow one or more of his clergy 'to obtain ordination from the English Church'; while, to save the interests of his own Church, persons thus admitted to English orders were to declare their assent to the Confession of Augsburg. He had no further intention of uniting the Churches of England and Germany, though he hoped that both nations might be drawn nearer to each other in the name of evangelical Christendom. According to the High Church party, the King of Prussia was an anathematised heretic, and his so-called Church not a church at all, though it might be described as a section of 'Evangelical Christendom.' The Christians in the East ought to submit to the oriental bishops, not to summon intruders from the West. The real objection in their eyes was that the plan seemed to point to ultimate union in discipline and doctrine between the English Church and the German Protestant churches.

High Church objections to the scheme.

The *Times*, which was at that moment in the High Church interest, denounced the scheme of organising a rival communion to the Greek Orthodox Church within the Patriarchate of Jerusalem, which was like sending an English-made bishop to Rome. Great Britain ought to protect and consolidate the only possible Christian centres, the Apostolic and Orthodox Churches. Why should Protestantism 'lift up its heel against the prelate who occupies

The *Times* leads the opposition.

by legitimate succession the episcopal throne of St. James?'
Moreover, there was danger of being tainted with Eastern
heresies as well as Western.

Archbishop Howley and Bishop Blomfield were willing to
forward the plan of an Anglo-Prussian Bishopric at Jerusalem,
on condition that such Protestants as should ask
to enjoy protection should be admitted to communion with the Church of England. The Bishopric
was established by Act of Parliament on October 5,
1841; the British and Prussian Crowns were to nominate
alternately to the see; the King of Prussia endowed it with
£15,000, and English subscriptions were to make
up the same sum, £3000 of which was promised
by the Society for Propagating Christianity among
the Jews.   Dr. Michael Solomon Alexander was
consecrated 'Bishop of the United Church of
England and Ireland in Jerusalem,' and authorised to ordain
German Protestants on their signing the Thirty-nine Articles
as well as the Confession of Augsburg.

Archbishop and Bishop of London approve.

Bishopric of Jerusalem constituted. Bishop Alexander, 1841.

Pusey, from his friendship with Bunsen and his interest
in the religious affairs of Germany, was at first inclined to
favour the project, believing that there was a
congregation of Jewish converts at Jerusalem who
did not understand Turkish or Arabic.   But the
High Church party as a whole strongly disliked the scheme,
though Samuel Wilberforce and Hook approved it; to Newman it was one of the blows which 'finally shattered his faith
in the Anglican Church.   That Church, in his view, was not
only forbidding any sympathy or concurrence with the Church
of Rome, but it actually was courting an intercommunion with
Protestant Prussia and the heresy of the Orientals';
and in the protest which he sent personally to
the Archbishop and to the Bishop of Oxford
on November 11, he speaks of Lutheranism and Calvinism
as 'heresies, repugnant to Scripture, springing up three
centuries since, and anathematised by East as well as West.'
He denounced such a course of action, 'as removing our
Church from her present ground, and tending to her dis-
organisation.'   'It seems,' he writes in October, 'we are *in the
way* to fraternise with Protestants of all sorts—Monophysites,

Pusey approves.

Newman's protest, 1841.

half-converted Jews, and even Druses'; and again: 'the Bishop, who has no Church principles, *is not to be made under the jurisdiction of the English Bishops*, and thus you have an Episcopate set up to gather, literally, Jews, Turks, infidels, and heretics from all quarters'; and again : 'to admit maintainers of heresy without formal renunciation of their errors goes far towards recognising the same.' What startled and stung him was 'the corroboration of a present, living, and energetic heterodoxy' by this action of the rulers of Church and State.

The point to which objection was taken was the assumption on the part of the King of Prussia, whose proclamation was issued in the *State Gazette* of November 17, 1841, that the Anglican Church was on an equal footing with the Protestant communities of the German nation, that there was such an institution as 'the Protestant Church,' and that the Church of England was, 'in its origin and doctrine, closely allied to the German evangelical Churches.' Especially it seemed strange that such an Act of Union could be passed, without any synodical action or conference among the English episcopate, by the mere authority of the Archbishop of Canterbury and the Bishop of London, aided by a permissive Act of Parliament. William Palmer of Magdalen, a young man of thirty, who in later life joined the Church of Rome, with his father and his brother Roundell, afterwards Lord Selborne, and with the assistance of Ranke the historian, drew up a protest against the doctrine of 'the essential unity of Protestant Christendom.' Much offence was given by an expression used by Palmer, 'I utterly reject and anathematise the principle of Protestantism as a heresy, with all its forms, sects, and denominations.'

The opposition of Newman and his friends brought the Jerusalem Bishopric into the front of doctrinal controversy; and Liberals, such as Maurice, Julius Hare, Lord Ashley, and Palmer of Worcester warmly supported the movement on the ground of a common Christianity, barely recognised by Rome, but allowed by the Oriental and Protestant churches. This was the standing ground of the latitudinarian school, as well as the Evangelicals, as Newman's was that of the 'Apostolicals.'

Liberal view
of the
Jerusalem
Bishopric.

Though the incident was trifling in itself, and not likely to lead to any shining results, the principle involved was important, being no less than the question whether Protestant communions, such as the Scottish Presbyterian Church, the English nonconformist congregations, and the evangelical Churches of the Continent, are or are not excluded from the Catholic Church because they have not adhered to the apostolical or episcopal succession. Maurice did not like the term 'the Protestant Church'; but the idea of a central unity independent of 'diversities of Christian worship according to languages and nations' had his sympathy. His view was that nations may be Protestant, but the Church is Catholic; and that 'the two are not contradictory, but complementary truths'; and he welcomed a step towards union which accepted the order of bishops, an institution which he himself believed to be primitive.

Frederick Maurice's view.

Julius Hare dwelt at length on the subject in his archidiaconal charge of 1842. He spoke with approval of the wish of the King of Prussia 'to obtain a centre for all the national churches of the evangelical confession, that might be willing to join in the scheme either now or hereafter.' 'The present aspect of Turkish affairs . . . and especially the political relation of England and Prussia with Turkey, has for the first time afforded a possibility for evangelical Christendom to demand a position in the birthplace of Christianity, by the side of the ancient Churches of the East, and over against that of Rome, as a co-ordinate member of the Universal Church of Christ. . . . To all the members of our Church the name of Protestant was for centuries a matter of glory. . . . Both politically and ecclesiastically the English nation and Church regarded themselves as intimately united to every Protestant body, and as the appointed champions of the Protestant cause. . . . Our brotherhood with the Protestant Churches on the Continent was affectionately recognised, not by Low Churchmen and Puritans, but by the very persons whom our modern Romanisers used to hold up as the exemplars of English Churchmen, by Archbishop Sancroft and by the Lower House of Convocation in 1689 and in 1705. . . . So alien is

Julius Hare, 1842.

the mind of the English Church from that new-fangled upstart heresy which disclaims the name of Protestant, and audaciously denies the name of Church to the German Lutherans.'

On the death of Bishop Alexander in November 1845, the appointment fell to the King of Prussia, who nominated Samuel Gobat, the son of a Swiss pastor, a linguist and orientalist, who had spent some time in Abyssinia and was a zealous missionary and a man of vigorous intellect and strong character. Gobat had been trained at Islington College, and was already in Anglican deacon's orders. But in dealing with the monophysite clergy of Abyssinia he had used language which, as Pusey thought, seemed to suggest unsound opinions. He had certainly, whilst blaming Nestorius, refused to anathematise either him or Eutyches; 'we only anathematise those who love not our Lord Jesus Christ'; he also said that 'the Bible speaks of neither one nor two natures in Christ; it only says that He is God over all.' On Baptism Bishop Gobat held the current evangelical view, that Baptism is rather a seal and symbol of grace than an effectual means of grace.

Samuel Gobat nominated to succeed Bishop Alexander, 1846.

Pusey had in 1841 'tried to make the best of the experiment.' But he had seen the effect upon others, especially upon Newman, of this attempt to bring the English and the German churches nearer to each other, and now it was to him 'like a sword in his bones.' 'What a misery,' he wrote, 'it would be if the ultimate object of the Prussian Government were obtained, and they were to receive episcopacy from us, and we were to become the authors of a heretical Succession.' Such a doctrine as this ignores the history of the English Reformation and 'unchurches half Europe'; and how material is the conception of episcopacy as a kind of spiritual possession conferred *ex opere operato* upon a church which, nevertheless, being heretical, could not derive benefit from it.

Pusey changes his mind.

It would have been a breach of faith to refuse to consecrate on the King of Prussia's nomination, whether or not it had been good policy in the first instance to enter into the agreement; and Pusey's proposal to protest against the Archbishop's act in conferring Priest's Orders upon Gobat without his 'publicly recanting heresy publicly put forth'

would seem to be merely impertinent.   The Bishop of
Exeter came forward with a protest founded on general
Bishop Gobat considerations, not on Gobat's religious views ; and
consecrated, Gobat having, to avoid scandal, explained certain
1846. remarks in his Journals, and subscribed to the
Creeds and Articles, was ordained priest and consecrated
Bishop on July 3, 1846.

This 'fancy Church,' as Gladstone called it, languished,
and indeed hardly came into effective existence.   Three
bishops on the Anglo-Prussian foundation were successively
consecrated ; then the joint arrangement was abandoned.
From the *via media* point of view the experiment was a
dangerous tampering with heresy : to Roman Catholics it
was little if at all more visionary and amateur than the *via
media* itself.   Newman's words are memorable : ' As to the
project of a Jerusalem Bishopric, I never heard of any good
or harm it has ever done, except what it has done for me.'
The memory of the controversy was only revived by the
mention of it in his *Apologia*.   There is a bishopric of
Jerusalem at this day, but it is an Anglican bishopric like
others, not a compromise between an episcopalian and a
non-episcopalian community.   The Anglo-Prussian Jerusalem
Bishopric was an ill-devised scheme, perhaps little more than
a Royal whim ; but it embodied a noble idea, and one in
harmony with the early Stuart times, to which Tractarians
looked back as the palmy days of the English Church.

AUTHORITIES.—Cf. Chapters XI. and XII.   For the Hampden Contro-
versy, R. D. Hampden, *Bampton Lectures*, 1832 ; *Observations on Religious
Dissent* ; H. Christmas, *Concise History of the Hampden Controversy* ;
J. H. Newman, *Elucidations*, etc. ; *The Hampden Controversy*, 1847 ; E. B.
Pusey, *Dr. Hampden's Theological Statements*, etc., 1836.   For the Jerusalem
Bishopric ; J. H. Newman, *Apologia* ; Liddon's *Life of Pusey* ; *Life and
Work of Samuel Gobat* ; J. C. Hare, *Charge to the Clergy of the Arch-
deaconry of Lewes*, 1842.

CHAPTER XIV

TRACT NINETY AND THE SECESSION

THE Tracts continued to appear, but excited less public interest, as they demanded more studious attention and appealed less to questions of the moment. Oxford was interested in such questions as the abolition of subscription at matriculation in 1835, the Hampden controversy in 1836, Newman's lectures in Adam de Brome's chapel and his sermons at St. Mary's, the Martyrs' Memorial in 1838, and the Jerusalem Bishopric and the Poetry Professorship in 1841. Meanwhile the progress of the Movement followed unconsciously the progress of Newman's mind; and, as he wrote in 1835, 'the controversy with the Romanists has overtaken us like a summer cloud.'

One of the most remarkable of the Tracts was No. 85, written by Newman in 1838. Though it did not receive much general notice, it made a deep impression upon thinkers, such as Ward of Balliol. It is composed in the form of lectures, and deals with difficulties in the Scripture proof of the doctrine of the Church; difficulties of latitudinarianism, which holds to Scripture but does not find a definite creed in Scripture; difficulties of the Christian and Catholic record contained in the history of the Church, and of the Canon of Scripture, from the incredibility or improbability of events recorded in Scripture and accepted by the Church,— an argument drawn out later by Newman in the *Essay on Ecclesiastical Miracles*; difficulties involved in the reception by Protestants of the Canon of Scripture as settled in the fourth and fifth centuries, unless the doctrines also which were held by the Church at the same time are accepted on the same authority. The conclusion is that neither the doctrines, nor the history of the Church, nor the Canon of Scripture can be maintained without the supernatural assurance of inspired Church authority behind all. God 'has given us doctrines which are but obscurely gathered from Scripture, and a Scripture which is but obscurely gathered from history.' The writer employs with consummate skill the artifice of unimpassioned rhetoric, removing stone by stone the foundations of belief for the Latitudinarian and the Protestant, till the climax suddenly comes in an appeal to the heart ; if this is so, the only answer to these reasonable doubts is the answer of St. Peter, 'Lord, to *whom* shall we go ?' Somewhither he must go. Love is the parent of faith. Why should not the Church be divine ? 'I love her Bible, her doctrine, and her rites, and *therefore* I believe.' The argument is that of universal scepticism, but scepticism is barred by faith and love.

The Tracts which were most discussed and roused most opposition were Nos. 80 and 87, published in 1838, which were written by Isaac Williams, by no means an incendiary, but a quiet retired poet. His works, *The Cathedral*, *The Baptistery*, *Thoughts in Past Years*, had merit as poetry, and counted for something in spreading High Church doctrine, and sentiment of the type represented by Herbert, Ken, and Keble. But in theology Williams was one of the most uncompromising of the party, 'of the straitest sect,' as Newman told him ; never completely under the spell of Newman ; notably of that section of the party which could go very near to Rome yet remain untempted.

Isaac Williams's Tracts, Nos. 80 and 87, on 'Religious Reserve,' 1838.

The subject chosen by Williams in Tract No. 80, and its sequel, No. 87, was 'Reserve in communicating Religious Knowledge.' The writer's intention, as he tells us himself, was to maintain the argument 'that religious truth cannot be known without serious attention.' It follows from this that the emotional and unintellectual methods of conversion, the display and, as it were, advertising of the Atonement to minds unprepared by discipline, the stress laid by some religionists upon promiscuous preaching, general religious education without catechising, the subordinating of worship to exposition, the use of extempore prayer and popular services, the theory of the 'open Bible,' the 'speculative mind' in religious inquiry, the literal and critical interpretation of Scripture, the ignoring of a mystical sense in the sacred history, poetry, and discourses,—all this is unscriptural and uncatholic, out of harmony with the methods prescribed and followed by the early Church.

These Tracts, like the whole series, but in plainer language, made a direct attack upon that school of thought which held 'that theology, like other sciences, improves by time . . . that Christianity was in its infancy, at most in its childhood,' when the Fathers wrote. The spirit of the times was the spirit of Antichrist; arrogance must be met by a call for humility, illuminism by obscurantism, since the darkness of reverence and mystery is better than the dazzle of false light. 'Modern and ancient theology are to a great extent irreconcilable.' The danger of such teaching is that under reverence may lurk superstition ; and when the author of the Tract introduces Archbishop Laud's journal and its supposed providential warnings, we are sensible that superstition is not far off.

Tract 89, by Keble, 'On the Mysticism attributed to the Early Fathers of the Church,' attracted much attention, and would probably have caused more stir but for a more important event, the publication of the famous Tract 90, which bears date 'The Feast of the Conversion of St. Paul, 1841.' *Tract 89, by Keble, Tract 90, 1841.*

The use and wont of the Church of England, as the Churchmen of the day and their fathers and grandfathers had known it, was condemned in every particular by the Tracts ; and a window seemed at the same time to be opened in the direction of Rome. No wonder that quiet people were astonished and scandalised at the audacity of these reformers ; no wonder that the heads of the *Advance in the direction of Rome.* universities, the bishops, and all persons in authority opposed innovations so recklessly introduced. Strictly speaking, they were not innovations, but a revival and extension of Prayer Book teaching as understood by those Caroline divines who are the great and peculiar glory of the Church of England ; but the doctrine of apostolical succession 'had gone out with

the non-jurors,' as Bishop Blomfield said; the theology of
the eighteenth century was evidential and latitudinarian; the
Roman question slumbered whilst the enemy in the field was
nonconformity; the Articles, not the Liturgy in its catholic
sense, had become the standard of theology; and when the
Tracts showed the Church of England her natural face in
the glass of the seventeenth century, she did not recognise it.

Students of Anglo-Catholic theology could not but observe
that the denunciation of Rome by the Caroline divines was
more thoroughgoing than that of the Tractarians. When
Pusey in 1840 wrote down heads of the tractarian creed
and mentioned among them high thoughts of the two Sacraments, of episcopacy, the visible Church, seemly ritual, reverence for and deference to the Ancient Church, he proceeded
to define the points of difference between 'Puseyism' and
Calvinism; he did not define points of difference between
Puseyism and Romanism. The younger generation of the
Tractarians, with W. G. Ward as their spokesman, were
openly expressing sympathy with Rome and desire for re-
union; and in the summer of 1839, as Newman was studying
the history of the Monophysite controversy, an article on the
Anglican Claim in the August number of the *Dublin Review*,

Wiseman's quotation of *Securus judicat*, etc., 1839.
written by Bishop Wiseman, brought to his notice
what the Bishop called 'an axiom in theology,' St.
Augustine's canon *Securus judicat orbis terrarum*, 'a
simpler rule than that of Antiquity.' He had seen
'the shadow of a hand upon the wall.' The thought came
into his mind, 'Rome will be found right after all'; and
though he would not listen to it, the thought returned. 'He
who has seen a ghost cannot be as if he had never seen it.'
He speaks four years later of the strange effect produced on
the mind when the conviction flashes, or rather pours, in upon
it that Rome is the true Church. 'By those great words of
the ancient Father, the theory of the *via media* was absolutely
pulverised.' A strange argument; for it upsets the maxim
'*Athanasius contra mundum.*' Though half convinced, he did
not give in; for five years more he wrestled with the problem.
He still believed that the theory of interpreting Anglican
formularies in the 'catholic sense' was sound, and his object
in writing Tract 90 was to keep the younger men from

'straggling in the direction of Rome,' by offering them here
what they sought at Rome. 'We must consent,' he writes,
'either to give up the men, or to admit their principles. . . .
Their tangible difficulty was subscription to the Articles, and
thus the question of the Articles came before me.'

The question of the Articles was to Protestants the most
critical question of all. The body of tractarian doctrine
was complete, including the tenet of the 'catholic
sense' in which the formularies were to be read;
but the Articles still remained as a hedge, on this
side and that side of which stood the English Church and
the Roman Church. It was the 'catholic sense' of the
Articles with which Tract 90 dealt. Newman's logical mind
saw no obstacle to prevent his drawing a conclusion from
premisses already arrived at; and he did not think the Tract
would create a great stir. He was 'quite unprepared for the
outbreak, and was startled at its violence.' But his treatment of the Articles did away with the conventional and
traditional meaning which they had borne for a century and
more, and it could not be ignored. Articles, it was thought,
which have been supposed to teach doctrine, lose all collec-
tive meaning if they are held to be meant only as terms
of comprehension, allowing all divergences of opinion;
the method of interpretation recommended in Tract 90
took away their authority from the Articles and transferred
it to the Liturgy, nay, to some unauthorised and undesig-
nated body of so-called 'Catholic' doctrine behind the
Liturgy.

The question of the Articles.

This momentous publication bears the harmless title,
'Remarks on Certain Passages in the Thirty-nine Articles.'
The opening words are these: 'It is often urged,
and sometimes felt and granted, that there are in
the Articles propositions or terms inconsistent with
the Catholic faith.' The object of the Tract is 'to show that,
while our Prayer Book is acknowledged on all hands to be of
catholic origin, our Articles, alas! the offspring of an uncatholic
age, are, through God's good providence, to say the least, not
uncatholic, and may be subscribed by those who aim at being
catholic in heart and doctrine.'

Analysis of Tract 90.

This thesis laid down, the interest of the Tract lies chiefly in the method of proof. The writer assumes that Scripture as interpreted by the Catholic Church is the rule of faith; he does not define 'the Catholic Church,' but implies that its authority to interpret rests upon the consent of primitive times. Since the Articles declare that the Homilies contain sound doctrine, he uses the Homilies as a storehouse of texts, almost as Scripture itself, ignoring the fact that from the same storehouse may be drawn texts open to an opposite construction. His method here—and may not this be said to be Newman's usual method?—is to accumulate instances on one side, whilst omitting important considerations on the other, which if stated might give a different turn to the whole argument. Thus, for instance, the history of the Reformation shows that the English Reformers looked upon the Lutheran and Calvinist bodies as engaged in the same cause with them, and allies in the common quarrel with Rome, whatever their differences among themselves and from us might be : Newman passes over this, and considers Rome a friend, Protestantism an enemy. The history of the Reformation shows that the English Reformers, though they honoured Councils and deferred to the authority of the primitive Church, set the rule of faith in Holy Scripture, not in Councils or patristic texts, and claimed the right of interpreting Scripture by its own light : Newman, with his apparatus of Fathers and Homilies, whittles away private judgment, and looks at the whole question in an unhistorical perspective. The history of the Reformation shows that the Reformers, English and others, wished to destroy, on account of its practical abuses, all belief in Purgatory, and that they did in practice destroy it, so that in the churches of all Protestant countries, including England, belief in Purgatory came utterly to an end : Newman, by a dexterous use of the word 'Romish,' makes out that Article XXII. condemns, not the doctrine itself, but the 'Romish' form of it ; not the Tridentine form, for the decrees of Trent are later in date than the Articles, but the popular abuses of the doctrine.

The conclusion to be drawn, said Tract 90, was that there were corruptions in the Roman Church, as in the Church of England, which sober-minded Romanists deplored ;

that the Articles were directed against these, but not against the mind of the Church deliberately expressed in formal decrees.   The distinction may be stated as a distinction between *Romish* and *Roman* doctrine; the former being the teaching prevalent throughout the Roman Church, promulgated by persons in authority and not contradicted by authority; the latter 'the authoritative statements of that Church herself,' as formulated in ecclesiastical decrees.   'The Articles are not written against the creed of the Roman Church, but against actual existing errors in it, whether taken into its system or not.'   This is an unhistorical distinction.   The Tridentine decrees may have approved reforms already made— for since Luther's revolt much had been reformed,—but in substance they confirmed the current opinion of the Roman Catholic world : how could they not, seeing that the Tridentine fathers held that the Church, not only General Councils, is divinely governed?   'Romish,' if it has any meaning, means in effect 'Tridentine,' although all that is Romish is not Tridentine.

So of 'the sacrifices [1] of Masses'; the distinction between this and 'the sacrifice of the Mass' will not hold.   The *animus imponentis* was to discredit the Mass and all the doctrine and practice connected with it, not to The sacrifice of the Mass. draw a fine distinction between the sacrifice of the Mass and 'certain observances, for the most part private and solitary . . . which involved certain opinions and a certain teaching.'   The Reformers' intention is illustrated, to take one instance, by the omission of the word 'Mass' in the second Prayer Book of Edward VI.   With the history of the times open before him it is surprising that Newman should have written as follows : 'On the whole . . . it is conceived that the Article . . . neither speaks against the Mass in itself, nor against its being an offering [though commemorative] for the quick and dead for the remission of sins.'   The plain historical meaning of the Article is that Christ's sacrifice was offered once for all, as opposed to repeated sacrifices of Masses ; it includes all Masses, private and other ; the money payment is *perniciosa impostura*, no doubt : but that is not the thing principally condemned.

[1] Newman prints 'sacrifice,' but the text of the Article is 'sacrifices (*sacrificia*).

Thus, again, on Article XXII., 'Of Images and Relics,' two doubtful instances in favour of relics are quoted from the Homilies; but the intention of the Article, viewed historically, is to condemn all veneration of images and relics. Again, in the matter of the Invocation of Saints, in the same Article, history tells us that in the interval between the First Book of Edward VI. and Elizabeth's Prayer Book, Invocation of the Saints had disappeared from the Church of England. As for Transubstantiation (Art. XXVIII.), the framers of the Articles went to the fire for denying it; and if a second Mary had reigned after Elizabeth, Elizabeth's bishops must have recanted or gone to the fire. The Articles, says Newman, are not against a real superlocal Presence; and Andrewes held doctrine closely approaching to the Roman definition. The *via media* is here plainly marked in our formularies; the *animus imponentis* is to admit all shades of opinions but the two extremes, that which denies that the bread and wine remain in their natural substance after consecration, and the opposite doctrine, that the Sacrament is no more than a memorial. The true meaning of the Articles is to be found not merely in the plain literal and grammatical sense, nor in a sense favouring the 'catholic' and 'primitive' opinion, nor by the interpretation of the Homilies; but in the history of the times when they were drawn up, by the light of relations and reactions, political and national as well as religious, which made it desirable to define little, and within certain prudential limits.

As for the true sense of the Articles, the *animus imponentis* is hard to seize, and the attempt to arrive at it may easily mislead. The 'imponent' is, in the first place, the Council of Edward VI., and especially Cranmer and Ridley in 1551; in the second place, Convocation and the Council of Elizabeth in 1562-63, and finally the Parliament of 1571. The first of these dates coincides with the influence of Helvetian doctrine, the second and third with the establishment of Elizabeth's Church and State system, in which discipline (that is to say, the attendance of all her subjects at church), was thought more of than correct doctrine. The object of Edward VI.'s advisers was to form a body of Protestant doctrine which should not be incompatible with the use of ancient forms ; and the experience of three centuries shows that it was successful ; the object of Elizabeth was to retain Catholics in their allegiance by giving them a form of worship which was not wholly abhorrent, and to obtain unanimity among English Protestants by laying down a broad basis of doctrine ; certainly not to set up Roman doctrine in the place of Protestant. From either point of view the consideration of the dates of Tridentine sessions, which was made much of in the controversy, is an irrelevant intrusion. But in point of fact the greater number of the Tridentine decrees were already promulgated in 1551, before the sessions of the Council were suspended, and all by 1563, when the Council was broken up ; so that, as Bishop Phillpotts noted, if the true sense is that of the authority imposing the subscription, *i.e.* the legislature (in this case the Parliament and Convocation of 1571), that date is eight years later than the promulgation of the last Canons of Trent ; and the Convocation of 1571 declared the true sense to be that of Holy Scripture and 'Catholic Fathers.'

In both cases, 1551 and 1571, and certainly in the second, the legislation was more for the sake of discipline and political expediency than of orthodoxy. Thus the 'plain literal and grammatical sense' of the words, to which Newman professed to adhere, depends partly upon history. Newman, however, is justified, as a matter of history, in his main contention that where the words will bear a 'catholic' interpretation that interpretation is not to be ruled out. He points out that this was the theory of Melanchthon, 'from whose writings the Articles are principally drawn' ; the framers, therefore, meant to give a reasonable latitude of interpretation. From his own point of view the *animus imponentis* is of no importance. 'I have asserted,' he writes on March 15, 1841, 'a great principle, and I ought to suffer for it ; that the Articles are to be interpreted, not according to the meaning of the writers, but, so far as the wording will admit, according to the sense of the Catholic Church.'

The common opinion of the ethics of subscription in the Church of England at this time may probably be summed up in the common sense eighteenth-century arguments of Paley in his *Moral Philosophy*. The rule of subscription,

Ethics of subscription. says Paley, is the *animus imponentis* ; the inquiry, *quis imposuit et quo animo*? The bishop is not the imposer. The compilers of the Articles are not the imposers. The legislation of the 13th year of Elizabeth is the imposer, whose intention the subscriber is to satisfy. The authors of that law intended to exclude from offices in the Church (1) all abettors of Popery, (2) Anabaptists, (3) Puritans. 'Whoever finds himself comprehended with these descriptions ought not to subscribe.' To this it may be added, that the intention of the imposer is to be judged according to a true understanding of the religious history of the sixteenth century, the language of which does not easily adapt itself to the religious thought of a later age, and is coloured by political conditions which have long ago passed away.

To Newman himself Tract 90 was no more than the application to a part of the Anglican formularies what had been asserted of the whole body of Anglican doctrine ; to the

Tridentine doctrine in the Church of England. majority both of friends and enemies it seemed a hazardous step forward into a doubtful region, a breaking down of the hedge between England and Rome. And so in the event it has proved. Though Tridentine doctrine has not been formally accepted by the Church of England, and though Rome has not abated anything of her claim to absolute obedience, professors of Tridentine doctrine now occupy English benefices, whilst they use Roman ritual and uphold Roman practice. And as the corner of the Anglican pentagram broken into by Tract 90 admitted those who were avowedly Romanisers, so by the same way Latitudinarians came into the fold, men who subscribe the Articles neither in a literal and grammatical, nor in a catholic sense. The Articles, in becoming articles of comprehension, have ceased to be articles of faith. The twentieth century cannot be bound by the mind of the sixteenth : and if the Articles remain in evidence, the standard of subscription to them has been

Practical result of Tract 90. lowered in every direction by legal authority. The binding force of subscription is relaxed, at the sacrifice of scrupulous veracity ; and it becomes increasingly doubtful whether any verbal test will hold an antiquated formula together. The new sense on the old Article is the new patch on the old garment.

Tract No. 1 was published in September 1833, Tract No. 90 in February 1841. The earlier Tract looked back to primitive tradition, the later to the growth of tradition and its expansion into the modern Roman system. The progress of the movement had been consistent; Tract 90 grew naturally, though not inevitably, out of the premisses of Tract 1. But storm was in the air; the bishops began to speak strongly against this rule of interpretation and the tractarian teaching in general; Lord Morpeth, in the House of Commons, attacked Oxford as a seedplot of Roman teaching; the *Times* stood up for the Puseyites; Oxford Common Rooms talked of nothing but Tract 90.

The bishops' charges.

Ten days after its publication, Churton of Brasenose, Wilson of St. John's, Griffiths of Wadham, and Tait of Balliol, all senior Tutors of their respective Colleges, addressed a letter to the editor of the series calling upon the writer to give his name to the Tract, on the ground that though liberty of interpretation should be allowed, such new and startling views, tending to obliterate the distinction between Anglican and Roman doctrine, and to open the way for teaching 'the most plainly erroneous doctrines and practices of the Church of Rome' in Oxford lecture-rooms and pulpits, ought not to be treated in an anonymous publication. Tait was the author of the letter. The points enumerated by the four Tutors as calling for comment were the doctrines of purgatory, pardons, worshipping of images and relics, invocation of saints, and the Mass, all of which the Tract declared to be within the scope of the Articles, as forming part of the Catholic Creed formulated and decreed by Rome as *de fide*, and not to be understood as included in the expression of Article XXII., 'Romish doctrine,' *i.e.* the commonly accepted and practically authoritative teaching of the Roman Church.

Protest of the four Tutors, March 8.

The protest appeared on March 8. Newman immediately acknowledged the 'very courteous communication' of it, and expressed no ill-will on account of the Tutors' action. Though he did not immediately give his name, he did not deny the authorship, and was known to be preparing an answer. But Golightly of Oriel stirred up the dust like a March wind, put the *Standard* in motion, sent copies of the Tract all over the country, and to the bishops, and by ceaseless activity prevailed upon the Heads of Houses to sit in judgment on the Tract and its author, without waiting for his answer. The Heads met on the 15th, and decided 'that modes of interpretation, such as are suggested [in Tract 90], evading rather than explaining the sense of the Thirty-nine Articles, and reconciling subscription to them with the adoption of errors which they were designed to counteract, defeat the object, and are inconsistent with the due observance of the [University] Statutes.'

Judgment of the Heads of Houses, March 15.

Newman's letter to the Vice-Chancellor, in which he acknowledged the authorship of the Tract, came out on March 16, the day after the censure of the Hebdomadal Council, and almost at the same moment his explanation of it, in a letter addressed to his friend Dr. Jelf, a Canon of Christ Church, and dated March 13. This letter passed through the press at the moment when the Heads were formulating their censure, and it would have been more courteous to the author of the Tract, though perhaps less convenient, to wait till it appeared. In this letter he used strong language against Romanism, and insisted on the distinction drawn between the decrees of Tridentine divines and 'the authoritative teaching of the present Church,' *i.e.* the doctrine of the schools, which 'is at present, on the whole, the established creed of the Roman Church; and this I call Romanism or Popery, and against this I think the Thirty-nine Articles speak . . . not certain accidental practices, but a body and substance of divinity, and that traditionary, an existing ruling spirit and view in the Church.'

Newman's letters to the Vice-Chancellor and Dr. Jelf.

It is not necessary to go into the details of the dispute. The Bishop of Oxford (Bagot) did his best to make peace, and showed much consideration for Newman; but the situation did not admit of peace. The Bishop's wish that the series of Tracts should be stopped was obeyed by Newman, but not without disappointment, and some sense of injury.

The Tracts are discontinued.

The result of the 'immense commotion consequent upon
the publication of the Tract' was that Newman 'weathered the
storm': No. 90 had not been censured, nor even
withdrawn from circulation.   The Bishop had said
that a certain Tract was 'objectionable,' but given

'Understand-
ing' with the
Bishop.

no reason.   There was an 'understanding' between Newman
and Bishop Bagot that he should 'publish his own condemnation' in a letter to the Bishop.   It was also understood
that no more Tracts should be issued, and no more were
issued.   But an 'understanding' often means a misunderstanding; and such an understanding could not bind even the
Bishop of Oxford, who had made it, much less his brethren.
The bishops used much hard language in their charges.
They could not be silent on so important a subject.
John Sumner of Chester upheld Justification by Faith as 'the
corner-stone of all the Reformed Churches'; his brother Charles,
of Winchester, took exception to the Tract on Reserve, to
expressions of admiration, love, and reverence for Rome, and
disparagement of the Reformers and their work, the new interpretation of the Articles, the doctrine of tradition, and the view
that 'Scripture was never intended to teach doctrine to the
many.'   Phillpotts of Exeter paid a high tribute to the
Tractarians, who had taught the Church that the Christian
life is not an individual but a corporate life; but he also
used such adjectives as 'offensive,' 'indecent,' and 'sophis-
tical.'   Blomfield of London and Copleston of Llandaff
also condemned the Tract, but in moderate terms.   Bagot
himself spoke with much respect of the temper of the
Tractarians, their dutifulness and ready submission, the
affection and kind feeling shown to himself personally,
and deplored the violence of attacks made upon them.
But he could not reconcile himself to the principle of Tract
90.   'I have already expressed my opinion that it was
objectionable'; and he went on to say that 'the plain obvious
meaning [of the Articles] is that which as members of the
Church we are bound to receive,' and to object to 'a system
of interpretation which is so subtle that by it the Articles
may be made to mean anything or nothing.'   If Newman
had known what was in the Bishop's mind, he would have
entered into no understanding with him.   No wonder that he

'hated "understandings"' ever after.   But could the Bishop honestly have said less?

The Tracts had done their work, and the action of the bishops was neither united nor uncompromising.   Newman had gained that point through the kindness of his own bishop, who could have given the matter a different turn. But disapproval on the part of the bishops affected Newman himself, to whom episcopal authority stood in the place of papal: 'a bishop's lightest word, *ex cathedra*, is heavy.'   The charges may even have set the tone of thinking in the Church in the sense of the Tracts generally, though not of Tract 90.

Bishops' charges are floodmarks; they show how high the water has stood, and indicate a normal level, they neither create nor check the growth of opinion; and the *Times* (6 March 1841) said significantly that 'the younger clergy are said to be very generally of this school.'

The bishops' charges.

Keble vacated the Professorship of Poetry in 1841, and his friends put forward Isaac Williams as a candidate for the chair.   He was known as a poet of some reputation, as a follower though not an imitator of Keble, a contributor to *Lyra Apostolica*, author of *The Cathedral, The Baptistery*, and other poems, and closely allied by friendship and family connexion with the Kebles and their circle.   In quiet times he would probably have been elected, for there was little doubt of his superior fitness for the chair, though his competitor Garbett had some claim as a scholar and student of literature.   But in unquiet times everything turns to party—*quodcumque infundis acescit*— and Williams, as a prominent Tractarian and author of the Tracts on Reserve, was not likely to escape.   Pusey was so ill-judged as to write a circular of recommendation on the ground of Williams's religious opinions, which was taken up as a challenge, and insured his defeat if he had gone to the poll; and after a comparison of votes Williams withdrew without a contest (January 1842).

Election to Poetry Professorship. Williams and Garbett, 1842.

At the same time an unsuccessful attempt was made to rescind the vote passed in 1836 against Hampden, which gave that unfortunate controversialist the opportunity for

striking a blow at the High Church party, by imposing, as
Professor of Divinity, a new and unauthorised test of
doctrine for the degree of B.D.   A High Church-   Macmullen's
man, R. Macmullen of Corpus, 'applied for theses'   degree.
to the Professor, as was the custom, and received from
him two theological propositions to support, which it was
known he could not support conscientiously.   The Vice-
Chancellor, Dr. Wynter, President of St. John's, wishing to
avoid dispute, made dispute inevitable by stopping Macmullen's
degree; and actions were brought in the Vice-Chancellor's
and other courts, which dragged the contest on through more
than two years; and when the Hebdomadal Board in February
1844 brought in a Statute to confer upon the Regius Professor
the power which he had attempted to exercise, the Statute
was thrown out by 341 to 21.   The Heads were out of touch
with the University.   They had more power than authority;
an unnatural position.

Some of them, with Hawkins the Provost of Oriel to lead
them, determined to attack Pusey himself.   They thought
that in virtue of their irresponsible position they
could cut off the tallest poppy-head in Oxford,   Pusey's
and deal a blow at the new heresy, on the plea   sermon on
of unorthodox doctrine put forward in a sermon on   the Eucharist,
1843.
the Holy Eucharist preached in Christ Church Cathedral on
May 24, 1843.   The views set forth in this sermon were,
as some thought, undistinguishable from Roman doctrine.
Dr. Faussett, Margaret Professor of Divinity, was the *delator*,
and was also one of the Six Doctors before whom the
complaint came.   The Statutes of the University gave the
Vice-Chancellor power to suspend, or to require a recantation.
It was decided to take the latter course, and if possible to
keep all secret.   The accused had no opportunity of meeting
his judges or saying a word in his own defence; he did not
know the name of his accuser, the definite charges laid against
him, the method under which the examination of the sermon
was conducted, nor what were the passages condemned.
Pusey, in his desire for peace, entered into private negotiations,
and was even willing to sign explanatory statements; but his
judges would not trust him, fearing that he 'would be able
by ingenuity to evade any direct charge of heterodoxy,' and

demanded a formal recantation. As his explanations did not
amount to so much as this, the Vice-Chancellor
proceeded to pass judgment upon him (2 June
1843), on the ground that he had 'taught certain
things disagreeing with and contrary to the doctrine
of the Church of England'; and pronounced sentence of
suspension from preaching within the University for two
years. It was an expression of opinion, not a judgment,
though it carried a penalty: a practical confusion of disciplinary and judicial action, not unknown in scholastic and
clerical affairs.

*Pusey sus-
pended for
two years,
1843.*

Pusey protested against the sentence as 'unstatutable and
unjust.' But the personal, legal, and ecclesiastical difficulties
connected with the affair made it impossible for him to
obtain redress, and the sentence was not openly challenged.
It is not wonderful that much suspicion and alarm should be
caused by the doings of the Tractarians; but to proceed in so
arbitrary a manner against so eminent and blameless a person
was, says Dean Church, 'a great injustice and a great blunder.'
It was an injustice, because the accused was not heard;
a blunder, because the sentence was merely disciplinary,
imposed no silence except in a single place and for a limited
time, discredited the University as a judge of doctrine, and
finally drew attention and gave publicity to a tenet which
had been hardly heard of in the Church of England thirty
years earlier. If the tractarian teachers were successful in
spreading high sacramental doctrine, some part of their success
is due to the action of the Vice-Chancellor and the Six
Doctors in 1843.

The effect of the whole controversy was to strengthen
and unite the high Anglican party for the time, but it
tended also to widen the road that led to Rome, and
to shake Newman's position both as a leader and as a
Churchman. He could not be sure of controlling his
followers, and he was no longer quite sure of himself.
He did not give up the living of St. Mary's, as he
had contemplated doing, from a belief that such
action would do more harm than good: but he had
lost heart. 'I saw clearly,' he says, 'that my place in the
Movement was lost; public confidence was at an end; my

*Newman at
Littlemore.*

occupation was gone'; and he retired more and more into solitude, though he still preached at St. Mary's, counsels of quietness.

A new turn was given to the dispute by William George Ward (1812-1882), Fellow and Lecturer of Balliol, who, going beyond his master, proclaimed in two pamphlets written immediately after Tract 90 that the Church W. G. Ward of England being part of the Church Catholic, of Balliol. her formularies must have a catholic sense read into them, whatever violence might be done to language and grammar, and that Catholic and Tridentine are identical. He claimed to hold 'all Roman doctrine' within his subscription to the Articles, and to subscribe these 'in a non-natural sense.' There were thus four theories of interpretation in the field: the old traditional Protestant theory, the *animus imponentis* theory, the theory of the literal and grammatical meaning, but with a Catholic intention, and now the Tridentine theory, Ward's theory, which only wanted the acceptance of papal infallibility to complete it.

Ward was a sanguine and eager character, a keen and invincible arguer, as skilled in logic as a schoolman, and shrinking from no conclusion to which logic led him. His dialectics were unmerciful; he put innumerable questions and insisted on answers; he delighted in transgressing the maxim of Epictetus to 'take things up by the handle which will bear it.' The exacerbation of feeling which set in suited him. He was at once the kindliest and the most irritating of men. He was also a man of warm friendships and loyal to his friends, who sometimes found he travelled too far for them. He now made wild work with the *via media*, the party, and himself.

His two pamphlets, 'A Few Words in Defence of Tract 90,' and 'A Few Words more in Defence of Tract 90,' neither defended nor explained, but opened a new question. 'A Few Words Interpretations of Articles in the Tract had been in Defence of thought forced: Ward wished them to be forced, Tract 90.' and propounded the doctrine of the 'non-natural sense.' Newman had spoken with reserve; Ward tore away the veil. He insisted on showing Newman whither his premisses led; and Newman, who liked logic too, was put in a difficulty.

Newman had spared the Reformers, partly out of tenderness for Pusey and his followers; Ward gloried in showing their uncatholic temper. Newman had said in effect, the letter of the Articles is not incompatible with the Tridentine decrees; they are not directed against the Tridentine decrees, because they are earlier in date; they are directed against errors accepted by the authoritative teaching of Rome, some of which may have been incorporated later into the decrees of the Council; we are concerned only with the words of the Articles and the Roman definitions *de fide*, not with popular or even authoritative theology. He did not state clearly where the authority to make definitions resided, and put aside the question of Trent. Ward said that the same authority imposed earlier definitions, Tridentine definitions, and the practical system of the Roman Church. That is the Catholic faith; the Church of England is a branch of the Catholic Church, therefore the Church of England holds the whole of that doctrine, and if the Articles do not teach it, so much the worse for the Articles; they must be subscribed, not in their plain literal and grammatical sense, but in a 'non-natural sense.' He does away with Newman's distinction between 'Romish' and 'Roman'; he does away also with the claim of the Church of England to an independent existence.

Thus there came to be a division between the older men, Keble, Pusey, Isaac Williams, and Palmer of Worcester, who did not wish the Reformation undone, and rever-

Division between old and new Tractarians.

enced those stout opponents of Rome, the Elizabethan and Stuart divines, and the younger and more extreme partisans, led by Ward. Newman, in bitter perplexity and sorrow of heart, was silent. Pusey asked Ward for a distinct pledge that he would not join the Church of Rome, which pledge Ward would not give. Ward visited the Roman Catholic College at Oscott. Sibthorp, a fellow of Magdalen, had been received into the Church of Rome in October 1841. Old friendships and mutual tolerations were breaking down; the University was not at peace with itself.

The Tractarians themselves were not silent about their divisions. Palmer of Worcester published in 1843 a *Narrative of Events*, which represents the grievance of the old Tract-

arians, who did not wish to follow the dangerous leadership
of the *British Critic*. He complains of 'a spirit
of dissatisfaction with the Church's principles, of William Palmer's
enmity to her Reformers, of recklessness for her *Narrative*, 1843.
interests, . . . of almost servility and adulation to
Rome ; . . . the blame of separation, of schism, is openly and
unscrupulously laid on the English Church. . . . The theory
of development . . . according to which the *latest* form of
Christianity is the most perfect . . . is openly sanctioned,
advocated, avowed.' Palmer and his friends wished to run a
new Review in opposition to the *British Critic*.
But the publisher preferred to suspend the *British* Ward's *Ideal of a*
Critic ; and Ward, now left without an organ, *Christian Church*, 1844.
answered Palmer's *Narrative* in the summer of
1844 by his famous book, *The Ideal of a Christian Church,
considered in comparison with existing Practice*.

Ward was one of those logical enthusiasts who from
intellect and temperament are incapable of reticence. Convinced of his own rectitude and intellectual power, he took
his premisses as certain, and had no misgivings as to any of
his conclusions. He accepted the Roman dogma in full ;
he considered the schism of the sixteenth century, the
desertion of the Roman Church, 'a great sin,' and held
that the Church of England ought to 'repent in sorrow and
bitterness of heart, and sue humbly at her feet for pardon and
restoration '; and yet subscribed the Articles of the Church
of England, ministered in her churches, and believed sacramental grace to be in the Church of England in virtue of
her apostolical succession. In a well-known passage he
declared his joy at seeing 'the whole cycle of Roman doctrine'
professed within the Church of England, and dared his
opponents to contradict him. 'Three years have passed
since I said plainly, that in subscribing the Articles I renounce
no one Roman doctrine : yet I retain my fellowship, which
I hold on the tenure of subscription, and have received no
ecclesiastical censure in any shape.'

The book has the manner of an argumentative work. But
it has little cogency. It is entirely unlike such books as
Newman's *Development of Doctrine* and *Grammar of Assent*.
There, the argument, however one-sided and incomplete, is

carefully conducted from point to point. Here there is but one syllogism—of which the major premiss is, that that which is ordained and practised by Rome is alone true and right, the minor, that the common forms, methods, and rules of the Church of England are opposed to those of Rome ; and the conclusion follows : Rome is right, and all else is wrong. Ward can see no good to set against the evil contained in Lutheranism, Evangelicalism, Protestantism of all kinds, and Rationalism. He is too full of matter to pause and reread what he has written. There is no reticence or discipline. Incidentally, however, the *Ideal* has interest as a contrast between Roman and Anglican doctrine and practice. We need not draw the author's conclusions, but he marshals the facts. Indeed, he did not draw his own conclusion. He remained in the Anglican Church, in spite of her denial, by the schism of the Reformation, of the great principles of obedience and faith ; in spite of her inferiority, in the fruits of religion, to the continental churches of the Roman obedience, her pride ('for three hundred years our peculiar note of disgrace'); in spite of her neglect of asceticism, of sacramental confession, of catechetical instruction, of duty to the poor, of all fixed religious principles; in spite of her 'absolute and pointed opposition' to Rome 'in government, in authoritative formularies, in discipline.' 'Newman is my pope,' he said to his friends ; and this, together with a sense that to change his religion would be an act of private judgment, and that if he became a Romanist the temptation to use private judgment might still be present, kept him for a time within the limits of the Church of England.

Ward's book would have been quickly forgotten, if it had not been chosen as the battle-ground of opinion at Oxford. It was thought necessary to pronounce with authority that an English Churchman cannot accept all the doctrines laid down by the Church of Rome, and retain his orders in the Church of England. The *Edinburgh Review* of October 1844, in an article entitled ' Recent Developments in Puseyism,

Edinburgh and Quarterly Reviews, 1844. after attacking Dr. Pusey's Sermon on the Eucharist, Newman's Essay on Miracles, and Keble's Tract, No. 89, on the ' Mysticism of the Fathers,' as affording indications both of the superstitious tendency of the

Oxford School, and of their disloyalty to the Church of
England, as well as of their disagreement among themselves,
spoke of Ward's book as 'a practical exemplification of the
principles of the Tracts of the most odious kind.' The
Quarterly Review in December, in an article written by
Gladstone, and therefore in no unfriendly spirit, compared
Ward to a child who should strike a parent before leaving her,
found fault with his theory that the supremacy of conscience
in religious inquiry is subjective, and is another name for
private judgment,—in Ward's own words, 'doing what we
think right because we think so,'—and exhorted him to
humility.

The movement against Ward was conducted, most un-
necessarily, it would seem, with all the secrecy of a conspiracy.
After some months of private consultations he was *The proposi-*
summoned, early in 1845, before the newly elected *tion of the*
Vice-Chancellor, Dr. Symons, Warden of Wadham, *University*
and the Hebdomadal Board, and asked to retract *1845.*
'six of the most startling and extreme passages from the *Ideal.*'
On his refusing, by legal advice, to commit himself, it was
resolved to submit proposals to Convocation, first, to condemn
the book and censure the author for want of good faith;
secondly, to deprive him of his degrees of B.A. and M.A.;
and thirdly, to impose on all graduates for the future a test
defining the sense in which the Articles were to be signed.
Convocation had as much or as little right as any private
association to pronounce upon the good faith of any graduate
of the University. It had the right to degrade on the ground
of opinions disentitling to 'the rights and privileges conveyed'
by degrees, but not in cases unprovided for by statute. As
for the imposition of a new test, apart from all legal and
technical difficulties, apart from all considerations of prudence,
propriety, and charity, the terms of the new definition were
ambiguous and elusive, and would hold no one. The
candidate for a degree was to affirm that he signed the Articles,
all and each, 'in the sense in which I sincerely believe that
they were originally put forth, and now proposed to me by
the University.' Since the University, that is, Convocation,
contained men of all opinions, and since this 'sense' was
nowhere defined, the latter clause said nothing, and might

be subscribed by anybody.   Or, if the two clauses had any
meaning, they could be pressed against Whately or Hampden,
as well as against the Tractarians.

The indignation and alarm created by the third proposition (for no one can predict a vote of Convocation) was so
The third great that it was withdrawn on January 23; and
proposition is at the request of 474 members of Convocation
withdrawn. a censure of the modes of interpretation advocated
in Tract 90 was substituted for it.   The attack was thus
diverted from Ward personally, and extended to the whole
tractarian party, and Newman in particular, the author of the
Tract, who was 'supremely indifferent as to the fate of this
new move about himself.'   The situation was curiously parallel
to that of 1836, when Dr. Hampden was censured, and the
outcome was much the same.   In both cases the University,
unwisely and with doubtful legality, assumed the office of
a judge of heresy, and much ill-feeling was stirred up; and
in both cases the judgment given was that of the University,
not of a party, and fairly represented the state of public
opinion.

Dr. Tait, now Head Master of Rugby, who had led the
attack upon Tract 90 in 1841, came forward at this point
Tait's with a pamphlet in which he admitted that Ward's
pamphlet. opinions ought to be censured, and even his degrees
taken away, but protested against the third proposition as tending to narrow the Church of England.   'It would
operate,' he said, 'to the exclusion of the best, because the
most conscientious men.'

The discussion came on on February 13, 1845 ; Ward
defended himself ably before the University ; he was
Ward's trial allowed to speak in English, the rest of the speeches
before the
University being, as usual, in Latin.   Indeed throughout the
Convocation. proceedings he was treated with much forbearance
and courtesy.   The first resolution, censuring certain passages
from the *Ideal of a Christian Church*, was carried by a majority
of more than 300 ; and the second, taking away the
Veto of the author's academical degrees, by about fifty.   When
Proctors. the Vice-Chancellor rose to read the third resolution,
condemning Tract 90, the Proctors, Guillemard of Trinity
and Church of Oriel, afterwards Dean of St. Paul's, rose and

pronounced the words *Nobis Procuratoribus non placet*; which, as in the case of Dr. Hampden, the only other case on record in the century, *ipso facto* suspended the vote.

Ward took the rebuke with characteristic light-heartedness, not levity, though Archdeacon Manning so mistook it. He retired from Oxford, an undergraduate Fellow of Balliol, six weeks later astonished and amused the world by suddenly announcing his marriage, and in September was received into the Roman Church. His grounds for this action were twofold : first, that church authority, no less than university authority, had pronounced against the principle of Tract 90 ; secondly, that he could not find for himself or others that sustaining grace in the ordinances of the Church of England which he had once believed her to possess. We may easily believe that his state of mind was much affected by the action of Newman, who made his submission to the Roman Church a few weeks later.

Ward is received into the Church of Rome.

If the Convocation of the University of Oxford had passed a censure on the principles of Tract 90, the controversy would not have ended there. Those principles might have been censured by the Convocations of the two provinces, and by all the bishops, but still no clerk could have been deprived of his benefice by their vote of censure : nothing but a judicial sentence of the highest ecclesiastical court could carry practical results. Tract 90 contained in it a principle of comprehension to which its author would not have subscribed, a principle admitting impugners of sacramental doctrine and biblical infallibility, a principle not excluding Erastian government and lay interpretation. This principle of comprehension, enlarged and applied to other forms of belief than the Roman, is now accepted by men of all parties in the Church, and has had momentous issues.

Ward's censure and secession caused much stir in the world. But a greater event occurred within a few weeks of his conversion, the conversion of Newman himself. The story of Newman's conversion has been told in his own matchless words, and all that remains to do here is to chronicle the date of his reception into the Church of Rome, October 8, 1845.

Newman received into the Church of Rome, 1845.

Tract 90 was meant to reconcile with subtle reasoning two irreconcilable positions, the Anglican and the Roman; and, as a practical result, to keep such men as Ward and his friends in the Church. 'We must consent either to give up the men, or to admit their principles.' Ward's *Notes* showed that the resting-place, if anywhere, was farther down the slope; and Newman, soon recognising this, ceased to officiate as an English clergyman. He did not retire at once; to hesitate was due to his own character and his position, and to those whom he had led so far. Indeed, the patience and resolution in which he armed himself to endure four years of 'deathbed' are not the least wonderful part of the story of his conversion. He gave up in 1841 the editorship of the *British Critic*, and desired that his name should be kept out of its pages as far as possible. In 1842 he left his rooms at Oriel, and migrated with a few disciples, to Littlemore. Here the little company fasted, prayed, and studied, said the daily office of the Church, and lived according to strict monastic rule. The services at St. Mary's were, for the most part, left to the curates, and the Vicar's familiar form seldom appeared in the streets of Oxford. Curiosity was awakened; what was he doing at Littlemore? All eyes were upon him, and he was subjected to much unkind criticism. He resented this; *secretum meum mihi*, he said; but he had created his own position by speaking out, and his long silence perplexed both friends and enemies. He was still the Vicar of St. Mary's, and the most conspicuous figure in the University, nay, in the Church of England, and he could not, as it were, cease to be. Still he lingered. In February 1843 he published, in the *Conservative Journal*, a formal retractation of 'hard things' said against the Church of Rome. On September 18 he resigned the living of St. Mary's, including the cure of Littlemore. On September 25 he preached at Littlemore, to a weeping congregation, that most affecting appeal, his last Anglican sermon, 'The Parting of Friends.' On October 15 he celebrated the Holy Communion for the last time at St. Mary's, 'while,' says Liddon, 'the friends who owed everything to him gathered round the altar with conflicting emotions of hope and fear.' Two years more passed, during which he was composing and writing his *Essay on*

the Development of Christian Doctrine, the motto of which,
telling of his 'deathbed' pangs, is '*Oculi mei defecerunt in
salutare Tuum, et in eloquium justitiae Tuae*,' and which ends
with the words, '*quia viderunt oculi mei salutare Tuum*.'
The passage of a 'dedicated spirit' into another world is a
solemn spectacle.

Meanwhile events were proceeding. In February 1845
came Ward's condemnation, and in September his secession.
Frederick Oakeley, one of Newman's special followers, was
deprived of his chapel in Margaret Street by the Arches
Court in July, and was received into the Roman communion
in October, Dalgairns in September. Capes, St. John, Faber
and others followed. At last the moment came, and Newman
passed out of the sight of the Church of England; but not
out of mind, for his sermons still live, and the *Essay on
Development, Loss and Gain*, and *Callista* are read. But
above all the *Apologia pro Vitâ Suâ* remains to remind
Englishmen, whether they follow to his conclusion or not, of
their countryman's struggle for conscience against inclination
and interest, and all the ties of home, friendship, and association. Newman was half forgotten when he wrote the *Apologia*
in 1864; since then he has become one of the permanent
possessions of the English people.

The argument which persuaded Newman was in effect
this: If there is, since there is, a God, from whom His
creatures are in some mysterious way alienated, and
above all man, whose consciousness of choice   Newman's
and knowledge of good and evil introduced sin   religious position.
into the world, and since the consequence of sin, as appre-
hended by man, is moral death; and since God is good, and
a God of love,—it is probable that He has not cast off His
creatures, but has a scheme for their redemption from death.
Such a scheme is found in the Gospel, which sets forth the
method in which God planned the salvation of the world,
by a revelation unlike any other. But a revelation which
each man's several conscience may severally interpret is not a
complete revelation. Man requires an authoritative guide. This
authoritative guide, say Catholic and Protestant alike, is found in
the Bible. But who is to interpret the Bible? The private
conscience of each believer, says Protestantism. Those, says

the Church, to whom Christ gave the *depositum fidei*, and with whom He has promised to remain till the end. Amongst all the jarring assertions of authority Newman found no church or philosophy which could claim authority with so good a right as the church which has always called itself Catholic. 'Either the Catholic religion is verily and indeed the coming of the unseen world into this, or there is nothing positive, nothing dogmatic, nothing real in any of our notions as to whence we come and whither we go.' The steps of his conversion are noted by himself, and have been read by all the world, in the *Apologia*. In his study of the Monophysite controversy in 1839 he saw 'the shadow of a hand upon the wall'—'a vista to the end of which he did not see.' 'My condemnation of the Anglican Church,' he wrote, 'arose out of my study of the Fathers.' In 1841 the doctrine of Tract 90 was condemned by the bishops; he saw in the Arian controversy what he had seen in the Monophysite controversy, the English Church in the position of the heretics; in the Jerusalem bishopric he saw the Church of England 'courting an intercommunion with Protestant Prussia and the heresy of the Orientals.' These, he says, were 'the three further blows which broke me.'

It has often been said that Newman accepted the Roman dogma as an alternative to scepticism. It should rather be said that the principle of dogma was held by him so fundamentally, that the only question before his mind was, where authority was to be found. The existence of God was to him self-evident, and upon this conviction his creed was built. His method of reasoning was deductive, and in establishing premisses there entered into his mind, as motives for deference to antiquity and constituted authority, a strong Hebraistic fear of God's judgments, a tender sentiment for the severe and ascetic virtues, coloured by the spirit of the age, the romantic mediævalist spirit, unlike that of the Reformation or of the eighteenth-century revival, and only partially akin to that of George Herbert and the High Churchmen of Charles I.'s time. Add to this strong repellent forces; anger against liberalism, against old-fashioned, professional, academical religion; impatience of self-reputed learning and conventional wisdom; and with this, vivid personal

Dogma and scepticism.

sympathies and antipathies; strong personal pride and self-will, sternly repressed; a delicate reserve and dislike of publicity; above all zeal for truth, and long-continued discipline in holy living, which more and more followed the guiding of the Roman Church, and made Roman usages and devotion seem to him the natural expression of religious emotion.

But though Newman's faith in dogma was never shaken, though dogma was to him a primary fact, and his first impressions of dogma were, as he tells us in the *His desire for enlightenment.* *Apologia*, 'never effaced or obscured,' his intellect was of that kind which, if his conscience had taken that line, might have made him a heretic. He wrote to Pusey in March 1845, 'each one has his own temptations. I thank God that He has shielded me from what intellectually might easily come on one—general scepticism.' Like Pascal, he was, by the natural turn of his intellect, next to a believer, a sceptic; but the weaker side of his mind, the tendency to assent, was corrected by no scientific training; the mould in which his mind was cast was ecclesiastical, and so was his estimate of probabilities. Questions of origins, of the comparative method in the history of religion and dogma, interested him little; but he said enough to show that there was in his mind, though strictly disciplined under authority, and firmly settled upon revealed truth, *His method of reasoning.* that desire for enlightenment which inspires what it is the fashion to call 'modernism,' one of the elements in which is faith in the continued revelation of God by methods and in directions as yet unknown.

It is characteristic of Newman's reasoning that it is cogent by clearness rather than by breadth. His principles once laid down, he argued fearlessly from them, and did not willingly re-interrogate them. It would seem as if intellectual light came to him entirely from one quarter, and that he distrusted all other illumination. His subtlety misled himself as well as others. Newman uses rhetoric as an aid to logic, he is supreme in commending a point of view by marshalling arguments and instances that point one way; and one of his greatest rhetorical advantages, as is acknowledged by all who read his sermons, is his deep insight into human nature.

Newman's secession could not surprise any one, but it affected many people very deeply. Even in the last days of Newman's sojourn at Littlemore Pusey's tender heart had clung to the hope that he would not desert the cause. His departure shook the whole High Church party; it sundered a company of friends who had worked together from the beginning of the movement which they created. The authors of the *via media* theory and the 'non-natural sense' theory proclaimed their own theories to be unsound, and submitted them to the only Church which claims to know with certainty. The enemy triumphed openly, whether Roman or Anglican or Evangelical or Liberal. They had all foretold it, and they were not wrong. It was an hour of deep humiliation.

AUTHORITIES.—As before, for Chaps. XI.-XIII. *Tracts for the Times*, Nos. 85, 87, 90; Pusey, *The Holy Eucharist a Comfort to the Penitent*, 1843; W. G. Ward, *A few Words*, etc., and *A few Words More*, etc., 1841, *The Ideal of a Christian Church*, etc., 1844; Wilfrid Ward, *W. G. Ward and the Oxford Movement*; J. H. Newman, *Essay on the Development of Doctrine*.

CHAPTER XV

LIBERAL REACTION

SCARCELY had Newman and his friends left the scene when the attention of the Church was called once more to Hampden. Between the attack made upon him in 1836 and his appointment to the See of Hereford, which took place in 1847, much had happened. He had not recanted; he maintained that he had nothing to recant, and that the declarations of orthodoxy which he was always ready to make were in harmony with the passages which enemies extracted from his books. It is impossible to recant confusion of thought and obscurity of style. Hampden knew more about his subject than his adversaries did; those who read him carefully found *Dr. Hampden's progress, 1836-1846.* that he needed elucidation less than they had supposed; but his subject was obscure in itself and little known, and he did not make its terminology sufficiently clear. Since his double condemnation by the University of Oxford in 1836 and in 1842, he had been appointed chairman of the Board of Theological Studies in 1842, and also examiner in the theological examination founded in the same year. Though his sentence remained unreversed, his position as Regius Professor and Canon of Christ Church, and his reputation as an active opponent of the Tractarians made him a prominent personage : and no one was surprised when in 1842 he objected to giving the Regius Professor of Hebrew the office of Examiner in Theology, avowedly because the then Professor was Pusey, the reputed leader of the Tractarians. Prophecies about the tendency of tractarian teaching had been fulfilled in the recent secession to Rome of Newman and many of his disciples. Keble and *The Christian Year* remained, the movement of 1833 had not spent itself; but Puseyism was unpopular, and the English fear of Rome and dislike of system and ceremony was awake.

Lord John Russell, who became Prime Minister in July 1846, had Whig notions of Church policy, robust Protestant prejudices, and a full share of that contempt for clerical ways of thinking and acting which is not uncommon among statesmen. The See of Hereford became vacant in the following year by the promotion of Bishop Musgrave to York; and Russell looked for a sound Protestant to recommend to the Queen in his place.

Divinity professors stand in the line of promotion, and Hampden was a Liberal as well as an anti-Tractarian.

Lord John Russell recommends Hampden as Bishop of Hereford, 1847. Lord John 'felt no doubt that the Archbishop had become reconciled to Hampden's promotion by the orthodox and Christian character of his subsequent writings'; he considered the precedents, and saw in Hampden's zeal for the Protestant religion a reason for his promotion. He recommended Hampden to the Queen, and Her Majesty accepted him; and having so recommended him he could not go back without discrediting both himself and his nominee. Lord John probably thought that Hampden's unpopularity had died out, and that no objection would be raised to his appointment as Bishop of Hereford. He showed a want of sagacity if he thought so. The vote of 1836 was irregular, tumultuary, and unjust, but it represented a formidable body of public opinion; the vote of 1842 showed a change but not a reversal of opinion; if he wanted to make a protest against the Romanising party he could easily have found a better champion than Hampden, who had little personal ascendency, and whose orthodoxy was suspected by Churchmen of all parties. Hampden belonged to no definite party, but though he denied it, he was more of a Latitudinarian than anything else, and the latitudinarian school was looked upon as dangerous.

There were reasons enough for objecting to Hampden's promotion; and they were expressed by Julius Hare, a

Liberal of middle views, who, whilst arguing that the clamour which had arisen against Hampden was founded in party spite rather than in truth, and that he was innocent of the charges brought against him, nevertheless thought the appointment 'a very unfortunate, nay, disastrous measure.' Thirteen bishops addressed the Prime Minister in the same sense. Among them were Blomfield of London, Sumner of Winchester, Phillpotts of Exeter, Denison of Salisbury, Bagot of Bath and Wells, Wilberforce of Oxford; but not Thirlwall of St. David's, Stanley of Norwich, nor Copleston of Llandaff. Some said the fiery and impetuous Bishop of Exeter was at the bottom of it, some, the Bishop of Oxford. If it was the Bishop of Oxford, he found out his mistake, and wrote to Hampden that he had trusted to extracts from the Bampton Lectures, and formed his opinion of the book without having read it, and that having read it he could find no heresy in it. The very awkwardness of the retractation is evidence of its sincerity, though Charles Greville surmised that his conscience had been awakened by cold looks at Windsor. The bishops' protest was made on the ground that the University of Oxford had solemnly affirmed its want of confidence in the soundness of Hampden's doctrine; that a deep and general feeling prevailed on this subject, and that his appointment would interrupt the peace of the Church, and diminish the confidence which it was desirable that the clergy and laity should feel in any exercise of the Royal supremacy.

Protest of the bishops.

Lord John answered courteously, if not logically, pointing out that the thirteen bishops did not express their own doubt of Hampden's orthodoxy, but only referred to a decree of the University of Oxford eleven years old; that since that time Hampden had received the approbation of several bishops; that the Archbishop when consulted had given 'no discouragement'; that to withdraw the nomination after the Queen's sanction had been given would be tantamount to saying that the Royal supremacy was transferred to one of the universities; and that many of Hampden's opponents in 1836 had since that time joined the Church of Rome. The main point of the petitioners,

Russell's answer.

the distress and disapproval which attended the appointment, was ignored.

The Bishop of Exeter also addressed a pompous and clamorous letter to the Prime Minister, which contained, however, one practical suggestion, that Hampden's writings should be subjected to 'a fitting and adequate tribunal.' Meanwhile no less than fifteen out of twenty-three Heads of

The Oxford Heads of Houses.

Houses at Oxford addressed a letter of confidence to Hampden, which was signed amongst others by Symons of Wadham, Vice-Chancellor, Hawkins of Oriel, Wynter of St. John's, Gaisford of Christ Church, Thomson of St. Edmund Hall (afterwards Archbishop of York), and was, it is said, approved by Dr. Routh of Magdalen, the respect for whose character was based not only upon his theological learning and his venerable age, but also upon his reputation for wisdom and courage.

It would have been as difficult for Russell now as for Melbourne on the former occasion to withdraw his recommendation. The *congé d'élire* was accord-

Congé d'élire issued.

ingly issued to the Dean and Chapter of Hereford, and then followed the strange series of occurrences which has preserved the memory of the incident. According to Charles Greville, Dr. Merewether, the Dean of Hereford, was sulky; he had expected to be made Bishop of Hereford himself, trusting to an alleged promise

Dean Merewether.

or 'deathbed injunction' of William IV., to which, with questionable taste, he referred in his correspondence with the Prime Minister, and so was disposed to make difficulties. His conduct of the proceedings does not lead to the conclusion that he would have made a good bishop, but there can be no question as to his sincerity. He wrote a letter to the Queen, in which he laid stress on the words 'a person meet thereunto' in the *congé d'élire*, as acknowledging some liberty of action residing in the Chapter with respect to the person recommended to them for election; he recited the Oxford Statute of censure, still unrepealed, and begged that the Chapter might be allowed not to proceed to election till Hampden's published writings should be submitted to the two Houses of Convocation, or some other competent tribunal. The receipt of the Dean's letter was acknowledged, but no further notice of it was taken. He then wrote a lengthy letter to the Premier, in which he announced that he would not vote for Dr. Hampden's election, to which Lord John replied as follows :—

'WOBURN ABBEY, *Dec.* 25.

'SIR—I have had the honour to receive your letter of the 22nd inst., in which you intimate to me your intention of violating the law.

'I have the honour to be your obedient servant,—J. RUSSELL.

' The Very Rev. the Dean of Hereford.'

This smart letter meant nothing, for the threat which it implied could not be carried out. If the Dean and Chapter proved contumacious, they incurred the penalties of *præmunire*, but it would not have been worth while to prosecute them ; the Crown would have dispensed with the formality of election, Hampden would have been consecrated as Bishop of Hereford under letters patent, and no one would have been molested.

The Dean and one Canon, Dr. Huntingford, voted against Hampden, the rest of the greater Chapter, fourteen in number, including the non-residentiary Canons, voted for his election ; and as no provision was made for a dissentient dean, the necessary documents were *Election of Hampden.* sealed by the ' Dean and Chapter' as if unanimous, with no mention of the Dean's vote. If the Dean meant to protest effectively, he should have refused the use of the capitular seal, or by some act of disobedience tried the strength of his position in law. The statutes required a unanimous election, an election notified under the capitular seal was in the eye of the law unanimous, and the Dean's protest in Chapter is 'a literary curiosity,' and nothing more.

Petitions and counter-petitions were signed, and the press took up the question on both sides. Proceedings against Hampden for heresy were taken in the Court of Arches by certain members of the University of Oxford, with the sanction of Bishop Wilberforce ; but he, having reconsidered the matter, withdrew his consent, and wrote the letter which is noticed above. The question of law was tried on the occasion of the confirmation of Hampden's election in the Archbishop's court held for that purpose in the Church of St. Mary-le-Bow. On such occasions notice is given for objectors to come forward and be heard. But the objectors were not heard, the court deciding that the Archbishop's confirmation was a ministerial act, and valid. The next step was to apply to the Court of Queen's Bench for a rule to show cause why a mandamus should not issue to compel the Archbishop or his Vicar General to oppose the appointment. The application was heard before four judges, two of whom, Coleridge and Patteson, gave judgment in favour of the application on February 1, 1848, Denman and Erle against it.

Confirmation of Hampden's election, 1848.

Judgment on mandamus.

The nomination to the Chapter having been made, the Queen's nominee elected, the election confirmed, the legal objection to confirmation quashed, this string of blunders and inconsequences came to an end; having in its course damaged the reputation of the person in question, the tractarian party, the Heads of Houses, the University of Oxford, the Bishops, the Archbishop, and the Prime Minister, besides several individuals who had intervened at one point or another; and above all, the cumbrous system of *congé d'élire*, which preserved the mediæval forms without the mediæval spirit. It is to be noted that no one concerned impugned the validity of the Royal nomination to vacant sees. Dr. Hampden was peaceably enthroned at Hereford, and was heard of no more except in his own diocese, which he administered well.

The impression left on the minds of lawyers and men of the world was that the law ought to be altered and bishoprics made donative, as in Edward VI.'s reign. But the incident passed, and the *congé d'élire* still exists. A Bishop of Rochester is appointed by *congé d'élire*, a Bishop of Birmingham by letters patent, and the most orthodox clergymen appear to think one method as good as the other, though the one may involve a vote against conscience, and the other gives up the whole question of the right of the Church to elect bishops. Such anomalies are inseparable from the

English church-and-state system.   But it is not difficult to conclude from the whole affair that if Lord John Russell had shown more tact and apprehension of Church feeling he would not have made the appointment; and that if, when moderate men of different parties asked that Hampden's writings should be examined by a competent authority, he had consented, he would have saved a scandal, and not provoked unnecessary jealousy of the manner in which the Royal supremacy was exercised.

Almost at the same time as the Hampden affair at Hereford an episcopal election at Manchester became a subject of political discussion.   The See of Manchester was created by Act of Parliament 1847, and the ancient process of election by Chapter was adopted, since there was a Chapter connected with the Collegiate church; partly perhaps from archæological sentiment, partly to give dignity to the Chapter, though it is not easy to see what dignity can accrue from the privilege of registering a Prime Minister's nomination.   James Prince Lee, Head Master of King Edward's School at Birmingham, was nominated, and elected without opposition by the Chapter.   Dr. Lee had been accused of intoxication, malversation, and falsehood by a surgeon in Birmingham of the name of Gutteridge, and the accusation had been made the subject of private and public inquiry in the town; but no legal or official notice had been taken of the affair, except by the Bishop of Worcester, and the character neither of Lee nor of his accuser had been cleared.   Dr. Molesworth, Vicar of Rochdale, took up the question on public grounds, representing it as unfair to the Church, the accused, and the accuser, that a person against whom grave accusation had been brought, but neither proved nor disproved before a regular court, should be imposed for election upon the Chapter of Manchester and for acceptance upon the diocese, by a mere act of authority.   Opposition here also was made to the confirmation of the elected Bishop (10 January 1848), but was overruled, as in the case of Hampden.   Ultimately the charges made against the Bishop were completely disproved, Lord Denman, who tried the case, declaring (April 1848) the charges to be utterly groundless; and Prince Lee's name stands high among the bishops of the time, but the scandal

Election of Prince Lee as Bishop of Manchester, 1847.

Lord Denman's judgment, 1848.

remained of an election persisted in without opportunity for objectors to be heard.

The Cambridge petitions of 1834,[1] showing as they did a large majority in favour of the retention of religious tests, were not followed by legislation; for though the Commons passed an Oxford and Cambridge Bill in that year, it was, as we have seen, thrown out in the Lords on the second reading; nor was any substantial progress made till a reaction against tractarian teaching set in after the secession of Newman, which was contemporaneous with the revival of Liberal opinion throughout the country. One of the first indications of a change of opinion was a pamphlet on University Reform published by Tait in 1839, which recommended changes in the professorial and tutorial systems. In 1843 W. Douglas Christie, a nonconformist Member of Parliament, brought forward a bill 'to abolish certain oaths and subscriptions in the Universities and to extend education in the Universities to persons who are not members of the Church of England.' The bill was thrown out on the first reading. In 1845 he moved, but did not carry, an address for a Royal Commission to inquire into 'all matters relating to the privileges, revenues, and trusts, and to the state of education, learning, and religion in the Universities of Oxford and Cambridge and the Colleges of those Universities.' In 1846 some of the leading Oxford Liberals, with Jowett and Stanley at their head, petitioned Parliament for a Commission of Inquiry; they had the support of Goldwin Smith, Pattison, Jeune, Master of Pembroke, Tait, and Liddell of Christ Church. An Oxford Tutors' Association was also formed.

Oxford and Cambridge Bill, 1834.

Tait's pamphlet, 1839.

Christie's Parliamentary notices, 1843, 1845.

Liberal movement at Oxford.

The movement for opening the universities was strengthened by sympathy with the nonconformist movement throughout the country, and perhaps by rivalry, one symptom of which was the founding of non-sectarian colleges and universities; to some extent also by the partial absorption of the old tractarian party in the neo-Roman party, which weakened the forces of orthodoxy by division,

Need of University Reform.

[1] See p. 176.

since the Church was no longer at unity in itself. How much need there was of reform may be judged from the fact that out of more than five hundred Oxford fellowships only twenty-two, at Balliol and Oriel, were at this time open to competition; for though the Christ Church studentships were not restricted by statute, they were in the gift of the Dean and Canons, and were treated as private patronage.

No reform of the universities or the colleges within them could be carried out without the aid of Parliament, since both colleges and universities were restrained by the letter of their statutes from remodelling their institutions. It was a further question whether, supposing those restrictions were removed, the ruling powers at Oxford and Cambridge would voluntarily carry out the desired reforms. Even moderate reformers thought that some measure of compulsion was necessary, if only to set free the hands which were bound by unalterable statutes.

On April 23, 1850, James Heywood, Radical Member for North Lancashire, moved to address the Queen for a Royal Commission of Inquiry into the Universities of Oxford, Cambridge, and Dublin. He spoke of 'promoting the interests of religion and useful learning'; interests which many who held rule at Oxford thought to be independent of each other, if not antagonistic. The University members, Inglis and Gladstone, with Roundell Palmer, afterwards Lord Selborne, already a defender of the Church, protested against so sacrilegious a proposal, and Gladstone declared that there was not 'the shadow or the pretext of a case for inquiry,' and pleaded for the rights of self-government against 'an intermeddling and inquisitorial power, supported neither by history nor by law.' Lord John Russell, the Prime Minister, though he did not vote for the resolution, unexpectedly acceded to the proposal, and in August two Royal Commissions were appointed, which included amongst them the names of George Peacock, Dean of Ely, Bishop Hinds of Norwich (chairman), Sir John Herschel, Adam Sedgwick the geologist, Tait of Balliol, Dean of Carlisle, and Liddell of Christ Church, Head Master of Westminster. The secretary of the Oxford Commission was Arthur Stanley, afterwards

Heywood's proposal for Royal University Commission, 1850.

University Commissions, 1850-1852.

Dean of Westminster, and the assistant secretary Goldwin Smith, whose letters to the *Times*, signed 'Oxoniensis,' had already attracted notice; the secretary of the Cambridge Commission was William Bateson of St. John's College, and the chairman Bishop Graham of Chester. These Commissions reported in 1852 in favour of the enlargement of the professorial system by creation of new professor-fellowships, and the strengthening of the universities as distinguished from the colleges; the introduction of students residing, not in colleges, but in licensed halls or hostels; the increase of the number and value of scholarships, and the removal of local, school, and family restrictions affecting admission to scholarships and fellowships.

The Oxford Commissioners, though they did not consider themselves at liberty to propose the admission of Dissenters, spoke with disapproval of the system of requiring subscription at matriculation. Such subscription, said the Report, 'habituates the mind to give a careless assent to truths which it has never considered, and naturally leads to sophistry in the interpretation of solemn obligations.' They advised that fellows of colleges should no longer be required to take Holy Orders; but they did not wish to relax the obligation of celibacy. 'Broadly speaking,' says the Oxford Report, 'the aim of the Commission is to popularise the University, first by giving to its governing body a quasi-representative character; secondly, by opening the University to a much larger and poorer class than that from which the students previously had been taken.'

Oxford Report, 1852.

The Cambridge Commissioners, whose Report bore date August 30, 1852, gave the University credit for introducing wise reforms, and recommended legislation. On the question of celibate fellowships the Oxford Commissioners were more conservative than those from Cambridge. They notice with pleasure that the University Syndicate for Revision of Statutes had recommended that no change in the form of subscription required for degrees in theology should take place; and they advise that the test required for other degrees should be the same as that required since the vote of June 23, 1772, of persons

Cambridge Report, 1852.

admitted to the degree of B.A., viz. a declaration of *bona fide*
membership of the Church of England as by law established.
The larger question, that of admitting others than Churchmen
to degrees in the Arts, Law, and Physic, they leave untouched.
They express, however, their opinion that since the University
is a great national institution, invested with important privileges
by the favour of the Crown or the authority of the Legislature,
and exercises a most extensive influence on the education of
the higher and middle classes of the community, and consequently on the intellectual, moral, and social character of the
nation, it ought to keep pace with the progress of enlightened
opinion, and to be more in sympathy and unison with the
spirit of the age.   They speak of the removal of barriers
which excluded fellow-subjects from equal enjoyment of civil
rights on account of differences in religious opinion as 'one
of the noblest characteristics of our times.'   'The University
will be placed more or less in a false position if it estranges
itself from this great movement of Liberal progress.   There
is a manifest challenge to it to throw open the advantages of
its system of education, under proper securities, as widely as
the State has thrown open the avenues to civil rights and
honours.'   In this language, as well as in that of the Oxford
Report, are set phrases, then novel and much disputed, the
language of the school of Mill and his contemporaries, but
now either accepted as commonplaces, or only questioned
by those who most strongly, in our own or the Roman
communion, uphold the claims of ecclesiastical authority.

After the publication of the Report on Oxford, the
Hebdomadal Board appointed a delegacy to collect opinions
on the spot.   The question lay between professorial
education and collegiate, and between lay education   Opinion at
and clerical.   And further, it was a question whether   Oxford.
the University should belong to the Church of England or
not.   The authorities of Oxford were for maintaining its
connexion with the Church, and its conformity to founders' intentions; no less than 249 members of Convocation against
105 petitioned Parliament against the Commission as unconstitutional and illegal; the majority of the juniors were for removal
of all restrictions of creed, and all local or family privileges.
Ultimately, the phrase 'a national institution' carried the day.

'The Church,' it was agreed, did not mean the same thing as it did before the Reformation, and for a century later, when the Church and the nation were the same thing. As at the Reformation all had agreed to disregard the pious intentions of Catholic founders, so now regulations made in former centuries were interpreted in the light of altered political conditions.

The outcome of the Universities Commissions in 1850-52, and of the publication of the Commissioners' Reports, was Lord John Russell's Oxford University Act of 1854. This Act abolished religious tests at matriculation and for the degrees of B.A., B.C.L., and B.M.; it admitted Dissenters as students, but denied them the M.A. degree, and with it a share in the government of the University or the colleges. The clauses which did away with these restrictions were moved by Heywood in the course of debate; they were no part of the original bill; indeed, the Prime Minister voted against the amendment, which allowed Nonconformists to matriculate; but this being passed, he supported the admission to the B.A. degree. The Government had not intended to mix up the question of the admission of Dissenters with the general question of university reform; it was to be reserved for a separate consideration and a distinct measure. Russell was willing to admit Dissenters by the means of new halls to be established; Gladstone would, in justice to the University, leave it free to settle that point for itself. 'To effect this object by forcible intervention of Parliament, he said, would be a great evil.' He also compared the national character of the universities with that of parochial benefices. 'Every parochial benefice in the country is also a national institution; but there is no immediate or necessary sequence in the proposition that therefore we should admit to their possession the holders of all descriptions of religious opinions.' But the Government was beaten on the matriculation question on June 22, 1854, and this being so, Gladstone voted for Heywood's amendment, which admitted Dissenters to the B.A. degree. Speaking of a settlement of the religious question, he wrote as follows to the Provost of Oriel, Dr. Hawkins: 'The basis of that

Lord John Russell's University Act, 1854.

Gladstone's opinion.

settlement should be that the whole teaching and governing function in the University and in the colleges, halls, and private halls, should be retained as now in the Church of England, but that everything outside the governing and teaching functions, whether in the way of degrees, honours, or emoluments would be left open.' The bill, as amended, was passed in July, and received the Royal assent on August 7 (17 and 18 Vict. c. 81).

The Cambridge University Bill was introduced by Edward Bouverie, Member for Kilmarnock, in 1856. It abolished tests at matriculation and for the degree of Bachelor in all faculties but that of divinity, and would have gone further; but an amendment was introduced and carried in the Lords, which retained the existing declaration of conformity as a condition for the degree of M.A., for fellowships, and for all university and college offices. The bill received the Royal assent on July 29 (19 and 20 Vict. c. 88).

Bouverie's Cambridge Bill, 1856.

During Lord Palmerston's Government from 1859 to 1865, Liberal measures were laid on the shelf, and university reform among them. But young members of Parliament did not lose hope. In 1863 Bouverie proposed to abolish tests. Gladstone, who was still Member for the University of Oxford, was unwilling to move: 'the principle of a general mixture of belief in the governing body' was abhorrent to his mind, and he thought it 'a fair and just demand' that the governors of the universities and of the colleges should be Churchmen. But in 1864, in the debate on Dodson's Bill for abolition of tests, he intimated that concessions would be made, and warned the friends of the Church against a policy of indiscriminate resistance.

Bouverie's Bill, 1863.

The continued exclusion of Nonconformists from all places of emolument and power in the universities became intolerable when the principle was once accepted that the universities, like the great public schools, were national institutions, and not exclusively the property of the Church. Universities, it was said, are not ecclesiastical or spiritual corporations; still less are they seminaries; the education of the country is not to be sacrificed to the exigencies of the clergy, present or future. True, the universities and colleges had been founded and endowed in the name of the National Church; the Dissenters could show no legal title; the interests of religion were incompatible with the secularism which was the logical consequence of equality. But partial exclusion was more galling even than total exclusion; for an excluded class could have provided their own education: but to entice Dissenters to the University and give honourable distinction to those of them who proved themselves worthy, and yet refuse a vote in university business, the common title of M.A., and the privileges which went with it, was something like an insult. The principle of Dodson's Oxford Bill of 1864 was not the admission of Dissenters to the University as students; it was the principle that university degrees should be independent of religious tests; that subscription to the Thirty-nine Articles and the 36th Canon should no longer be required from Oxford graduates, such tests having already been removed at Cambridge and Dublin.

Oxford itself was deeply stirred. At no time was the liberal and latitudinarian element stronger among the leaders of the University. After much correspondence and conversation, a public meeting was held at the Freemasons' Tavern on June 10, 1864, at which resolutions were passed in favour of Dodson's Oxford Bill and Bouverie's Oxford and Cambridge Bill, which extended abolition of tests to college fellowships. Among the speakers were Goldwin Smith, Charles Bowen, Jowett, Henry Smith, Bright, Goschen, Dean Stanley, and Thomas Hughes; and Fawcett, W. G. Clark, Maurice, and many of the best Cambridge men, though Oxford was more fully represented. The Oxford bill passed the Commons by the Speaker's vote only, and on a second division was thrown out by two votes.

Liberal Meeting at Freemasons' Tavern, 1864.

In 1865 Gladstone was 'unmuzzled' by the loss of his seat for Oxford, and was free to pursue what was now his natural career of liberalism. The bill for that year was brought in by Gordon and Grant-Duff. In 1866 John Duke Coleridge, the newly elected member for Exeter, proposed entire abolition, taking up the position, already maintained by Goldwin Smith and Goschen, that the universities are national institutions, essentially and legally lay

Coleridge's Bill, 1866.

corporations, neither more nor less clerical seminaries than the public schools, and that the imposition of any tests, the erecting of any barrier against Nonconformists, was an unjust and intolerable humiliation. He wished to extend the benefits of university education to the Dissenters. The Church could take care of itself, but must not shut the door to inquiry. 'The university,' he said, ' is just the place where inquiry may be conducted under the most softening and healing influences. . . . Free inquiry you must and will have . . . there has been too much fear of inquiry. . . . The fear of free and sound inquiry is a baseless one ; it is one in which I cannot share, and as a believer and a Churchman I protest against it.' It might be said, he added, that the University of Oxford owed much to its connexion with the Church of England. But the time, since the Reformation, when the University of Oxford was most under the dominion of the clergy was also the time of its greatest intellectual stagnation. Orthodoxy and religion may flourish in a congenial atmosphere, from which doubt is excluded, but the atmosphere which admits science is more wholesome.

Coleridge's bill passed the Commons, but went no further. He brought forward the same measure in 1867. The onus of exclusion, he said, rested on those who objected to the proposal. The Church of England must greatly widen her gates and liberalise her tests, or she would cease to be national, and would invite disestablishment. If national, she must be very comprehensive. ' The Thirty-nine Articles are costing us dear.' Whatever disabilities existed had been imposed for reasons which were no longer valid. Nonconformists were already there as examiners and private tutors. The bill, however, did not propose to touch the colleges or to make Dissenters eligible to fellowships. It only set the national character of the universities against the exclusive claim of the Church of England. In short, he seemed to say, 'the tide is flowing, you cannot resist it ; as you must give way, why not do it with a good grace ?'

Henry Fawcett, Member for Brighton, moved to extend the provisions of the Act to Cambridge ; this was accepted, and the bill was passed, but lost in the Lords, after an interesting debate in which the Duke of Devonshire, Chancellor of the

University of Cambridge, spoke, as he confessed, against the sense of the University in pronouncing for the bill. He

Oxford Bill extended to Cambridge, but rejected, 1867.

thought that the Church was sufficiently guarded by the colleges, their Heads and fellows, and the Council, the governing body of the University, all members of the Church; and he drew attention to the recommendations in favour of a wider policy to be found in the Report of the University Commission. The bill was thrown out on July 25 by a majority of twenty-eight.

In 1868 Grant Duff reintroduced the bill. He contrasted the mediæval spirit of bondage with the modern spirit of

Grant Duff's Bill, 1868.

liberty. 'The spirit of old Oxford spoke in *Lyra Apostolica*; it was in complete antagonism to the spirit of the democracy, which must henceforth rule the rulers, and put an end to semi-monastic Utopias.' There is no argument in these words; they are merely *la raison du plus fort*, and Beresford Hope's rhetoric was more to the point, when he spoke of 'the party of relentless progress,' and foretold the danger of 'unqualified and unblushing nihilism'; contrasted philosophy with religion, and described a state of things in which the university supply of clergy would fall off, partly from the irreligious temper which was likely to prevail, partly because serious Churchmen would erect seminaries, and so a race of clergy might grow up without the liberal and human influences of university life and traditions. Trust the universities, he said, and leave them to themselves.

The nonconformist grievance was put forward by George Melly, Member for Stoke, who spoke as a representative of

Nonconformist grievance.

Lancashire business men, in great measure Unitarians, who could not conscientiously send their sons to Oxford and Cambridge, and regretted the opportunities so lost. H. S. P. Winterbotham, Member for Stroud, a radical Nonconformist, said that the Act of Uniformity, which was intended to make all the people members of the Church of England, had created dissent, and that the result of exclusion from the universities was that the Dissenters had an unlearned clergy. The Dissenters asked for nothing more, and would be contented with nothing else, than religious equality. The second reading was passed on July 1, 1868, by a majority of fifty-eight; but neither in that year nor in the next did it become law.

In November 1869, at a meeting held at St. John's College, Cambridge, under the presidency of the Master, Dr. Bateson, resolutions were proposed by the Master of Trinity (Thompson), Sedgwick, and Maurice, in support of Coleridge's bill, but deprecating the permissive clauses under which the colleges were at liberty to maintain or abolish clerical restrictions. *Liberal meeting at Cambridge 1869.*

The bill of 1870, which was included in the Queen's speech as a Government measure, and was introduced by Sir John Duke Coleridge, now Attorney General in Gladstone's Government, left all university appointments free except clerical fellowships, degrees in divinity, and theological chairs. *Bill of 1870.* The main change, since the preceding year, said the Prime Minister, was that it was no longer proposed to allow any college to pass from under the operation of the measure; the bill proposed 'an absolute and universal repeal of that permissive power.' Lord Salisbury, however, when the bill came up to the Lords, moved to refer it to a select committee, and the measure was thus put off for another year.

At length in 1871 the bill passed both Houses and received the Royal assent (35 and 36 Vict. c. 26), and thus the national principle asserted in the preamble to the Act, which was drawn by Charles Bowen, was finally accepted. *Universities Tests Act passed, 1871.*

By the legislation of 1871, says Professor Lewis Campbell, 'the citadel was taken.' Some colleges at Oxford had reduced the number of their clerical fellowships, but this process had not been made compulsory. Merton and Oriel were still the only colleges of which it was possible for a layman to be elected Head. *Executive Commission (Oxford), 1877.* But the power to alter their statutes existed, and an Executive Commission, appointed in 1877, replenished the university chest at the expense of the colleges, and, co-operating with the governing bodies of the several colleges, abolished most of the clerical restrictions still remaining. In 1880 Charles Roundell, Member for Grantham, presented a petition to the House of Commons, signed by 131 resident graduates of Oxford, among them six Heads of Colleges and fifteen professors, being half of the Hebdomadal Council and half the professoriate, the prayer of which was for the abolition of the restrictions still existing. Again was urged the plea of the national character inherent in the universities, and the measure was recommended on the grounds of being inevitable as well as being in the best interests of education.

As the Commission had not reported, the decision of the question was put off till 1881, when a resolution was passed without a division, which was taken as an instruction to the Commission to do away with the remaining clerical restrictions. The exceptions still maintained related to the cathedral-collegiate chapter of Christ Church and the divinity professorships, but not those of Hebrew and ecclesiastical history; and to all colleges established on a Church of England foundation since the nationalisation of the University, such as Keble, founded in 1870 in memory of John Keble, and Hertford, refounded in 1874. Selwyn College (1882), Ridley Hall Clergy Training School (1882) at Cambridge, and Wycliffe Hall at Oxford, which in some respects resemble Keble and Hertford, are not, like them, incorporated in the University.

Whatever may have been the effect upon religion and religious teaching at the universities produced by the legislation completed in 1871, there can be no doubt that the atmosphere of the universities has been largely affected by that legislation, or by the causes which produced it. The result justified High Churchmen like Gladstone, or Low Churchmen like Newdegate, who prophesied the downfall of clerical rule at Oxford and Cambridge and the rise of a critical and negative spirit in the headquarters of the Church. The quiet clerical Oxford and Cambridge of fifty years ago exist no longer. The universities are the homes of new ideas, not the seat of undisturbed orthodoxy. And here it may not be out of place to recall Archbishop Tait's words spoken in the House of Lords, 1868. He saw no danger to the University in admitting a few Nonconformists. But the colleges were different. A college was a home, not a republic. He would wish the government of the colleges to be reserved to the National Church. Let the university, through the college, educate the clergy. If not, we shall have seminaries.

OXFORD UNIVERSITY ACT, 17 and 18 Vict. c. 81
(7 August 1854)

§§ 1 and 2. Commissioners appointed till 1858.

§ 5. Powers of the Hebdomadal Board, or Council of Heads of Colleges, transferred to a Hebdomadal Council of twenty-two persons holding office in the University, to be elected by Congregation and to hold office for six years from election.

§ 12. Convocation to retain its present powers.

§ 16. Congregation re-constituted.

§ 24. Certain oaths of secrecy or against altering the institutions of the University or any of the colleges are declared illegal, and none such are hereafter to be administered or taken.

§ 27. Private Halls may be established.

§ 28. Colleges may amend their own statutes.   If (§ 29) they omit to do so the Commissioners may frame ordinances.

§ 30. Trusts more than fifty years old may be altered for the advancement of religion and learning and the main design of the donor.

§ 36. All ordinances, statutes, etc. to be laid before the Queen in Council and before Parliament.

§ 43. No declaration or oath to be made at matriculation.

§ 44. No declaration or oath to be made at taking degree of B.A., B.L., B.M., or B.Mus.

SUMMARY OF CAMBRIDGE UNIVERSITY ACT,
19 and 20 Vict. c. 88 (29 July 1856)

Commissioners appointed till 1860.

§ 5. Council of the Senate appointed, consisting of eighteen persons.

§ 22. No oath of secrecy or of resisting any change in university or college statutes to be taken.

§§ 23-26. Members of the University may open Hostels under certain conditions.

§ 27. Colleges may make or alter statutes, or, in default (§ 29), the Commissioners.

§ 30. University may frame statutes, or in default (§ 31), the Commissioners.

§ 45. No person to be required to make oath or declaration of religious belief upon matriculation or upon taking degree of B.A., B.L., B.M., or B.Mus., nor (§ 96) on obtaining any Exhibition or Scholarship.

(Mem.—There is no saving clause for maintenance of religious service in the college chapels, as in the Oxford Act of 1854, 17 and 18 Vict. c. 81, §§ 4-6.)

SUMMARY OF UNIVERSITIES TESTS ACT,
34 Vict. c. 26 (16 June 1871)

§ 3. Persons taking lay academical degrees or holding lay academical or collegiate offices not to be required to subscribe any formulary of faith or to make any declaration or take any oath respecting religious belief or profession, or to conform to any religious observance or to attend or abstain from attending any form of public worship, or to belong to any specified church, sect, or denomination.

§§ 4-6. The lawfully established system of religious instruction and worship not to be interfered with. Religious instruction and public worship, according to the use of the Church of England, to be maintained in all existing colleges.

§ 7. No person to be required to attend any lecture to which objection is made by himself, or, if a minor, by his parent or guardian.

AUTHORITIES.—As before, Chapter IX. H. Christmas, *Hampden Controversy* ; Davidson and Benham, *Life of Archbishop Tait* ; Lord Morley, *Life of W. E. Gladstone* ; Goldwin Smith, *A Plea for the Abolition of Tests,* etc. ; *Report of Oxford and Cambridge Commission,* 1852 ; Lewis Campbell, *The Nationalisation of the Universities.*

CHAPTER XVI

THE GORHAM CASE

BAPTISMAL regeneration did not come prominently forward as a debatable question at the English Reformation. The language of the Fathers and the Schoolmen, as re-produced in Protestant formularies, was used by the framers of our Prayer Book, though a new and less literal sense might be given to the words used. The doctrine of Trent is that 'Baptism is the sacrament of regeneration by water in the word,' and 'water is used in baptism to signify the washing of the soul which it effects.' The Ten Articles of 1536, coming from a Lutheran source, had asserted the necessity of faith and repentance and the co-operation of the grace of the Holy Ghost with the sacramental act. Hooker, while blaming those who ' elevate ' (*i.e.* make light of) 'the ordinary and immediate [sacramental] means of life,' says that the eternal election ' in-cludeth a subordination of means, without which we are not actually brought to enjoy what God secretly did intend.' The full Calvinist doctrine, as set forth in the Westminster Confession, is that in baptism are conferred 'ingrafting into Christ, regeneration, and remission of sins '; but only upon the elect. For those who are not elect the sacrament can do nothing ; but to the elect pre-venient grace is granted to enable them to have faith and repentance, the conditions of effectual baptism. Since, in this view, some infants not sinning are predestined to perdition, it follows that original sin is not remitted to all recipients of baptism. Luther and Melanchthon, and presumably the Church

(marginal notes:) Baptismal doctrine of the English Church.

Hooker.

Westminster Confession.

319

of England, held with the Church of Rome that baptism remits
sin both original and actual, and that therefore all infants
baptized and not actually sinning are saved.   All agreed
that those who come to baptism without faith and repentance
do not receive the benefit of the sacrament.   The
Point left question left undecided by the English formularies
undecided. was this, whether the efficacy of baptism depended
upon prevenient grace enabling to have faith and repentance,
in which case the sacrament was only a symbol, or whether it
depended upon the sacramental act, in which latter case grace,
prevenient or co-operating, was imperfect till completed by
the sacramental act.

The Puritan doctrine of the sixteenth and seventeenth
centuries, as expressed in the Westminster Confession, affected
in this, as in other particulars, current belief in the Church
of England.   In a point of such high theology few Churchmen can have held very definite opinions.   Baptism was considered necessary by all, but the precise method of its operation was not closely inquired into.   The Methodists preached
regeneration as a consequence, by divine grace, of conversion,
a process in which the human will and divine grace co-
operated, as something independent of baptism, which nevertheless worked efficaciously, but by inward grace, not as the
opus operatum necessarily effected by a sacrament.   The High
Church school, represented by Richard Mant, afterwards
Bishop of Down, Bampton Lecturer of the year 1812, taught
High Church that the sacramental grace of regeneration always
school. accompanies the ceremony.   Men may and do
Bishop Mant. fall away, but regeneration or conversion in the
Methodist sense, a conscious act of accepting and being
accepted, is not necessary for all, since regeneration accompanies baptism, and many baptized persons do not fall away,
and so do not need conversion.   Mant's opponents
Evangelical showed that in the texts quoted by him from Scrip-
school. ture the spiritual side is never omitted.   They held
baptism to be the seal of grace granted, the means and the
declaration of grace, indissolubly connected with the grace
itself, but not to be confounded with it.   Regeneration is
possible without baptism, baptism without regeneration.   Faith
and repentance are necessary conditions of regeneration in

baptism; and the Church charitably speaks of the baptized generally as regenerate, as in the Order of Confirmation, on the supposition that they have faith and repentance. This hypothetical principle, they said, pervades all the services of the Church, and they instanced especially the expressions of hope to be found in the Burial Service.

Apart from theological subtleties, which, by defining too much, often put ignorance in the place of knowledge, the question is that of the efficacy of sacraments. The disparaging of ceremonies and exaltation of immediate grace is a note of the Reformation, and Pusey in his Tract on Baptismal Regeneration (Nos. 67, 69) insists, against the Reformers, on the necessity of this sacrament and its mystical character. The language of Article XXVII. is, 'Baptism is . . . a sign of Regeneration or new Birth, whereby, as by an instrument, they that receive Baptism rightly are grafted into the Church; the promises of the forgiveness of sin, and of our adoption to be the sons of God, by the Holy Ghost, are visibly signed and sealed.' It is obvious that this definition does not settle the question whether forgiveness of sin and adoption are conferred by means of this sacrament exclusively; which is a reasonable but not an inevitable conclusion from the definition in the Church Catechism that the two Sacraments are 'generally necessary to salvation.'

George Cornelius Gorham (1787-1857), Fellow of Queens' College, Cambridge, and a man of some university distinction, an antiquary and naturalist, was a Cambridge Evangelical, and therefore 'suspect' to High Church divines. He belonged to the school and the age of Simeon, and his doctrine might be expected to be limited and old-fashioned. He held the benefice of St. Just-in-Penwith, in the diocese of Exeter, and on his presentation by the Lord Chancellor in 1847, at the age of sixty, to another living in the same diocese, Brampford Speke, Bishop Phillpotts, who saw an opportunity of sifting him, subjected him to a searching examination in December, and again in March. In this he was following the example of Bishop Marsh of Peterborough, who in 1821 had issued a paper of eighty-seven questions to candidates for

Pusey's Tract on Regeneration.

Doctrine of the Church of England.

G. C. Gorham.

Bishop Phillpotts 1847.

Orders, with the intention of purging out Calvinism from his diocese. Marsh failed, and Phillpotts was to fail too. He improved on Marsh's precedent; for Marsh's examination was general, and came before admission to Orders, when it is the Bishop's duty to examine the candidates, Phillpotts's questions were addressed to a particular person, who had been in Orders for nearly forty years, and had been lately instituted by himself. The number of written questions propounded by the Bishop was no less than a hundred and forty-nine. They were not drawn up and presented beforehand, but arose out of the verbal examination, which in itself occupied altogether some thirty-eight hours. The examination, moreover, was intolerably inquisitorial; 'wholly unprecedented for length and severity,' as Gorham's counsel described it.

Examination of Gorham, 1848.

The main point involved in the controversy, for such it came to be, was whether regeneration in baptism is absolute or conditional on an act of prevenient grace. If the high sacramentarian view held by the Bishop had been declared by the authority of ecclesiastical law to be the doctrine of the Church of England, and no way of escape provided, there would thenceforward have been no place for the evangelical party in the Church of England. The controversy, therefore, was of great moment, and attracted much attention.

The Bishop having refused to institute (21 March 1848), on the ground that 'he had upon the examination found Mr. Gorham unfit to fill the vicarage by reason of his holding doctrines contrary to the true Christian faith and the doctrines contained in the Articles and formularies of the Church of England,' Gorham instituted proceedings against him in the Court of Arches (15 June), the form of proceeding being, not under the Act of 1840, but by *Duplex Querela*;[1] but the parties, instead of propounding a definite statement of doctrine on one side and the other, agreed to submit the whole volume of questions and answers to the decision of the Court. The Bishop's

Gorham v. Phillpotts in Court of Arches, 1848.

---

[1] *i.e.* 'a complaint made by any clerk or other to the Archbishop of the province against any inferior ordinary for delaying justice in any cause ecclesiastical; as to give sentence, or to institute a clerk presented, or such like' (Burns).

accusation was that Gorham held that spiritual regeneration is not given or conferred in baptism. Gorham said, in answer to the Bishop's questions, that regeneration is a change of nature, a gift bestowed before, in, or after baptism, not given unless baptism is rightly received. He defined 'rightly' as 'not merely by lawful administration, but by worthy reception.' Grace is not conferred in baptism unconditionally, but is given to those only who receive baptism worthily, and on condition of their fulfilling certain promises. Worthiness is of the essence of the sacrament; and worthiness means faith and repentance, personally in the case of adults, sponsorially for infants. Baptism is not absolutely necessary to salvation; 'born of water' and 'born of the Spirit' are not so indissolubly tied together as to be of equal necessity; faith is absolutely necessary, baptism generally necessary. The acceptance of infants, and the certainty of their salvation if they die baptized before committing sin, are a corollary from the doctrine that original sin is always washed away in baptism. Now, as all infants are born in sin, there must have been a prevenient act of grace to give them faith and repentance, and so make them worthy recipients of baptism and its benefits. He did not hold that infant baptism is effectual *per se* without an act of prevenient grace, but he did not define under what conditions, and to whom, prevenient grace is given. It is curious, and is an instance of the fallibility of divines and lawyers, that neither counsel nor judges seem to have heard of 'prevenient grace,' till they found the term in Gorham's answers.

Doctrine of prevenient grace.

No evidence was adduced beyond the Bishop's questions, and the answers given by Gorham; and on this evidence the Dean of Arches, Sir Herbert Jenner Fust, pronounced sentence against him on August 2, 1849, on the ground that, according to the doctrine of the Church of England, spiritual regeneration is given in baptism unconditionally. Gorham took his stand principally upon the Articles. But as Article XXV. (Of Sacraments) does not define the word 'worthily,' a definition (said the judge) must be found elsewhere, and is found in the Office for the Baptism of Infants; where a prayer is offered for regeneration before baptism, and a declaration is made after baptism that the

Jenner Fust's judgment, 1849.

child baptized is regenerate, and thanks are given for this. Regeneration, therefore, at and through baptism is the doctrine of the Church of England. Gorham had introduced the question of predestination and election, on which subjects Article XVII. gives no certain decision. The judge decided against his allegation that the known Calvinistic leanings of the Reformers should be taken into account, seeing that no clear enunciation of such views was made in the Articles. Private interpretation was out of place. So long as the Articles and services of the Church are reconcilable, they are to be understood in that sense only in which they can be reconciled. On these grounds the rule against the Bishop was dismissed. Gorham appealed against this judgment, and was heard on December 11, 1849, before the Judicial Committee of the Privy Council.

This was the first case in which the limits of clerical liberty in matters of doctrine were brought under the cognisance of the Judicial Committee, and is therefore taken as the leading case in the construction

Appeal to the Judicial Committee, 1849.

of the formularies of the Church of England in similar proceedings. There was some difficulty in forming a competent court; and the two Archbishops (Sumner and Musgrave), and the Bishop of London (Blomfield), assisted by special command. The prelates were to give their opinion as assessors, but not to vote as judges,

Ecclesiastical assessors.

since the Church proceedings were not under the Act of 1840. In the event the Archbishops expressed their opinion in an antisacramentarian sense, taking the view that many Churchmen of good repute and authority had held views similar to those of Gorham, and so following a practical rather than a legal line; the Bishop of London, a High Churchman, but moderate and practical, agreed with them in the main, but thought Gorham had gone too far in disparaging the sacramental efficacy of baptism, and therefore dissented from the judgment. It is possible that the spiritual assessors were influenced by fear of tractarianism,—for it must be remembered that this was the time of many important secessions to Rome, and Romanism was aggressive and Puseyism unpopular,—as well as by a tenderness for the evangelical body.

The judges, with the exception of Vice-Chancellor Knight Bruce, were unanimous; and the Master of the Rolls, Lord Langdale, delivered the judgment of the Committee on March 8, 1850. He complained that in con- sequence of the mode of action pursued in the previous trial, the Court had before them no clear statement of what the Bishop alleged to be the doctrine of the Church of England, nor of what he imputed to the appellant and alleged to be unsound, nor of the appellant's own views. Instead of this they had to consider a long series of difficult questions, 'upon a subject of a very abstruse nature, intricate, perplexing, entangling, and many of them not admitting of distinct and explicit answers'; and the answers were 'not given plainly and directly, but in a guarded and cautious manner,' as indeed was natural.

Lord Langdale delivers judgment, 1850.

The judges' opinion was that Gorham held baptism to be a sacrament generally necessary to salvation, but believed that regeneration does not invariably take place in baptism, being conditional upon worthy reception. They did not define the term 'generally,' which Gorham distinguished from 'universally.' Whether these views were theologically correct or not, they said, was not their business; their business was to decide whether the opinions under consideration were contrary or repugnant to the doctrine of the Church of England as enjoined upon the clergy by its Articles, Formularies, and Rubrics, interpreted with regard to the following considerations: (1) that the framers of the Articles did not propose to include in them an authoritative statement of all Christian doctrine, but left some things undecided and others ambiguous in statement; (2) that in the case of ambiguous statement nothing can be insisted upon beyond the literal and grammatical sense conveyed or implied; (3) that different opinions as to the Sacrament of Baptism were held by different promoters of the Reformation, and expressed by alterations made in the Articles; and (4) that opinions not to be distinguished in any important particular from those of the appellant had been propounded and maintained without censure or reproach by eminent divines in the Church of England, from the time when the Articles were first established.

The argument of the Court, in short, was that the Church

of England did not profess to include in the Articles 'an authoritative statement of all Christian doctrine'; that language must have some latitude of interpretation; and that some such latitude was probably intended by the framers of the Articles themselves. It is indeed impossible to construct a complete and consistent body of theology from articles and formularies accepted, adapted, or framed in view of controversies of three hundred years ago, and coloured by political and personal sympathies, and by the great events of the Reformation period.

It will be seen that the Court pronounced no opinion as to the 'theological correctness or error' of Gorham's doctrine, and that their decision rested mainly upon the argument *secundum libertatem*, that in any case of doubtful language the larger interpretation was lawful, and had been held to be lawful. If the judges had been infallible in grammar they might have pronounced 'generally' to be equivalent to 'universally,' and the judgment would have gone the other way; for the distinction drawn by Gorham is not allowed by lexicographers at the stage of the English language represented by the Anglican formularies. In the Church Catechism 'generally' means 'universally,' as a 'general' council means a 'universal' council, and a 'general' order an order to all concerned. But Gorham's distinction was tacitly admitted by the judgment; the point was not raised, and the judgment went mainly upon the question of prevenient grace, not upon that of the necessity of sacraments. The judges took the line suggested by Newman's principle of interpretation according to 'the plain, literal, and grammatical sense'; but by omitting his proviso that such interpretation should be in a catholic sense, they turned the tables upon the supporters of Tract 90; and the precedent of this trial has been followed in later judgments. On these grounds the Court decided that Gorham's doctrine was not contrary or repugnant to the declared doctrine of the Church of England, and reversed the sentence of the Arches Court.

The decision of the Judicial Committee was received with dismay by the High Church party, and caused as great a storm as the promotion of Hampden, if not greater. Manning pointed out that 'a supreme interpreter is equivalent to a legislator.'   He describes how he went at once to Gladstone, who said, 'the Church of England is gone, unless it releases itself by some authoritative act.'   Meetings were immediately held, and different courses of action proposed.   Some trusted the bishops, some wished to stir them to action : a general protest from the Church was thought desirable, but how could it be obtained ?   James Hope appears to have been the most prominent promoter of action ; Gladstone, who at first was eager, withdrew, and pleaded for delay.

A declaration was drawn up, dated March 20, 1850, and signed by Manning, Pusey, Keble, Dr. Mill, Professor of Hebrew at Cambridge, Robert and Henry Wilberforce, and several other clergymen and lead- *Declaration against the* ing laymen, purporting that the Church was bound *judgment, 1850.* by the sentence unless it openly and expressly rejected the erroneous doctrine sanctioned thereby ; and that any portion of the Church consciously, wilfully, and deliberately admitting such doctrine thereby becomes formally separated from the Catholic body.   The practical conclusion was that 'an authoritative declaration by the Church of the doctrine of Holy Baptism, impugned by the recent sentence' should be obtained ; or that at least the bishops should be moved to reaffirm the doctrine so impugned.

Bishop Phillpotts, never sparing of language, published a letter to Archbishop Sumner, in which he declared that so long as the Archbishop persisted in licensing Mr. *Bishop* Gorham to the living of Brampford Speke, he would *Phillpotts, Gladstone,* not hold communion with him.   'Call together your *and Roundell* comprovincial bishops,' he cries ; 'invite them to *Palmer.* declare what is the faith of the Church.'   Thus a bishop ex-communicated an archbishop.   Gladstone took his own line, and in a letter to the Bishop of London, dated June 4, 1850, elaborately examined the question from historical and legal points of view, and showed from authorities such as Lord Coke that Henry VIII. in transferring the Papal prerogative to himself did not transfer any purely spiritual functions, and that the ancient law of the Church remained unrepealed, viz. that the bishops, not the King's courts, were the judges of heresy.   Roundell Palmer wrote that the Church was dis-honoured by the judgment, which was founded neither on

Holy Scripture nor Church tradition, nor on any principle whatever. The King is Head of the Church only as the Church is incorporated in the law; his supremacy does not extend to the province of religious belief; and he declared that no such anti-Christian profession had been made by any sovereign since Henry VIII. It was represented from other quarters that the judges were wrong in going to the Articles for doctrine in preference to the Prayer Book. The Reformers could not have meant to leave in ambiguity so important an article of the Faith; and if ancient language is used, the probability is that it is used with the ancient meaning, and therefore implies a declaration of the Church that the thing signified in the Sacrament is given at the moment. Other writers held that the doctrine of the Church on baptismal regeneration was clearly recognised though not declared by the court, a certain latitude of opinion being permitted on an obscure point, that of the condition of baptized infants; that the extreme sacramental view was dangerously near the Roman doctrine of *opus operatum*; that Gorham declared his belief in the doctrine of baptism as expressed in the Nicene Creed, and ought not to be condemned because he did not accept a particular interpretation of it; that some latitude of interpretation is lawful in a matter confessedly mysterious. Even Dr. Pusey thought that Christians who did not hold the doctrine of regeneration absolutely might hold it charitably, with Hooker and other divines; and Joshua Watson acquiesced in Blomfield's refusal to concur with the decision of the judges. 'It will do as much good, *à mon avis*, at least, as the judgment can do harm.' There was, he said, no new heresy to condemn, and all sound doctrine had been long since established in our Liturgy and Articles.

Various opinions on the Gorham case.

Dr. Pusey.

The press discussed the event from lay and clerical points of view. The *Times* thought that 'no other decision could be arrived at consistently with strict rules of legal construction, and . . . high considerations of public policy. The Queen in Council does not legislate for the Church, nor pronounce dogmatically on points of doctrine, which would manifestly be to arrogate to such

Comments of the press.

courts as the Privy Council the powers of Convocation . . .
but taking the Church as it is established by Act of Parliament
and by the Canons, the Crown as Head of the Church admini-
sters it under the advice of its judicial counsellors.' This is
sound doctrine, so far as it goes ; but it waives the question
who are the judicial counsellors of the Crown in cases of
heresy ; it omits the consideration that in ' words of art' expert
opinion is required, and that lay judges may from want of ecclesiastical learning mistake the meaning of words. As the *Morning
Chronicle* put it, the court consisted of six gentlemen, one of
whom was a Presbyterian, and the rest wholly unfamiliar with
the subject matter and the law affecting it. It may, however,
be urged in answer to this argument that it is the business of
lawyers to make themselves familiar with other aspects of law
than those with which they are most conversant, and that
judges have every day to try causes connected with minutiæ of
science, commerce, navigation, and art, of which they have no
acquaintance at first hand. In so difficult a question, and one
so interesting to a vast number of Christians, the court did not
do ill to ' decide by avoiding a decision,' and so refrain from
driving conscientious people into schism. And in the same
sense the *Daily News* rejoiced over the rebuff of a party which
wished to revive such 'ante-Reformation things' as Church
Councils. 'The Roman Church desires definitions ; Protestant Churches, freedom of speculation.'

On July 2, 1850, Archdeacon Manning wrote a letter to
Bishop Gilbert of Chichester, arguing that to dispute the
doctrine of baptismal regeneration was heresy, and that this
heresy had now received the sanction of the law.
'I do not see how the Church of England can
permit two contrary doctrines on baptism to be
propounded to her people, without abdicating the
divine authority to teach as sent from God'; and he writes
in a letter, 'It is no question of more or less, better or
worse, but whether we are in or out of the faith and Church
which our Lord founded by His Apostles.' About the same
time Keble published anonymously a powerful and
temperate pamphlet (*Church Matters in 1850*) on
the competency of the Court. The Judicial Committee, he argued, was not only a lay court, but an alien

[marginal note beside paragraph:] Manning's letter to Bishop Gilbert.

[marginal note:] Keble's pamphlet.

court, appointed nominally by the Crown, but really by the Prime Minister, a nominee of the House of Commons, which is no longer, as in Tudor times, an assembly of Churchmen. Such a state of things would be impossible and incredible in the case of a nonconformist body or an established church like that of Scotland. The Church of England had never assented to this court, as it had assented to the Royal supremacy and the establishment of the Court of Delegates. The Church submitted to Henry VIII. on the understanding that he would be bound by the law of the land in temporal things, and by the law of the Church in spiritual things. But now Parliament had taken to itself to interfere with Church legislation ; and the court set up by Parliament was neither accompanied with the same safeguards nor appointed by the same authority as that which it superseded. The Crown cannot make statutes without Parliament nor settle doctrine without Convocation, since the Church 'hath authority in controversies of faith.' The Church had suffered her powers to lapse, but had not lost the right or power to resume them.

In July, Manning, Robert Wilberforce, and Mill, separating themselves from Keble and Pusey, circulated another Declaration among the clergy and other persons of whom subscription to the Royal supremacy was required, to the effect that the Royal supremacy did not rightly extend to the decision of questions of doctrine or discipline. But the great majority of those to whom the protest was sent refused to sign it ; 20,000 copies were sent out, 1800 signatures were received, and Manning 'saw that the game was up. It was a fair test fairly applied ; and it received next to no response.'

This was not known till the autumn. In the meantime

Sermons at St. Barnabas', Pimlico. Bishops Blomfield and Wilberforce, Pusey, Keble, Manning, and other prominent High Churchmen preached in turn at St. Barnabas' Church, Pimlico, during the services held in connection with the consecration

Meeting in St. Martin's Hall, July. of the church on St. Barnabas' Day, June 11, and in turn condemned the Gorham judgment. A meeting to protest was held in St. Martin's Hall on July 23, at which J. G. Hubbard, afterwards Lord Addington, was chairman, and all the principal High Churchmen, clerical and lay, were present, and among them one bishop, Bagot of Bath and Wells, Newman's friend. The meeting agreed in a Declaration in which, after fully setting forth reasons, they solemnly repudiated and protested against the judgment, and appealed to a free and lawful synod of the Church of England.

The Bishop of London, who was brought prominently forward as having been an assessor to the Court, and having, as such, partially disallowed its judgment, was addressed by lay members of the Church to take measures with the other bishops for procuring an authoritative statement of the Church's doctrine on Baptism. *Demand for a statement of doctrine.* But since the Archbishops, who had agreed with the judgment, and most of their suffragans, thought any such action unseasonable, nothing was done. The next step was to urge the Archbishop of Canterbury to represent to the Prime Minister that a proper Court of Appeal might be found in the Upper House of Convocation, if restored to functions which had never been abrogated, and fortified by the opinion of lay judges. This view was advocated by some of the daily papers, which announced to a surprised public that the Church ought to speak, as it had the right to speak, through Convocation. Lord John would have nothing to say to this, and went out of his way to talk about 'dogmatic decrees of a dominant hierarchy' which might 'totally alter the Protestant character of the Church, and in the end substitute the supremacy of the Pope for that of the Queen,' —a strange utterance for a bishop-maker.

The Bishop of London, finding no support from his superiors in Church or State, had already, on June 3, on his own authority, brought forward a bill in the House of Lords, which, if it had passed, would have saved much trouble, and satisfied all except the extremest *Blomfield's bill, 1850.* High Churchmen and the extremest Erastians. He introduced his bill with an earnest appeal to his hearers to bear in mind the great importance of the issue to the integrity of the Church and even the tranquillity of the Empire. Twenty-five bishops had approved the principle of the bill, which was to carry out Henry VIII.'s intention that the Royal supremacy should be exercised in causes spiritual by judges of the spiritualty, and in causes temporal by the temporal judges. The present court, he said, left nothing to be desired when matters of fact and clear enunciation of the law were concerned: but according to the original constitution of the court it was not so, when faith and doctrine were in question. He could conceive questions so new to members of the Judicial Committee of the Privy Council that they would not understand the terms in which they were couched, while to a prelate of the Church these would be the mere alphabet of theology. The constitutional doctrine was that 'it doth not appertain to the King's Court to determine schisms or heresies,' but that 'the King's Court is to consult with divines to know whether it be schism or not.' So the Chancery inquires from the Common Law judges on a point of Common Law; in matters of foreign law, science, navigation, and so on, the decision goes by the decision of witnesses practically conversant with the subject. The same principle obtained in the Established Church of Scotland, and it was the purpose of this bill to introduce it in the Church of England also. From this reference to custom and precedent it was not to be supposed that he intended to put out of view the fundamental and vital principle of the indefeasible inherent right of the bishops of the Church of England to determine finally all points of doctrine. The speech was delivered with much emotion, which was the more remarked because of the equable and moderate character of the speaker.

Lord Lansdowne, on behalf of the Government, gave the official answer that interference was undesirable, because it would be an imputation and censure on the Judicial Committee as well as an infringement of the Queen's prerogative, and would restore an obsolete and dangerous jurisdiction. He would, however, approve that every bishop should be *de jure* a member of the Judicial Committee. Lord Brougham thought that bishops might be admitted as assessors, not as judges; Bishop Thirlwall, who spoke with great authority, feared that such an enactment would cause division in the episcopate, and favour the Romanising party. Lord Stanley wished the bishops, or some of them, to act as assessors. The course of the debate showed that public opinion would not support so

Blomfield's bill rejected by the Lords.

large a measure, and the bill was thrown out by 84 to 51.
It would have had no better fortune if it had reached the
Commons, for the temper of the time was more than usually
anti-clerical.

The Bishop of London, at a later date (November 1850),
explained his position by going at length into the whole
question : he stated Gorham's doctrine to be that
infants are not regenerated in and by baptism, Blomfield's letter.
but that if they are regenerated, it is by an act
of prevenient grace, so that they come to baptism already
regenerated ; a doctrine directly contradicting the words of
the Catechism, and destroying the nature of a sacrament.
His belief was that the true defence of the Church was
to be found in the Liturgy rather than the Articles.   He
considered that there was no necessity for synodical action
on the part of the bishops, still less was there any excuse for
individual secession to Rome ; partly because the judgment
was no act of the Church, though it affected the Church ;
partly because it did not deny or even call in question the
doctrine of baptismal regeneration, though it allowed too
great latitude of explanation.   'I hold,' he wrote, 'that until
the Church's articles and formularies are altered by the
authority of Convocation or of some synod equivalent to
Convocation, her character as a teacher of truth remains
unchanged ; and that nothing short of a formal act of the
Church, itself repudiating what it has hitherto asserted as
truth, can warrant a man in quitting its communion.'   He
also said, but guardedly, as was his custom, that Convocation, though not perfect nor infallible, ought to be allowed
freedom of speech, and would speak with more His opinion on Con-
weight if laymen were admitted to its counsels.   'I vocation.
would not be understood to express an opinion unfavourable to the removal of those restrictions which hinder
the Church from deliberating . . . on doctrine and discipline.'
The Court 'deduced, from some questionable instances of
published opinions of divines in former times, which had been
suffered to pass without censure, the conclusion that a
clergyman might lawfully call in question in his writings and
teaching the certainty, or even the possibility, of any knowledge
of the truth or falsehood of that which, as often as he baptized

an infant, was positively and unconditionally affirmed in the words put into his mouth by the Church.' A synodical decision was needed, to clear away misunderstandings.

The High Church party had now done all that was in their power, short of secession, and had been courageously led by Manning. For himself, Manning felt that the situation had become intolerable, and on April 6, 1851, he was received with James Hope (afterwards Hope Scott) into the Church of Rome. Manning's position in the Church of England had been next to that of the first three tractarian leaders. He had a high reputation for sanctity; as a preacher he was surpassed by none but Newman; he was a bold controversialist, an accomplished speaker, and a good man of business. He had the faults as well as the merits of the priestly type: he was ambitious, because he commanded; an actor, but sincere; a convinced rhetorician; clear in his ends, not always scrupulous in his means; a powerful administrator and ruler, one whose place must always be in the front rank; a character so complex as to baffle analysis. So conspicuous a desertion caused much dismay in the Church, but in the event strengthened the hands of Keble and Pusey.

Manning's secession, 1851.

The conclusion of the whole controversy was to establish by a decision, protested against by the High Church party, but approved by Evangelicals and Latitudinarians, and valid in law, the position that a clergyman holding Calvinistic or uncertain doctrine on the subject of baptismal regeneration was not on that ground to be excluded from the ministry of the Church of England; and, like other judgments coming from the same quarter, it tended to enlarge the interpretation of the terms of subscription. It has been called by some the charter of religious freedom, by others a soul-destroying judgment. It extended the bounds of comprehension; it did nothing to settle the principles of comprehension.

NOTE ON BAPTISM

The doctrine of baptism includes: (1) God's intention, *i.e.* His purpose in electing certain persons to eternal life, an abstruse and greatly controverted subject, upon which the Church of England abstains from strict definition; (2) God's action, whether by means of sacraments or otherwise, concerning which the Church of England maintains the efficacy of sacraments, but does not formally deny that grace may be given by other means, repentance and faith being present; (3) the question whether sacramental grace is given instrumentally, by and at the moment of the act, or in consequence of an act of prevenient grace rendering the receiver worthy, *i.e.* whether sacramental grace in baptism is given absolutely or conditionally.

The biblical record is that the baptism of St. Peter's disciples at Jerusalem, and Philip's at Samaria, was followed by the gift of the Spirit, whereas in the case of Cornelius the sacrament succeeded the gift. St. Paul also was baptized; the language of St. John iii. 5, Rom. vi. 3, 4, 1 Pet. iii. 21 admits of more than one interpretation.

According to the doctrine of the Church of England, three effects of baptism are affirmed : remission of the guilt of original sin, admission to the Christian community, and a title to future spiritual benefits.

The word Regeneration, which came so prominently forward in this controversy, was used, like many theological terms, both in a biblical and in an ecclesiastical or traditional sense. To dogmatise as to the biblical sense of the new birth would be to assume the question at issue, since all Christian confessions of faith are based upon the words of the Bible ; the ecclesiastical or patristic, *i.e.* historical sense, is never dissociated from baptism, and is often a synonym for baptism. To these we may add the meaning frequently assigned to the word in and after the Reformation period, as synonymous with conversion, or the rise after a lapse. Since these three types of thought, the biblical, the traditional, and the neo-biblical were all present in the minds of the adapters and framers of the Anglican Services and other formularies, it is difficult to assign exclusive meanings to the terms used ; and a legal interpretation according to strict and consistent definitions is not properly applicable to language loose in expression and rather technical than exact.

From a historical point of view it must be observed that :—

(1) The question of baptism had not become controversial in a high degree at the time when the Baptismal Service was drawn up, the form of which differs only slightly from that in which it was fixed in 1661. In making such alterations as were made, recourse was had to Archbishop Hermann's *Consultations*, based upon Luther, Bucer, and Melanchthon, all of whom held Catholic doctrine on the question, following Augustine, and Cranmer and Ridley agreed with them, and determined to retain the sacramental language. 'The model,' says Bishop Browne in his book on the Articles, 'on which [the English] Baptismal Services were formed was not Calvinistic nor Zwinglian, but Lutheran. . . . The parts of the more ancient services which were deemed superstitious, such as chrism and exorcism, were omitted. But the doctrine involved is evidently the same as that held by Luther and Melanchthon, who . . . followed and symbolised with St. Augustine.'

(2) On the other hand, since the Prayer Book, as we have it, is in a large degree the work of Cranmer, it was modified by later influences, and especially by the views of Zwingle and his followers, with whom Cranmer came to associate himself, and whose anti-sacramentarian doctrine

and dislike of *opus operatum* and 'magic' were strongly expressed in the reign of Edward VI. It is worthy of remark, as was noticed by Arthur Perceval, that the language of the Article of 1552 is more ambiguous than that of 1536, and that in those eventful sixteen years Calvinism had begun to take root in the English Church, so that many clergy who would not have subscribed the earlier article could subscribe the later.

(3) The Calvinistic ideas of grace given to the elect and not to the non-elect do not come into the history of the Prayer Book, though they have largely affected its interpretation since. Had it been otherwise, the formularies would have been altered to deny or affirm Calvinistic doctrine.

There can be little doubt that the Anglican baptismal formularies were drawn up in a Catholic sense ; nor, on the other hand, is it doubtful that a non-sacramentarian sense was read into them by the Puritans or ultra-Protestants of the times of Edward VI. and later, and was not condemned by authority.

The point at issue is clear. One party holds that grace is given to infants in and by baptism, whereby original sin is forgiven, and (by the same act) regeneration is conferred. This view points in the direction of grace *ex opere operato*. The other party holds that all sacramental efficacy depends on the worthy reception of sacraments. In the case of baptism, in order that an infant may receive it worthily, a prevenient grace is necessary. We cannot affirm that this grace, without which baptism is inoperative, is granted in the case of every infant baptized ; and the declarations to that effect in the Prayer Book are to be understood as the language of charity and hope, not as dogmatically exact. This view tends to make sacraments merely a seal or symbol, not a necessary means. The Church of England holds the former doctrine, but it is not certain that she excludes the latter.

AUTHORITIES.— *Tracts for the Times,*. Nos. 67-69 (on Baptism, by Pusey); *Gorham* v. *Bishop of Exeter. Full Report*, etc., 1850 ; Bishop Browne, *Exposition of the Articles.* BIOGRAPHIES : *Pusey, Keble, Gladstone*, etc., as before ; *H. E. Manning*, by E. S. Purcell; *Bishop Blomfield*, by A. Blomfield. Brodrick and Fremantle, *A Collection of Judgments*, etc. ; Brooke, *Privy Council Judgments* ; Strange, *The Bennett Judgment* ; Denison, *Notes of my Life*.

CHAPTER XVII

THE PAPAL AGGRESSION

IN 1839 Pope Gregory XVI. increased the number of Vicars-Apostolic in England from four to eight. A Roman Catholic revival was in progress there, as the Court of Rome well knew; and to present Catholicism in a dignified form and to clear away the squalor with which the Roman Church had been encumbered during three centuries of persecution or contempt was a step towards fuller recognition and wider influence. Time has shown that this was a prudent policy. The Roman Church now holds its head high in England. Sixty years ago it was hated as an enemy to true religion, or despised as obscure and uneducated. But the times were changing; the Romantic movement had its religious side, and when Scott's magic glass had shown a reflection of the Middle Ages, such Roman Catholics as Augustus Welby Pugin, the architect, and Kenelm Digby, the author of *The Broad Stone of Honour*, counted for more than was known at the time. The stir of life and intellectual interest which accompanied the Romantic movement was felt in Roman Catholic circles, and Oscott, the seminary near Birmingham, became a centre of intellectual activity. 'Oxford,' says Mr. Purcell, in his *Life of Cardinal Manning*, 'perhaps helped Oscott, and encouraged it; but Oscott had begun of itself.' Nicholas Wiseman, the head of Oscott, was more cosmopolitan than most of his brethren; he had spent much of his life at Rome, he was a learned divine, a linguist and an orientalist of high reputation, and in culture and attainments of every kind the superior of those whom he was called upon to rule.

(margin note: Papal vicariates in England.)

Bishop Milner, Wiseman, and Lingard, the accomplished scholar and historian, were among the Roman Catholics whose efforts to introduce their Church to the notice of England pointed forward to a fuller revival, and offered to the converts who followed the lead of Newman and Manning a dignified habitation, not the obscure cell, the foreign *enclave* within the limits of England, in which a small, proud, and shy community had worshipped, nursed in family and local traditions of persecution and concealment. English Catholics were little affected by the movements of religion and politics at home or abroad, except when Emancipation was being offered to them rather than sought by them, or as the wrongs and sorrows of Ireland moved them to sympathy. The ancient Catholic families intermarried with each other, lived on their estates, or, if they came to London, in a narrow circle of their own. There were scarcely any Roman Catholics amongst the middle classes, and few amongst the poor, except the Irish settlers to be found in great cities, and in parts of Yorkshire and Lancashire the tenants and dependants of local land-owners. To the English at large they seemed not part of a vast organisation and a universal body, but an obscure half-foreign and negligible sect. Catholic emancipation opened the door; Wiseman, more than any one else, stood on the threshold welcoming the newcomers, helping them to feel that by becoming Romans they did not cease to be Englishmen, and at the same time bringing a larger atmosphere into the lives of his own co-religionists. He was the first Roman ecclesiastic who was recognised as a leader outside the circle of ecclesiasticism.

Revival of Roman Catholicism in England.

Dr. Wiseman's position.

In 1840 Dr. Wiseman was consecrated by Gregory XVI Bishop of Melipotamus *in partibus*, and appointed president of Oscott College. Since he had had constant and intimate relations with Rome, his mission had importance; and he saw at once the great issues that lay in the Oxford Movement. He was always ready to welcome inquirers. His correspondence was large, and he had the personal authority which a wide correspondence implies and maintains. To the English Catholics, though by original extraction one of themselves, his high birth and

Wiseman at Oscott, 1840.

Roman education made him seem un-English, and his appointment as Vicar-Apostolic in London in 1849 was disliked as that of an Ultramontanist and friend of the Jesuits. His activity in reviving or founding guilds and confraternities, organising retreats and missions, and generally waking up the Church by modern alarums, set slovens against him and made the willing more alert. Wiseman's influence worked in harmony with the general stirring of thought and practical activity in religious and secular matters throughout the country, though on different lines. Under this influence the bonds of ecclesiastical discipline were tightened. *His ultramontane policy.* Daily mass was insisted on, monastic orders were revived, the Jesuits were welcomed, the tie with Rome was made closer, everything was done to strengthen the Papal autocracy, and to substitute the imposing fabric of ultramontanism for the old-fashioned simplicity and easygoing custom under which many generations of Englishmen had preserved their religion, and with it their national feelings and loyalty.

When in 1841 a Roman Catholic peer, Lord Beaumont, proposed the repeal of certain Acts which affected Roman Catholics vexatiously, on the ground that the offences against which they were directed were obsolete, the obnoxious Acts were repealed in part. In 1845 Lord John Russell said in Parliament that it would be 'absurd and puerile' to make a fuss about identical titles; and so it appeared to be generally thought. But in 1846, when this legislation was extended further, Lord Brougham objected to the removal of all hindrances to the publication of Papal bulls in England. Accordingly, the penalty was taken off; but the offence remained on the statute book, to be dealt with, if a case should occur, which seemed most unlikely, by the common law. Four years later the case did occur; and the means of punishment, if any existed, turned out not to be applicable without great difficulty and delay. The obvious remedy, said the *Quarterly Review* of October 1851, was to enact a specific penalty; this penalty (for a different offence, it is true) was imposed by the Ecclesiastical Titles Act of 1851; but at what a sacrifice of dignity and even decency, and with what result?

The traditional Protestantism of the English nation has

persistently refused to allow any official correspondence between the Court of St. James's and the Papal Curia, and misunderstandings have arisen in consequence. The delicate problems connected with a divided allegiance are a reason for, not against, regular and authorised communications. Centuries of oppression are not wiped away in a few years ; and the removal of disabilities did not unite the two nations, for such they may be called, in one. Concealment on the one side and distrust on the other prevented harmonious action. An accredited representative at Rome would at least have broken down mutual ignorance ; occasional messengers had no official position, and yet were supposed to act with some authority. Such an envoy was Lord Minto, the father-in-law of the Prime Minister Lord John Russell, who being sent on a political mission to the Italian Courts in the autumn of 1847, had a personal interview with Pius IX., in which he informed the newly elected Pope that the British Government was prepared to send a representative to the Quirinal, and that a bill to give powers was being prepared.

Lord Minto's negotiations at Rome, 1847.

A bill was accordingly brought in by Lord Lansdowne, President of the Council, at the beginning of the session of 1848, to enable Her Majesty to open and carry on diplomatic intercourse between this country and the Court of Rome. The debates in both Parliaments were generally temperate, though intemperate things were said, and the bill passed both Houses and received the Royal assent on September 4, 1848 (11 and 12 Vict. c. 108) ; but with an amendment, that no person in Holy Orders should be received in England as the Pope's representative. In the course of debate Sir Robert Inglis asked the Prime Minister, Lord John Russell, whether he had heard of any project of the Pope to divide England into dioceses, and to appoint an Archbishop of Westminster, and whether he had given his assent to any such project ? To which Lord John replied that he did not know of any such intention on the part of the Pope, and that he should not give his assent to the formation of any such dioceses in the Queen's dominions. Yet the *Quarterly Review* had declared six months before, in December 1847, the Pope's ' intention of proving that

Act to open diplomatic relations with Rome, 1848.

he has power and authority, both temporal and spiritual, here in
England itself, by erecting those ecclesiastical officers hereto-
fore tolerated under the modest and sufficient title of Vicars-
Apostolic, into the dignities of archbishops and bishops—not
merely nominal, not *in partibus*—but of Pope-created dioceses
. . . Bishops of Westminster and Birmingham.'   Lord Minto
was still at Rome in June 1848, when the *Roman*
Gazette spoke of Dr. Wiseman as 'his Eminence the   An 'enormous
Most Reverend Monsignor the Vicar-Apostolic, now   misunder-
                                                     standing.'
Archbishop of Westminster.'   It is asserted that the documents
referring to the re-organisation of Roman Catholic England had
been shown by the Pope himself to Lord Minto, and that Lord
Minto gave some sort of assurance that the British Government would not object to the design.   If so, there was a strange
inadvertence or forgetfulness on the part of one or the other
of the noble lords.   Nor has it ever been explained how
Lord Minto, if he saw the papers, took no notice of them,
nor how Lord John Russell, if Lord Minto reported them to
him, forgot all about the matter, nor how the Papal Court
was satisfied, from so entirely informal a sanction, that it
could proceed without giving offence to Protestant England,
especially after Russell's disclaimer; nor finally, how the
whole 'enormous misunderstanding,' as Lord Lansdowne
called it, was not cleared up in the debates on the Ecclesiastical
Titles Bill in 1851, if not long before.   The inadvertence, or
it may be contemptuous negligence, of the Vatican is an instance
of the victorious disregard of times and seasons and political
conventions which Newman mentions as a characteristic of
Papal action; and never was it more successful in the result.
In any case, the tone of the Act of 1848 was so grudging
and discourteous, in refusing the Pope any title but that of
'the Sovereign of the Roman States,' and debarring him from
the appointment of an ecclesiastic as his diplomatic representative, that it is not wonderful that the Curia should have
ignored its enactment, if indeed that fact was ever officially
communicated at Rome.

In July 1850 Dr. Wiseman was summoned to Rome, and
informed by Cardinal Antonelli that he was to receive a
Cardinal's hat.   'I leave England (for ever) next month,' he
wrote.   This action of the Pope condemned him to 'golden

fetters' for life, and cut off all his hopes of labouring for the conversion of England. In the same month the forward movement of the Roman Catholic Church in England was signalised by the consecration in full pomp of ritual, and in the presence of fifteen prelates from many quarters of the globe, of the new Cathedral of St. George in Lambeth.

Dr. Wiseman made Cardinal and Archbishop of Westminster, 1850.

Before going to Rome, Wiseman called upon the Prime Minister, and appears to have gathered from him in conversation that the Government would not oppose the establishment of a Roman hierarchy in England, if the Papal Court should decide on such a measure. When he arrived at Rome he learnt that he was to return to England as Archbishop of Westminster, and on September 30, Letters Apostolic were published, by which the eight existing Apostolic Vicariates were suppressed, and in their stead a Metropolitan see and twelve Episcopal sees created, having assigned to them districts defined according to the limits of counties, and bearing territorial titles. The reason for this action was plainly given : considering the increasing number of Catholics, the removal of hindrances to the spread of the faith, and the general desire of clergy and laity expressed by their petitions, the Pope declares that 'the time has come in which that form of ecclesiastical government may be restored in England which freely prevails in other countries.'

A few days later was published in England the Pastoral Letter, dated October 7, 1850, *ex Porta Flaminia*, 'from the Flaminian Gate,' and signed 'Nicholas Cardinal Archbishop of Westminster,' in which the new Cardinal spoke of the blessing conferred upon England 'by the restoration of its true Catholic hierarchical government, in communion with the See of St. Peter,' and the restoration of Catholic England 'to its orbit in the ecclesiastical firmament, from which its light had long vanished.'

Pastoral Letter *ex Porta Flaminia*, 1850.

The language of the Pastoral was inflated and rhetorical, and great exception was ignorantly taken to the dictatorial and authoritative tone which it appeared to assume. The result was an outbreak of popular excitement, such as it was hard to foresee, but not

Outburst of popular indignation in England.

difficult to account for, though it could not be justified in reason. The ordinary British mind is in a condition of invincible ignorance with regard to the Roman Church. Englishmen will neither learn the facts nor pass them by as unimportant. Their action, when they do act, is usually in accordance with a Liberal conception of Catholicism; but they preserve the prejudices of three hundred years ago, a time when the independence of England was threatened by the Catholic powers of the Continent. No such danger existed in 1850. The rhetoric of a Romano-Irish ecclesiastic is usually florid, and might have been recognised as official. But English Protestantism understood it literally, and took the document as a deliberate insult to the Crown, Parliament, Church, and people of England. The very dating of the Cardinal's circular from 'the Flaminian Gate' was thought to be ostentatious and aggressive, though it was merely an official address like 'War Office' or 'Downing Street'; and though the letter was addressed to none but 'the clergy and the faithful' of the Roman obedience, English men and women of all classes were angry because the English episcopate was ignored, as well as the existence of any church at all except the Roman, and a minority was addressed as if it were the whole nation. Such expressions as 'We govern and shall continue to govern and administer with ordinary jurisdiction the counties of Middlesex, Hertford,' etc., gave offence, because no mention of the Queen's authority was made, nor of the existence of other bishops in the country. But the grammatical subject to the florid and somewhat absurd sentence about a restoration of our country 'to its orbit in the ecclesiastical firmament, from which its light had long vanished,' was 'Catholic England,' not 'England'; and England as a whole had nothing to say to it. A document issued from the Roman Curia had no more existence in the eye of the English law than advertisements from the authorities of the Baptist or Wesleyan bodies; it had relation to the members of the Roman Church in the new archdiocese, and to no one else. Catholic emancipation, if it meant anything, was an invitation to the Church to come out of obscurity. The claims of Rome were exactly what they had been when the organisation of the Roman Church in England was on a less pretentious

scale.   The action of the Papal Court in appointing archbishops and bishops with territorial titles was no new thing.

Precedents
for the
Pope's
action.
In Ireland the assumption and recognition of such
titles, though illegal, was universal ; and Roman pre-
lates had been summoned by their territorial titles
to sit as Parliamentary Commissioners ; the titles of
'Grace' and 'Lordship' were officially given to Roman
Catholic prelates in Ireland, though the designation of 'Archbishop of Dublin,' etc., was avoided ; but 'the Roman Catholic
Primate' and 'the Roman Catholic Archbishop of Dublin'
were given precedence by the official *Dublin Gazette* of
August 7, 1849, under those titles, next to the Protestant
Archbishop of Dublin and before the Duke of Leinster, the
premier Irish peer.   In recent years, also, Roman sees had
been established in Australia, Canada, and Nova Scotia, and
with territorial titles, which were recognised by the colonial
and home Governments.

It should, however, be mentioned, as some excuse for the
violent language of Protestant alarmists, that a like intemper-

Exultation of
the Roman
Catholic
press.
ance appeared on the Roman side.   The Catholic
newspapers announced the new organisation in
tones of 'exultation and defiance' ; 'Rome,' the
Tablet wrote, 'has divided our land into dioceses
. . . the Anglican sees, those ghosts of realities long passed
away, are utterly ignored.'   The *Univers*, the organ of Louis
Veuillot, a well-known French ultramontane journalist, wrote
on November 3, 1850, 'As St. Gregory transferred the primacy
of London to Canterbury . . . so does Pope Pius IX. now
transfer the primacy of Canterbury to the Archiepiscopal See
of Westminster . . . since the promulgation of the Papal
brief, the Sees of Canterbury, of York, of London, and any
other sees established before this reform, have ceased to exist.'
The enthronisation of the new bishops was celebrated with

Newman's
sermon at
Birmingham.
ostentatious pomp ; and Newman, preaching before
Bishop Ullathorne at Birmingham, pronounced that
'the people of England, who for so many years had
been separated from the See of Rome, are about of their own
will to be added to the Holy Church.'

Nothing could exceed the excitement and indignation of
all classes in the country.   Meetings called by the Sheriffs

were held in every county in England and Wales; numerous
addresses and petitions were issued; representatives from
the universities and the City were received by the Queen in
person on December 10, 1850, and the tone of her answers was
Elizabethan. Both the Queen and her husband _{The Queen's}
thoroughly disliked the tractarian movement, and _{answer to}
this was implied in the replies given, though within _{deputations.}
the limits of constitutional reserve, which are narrower for a
sovereign than for a prime minister; but in private correspondence, however, she lamented the 'unchristian and unwise'
language of her subjects. Among the instances of extravagant
language made use of in high places was the speech of the
Lord Chancellor (Truro) at the Mansion House on November
9, 1850, when the bonfires of Guy Fawkes day were hardly
cold. He spoke of 'insult, triumph, and domination,' 'the
insidious within and the enemies without,' 'a cardinal's cap
equal to the Crown of England,' and so on; and none of his
hearers saw that such words were both insolent and ridiculous,
since, as Newman had said in his sermon, 'the lion could
roar, but that was all he could do.'

'The clergy of the Church of England,' said the *Annual
Register*, 'were roused from their tranquillity. . . . The papal
brief wholly ignored their commission, treated their
episcopate as null, their dioceses as vacant, their _{The bishops}
jurisdiction as superseded. . . . The evangelical _{and clergy.}
party saw in it a new incentive to their abhorrence against
popery, the High Churchmen resented it as an invasion of
Catholic unity, and of that rule of discipline which forbids the
intrusion of a second bishop into a diocese already occupied.'
'An excess of timidity,' says Dr. Liddon, treating of this
crisis, 'has always been thought to be the mark of the episcopate in the Western Church; and of the bishops it was said
in the Middle Ages, *episcopi in Anglia semper pavidissimi.*'
The bishops certainly showed no disposition to run counter to
the popular current on this occasion. It may be fairly said,
however, that if any one was insulted and outraged, it was
the bishops of the Church of England; and it _{The bishops.}
would have demanded a meekness in them beyond
that of Moses to feel and express no resentment, and so
incur the imputation of disloyalty to Church and State.

If the bishops had been silent their effigies would certainly have gone to the fire with those of the Pope and the Cardinal. As it was, they spoke their minds openly. In answer to addresses from their clergy they issued charges, in which they made use of such expressions as 'foreign bondage,' 'audacious aggression,' 'revolting and frightful assumption.' Even Bishop Blomfield spoke of an intended 'insult to the Sovereign and Church of this country,' and called the Romish invaders 'emissaries of darkness.' Finally, the whole episcopate, with only two exceptions, joined in an address to the Queen, whose answer was in the same strain, 'you may rely on my determination to uphold alike the rights of my Crown and the independence of my people against all aggressions and encroachments of a foreign power.'

Disraeli, whose business it was not to make things pleasant to the Liberals, but who nevertheless thought the indigna-

Disraeli's letter to the Duke of Buckingham.

tion of the country just, wrote a letter to the Duke of Buckingham, in which he put the responsibility on the Government, by whom 'the whole question had been reconsidered, and decided in favour of the Pope. . . . The Ministers who recognised the pseudo-Archbishop of Tuam as a peer and a prelate cannot object to the appointment of a pseudo-Archbishop of Westminster, even though he be a cardinal.'

In fact the negligence and inadvertence of the Government were highly reprehensible, and Lord John Russell, if he had

Lord John Russell's 'Durham Letter,' 1850.

attempted to excuse himself, would have found defence difficult. Instead of this he covered his laches by raising a cloud of 'indignation,' which may be thought to have had in it more policy than passion. The so-called 'Durham Letter' of November 4, 1850, may have been a sincere expression of feeling, but it was also a bid for popularity. Lord John was adroit enough to animate and give a lead to the popular fury which might have overthrown him. It is not impossible that he may have thought an antipapal demonstration a good parliamentary move for a tottering government. He gained no real victory, and if he had been a stronger man he would have exerted himself to calm the storm instead of blowing it up. The Government could not ignore so loud and universal an outcry, but it was hardly necessary for the Prime Minister to lead the chorus. The letter addressed by Lord John to his friend and former tutor, Dr. Maltby, Bishop of Durham, spoke of the late aggression of the Pope upon English Protestantism as 'insolent and insidious,' and complained of a 'pretension to supremacy over the realm of England, and a claim to sole and undivided sway, which is inconsistent with the Queen's supremacy, with the rights of our bishops and clergy, and with the spiritual independence of the nation, as asserted even in Roman Catholic times.' He adverted to the similar instances of the division of Scotland into dioceses by the Episcopal Church, and of England into districts by the Wesleyan Conference, only by denying that they were similar. But the danger which alarmed him much more than any aggression of a foreign sovereign was that which arose from 'the unworthy sons of the Church of England herself,' who, by advocating the honour paid to saints, claiming infallibility for the Church, and recommending auricular confession and the administration of penance and absolution, had been 'the most forward in leading their flocks, step by step, to the very verge of the precipice.' This attack upon the Puseyites, with some commonplaces about 'the glorious principles and the immortal martyrs of the Reformation,' 'the mummeries of superstition' and the like, concluded a document which seemed to anticipate by its date the riotous outbreak of religious absurdity which took place on the next day in London and many other towns, notably Salisbury and Exeter, where, in place of the ordinary burning of Guy Fawkes's effigy, the Pope and the new Cardinal Archbishop, with his suffragans, were carried in procession and thrown into the fire 'on a scale and with a significance much greater than common.'

It should be said that the tone of Lord John's letter was regretted by moderate men like Lord Lansdowne; that two Liberal bishops, Stanley and Thirlwall, refused to be alarmed; while from the other side the Duke of Norfolk, head of the English Roman Catholics, agreed with the Durham Letter, and said that 'ultramontane opinions are totally incompatible with allegiance to our Sovereign and with our Constitution.' Lord Beaumont also, another

Roman Catholic peers.

Catholic peer, who had in 1841 carried a bill for the repeal of certain anti-Catholic Acts, took a similar line.

So completely did the question of papal aggression capture the popular imagination, that for months together the newspapers were full of denunciation of the Pope and the Puseyites; the *Guardian* and the *Record*, the *Times* and the *Standard* sounded the same note. There is no better weathercock than *Punch* by which to tell the shifting airs of the popular gale; and *Punch* was as eager as the religious and political papers to protest in a tone of blustering vulgarity against the Roman pretensions, which, however, it treated as matter for mirth rather than for alarm, whilst a more angry and hostile manner was assumed in attacking the Puseyites, their childish affectation, their insidious manœuvres, the spiritual tyranny to which they were trying to subject Protestant consciences. The vigour and humour of the caricatures drawn by Leech and Thackeray increased the effect on the popular mind, and contributed to make moderation impossible.

The press: Punch.

In the midst of this hubbub Cardinal Wiseman returned from Rome, on November 11, 1850, much annoyed at the violent opposition to his mission, but not dismayed, and prepared to make the most of a good case. His 'Appeal to the English People,' written in a few hours, was, as was noted in the journal of Charles Greville, Clerk to the Privy Council, 'a very able manifesto, in which he proves unanswerably that what has been done is perfectly legal, and a matter of ecclesiastical discipline, with which we have no concern whatever.' He had a great opportunity, if he had written moderately; but the logical victory was so easy that he did not sufficiently consider the weight and unanimity of his adversary, and his 'Appeal to the English Nation' angered instead of convincing. Protestant feeling ran high and expressed itself, not only in burning Popes, but in riots in which both Roman Catholics and Tractarians suffered.

Wiseman's 'Appeal to the English People.'

Parliament met on February 4, 1851, and the Speech from the Throne made mention of ecclesiastical titles conferred by a foreign power, and addresses presented to the Queen by large bodies of her subjects. 'I have assured them,' said the

Queen, 'of my resolution to maintain the rights of my Crown and the independence of the nation.'

On February 10 Lord John Russell brought in a bill to deal with Ecclesiastical Titles. It was founded on an Act of George IV., which forbade the assumption of any ecclesiastical title already appropriated to the Church of England, under penalty of £100 on every offence. The action of this law certainly did not, as John Arthur Roebuck, Member for Sheffield, showed, prevent a Roman ecclesiastic from calling himself 'Archbishop *in* Westminster'; it was doubtful whether the titles of Archbishop *of* Westminster, Bishop *of* Beverley, Southwark, etc. were illegal, since they had not been used to designate prelates of the Church of England. Lord John Russell, he said, admitted that the law officers of the Crown thought the law had not been broken, and the argument of the bill rested on a 'whereas it may be doubtful' clause. No earthly power could prevent the spiritual authority of the Pope from being exercised ; the penal statutes of the Tudors had failed to do that; all that modern legislation could do was to make certain ecclesiastical titles illegal. If territorial archbishoprics and bishoprics were illegal, so were territorial vicariates-apostolic; and the action of Gregory XVI. in doubling the number of the vicariates and assigning districts to them was as much or as little a breach of the law as this of Pius IX.

Russell's Ecclesiastical Titles' Bill, 1851.

Debates in Parliament.

Bright accused the Prime Minister of appealing to the bigotry of the country. Gladstone spoke earnestly against the bill. If, he said, the Pope's rescript had a temporal character, why exempt the bishops of the Scottish Church from the penalties of the bill? if spiritual, why interfere at all? In a passage of noble eloquence he entered a solemn protest against the measure as 'hostile to the institutions of the country and the great principle of religious freedom, on which this wise and understanding people had permanently built its legislation of late years.' Other speakers of the High Church school, such as Roundell Palmer and Beresford Hope, followed in the same vein. Sir James Graham, a man of calm temper and dignified mind, pointed to the

Bright, Gladstone, Palmer, Hope, Beresford, Graham.

dilemma presented by Ireland, which the Government could neither leave out of the bill nor subject to its provisions, and spoke of 'a penal code with all its horrors,' and legislation which must be 'either contemptible or oppressive.' Radical speakers had no trouble in showing how inconsistent the present legislation was with that of 1829; that it established a similar mode of action in England, Scotland, and Ireland, whereas the conditions of the three kingdoms were wholly different; that the Queen's prerogative was in no way touched by the Pope's action; that there had been no intention to insult.

It may sometimes happen that a section of the political world, engaged neither in promoting and explaining nor in opposing ministerial action, may see more clearly than others who are in the heat and dust of the game. Sir Robert Peel died in the summer of 1850, and his followers Aberdeen, Graham, Gladstone, Herbert, and Newcastle had as yet joined neither party. Independently of each other this knot of capable politicians came to the conclusion that the Prime Minister, the Ministry, the clergy and the British public were making much of little in delivering themselves over to 'a transport of indignation'; and that however indignant people might be, it was difficult to do anything by means of legislation. Aberdeen and Graham felt this so strongly, that when in February 1851 Lord John Russell tried to form a coalition with them in the reconstruction of his government, they refused to consent, unless the Ecclesiastical Titles Bill was unconditionally withdrawn. Aberdeen wrote to his son, 'I might have been Prime Minister at this moment, had it not been for my resistance to the Ecclesiastical Titles Bill. Without doubt this is a most unpopular ground; but I feel quite satisfied that I am right'; and so some years later Lord John himself acknowledged. At the moment, Lord Aberdeen went so far as to speak of the existing popular excitement as 'a noble manifestation of Protestant spirit'; but his more considered judgment was that the 'complaints made against the "arrogance" of the Pope amounted to a complaint against his existence; there was evidently no intention on the part of the Pope to offer the least offence to the Crown of England.'

The Peelites.

Lord Aberdeen.

He concluded by saying that if the bill were passed, and proved to be anything but a dead letter, there would never again be peace in Ireland.

All reason and expediency were on one side, as the history of the Act has shown, or rather the absence of a history, for it was still-born.   But argument had no place in these debates.   On the side of un-reason was the violent Protestant feeling which had possessed the whole nation; the arguments used were little more than noise and claptrap, or else ingenious legal quibbles, that territorial bishoprics carried with them dangerous Canon Law precedents which would involve the Court of Queen's Bench in problems of mediaeval jurisprudence, or rodomontade such as that for which Lord Ashley, not usually given to rodomontade, was called to order, that 'if the Parliament of England submitted to the dethronement of the House of Hanover, the Queen would not.'   The bill was carried in both Houses by enormous majorities.   'It was something, however,' as Lord Morley writes, 'to find Mr. Gladstone, the greatest living Churchman, and Bright, the greatest living Nonconformist, voting in the same lobby.'

Ecclesiastical Titles Act, 1851.

The Act of 1851 remained on the Statute Book till 1871, when Gladstone repealed it.   No action was ever taken under it, and the Roman archbishops and bishops in England continued to use in public and in private the territorial titles which had been conferred upon them by the Pope.

Ecclesiastical Titles Act a dead letter.

The voice of wisdom is often loud after the event; it is refreshing to turn from so much intemperate language and unpractical action to the quiet good sense of Charles Greville, who protested against the popular fury in an able letter addressed to the *Times* on December 9, 1850, signed 'Carolus.'   He had written in his journal a month before, 'This odious agitation will continue till it is superseded by something else, or expires from want of aliment more solid than fanatical denunciations.   Already sensible people, even those who are indignant at the "Papal Aggressions," as they are termed, begin to think the clamour exaggerated. . . .   They begin to reflect that a great movement without a definite and attainable object is a very foolish thing;

Charles Greville's opinion.

and as it is quite certain that the Pope will not retract what
he has done, and that we can neither punish him nor frighten
him, that his ecclesiastical arrangements will be carried into
execution here whether we like it or not, and that as we shall
take nothing by all our agitation and clamour, we shall
probably end by looking very foolish.'

Greville's letter to the *Times*, the argument of which he
elaborated at great length and with much ability, is written in
no partisan spirit: he says plainly that the Pope's proceedings
exhibited 'rashness, want of courtesy to the Crown, and want
of consideration for the feelings of the people of England. . . .
The flourish of trumpets, the songs of triumph, the vain boast-
ing with which those measures were proclaimed, justify a large
amount of disgust and indignation; but the real injury which
the honour and the policy of England are required to redress
bears in my mind but a small proportion to the false assumptions and ridiculous pretensions which we might well afford to
regard with a scornful indifference.'

No popular frenzy is wholly irrational. The spark of reason
which lay hid under so much rubbish was that the rights of the
'foreign power,' non-existent in the political, but strong in the
spiritual forum, could not be asserted in a public and notorious
manner without the appearance of arrogance. The English
people were conscious of having been generous as well as just
when they abolished Catholic disabilities, and they were naturally incensed at the sudden publication to all the world of
what appeared to be a declaration of war against English Protestantism, without even the courtesy of a notice. It was also
commonly believed, and not without reason, that Puseyism
was a long step in the direction of Rome, and was welcomed
as such at Rome.

Since the first appearance of the Tracts the minds of
ordinary English people had been much disquieted by fear
that the Oxford Movement was tending towards
Rome. New doctrines, or what seemed to be new,
were preached; the clergy began to separate themselves from the world in manner, dress, and speech. The
customary ritual was changed, new sacerdotal claims were
advanced, and the faithful were bidden to have recourse to
the priestly offices of private confession and absolution. At

Effect of the tractarian movement.

the same time, and in consequence of developments in the same teaching, a large number of English clergymen and lay-men had become converts to Rome, resigning fellow-ships and benefices. The most conspicuous, of Secessions to Rome. course, was Newman, who, as has been said, left the Church of England in the autumn of 1845, followed by Ward, Dalgairns, St. John, Oakeley, and Faber, and in 1851 by Manning, driven out by the Gorham judgment. Manning's subsequent history as Cardinal Archbishop of Westminster, and as a leader in social and philanthropic activities, does not concern us here. Others who had been foremost in propagating tractarian opinions changed their religion at one time or another, and it was confidently expected by those who did not know their steadfastness, that Pusey and Keble would go the same way. It was remembered how strongly anti-Roman the language of the earlier Tracts had been, and how, since their publi-cation had ceased, denunciations of Rome on the part of the leaders who still remained in the Church of England had become less frequent in proportion as the apparent danger of secession became greater. These secessions were, of course, in no way connected with the Pope's action, but they were a predisposing cause for a great outburst of Protestant feeling against the aggression when it took place, and brought much unpopularity upon the 'Puseyites.' Pusey himself stood firm, with Keble at his side ; and it was greatly owing to their pre-dominating influence that no large secession took place, either at this critical time or afterwards, and that the growth of High Church teaching and ritual has continued to the present day within the limits of the Church of England, without visible breach of unity.

Hitherto the conflict between old and new, which was intro-duced by the issue of the *Tracts for the Times*, had borne, more or less, an academic character. It now became a matter of notoriety beyond religious circles, partly in consequence of the number of the secessions to Rome and the high character of those who seceded, especially Newman and Manning, partly from the innovations introduced in ritual, which entirely changed the character of the public services in many churches, and led to popular riots, further developments of ritual, attempts to check the ritualist movement by legal prosecutions, and the organisation of attack and defence, in matters both of ceremonial and doctrine.

We have followed in this volume the philanthropic and humanitarian movement which was set on foot by the evangelical school at the beginning of the nineteenth century; the growth of new religious societies and the revival of activity in the old societies; we have considered the origins of national education as conducted by the National Society and the British and Foreign School Society, and the beginning of the contest of the Churches over education; the effect upon the Church of England, both in spirit and in material results, of the Reform agitation and legislation; the rise of a school of liberal theology, and of a new generation of High Churchmen, and the striking and rapid development of High Church principles by the authors of the *Tracts for the Times*; the dissensions within the Oxford Movement itself, and the discouragement caused by the secession to Rome of some of its foremost leaders. The next volume will treat of the development of high doctrine, and of the ceremonial by which it was symbolised, beyond the limits of the *via media*, and the attempts, public and private, to deal with the ritualist movement, a subject which occupies nearly the whole field of Church history for many years; the growth of liberal opinion and critical research, and the counter action of orthodoxy; the spread of missionary enterprise, and the expansion of the colonial and external branches of the Church of England.

AUTHORITIES.—Wilfrid Ward, *Life and Times of Cardinal Wiseman*; *W. G. Ward and the Catholic Revival*; Wiseman, *Appeal to the Reason of the English People*; Disraeli, *Letter to the Duke of Buckingham*; Lord John Russell, *Letter to the Bishop of Durham*; Charles Greville, *Journals*.

APPENDIX I

DATES

	A.D.
S.P.C.K. founded (India)	1698
S.P.G. founded (N. America).	1701
Baptist Missionary Society founded	1793
C.M.S. ('The Church Missionary Society for Africa and the East') and R.T.S. (Religious Tract Society) founded	1799
Act of Union between Churches of England and Ireland . . .	1800
Samuel Marsden's Mission to Botany Bay	,,
Pitt resigns. Catholic Relief delayed	1801
Josiah Pratt, Secretary of C.M.S.	1802
Meeting of R.T.S., foundation of a Bible Society proposed . .	,,
British and Foreign Bible Society founded	1804
Henry Martyn sails for India	,,
C.M.S. Mission to Sierra Leone	,,
Fox moves the Roman Catholic question	1805
Death of Pitt	1806
Mutiny at Vellore	,,
Death of Fox	,,
Slave Trade Abolition Act	1807
Grenville resigns on Roman Catholic question	,,
British and Foreign School Society founded	,,
Royal Lancasterian Society established	1808
Endowment of Maynooth College	,,
London Society for promoting Christianity among the Jews .	1809
Synod of Aberdeen adopts the Scottish Communion office . .	1811
John Keble elected Fellow of Oriel	,,
Thomas Charles of Bala founds adult schools in Wales . .	,,
Robert Raikes of Gloucester founds Sunday Schools . . .	,,
National Society founded	,,
C.M.S. established in Salisbury Square	1812
C.M.S. meeting about East India Charter Bill	,,
Bristol Church Missionary Association formed	1813
Catholic Emancipation lost by Speaker's vote	,,
East India Charter Act	,,
Prayer Book and Bible controversy (Milner and Marsh) . .	,,
Unitarian Relief Act	,,
Grattan's Catholic Relief Bill defeated	1814
Thomas Fanshawe Middleton consecrated Bishop of Calcutta .	,,
Samuel Marsden's Mission to New Zealand (C.M.S.) . . .	,,

A.D.

Four missionaries (C.M.S.) sent to India 1814
Bishop Ryder consecrated to See of Gloucester 1815
St. Bees' Theological College founded 1816
Travancore Mission . . . . ,,
Grattan's Catholic Relief Bill defeated 1817
Government chaplains appointed for Australian convict settlements . ,,
Benares Mission (C.M.S.) . . . . ,,
Church Building Act 1818
Ceylon Mission (C.M.S.) . . . . ,,
Bengal Mission (S.P.G.) . . . . ,,
Catholic Emancipation Bill defeated by two votes . . . 1819
Bishop Marsh's questions to candidates 1820
Bishop's College, Calcutta, founded . . . . . . ,,
Death of George III. Accession of George IV. . . . ,,
Missions to Tinnevelly and Bombay (C.M.S.) . . . . ,,
Death of Bishop Middleton ; succeeded by Reginald Heber . 1822
Henry Williams sent to New Zealand (C.M.S.) . . . ,,
Lampeter College founded . . . . ,,
Archdeaconry of New South Wales added to See of Calcutta . ,,
Irish Catholic Association formed 1823
Newfoundland Society founded . . . . . . ,,
Sees of Jamaica and Barbadoes founded 1824
Apocrypha Controversy 1825
Burdett's Catholic Relief Bill thrown out by the Lords . . ,,
Islington Institution opened . . . . ,,
University of London founded 1826
Death of Bishop Heber . . . . ,,
Missions to Egypt and North-West America (C.M.S.) . . ,,
The Christian Year published 1827
University College buildings begun (Gower Street, London) . ,,
Repeal of Test and Corporation Acts 1828
Clare election . . . . ,,
Catholic Emancipation announced in the Speech from the Throne 1829
Peel resigns his seat for Oxford University . . . . ,,
Broughton sent out as Archdeacon of New South Wales . . ,,
Catholic Emancipation (Roman Catholic Relief Act) passed . ,,
Foundation of King's College . . . . ,,
Missions to Australia, Smyrna, Abyssinia (C.M.S.) . . . 1830
Royal Commission on Ecclesiastical Courts . . . . ,,
Trinitarian Bible Society founded . . . . . . ,,
Death of George IV. Accession of William IV. . . . ,,
Exeter Hall opened 1831
Russell's Parliamentary Reform Bill passes the Commons, thrown out
    by the Lords . . . . ,,
Royal Commission on Ecclesiastical Revenues, etc. . . . ,,
Report of Royal Commission on Ecclesiastical Courts . . 1832
Court of Delegates abolished. Jurisdiction transferred to Privy
    Council . . . . ,,
Reform Act . . . . ,,
Daniel Wilson consecrated Bishop of Calcutta . . . . ,,
Durham University founded . . . . ,,
Church Temporalities (Ireland) Act 1833
Ecclesiastical Appeals transferred to Judicial Committee of Privy Council ,,

A.D.

Keble's Sermon on ' National Apostasy'	1833
Association of Friends of the Church	,,
£20,000 granted to Nat. Soc. and B. and F. School Society . .	,,
Manchester church rate refused	,,
Affirmation for M.P.'s allowed instead of oath	,,
Tithe Composition Act (Ireland)	,,
No. 1 of *Tracts for the Times* published	,,
Death of William Wilberforce. Slaves Emancipation Act passed .	,,
Ashley on factory children	,,
Cawnpore Mission (S.P.G.)	,,
Cambridge petition for abolition of University Tests . . .	1834
Hampden's *Observations* published	,,
University Tests Bill defeated	,,
Church Rate Bill introduced	,,
Pusey's Tract on Baptism	,,
Tamworth manifesto	1835
Irish Tithe Resolution	,,
Bishopric of Madras founded	,,
Ecclesiastical Commission appointed ; issues first Report . .	,,
Brougham's Education Resolutions	,,
Bishopric of Durham Act	1836
Established Church Act	,,
Church Pastoral Aid Society founded	,,
Bishopric of Australia established	,,
Blomfield's Metropolis Churches Fund established . . .	,,
Hampden made Regius Professor of Divinity	,,
Ecclesiastical Commission permanently appointed . . .	,,
Tithe Commutation Act	,,
Act for carrying out recommendations of Ecclesiastical Commissioners	,,
Dissenters', etc., Marriage Act	,,
London University incorporated by Charter	,,
Death of William IV. Accession of Queen Victoria . .	1837
Additional Curates Society founded	,,
Pluralities Act	,,
Sees of Madras and Bombay founded	,,
Zulu Mission (C.M.S.)	,,
Brougham's Plan for National Education	,,
Irish Tithe Act	1838
Ashley's Factory Bill rejected	,,
Gladstone on *Church and State* published	,,
Froude's *Remains* published	,,
Church Building Act	,,
Pluralities and Non-residence Act	,,
Church Discipline Act	,,
Library of the Fathers begun	,,
Colonial Church Society founded	,,
Lord John Russell's education proposals rejected . . .	1839
Education Grant raised to £30,000	,,
System of Inspection introduced in Elementary Schools . .	,,
Martyrs' Memorial at Oxford (erected 1841)	,,
See of Toronto founded	,,
Marriage of Queen Victoria	1840
Church Discipline Act	,,

A.D.

Ecclesiastical Duties and Revenues Act 1840
Educational ' Concordat' . . . . ,,
Wells Theological College founded . . . . . . ,,
Agreement of Waitangi (New Zealand) . . . . . ,,
Tract 90 published, and condemned by Heads of Houses . . 1841
Tracts for the Times discontinued . . . . . . ,,
Colonial Bishoprics Fund established . . . . . ,,
Telugu Mission (C.M.S.) . . . . ,,
Colonial and Continental Church Society founded . . . ,,
Michael Alexander consecrated Bishop of Jerusalem . . . ,,
Selwyn consecrated Bishop of New Zealand . . . . ,,
Bishop Blomfield's Charge on ritual 1842
Braintree church rate case . . . . ,,
Sees of Tasmania, Guiana, and Antigua constituted . . . ,,
Garbett elected Professor of Poetry at Oxford . . . . ,,
Bishop Blomfield's Charge on rubrics . . . . . ,,
Five Colonial Bishops consecrated . . . . . . ,,
Lord Ashley's Motion on Christian Education 1843
Joseph Hume proposes Secular Education . . . . ,,
Graham's Factory Bill. Education clauses withdrawn . . ,,
Surplice Riots in London (St. George's in the East) and Exeter . . ,,
Pusey inhibited (Sermon on the Eucharist) . . . . ,,
Newman resigns the Vicarage of St. Mary's . . . . ,,
Missions in China (C.M.S.) . . . . ,,
Ordination of Samuel Crowther, a native African . . . ,,
Graham's Factory Bill carried 1844
Peel's Act for Endowment of Church Districts . . . . ,,
Ward's *Ideal of a Christian Church* . . . . . ,,
British Anti-State-Church Association founded . . . . ,,
St. Augustine's College (Canterbury) founded . . . . ,,
Consecration of St. Saviour's, Leeds . . . . . ,,
Missions to China and East Africa (C.M.S.) . . . . ,,
Archbishop Howley's Provincial Letter on Ritual . . . 1845
Park Village West Settlement opened . . . . . ,,
Endowment of Maynooth College (£26,000) . . . . ,,
Judgment in St. Sepulchre's case (Cambridge) . . . . ,,
Ward deprived of his Degrees by Convocation . . . . ,,
Evangelical Alliance founded . . . . ,,
Oakeley condemned in Court of Arches . . . . . ,,
Queen's Colleges at Cork, Galway, and Belfast founded . . ,,
Secession of Newman, Oakeley, Ward, Faber, and others . . ,,
Samuel Wilberforce consecrated Bishop of Oxford . . . ,,
Bishop Blomfield withdraws his ritual directions . . . 1846
Bishop Stanley's Charge upon Apostolical Succession . . ,,
Committee of Council on Education accepts the Denominational
    System . . . . ,,
St. Aidan's (Birkenhead) Theological College founded . . ,,
Borneo Church Mission Fund established . . . . ,,
Miss Sellon sets up a sisterhood at Devonport . . . 1847
Hampden appointed Bishop of Hereford . . . . . ,,
Factory Act . . . . ,,
Jews admitted to Parliament . . . . ,,
Bristol Church Union established . . . . . . ,,

A.D.

Dispute about Services at St. Saviour's, Leeds 1847
Sees of Melbourne, Newcastle, and Adelaide founded . . . ,,
See of Cape Town founded . . . . ,,
See of Manchester founded . . . . ,,
Prince Lee consecrated Bishop of Manchester 1848
Death of Archbishop Howley. John Bird Sumner succeeds . . ,,
Sisterhood of St. Mary the Virgin, Wantage, founded . . . ,,
St. Thomas' College, Colombo, founded by Bishop Chapman . . ,,
Gorham institutes proceedings against the Bishop of Exeter . . ,,
C.M.S. Jubilee . . . . ,,
Clewer House of Mercy founded 1849
Anti-State-Church Society becomes Liberation Society . . . ,,
Sir H. Jenner Fust gives judgment against Gorham . . . ,,
First Report of Metropolitan Church Union issued . . . ,,
Cumbrae Theological College founded . . . . . ,,
Irish Church Mission . . . . ,,
Bishoprics of Rupert's Land and Victoria (Hong Kong) created . . ,,
Prosecution of Shore by Bishop of Exeter . . . . ,,
Bethnal Green Churches completed 1850
Judicial Committee gives judgment in Gorham case . . . ,,
Society for the Revival of Convocation . . . . . ,,
Bishop Blomfield's Ecclesiastical Appeals Bill . . . . ,,
Exeter Diocesan Synod meets . . . . ,,
St. Barnabas', Pimlico, consecrated ; riots at St. Barnabas' . . ,,
Oxford and Cambridge University Commissions . . . . ,,
Pluralities Act . . . . ,,
Wiseman made Cardinal . . . . ,,
Bull of Pius IX. dividing England into Dioceses . . . . ,,
Wiseman created Archbishop of Westminster . . . . ,,
Bishop Blomfield's Charge. Wiseman's Pastoral *ex Portâ Flaminiâ* ,,
Russell's Durham Letter . . . . ,,
No-Popery Riots at Exeter and other places . . . . ,,
Bennett resigns the living of St. Barnabas' 1851
Joint Pastoral of Bishops on Ritual . . . . . . ,,
Petition to the Queen against ' Novelties ' . . . . ,,
Petition for increase of Episcopate . . . . . . ,,
Manning received into the Roman Church . . . . ,,
Ecclesiastical Titles Act . . . . ,,
Debate on Convocation in the House of Lords . . . . ,,
Riots at St. Barnabas', Pimlico . . . . . . ,,
Leeds Ruridecanal Chapter approves Evening Communion . . ,,
Missions to Palestine and Hudson's Bay (C.M.S.) . . . ,,
See of Sierra Leone founded . . . . ,,

APPENDIX II

SOVEREIGNS.	Accession.	ARCHBISHOPS OF CANTERBURY.	Accession.	ARCHBISHOPS OF YORK.	Accession.	BISHOPS OF LONDON.	Accession.
George III.	1760	John Moore	1783	William Markham	1777	Beilby Porteus	1787
George IV.	1820	Chas. Manners Sutton	1805	Edw. V. Vernon Harcourt	1808	John Randolph	1809
William IV.	1830	William Howley	1828	Thomas Musgrave	1847	William Howley	1813
Victoria	1837	John Bird Sumner	1848			Charles James Blomfield	1828

INDEX

THE END

Printed by R. & R. CLARK, LIMITED, *Edinburgh.*

A HISTORY OF
THE ENGLISH CHURCH

EDITED BY THE LATE

Very Rev. W. R. W. STEPHENS, D.D.

DEAN OF WINCHESTER

AND

The Rev. WILLIAM HUNT, D.Litt.

A Continuous History, based upon a careful Study of Original Authorities, and of the best Ancient and Modern Writers.

In Nine Volumes, uniform binding, Crown 8vo. With Maps.

Each Volume is sold separately, and has its own Index.

Vol. I. **The English Church from its Foundation to the Norman Conquest** (597–1066). By the Rev. WILLIAM HUNT, D.Litt. 7s. 6d.

Vol. II. **The English Church from the Norman Conquest to the Accession of Edward I.** (1066–1272). By DEAN STEPHENS. 7s. 6d.

Vol. III. **The English Church in the Fourteenth and Fifteenth Centuries** (1272–1486). By the Rev. Canon CAPES, late Fellow of Queen's College, Oxford. 7s. 6d.

Vol. IV. **The English Church in the Sixteenth Century, from the Accession of Henry VIII. to the Death of Mary** (1509–1558). By JAMES GAIRDNER, C.B., LL.D. 7s. 6d.

Vol. V. **The English Church in the Reigns of Elizabeth and James I.** (1558–1625). By the Rev. W. H. FRERE. 7s. 6d.

Vol. VI. **The English Church from the Accession of Charles I. to the Death of Anne** (1625–1714). By the Rev. W. H. HUTTON, B.D., Fellow of St. John's College, Oxford. 7s. 6d.

Vol. VII. **The English Church from the Accession of George I. to the End of the Eighteenth Century** (1714–1800). By the late Rev. Canon J. H. OVERTON, D.D., and the Rev. F. RELTON, A.K.C. 7s. 6d.

Vol. VIII. (In Two Parts). **The English Church in the Nineteenth Century.** By F. WARRE CORNISH, M.A., Vice-Provost of Eton College. 7s. 6d. each.

MACMILLAN AND CO., LTD., LONDON.

EARLY CHURCH HISTORY
TO A.D. 313

By HENRY MELVILL GWATKIN, M.A.

DIXIE PROFESSOR OF ECCLESIASTICAL HISTORY IN THE
UNIVERSITY OF CAMBRIDGE

Two Vols. 8vo. 17s. net.

OUTLOOK.—" Professor Gwatkin speaks with a tremendous sense of responsibility and from a toilsome knowledge of facts. . . . We can only hope fervently that our bishops will insist on the study of these volumes by candidates for holy orders. Their style is admirable, and no man should enter the ministry without having fairly weighed the opinions which they contain."

SPECTATOR.—" Professor Gwatkin's book, the result, it is clear, of long and close study, will be found illuminating by every serious student of the subject."

EXPOSITORY TIMES.—"The History of Early Christianity, having the Gifford Lectures in front of it, will be received without hesitation. . . . Just as surely as the Gifford Lectures take their place in the expositions of Christianity, this book will take the foremost place in the history of its earliest years."

LOLLARDY AND THE
REFORMATION IN ENGLAND

By JAMES GAIRDNER, C.B.

Two Vols. 8vo. 21s. net.

ATHENÆUM.—" A work of the highest standard, wherein is marshalled, with innate honesty of purpose, an abundance of facts concerning a most complex and perplexing period of English history in Church and State."

CHURCH TIMES.—"The first of these volumes, as has been already shown in these columns, is of great value as coming from the pen of an historian saturated with the very essence of original documents ; the second volume is of equal value and of thrilling interest from cover to cover."

SPECTATOR.—" A book which is invaluable to students, and of permanent importance as a work of reference."

MACMILLAN AND CO., LTD., LONDON.